HAPPINESS QUANTIFI

Happiness Quantified

A Satisfaction Calculus Approach
Revised Edition

BERNARD VAN PRAAG
University of Amsterdam, Tinbergen Institute and SCHOLAR

ADA FERRER -I- CARBONELL
ICREA and Institut d' Anàlisi Econòmica (CSIC)

OXFORD
UNIVERSITY PRESS

OXFORD

UNIVERSITY PRESS

Great Clarendon Street, Oxford OX2 6DP

Oxford University Press is a department of the University of Oxford.
It furthers the University's objective of excellence in research, scholarship,
and education by publishing worldwide in

Oxford New York.

Auckland Bangkok Buenos Aires Cape Town Chennai
Dar es Salaam Delhi Hong Kong Istanbul Karachi Kolkata
Kuala Lumpur Madrid Melbourne Mexico City Mumbai Nairobi
São Paulo Shanghai Taipei Tokyo Toronto

Oxford is a registered trade mark of Oxford University Press
in the UK and in certain other countries

Published in the United States
by Oxford University Press Inc., New York

First published 2004
Revised edition published 2008

British Library Cataloguing in Publication Data

Data available

Library of Congress Cataloging in Publication Data

Data available

Typeset by SPI Publisher Services, Pondicherry, India
Printed in Great Britain
on acid-free paper by
Biddles Ltd., King's Lynn, Norfolk

ISBN 978-0-19-828654-7 (Hbk.)   978-0-19-922614-6 (Pbk.)

1 3 5 7 9 10 8 6 4 2

Preface

This book was written when the first author was a university professor and the second author Ph.D. research associate at University of Amsterdam. We are grateful for the friendly climate and the support we received.

It is obvious that this book could not have been written without the help of other researchers before us. The line of research started more than thirty years ago with Van Praag (1968, 1971). However, the main part of this monograph may be considered as new. Many researchers have contributed to this line of research, which was initiated when the main contributors were affiliated with the University of Leyden. It is therefore sometimes called the Leyden School. Nowadays it is merged into the flourishing field of happiness economics. It is impossible to list here precisely who did what and when. In the following chapters we shall give the appropriate references when we deal with them. Here we mention the most important contributors without whom this work would not have been done. They are Arie Kapteyn, Aldi Hagenaars, Theo Goedhart, Huib Van der Stadt, Nico Van der Sar, Erik Plug, Barbara Baarsma, Paul Frijters, and Peter Hop. We are very grateful to them.

This book bears the traces of 'research in progress'. As it is mainly based on papers produced over a period of thirty years we use various data sets, which included Dutch, German, British, Russian, and data sets of other European countries. If we have tried to solve a specific problem with a specific data set, it is frequently not repeated on other data sets as well. This procedure is chosen for practical reasons of efficiency and in order to avoid tedious repetitions. We are also sometimes comparing competing methods but not always on the same data sets. Sometimes specific questions were included in one survey but not in another. However, as any scientific study is 'work in progress', which is needed at the time but superseded in the future by new insights, we dare to publish this book now, the more so as over the course of time colleagues have expressed the need for some kind of synthesis of the work of the Leyden School thus far. To avoid any confusion, it should be said, that after 1986 the work was in no way affiliated with Leyden any more.

The subject of this book, which we may loosely characterize as analysis of subjective questions, is not uniquely associated with the persons mentioned above and the Leyden School. First, there has been attention for this type of data in sociology (cf. Bradburn 1969, Cantril 1965) and in psychological literature (e.g. Kahneman and Diener). Most of the question modules we consider are actually stemming from those scientists. However, those data sets were not seriously analyzed by most economists except by Easterlin (1974). (Katona 1951, 1975 and his school constitute an exception.) The more so, because sociological and psychological surveys devoted only scant attention to so-called 'economic' variables. Till the seventies there were many surveys that did not provide information on household income, as being 'too difficult or too impertinent to be asked'. Sociologists and psychologists were not interested in the questions economists ask and their methods of analysis (e.g. factor analysis) are essentially different from the econometric models economists use. A lifelong pioneer in setting up the *World Database of Happiness* is the Dutch social psychologist Ruut Veenhoven. Major publications are Veenhoven (1989, 1996, 1999). Veenhoven also founded the *Journal of Happiness Studies*.

We mention that from about 1990 economists other than the Leyden School started to be systematically interested in subjective questions as well. We mention without being complete in (roughly) chronological order apart from Easterlin (1974), Oswald, Graham, Helliwell, Frey, Clark, Blanchflower, Ravallion, Frijters, Dolan, DiTella, MacCulloch, Senik, Stutzer, and Pradhan. We shall refer to their work in the following pages when relevant. It seems proper to see the early Leyden insights as a forerunner and part of the now maturing body of satisfaction research or as it is now frequently called 'happiness research'.

A considerable part of this book draws on earlier research. However, we have tried to rewrite all those parts, such that they fall into line and that tedious repetitions are avoided. Also most chapters are considerably extended and/or changed, compared to the earlier publications. A major part of Chapters 3 and 4 has been published in the *Journal of Economic Behavior and Organization*, the first half of Chapter 7 was published in Maital (Van Praag and Van Weeren 1988). Chapter 9 is based on a paper in *Health Economics*. Chapter 10 is based on an article in the *European Economic Review* and one in *Climate Change*. Chapter 11 is based on a paper in *the Economic Journal*. Chapter 12 draws from a publication in the *Journal of Public Economics*. Chapters 13 and 15 are partly based on articles in the seventies of the previous century in the *European Economic Review*, the *Journal of Human Resources*, the *Review of Economics and Statistics* and the *Review of Income and Wealth* and on more recent articles in the *Journal of Economic Inequality* and the *Journal of Happiness Studies*.

PREFACE TO THE REVISED EDITION

This revised paperback edition appears in 2007, three years after the first edition in 2004. In those three years the situation in 'Happiness Economics' has been drastically changed. As Clark et al. (2006) are documenting, the literature in those three years has roughly doubled in size and there is a real avalanche of studies underway. This raises some questions about the position of this monograph within the literature.

This book was and is not intended as a survey of 'happiness economics'. First, there are now several extensive surveys around like the monographs by Frey and Stutzer (2002*a*) and Layard (2005) and the survey papers by again Frey and Stutzer (2002*b*), DiTella and MacCulloch (2006), Graham (2006), and Clark, Frijters, and Shields (2006). We mention also a volume of classics, edited by Easterlin (2002). Second, the problem with this exponentially growing literature is that a survey is already practically outdated at the time of publication. This deterred us from that ambition.

Although of course we give due attention to our scientific environment, the first intention of this book is to introduce the reader in the research kitchen, where methods are developed and applied and discussed with a view on socio-economic policy problems. This gives our book a little bit of the character of a textbook. We think that it is still the first and only book of this kind in the field of 'Happiness Economics'.

Second, this book gives an account of the main points of our own research since 1971, when it started under the name Leyden School. Although the recent upsurge of 'Happiness Economics' provides us with many new insights and results, it seems only fair to acknowledge that a number of very similar models and results had been already found in the seventies by the Leyden School. In this monograph we aim at a harmonious blending of old and new stuff.

Third, we provide the reader with some concepts and models, which are not yet developed elsewhere, and which we see as new contributions to the field.

This revised edition has been changed on a number of points, compared to the first edition. First, we have completely changed section 2.6., where we introduce the POLS-methodology. Second, we have added a number of recent references and corrected a number of printing errors and added some sentences here and there. Finally, we have included a new chapter on multi-dimensional poverty. As the main focus of this study is methodological, we abstained from updating the data set used.

Contents

Figures

Tables

1

Introduction

1.1. SATISFACTION

One of the most interesting subjects for a scientific researcher is people themselves. As the researcher is also human, he or she is in fact investigating him- or
herself. If we use introspection we are able to formulate hypotheses and we can
easily predict, because we have much in common with our object of research.
However, it would be wrong to assume that all human beings are equal and that
it is sufficient for our research to study ourselves only. We have to extend our
studies by observing other individuals as well, by means of interviews, surveys,
monitoring, experiments, or observation of (market) behavior.

Humankind is the subject of the social sciences; namely, psychology, sociology, economics, anthropology, and political sciences. Probably, the historical
separation between these sciences is somewhat artificial and unfortunate. It is
artificial because it is hard to argue that economics has nothing to do with
sociology or psychology, or the other way round. And it is unfortunate because
those artificial scientific boundaries make it difficult to make a complete study
of phenomena that have economic, sociological, and psychological aspects. Evidently, this point is implicitly recognized by the creation of hybrid disciplines
like 'economic psychology', 'social psychology', or 'economic anthropology', to
name but a few. But these are still scientific backwaters, beyond the mainstream.

The subject of this book is *satisfaction* analysis. Humans evaluate many
aspects of their situation. This amounts to posing the question: Am I satisfied
with my job, my health, my family, the way I use my leisure time, my choice
of car, my choice of breakfast jam, etc.? The obvious reason for this almost
continuous monitoring of our own life is that we are always looking for the
best situation. If we are dissatisfied with something, we attempt, within our
possibilities, to change conditions so as to improve our satisfaction.

This continuous evaluation of how satisfied we are with aspects of our life
has the clear objective of changing our life if we can improve our satisfaction.
This change can materialize in changing one's habits, changing one's job,
changing one's family situation, buying new furniture, etc. Obviously, there are
situations in which we are dissatisfied but are unable to change our situation.
In those cases it is very frustrating to repeat the evaluation process over and

over again. We resign ourselves to our situation and stop consciously evaluating all the time. Similarly, if we conclude each time that we are satisfied with
something and see no reason for change, it would be a waste of time to
evaluate the situation again every day.

In fact, satisfaction is measured within our mind on a continuous scale
ranging from completely dissatisfied to completely satisfied. In practice, it is
sometimes difficult to express our satisfaction on a continuous scale. Mostly,
we use verbal scales like 'good' or 'bad', but we also use, and increasingly so,
numerical scales. Then satisfaction is expressed on a scale from 0 to 10 or on a
scale from 0 percent to 100 percent. We have heard someone say: 'I am feeling
100 percent today', which means 'I am feeling in an excellent mood'. Such a
satisfaction scale is a cardinal scale. That means that the satisfaction improvement of 30 percent to 40 percent is the same as the improvement from 70
percent to 80 percent. It is a ladder where the rungs are equidistant. Frequently
in survey questions those scales are discrete; for example, you may only
answer 0, 1, ..., or 10.

Let us assume that we have two situations, which are denoted by a_1 and a_2,
and let us assume that the satisfaction values or satisfaction levels attached to
both situations are $U(a_1)$ and $U(a_2)$, both scaled between 0 and 100 percent.
The present situation is a_1. Let us assume that $U(a_1) = 0.6$ and that
$U(a_2) = 0.7$. In that case, the individual will prefer a_2 to a_1 and consequently
try to *act* to change his situation from a_1 to a_2. This action may be a move to
another house, a divorce from his present partner, buying a new type of breakfast jam, etc. Here we ignore the possible existence of transaction costs; for
instance, the cost of moving or divorcing. It might be the case that if one could
begin from scratch one would choose a_2, but, given that the present situation is
a_1 and the transaction costs are high, one prefers to stay or is resigned to
staying in situation a_1.

At this juncture we encounter a point which was fairly crucial for the development of economic science in the last century. It is the question of whether
we can find out from observing that somebody prefers a_2 to a_1 what the values
$U(a_1)$ and $U(a_2)$ are. A moment's thought shows that this is impossible. This is
easily seen by realizing that $U(a_1) = 0.5$ and that $U(a_2) = 0.8$ would yield the
same choice as $U(a_1) = 0.4$ and $U(a_2) = 0.7$, or $U(a_1) = u_1$ and that $U(a_2) = u_2$
with $u_1 \leq u_2$. In that case we would have observed the same choice and the
same action. It follows that from the observation of actions we are unable to
estimate the difference between two satisfaction levels. Does this imply that an
individual is unable to express his degree of satisfaction on a numerical scale,
say from 0 to 100 percent? It will be obvious that the fact that we cannot
estimate the U-values from observing choices, presumably based on comparing
U-values, does not imply that an individual does not think or act on the basis
of such a U-function. The observation of acts just does not offer enough information to estimate the U-values. The only thing that a preference for a_2 over
a_1 reveals is that $U(a_1) < U(a_2)$.

Already in the nineteenth century economists investigated consumer behavior. The idea is that individuals consume bundles of commodities. More precisely, take the example that there are two commodities, bread and beer, which may be bought in quantities x_1 and x_2 at unit prices p_1 and p_2 respectively. Total expenditures are then $p_1x_1 + p_2x_2$. Assuming that the consumer evaluates each bundle (x_1, x_2) by a satisfaction value $U(x_1, x_2)$ and that the money which the individual may spend is y, the consumer problem boils down to the maximization of $U(x_1, x_2)$ with respect to (x_1, x_2) under the constraint that $p_1x_1 + p_2x_2 \leq y$. Economists did not use the term satisfaction but the seemingly more neutral terms *utility* or *ophelimity*. If one knows the maximum utility one can derive from an amount y at given prices p, one can also speak of the utility of the money amount y and denote it by $U(y; p)$. This function is called the *indirect* utility function or the utility of money. If y equals *income*, it is also called the 'income' utility function. This latter function is obviously very important from a socio-political point of view. We may compare the situations of citizens and evaluate the equity of the income distribution. It also gives a clue for a redistribution of incomes by income taxation which would yield higher average utility.

At the beginning of the twentieth century Pareto (1909) discovered that the observation of consumer behavior, defined in the way above, could not reveal the nature of the utility function, except for the statement that preferred bundles had to be associated with higher utility than bundles which were not preferred. But if the utility function could only be ordinally identified, such an ordinal utility function was not useful for the solution of the sociopolitical problems hinted at. Another problem was that if individuals with the same income bought the same optimal bundle it was still not obvious that they would be equally satisfied by that bundle. It might be that the two individuals A and B had different utility functions $U_A(.)$ and $U_B(.)$ such that both functions were maximal at the same bundle x, but that $U_A(x) \neq U_B(x)$. This could only be verified by interpersonal utility comparison and, as utility itself was assumed to be unobservable, comparison was consequently impossible. Gradually this was recognized by the entire economic profession, and the utility concept in its *cardinal* version, that is as a satisfaction function, became anathema. In nearly all textbooks students were and are still indoctrinated that cardinal utility is unmeasurable; whereas the exact statement should have been: Cardinal utility is unmeasurable by observing choice behavior only, for example purchase behavior.

According to Robbins (1932), Hicks and Allen (1934), Samuelson (1954/1979), and Houthakker (1961), to name but a few prominent economists, only the ordinal concept made sense. And, although some other equally prominent economists like the Nobel Laureates Frisch (1932, 1964), Tinbergen (1956), and Sen (1999) remained sympathetic to the idea of cardinalism, the utility concept fell into disregard in mainstream economics. Economists argued that if cardinalism made any sense then cardinal utility should be the research subject of psychologists. This erosion of the utility concept in economics was an example of reductionist science. If an assumption is superfluous, it should be removed from your body of axioms.

Notwithstanding this accepted conventional wisdom, the cardinal utility concept popped up in many economic subfields like the *theories* of savings, investments, decisions under uncertainty and macro economic theory. Alongside positive theory the cardinal approach proved hardly avoidable for sensible normative theory, where the welfare (or well-being) of individuals is to be compared or where economic policies have to be evaluated in terms of changes in a social-welfare function. We think especially of poverty and inequality issues, taxation, social-security problems, and game theory. However, the development in economics, in which the operationalization of cardinal utility is shunned, explains the present cul-de-sac, in which everybody talks about utility but nobody dares to operationalize the concept by measurement.

The question remains whether it is possible to observe satisfactions. For at least the last fifty years questions of the following kind have proliferated:

How satisfied are you with your financial situation, job, health, life, etc. Please respond on a scale from 'very bad' to 'very good' or on a numerical scale from 1 to 7 or 1 to 10.

We will call such questions 'satisfaction questions' (SQ). The empirical practice and success of these questions constitute ample evidence that individuals are able and willing to express their satisfaction on a cardinal scale. If we assume those questions to be interpreted in approximately the same way by different respondents and we find that similar respondents give similar answers, this is ample evidence that (approximate) interpersonal comparison is possible. The fact that such questions in practice demand the filling in of an answer category rather than an exact answer on a continuous scale adds inaccuracy to the analysis but it does not essentially change our position.

Psychologists try to measure and to explain satisfaction with 'life as a whole', with health, or with more mundane aspects of life like a cup of coffee. This is called 'stated' behavior or 'stated' preferences. If direct measurement of preferences is possible, we, as economists, should not take the dogmatic stand that it is impossible. Rather, we should seize the opportunity to enlarge our sources of information and try to measure preferences directly. Our aim in doing that is not to replace the usual tools and research methods of traditional economics but to enrich its methodology.

This book mostly deals with that which precedes decision taking; that is, with judgements and evaluations, likings and dislikings, from which preference orderings originate. Judgements and evaluations are studied by various disciplines. The subject is prominent in psychology, in economics, and in sociology. This book, although written by two economists, is explicitly intended for all social scientists, with the aim of promoting discussion between the disciplines. In this, we realize quite well that we make ourselves more vulnerable. In wooing an audience in related but distinctly different sciences, each with its own traditions, paradigms, and conventional wisdoms, the opportunity for critique, even relevant critique, will be considerably larger than if we had aimed at one homogeneous audience only. In particular, as it is clearly impossible to be an expert in all those social sciences, we trust to a special indulgence when we do not cite all the relevant literature or results. We are operating in a border region, or perhaps even in a no man's land, touching many sciences. Although we are economists by upbringing, we do not believe that our findings are exclusively relevant for economists. Rather, we believe that our findings will also be relevant for other social scientists and therefore we are willing, and we deem it even necessary, to transgress some scientific borderlines.

This approach also implies that at some points we use more words than would be necessary if we aimed at followers of one discipline, say economics, only. At other points psychologists will feel at home, while economists have to be carefully introduced to fields which are to them *terra incognita*.

As we shall see, for many problems we do not need to make a cardinality assumption. We can accept the idea that all individuals evaluating their life by the same number feel equally well without making any assumption on the equality of differences. This weaker assumption will be called the *ordinal* approach, favored by Robbins and most mainstream economists (see also Suppes and Winet 1954). In this study we will be rather practical. We shall use the ordinal approach when possible. For some problems we have to be cardinal and then we will assume that cardinal comparison is possible.

1.2. SATISFACTION AND NORMS

Alongside the satisfaction question we introduce another question module, which we call the 'income-evaluation question' (IEQ). It was first developed by Van Praag (1971) and extensively used by a research group in the seventies of the last century at Leyden university, the so-called Leyden School. The IEQ runs as follows:

Given your present household circumstances, what monthly household-income level would you consider to be:

A *very bad* income	$....
A *bad* income	$....
An *insufficient* income	$....
A *sufficient* income	$....
A *good* income	$....
A *very good* income	$....

It is obvious that the question may also be phrased for human length (short–tall), age (young–old), and many other aspects. The outcome is what we call a *norm*. This usage of the word 'norm' has no ethical connotations. It just specifies what the respondent considers to be 'tall' and 'short' or a 'good' income

and a 'bad' income. These norms will mostly differ between individuals. Therefore, we shall speak of *individual* norms. If we interpolate the respondent's own
situation, we find his or her self-evaluation with respect to his or her norm. For
instance, if his or her height is 1.90 meters and he or she responded that a
person of that length may be called 'tall', that is tantamount to saying that the
respondent evaluates himself as 'tall'. Similarly if a bad income is according to
him or her an income of $2,000 per month, and his or her own income is
$2,000, it follows that the respondent evaluates his or her own income as a bad
income. If we interpret this scale of bad to good income as a satisfaction scale,
we conclude that the respondent is badly satisfied with his or her own income.

This evaluation question differs in three respects from the satisfaction question with verbal labels considered on page 4. First, it does not refer to *own*
income. Second, it starts by presenting a verbal label and it asks for an income
level, which is described by the verbal label offered. That level may be called
the respondent's *income norm* for a 'bad', 'sufficient', etc., income. Third,
several verbal labels are offered. In the example we ask for six levels or income
norms, corresponding to the six labels supplied. The advantage of this question
compared to the income-satisfaction question is that we get much more
information per individual. Moreover, because the respondent has to supply six
answers he or she is forced to think better about the exact positioning of each
income level. Hence, we assume that the answers are more exact than in the
one-level case. It has been found that the answers heavily depend on the
respondent's own income; that is, the higher that income is, the higher he or
she will pose his or her income norms, although the relation is mostly not
proportional.

We may visualize such a norm by a graph, if we translate the verbal labels
into numbers from 0 to 1. For instance, if we have five labels we identify them
with the intervals [0, 0.2], ..., [0.8, 1.0]. It follows that the verbal labels are
translated into the midpoints 0.1, 0.3, ..., 0.9. Obviously, some inaccuracy is
introduced by the categorization procedure.

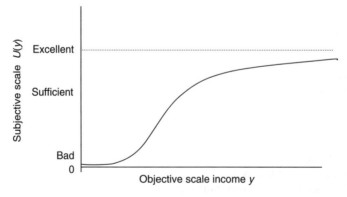

Figure 1.1. *Income-evaluation function*

However, it follows then that we may visualize the norm by a curve like that in Figure 1.1. It is a cumulative distribution function.

1.3. DOMAIN SATISFACTIONS

In modern surveys we find not only questions on *income* satisfaction. Similar questions are posed with respect to job satisfaction, health satisfaction, housing satisfaction, satisfaction with the marital relation, etc. For instance, in the British Household Panel Survey (BHPS) and the German Socio-Economic Panel (GSOEP), two data sets that will be frequently used in this book, we find such question modules. We shall speak of 'domain satisfactions' (DS), corresponding to the life domains income, job, health, housing, marriage, etc.

There is an essential difference between income-satisfaction questions and questions with respect to other aspects of life. We may evaluate our health in terms of 'good' or 'bad' or numerically on a scale of 0–10. However, if we look for a health satisfaction function $U_{health} = U(h)$, analogous to the income satisfaction function $U_{income}(y)$, we face a difficulty. There is an objective one-dimensional description of our income or financial situation in terms of a specific money amount y per month or per year. Is there, however, a one-dimensional objectively measurable variable h which describes our health status? Health economists try to evaluate health in objective terms by asking questions on health *aspects* $H_1, \ldots, H_k$, as to whether you can walk, run, see, whether you are sleepless, etc. In this way a number of indices referring to different health aspects are collected, and those indices are aggregated in some way or other, for instance, averaged into a health index $H(H_1, \ldots, H_k)$. However, it is unclear whether this construct H is the variable h we have in mind. This would only be so when individuals with the same value of H report the same level of satisfaction U_{health}. If this is not the case, the construct H may be the product of a nice expert-rating system, but it does not provide an adequate measure for the individual subjective health status. If we were to have a variable H, such that all respondents with the same value of H were to experience the same health-satisfaction level, this construct H would be ordinally equivalent with h. Apart from the fact that such a construct H does not seem to have been found yet by the medical profession in conjunction with health economists, there is the practical problem that there is insufficient information on H in general surveys. Those surveys are mainly based on self-reporting, and the collection of health aspects is incomplete or even hardly present at all. For instance, objective measurements of blood pressure, cholesterol, etc. are nearly always missing in such surveys. See for an exception Blanchflower and Oswald (2007). In some medical data sets with interviews by doctors or other medically qualified interviewers such data are found, but those surveys do not contain much non-medical information. For instance, in the British Household Panel Survey (BHPS) a wide variety of questions on health aspects are posed to the individual, but there are no independent judgements by medical experts on the health status of the individual. In the German Socio-Economic Panel (GSOEP) there is practically no question on health aspects to be found.

We may ask whether it is necessary to characterize health one-dimensionally. Is it not as interesting or even more so to consider $U_{health}(H_1, \ldots, H_k)$, where we try to model subjective health satisfaction as a function of various health aspects? This is indeed the method we will choose. It follows that we can estimate the relative impacts of changes in various health aspects on health satisfaction as a whole. If we find that subjective health satisfaction does not only depend on 'medical' aspects but also on age, income, education, in short a list of 'non-medical' variables x, we have to conclude that subjective health satisfaction is not determined by 'medical' factors only and we write $U_{health}(H_1, \ldots, H_k; x)$.

It follows that a question like the IEQ cannot be posed for health; there is no 'health-evaluation' question. Is it then reasonable to think of a cardinal health-satisfaction function? We think that that is fairly reasonable. In the question module quoted above respondents evaluate their health on a numerical bounded scale between 0 and 10 or 1 and 7. If individuals understand such a question and give answers that are clearly not haphazard but rather systematic, then those respondents have a cardinal evaluation function in mind. Hence, we assume that there is an underlying cardinal health-satisfaction function that is defined on a scale of 0–1. All monotonic transforms $\tilde{U} = \phi(U_{health})$ are ordinal equivalents of it.

Let us now consider job satisfaction. Here we can make the same observations as with respect to health. A job cannot be described by a one-dimensional characteristic. The same holds for almost all the other aspects we shall consider in this book. For housing satisfaction we notice that in some countries attempts have been made to evaluate (social) housing by means of 'objective' quality indexes. For instance, in Dutch social-housing policy housing units in the social (i.e. state-subsidized) sector are evaluated by 'points'. The evaluation in 'points' is based on aspects such as how many rooms the dwelling contains, how many floors, what the flooring in the living room is, whether there is a bathroom, and if so whether with bath or shower or both, etc. Here we face the same problem as with health. Such 'objective' quality indices do not have to reflect subjective housing satisfaction.

Other versions of satisfaction questions ask for a numerical evaluation on a scale of 1–7 (Likert 1932) or in terms of verbal labels like 'bad'/'good' or in terms of 'laughing' and 'weeping' faces (Shizgal 1999; Sandvik et al. 1993). In general, such answer formulations are not essentially different nor do they require a different mode of analysis from the questions we considered before.

1.4. GENERAL SATISFACTION AND DOMAIN SATISFACTIONS

We may also ask for satisfaction with 'life as a whole'. We call the answer 'general satisfaction (with life)' and denote it by 'GS'. Such questions are posed in many surveys as well. This question is the most widely used one in the now emerging happiness economics literature. For an overview of this literature we refer to Clark, Frijters, and Shields (2006), Di Tella and MacCulloch (2006), Dolan, Peasgood, and White (2006), Frey and Stutzer (2002*b*), Graham (2006), Layard (2005), and Senik (2005). For important methodological discussions, we refer to Bertrand and Mullainathan (2001), Bruni and Porta (2005), Kahneman and Krueger (2006), Bruni and Sugden (2007), and Van Praag (2007).

Now we may ask how far GS and the DS are related. Can we find a relation $GS = GS(DS_1, \ldots, DS_k)$ such that general satisfaction will be an aggregate of domain satisfactions? This is an essential question that we shall try to solve later on in the affirmative. The reader may find a picture of that relational structure on the cover of this book.

1.5. PLAN OF THIS BOOK

In Chapter 2 we shall consider the financial-satisfaction question as an example of how we will do our quantitative analyses. Here we will introduce in 2.6. a novel, intuitively and computationally more easy, methodological approach to deal with 'discrete reponse problems', which we will call the POLS–method. The acronym POLS stands for Probit OLS. The method is less generally applicable than Probit but in practice it mostly yields similar results as Probit. The reason for its introduction is that it is much easier to apply in more complex models than Probit and its offspring albeit that we have to accept an additional assumption which in our situation seems to be approximately true. It also leads to substantial reductions in computer time. Nearly all of section 2.6 may be skipped by those readers who are not interested in methodology. The chapter is partly analytical and partly methodological.

The financial-satisfaction question measures a feeling and the answers are cast in response categories. These two features (feelings, categories) make such analysis tricky. We shall show that there are at least four methods for analyzing such questions but that the outcomes are almost identical. We shall use the outcomes to define family-equivalence scales, a well-known tool for socioeconomic policy. Moreover, the differences and similarities will be indicated between the old Leyden results, which are based on the IEQ, and the recent subjective approaches, which use satisfaction questions. We shall also introduce and consider the preference-drift phenomenon. It will be seen that there is a close similarity with the concepts of decision utility and experienced utility introduced by Kahneman, Wakker, and Sarin (1997).

In Chapter 3 we apply the POLS-methodology introduced for the analysis of financial satisfaction to a variety of other domains of life with respect to which individuals may express their satisfaction or lack of satisfaction. We consider, for instance, the quality of health, job, housing, and one's marriage. We analyze these domains on two panel data sets; namely, the German Socio-Economic Panel Survey (GSOEP) and the British Household Panel Survey (BHSP). Our conclusion is that domain satisfactions, although they look a bit esoteric, are viable variables for quantitative analysis.

In Chapter 4 we pursue the analysis of Chapter 3. The main thesis is that satisfaction with life as a whole may be seen as a weighted aggregate of the domain satisfactions. This result, which is empirically confirmed on both data sets, indicates that satisfactions in different domains of life are *commensurable*. It then becomes possible to compute trade-offs between domains. Since all the domains in their turn depend on objectively measurable variables like income, age, etc., it is also possible to find the effect of additional income on all domains and to aggregate those effects into one effect with respect to life as a whole. It will be seen that this model does not depend on a specific cardinalization. The satisfaction model becomes a two-layered model, as pictured on the cover of this book.

The same model is then also applied to job satisfaction for the British data set. The job is broken down into several aspects, like salary, safety, permanence, etc. The worker/respondent evaluates his or her job with respect to these 'sub-domains', and it is seen that job satisfaction may be regarded as an aggregate of the satisfaction levels with respect to the sub-domains. As a consequence, we have constructed a three-layered model.

In Chapter 5 we apply the same methodology to 'political satisfactions'. We studied a large module in a population-wide Dutch survey which contains questions with respect to political satisfactions. Analogously to 'life as a whole' we consider the individual's satisfaction with government policy. Analogously to the breakdown with respect to life domains we consider satisfaction with government health policy, employment policy, migration policy, income policy, etc. It appears that the individual's satisfaction with government policy may be explained by (political) domain satisfactions which in their turn may be explained by objective variables. At the other end of the system 'satisfaction with government policy' acts as one of the constituents of 'satisfaction with life as a whole'.

In Chapter 6 we investigate whether males and females in the household have roughly the same opinion on satisfactions and what is the correlation matrix of male and female opinions. This is technically important for underpinning the assumption that we can accept one of the partners as representative of the 'household' opinion. If males and females were to disagree or if the correlation between the opinions of the partners were low, we could not assume that one respondent could be seen as representative of the household. The conclusion is that there is a strong correlation.

Chapters 2–6 are examples which illustrate the fact that we may deal with satisfactions as with other economic variables and that we may use them in econometric analysis in almost the same way as 'objective' variables. These chapters have a double objective. First, they may be considered as necessary standard investigations along the path of quantifying satisfactions and starting a calculus of satisfactions. Second, a standard methodology is developed which does not make use of cardinality assumptions.

At this point in the book there is a caesura. In the chapters that follow we apply both the methods introduced and ad hoc methods to specific problems.

In Chapter 7 we pose the question how far present norms are determined by past experiences and what one anticipates for the future. This question is difficult to answer in its generality, because individual norms are difficult to observe. Fortunately, we have one at our disposal. The individual-welfare function, which is derived from the income-evaluation question, is the individual's norm with respect to incomes. The question is then how past incomes determine our present opinion on what is a 'good' income and what level may be called 'bad'. And if the past determines our present norms, is it not reasonable to assume that our expectations for the future will have some impact as well? In Chapter 7 we assume that both the past and the future have an impact and that the impact distribution is described by a mass-density function on the time axis. That function is estimated, and it appears that the function varies its position and shape with age and other individual variables. It is found that young and elderly people place more weight on the past, while individuals in mid-life give more weight to the future.

In Chapter 8 we continue our quest for the genesis of income norms. Alongside the influence of our *own* experiences over our lifetime it is frequently assumed that the situation and composition of an individual's *reference group* will have a considerable impact on the individual's norms. Here we have to distinguish between two cases. In the first case we know what someone's reference group is; for example, defined as people of the same age, education, and job type. In that case we find very significant reference effects of the type we expected; that is, the higher the average income of the reference group is, the less satisfied the individual will feel. A second approach, which is much more ambitious, departs from the idea that we do not know the individual's reference group beforehand, and that we aim at *estimating* someone's reference group from his or her observed norms on income. The reference group is described by a 'social-filter function' on the social reference space, which assigns much value to individuals, who are 'nearby', socially speaking, and negligible weight to people, who are 'far away', socially speaking. We try to identify this social-filter model, with some moderate success.

Chapters 7 and 8 may be seen as incursions into the realms of psychologists and sociologists. We see these approaches as promising models, but we are painfully aware, especially for Chapter 8, that these are only the first steps towards a more comprehensive quantitative and empirically estimable model, in which individual norms are shaped by the individual's own experiences and expectations and by the social reference group.

Now we reach a second turning point in the book. Chapters 9, 10, 11, and 12 are devoted to the influence of external effects on well-being and welfare.

In Chapter 9 we consider the effect of health differences on well-being. Using the trade-off model developed in Chapters 3 and 4 we derive the compensation in money which would be needed to overcome the loss in well-being caused by the less than perfect health condition. These results are very relevant for modern health policy. Confronted with financial and personnel scarcity, health authorities have to evaluate the benefits of health measures with the measuring-rod of money. The present methods in health economics are based on health measures like 'quality adjusted life years' (QALYs). The benefits of health measures are evaluated in QALYs, but it is unclear what the money value of a QALY is. Sometimes it is set by practical health economists and politicians rather arbitrarily at $100,000 per QALY, but the scientific basis for such a valuation is virtually absent. It is very probable that the value of a QALY improvement varies over individuals; for example, according to age. The method that we propose and empirically operationalize for the British in Chapter 9 makes it possible to evaluate the benefits of health policies in terms of money. It should be kept in mind that such compensations may vary over countries, cultures, and sociopolitical environments.

In Chapter 10 we use the same methodology to estimate the effect of climate differences. It is obvious that the climate of Alaska is harder than that of Florida. Hence, we may look at the money compensation needed to make the individual indifferent between living in either place. This idea yields climate-equivalence scales. Here we face a problem, because it does not appear self-evident that climate can be characterized by one dimension; say, temperature or rainfall. Climate is a multidimensional phenomenon. We have to find a one-dimensional composite variable, which may be called the 'climate index'. Indices are estimated for the European Union and for Russia. The results are relevant for income policies of large states and remuneration policies of firms which operate in different climate zones. It is obvious that the technique developed in this chapter for climate may be applied to other external effects, for instance of public infrastructure.

In Chapter 11 we report on a study by Van Praag and Baarsma, who considered the living climate around Amsterdam airport. The external effect is here the noise produced by the air traffic. There are two extreme situations conceivable. In the first case houses with a noisy environment are cheaper than similar houses in a quiet environment. More precisely, the price differences are such that the individual becomes indifferent between the two houses. In that case the external effect (aircraft noise) is called 'internalized' by the market. In mainstream economics the standard hypothesis is that the market works. Hence, the problem of an external effect to the advantage or disadvantage of specific individuals is a temporary problem at the time of the introduction of the effect; for example, when a highway is built passing through a quiet suburb or when an airport is built. However, after a period of, sometimes painful, adaptation there will be no influence of the external effect which has been neutralized by adapted market prices. In the second case there is no price adaptation. This means, bluntly speaking, that houses may yield different contributions to well-being while fetching the same price. Obviously, this is a case where the market does not work, or at least not perfectly, and where there is accordingly no market equilibrium. Then, we find that aircraft noise must have an effect on individual well-being. It is well-known that the Amsterdam housing market cannot be characterized as being in equilibrium. In that case the external effect is not or not wholly internalized and there would be grounds for compensation by the airport which generates the external effect. In this chapter we estimate whether the external effect has influence and we estimate its size. We find that Amsterdam housing costs do not depend on the noise at all; hence, we conclude that there is not even a partial internalization. The methodology is clearly applicable to a wide range of environmental external-effect evaluations and it deserves a place next to the more traditional 'contingent-valuation' methods.

In Chapter 12, based on Plug, Van Praag, and Hartog (1999), we consider an application of the knowledge of observed utility functions to the construction of tax schemes. We return to the idea of Tinbergen's 'talent tax'. It is found that individual IQ and education determine individual income and that they also affect individual welfare. Building on this finding we can construct a lump-sum tax, which depends on IQ and education instead of income or consumption. As Tinbergen (1970*a*/*b*) pointed out, such a tax base eliminates the work-discouraging influence that is linked with an income tax and actually with nearly all tax types that are used in the civilized world. On the basis of empirical research on a Dutch database, it is found that the net result of introducing this IQ and education tax would, surprisingly, not lead to a tax system that differs dramatically from the present income-tax base. However, the data set was unfortunately restricted to individuals born around 1940, and it may be that results would be very different if the investigation were repeated on later cohorts. Unfortunately, we do not know of comparable data sets where information on the IQ of the respondents is known.

In the four chapters 13, 14, 15 and 16 we investigate the implications of our newly won knowledge for the definition and measurement of inequality.

We start in Chapter 13 with a look at income inequality. Inequality is an index of subjectively felt income differences. It stands to reason that we shall make use of our empirical observations of the income-evaluation question and the financial-satisfaction question. The resulting inequality concepts are not based on an axiomatic approach, which yields a specific inequality definition as the unavoidable outcome, as usual in the literature, but on measured satisfaction differences. This makes the derived index more credible in representing inequality feelings. As we shall explain in Chapters 2 and 13, the IEQ leads to an inequality index which varies among individuals. Hence, the same income distribution may be perceived as extremely unequal by a poor citizen, while the rich citizen perceives it as being quite equal. Apart from that, both questions yield a second concept of inequality, which is not the individual perception but a general index.

In Chapter 14 we extend the inequality concept. Alongside inequality with respect to income we may conceive of inequality with respect to health, job satisfaction, quality of one's marriage, and so on, culminating in inequality of satisfaction with respect to 'life as a whole'. It follows that we may define a social inequality with respect to every life domain distinguished and an inequality with respect to satisfaction with life as a whole. We may also define the correlation between satisfactions with two different domains. The result is a satisfaction covariance (and correlation) matrix. It is found empirically from the German and the British data sets that the correlation between domains is substantial. Hence, somebody who is discontented with respect to one domain of life is probably unhappy with other domains as well. When we look at inequality of satisfactions with life as a whole, and when we remember from Chapter 4 that satisfaction with life as a whole may be seen as an aggregate of domain satisfactions, it is no wonder that we can break down satisfaction inequality with life as a whole in terms of domain satisfactions inequality.

In Chapter 15 we look at the poverty phenomenon. Here, we can distinguish between the status of objective poverty and the subjective feeling of poverty. In our opinion an objective poverty definition in terms of a minimum income, or in terms of 'basic' needs runs the danger that some individuals who are officially declared to be 'poor' feel 'non-poor' and vice versa. The same subjective questioning that we used before may be utilized again to define subjective poverty. This also then leads to a subjective poverty line. The technique in one form or another has been applied by many statistical agencies in order to find out how far 'objective' poverty definitions coincide with subjective feelings. However, this has always been done as an experiment. In fact the classification into 'poor' and 'non-poor' can be seen as the extreme of a coarsened income concept, where the income axis is divided into just two brackets. It follows that the poverty ratio can be seen as a coarsened inequality index. It follows then that the road taken in Chapter 14 may also be taken with respect to poverty.

In Chapter 16 we generalize the subjective poverty concept by examining poverty in various domains of life, such as financial, health, house and job poverty. In short we define a multi-dimensional poverty concept conforming to the approach to multi-dimensional inequality. Using regression analysis as in Chapters 3 and 4, we predict the chance that an individual will be poor, given his objective situation X. The average of these individual chances provides, the expectation of the overall poverty ratio in the sample. Using this information, we look at the ways in which we can reduce the poverty ratio by changing individual's situation X. In the chapter we also distinguish between transitory and permanent poverty and explore the transitions from and out of poverty by using the panel character of the data.

The last chapter is a short epilogue.

The reader will see that there is a common thread running through this book from one chapter to another. But it is also clear that the book touches on many subjects and that it is not necessary to read all the chapters. We would advise the reader to read as a must Chapters 2, 3, and 4. After that you can read the chapters in any way, as they are reasonably self-contained, except the inequality chapters 13, 14, 15, and 16, which should be taken together.

2

The Analysis of Income Satisfaction with an Application to Family Equivalence Scales

2.1. INTRODUCTION

In the previous chapter we surveyed our instruments, namely question modules, and we explained what could be done with those instruments. In this chapter we start the empirical analysis by studying income satisfaction. We have seen that there is more than one way to tap information from respondents. We are especially interested in whether the different question modules will yield comparable and similar results. We shall study five methods that look different but which appear to yield roughly identical results. This chapter deals with methodology, but simultaneously we shall utilize our empirical results, derived from German and British data, to define and assess family-equivalence scales. In this way we introduce the reader to the methodology that we will use throughout this book.

If one is interested in the question of how satisfied someone is with his or her income, the most sensible thing to do is to ask him or her. There are various modalities. You may do it in face-to-face interviews, by phone, or by mail. From experience, we prefer a situation where the respondent feels as anonymous as possible. One has to avoid 'steering' the respondent. If somebody gets the idea that by answering that he or she is unsatisfied the direct or indirect effect will be an increase in his or her income, we may safely conclude that many respondents will give a biased answer. They will exaggerate their *dis*satisfaction. It is to be preferred that respondents fill out a multi-purpose questionnaire; by including income as one of many subjects we reduce the risk that individuals will respond strategically on income questions. This is best realized by asking a whole battery of questions on various non-related subjects. Examples are the German and British data sets we use in this book.

2.2. THE INCOME-SATISFACTION QUESTION

The income-satisfaction question we are using is part of a module that refers to various areas of life, including the financial aspects. It runs as follows:

How satisfied are you today with your household income? (Please answer by using the following scale, in which 0 means totally unhappy and 10 means totally happy.)

This question is posed in the German Socio-Economic Panel (GSOEP).[1] A similar question is posed in the British Household Panel Survey (BHPS).[2] The only difference is that the British analogue distinguishes seven categories, while the German question has eleven response categories.

There are two ways in which we may deal with this question: the ordinal and the cardinal way.

We start with an ordinal approach, which is the usual one in the literature. That is, we assume that the numerical evaluations 0, 1, 2, ..., 10 utilized by the respondent indicate just eleven income categories, where incomes in category 6 are felt to be 'sufficient' and those in category 4 to be 'bad', etc. Our approach would be cardinal if we were to assume that somebody who answers '4' is half as satisfied as somebody who answers '8.' We start by not making this cardinality assumption.

The first method of analysis we shall apply is the 'Ordered-Probit' (OP) method. We assume that there exists a latent (i.e. not directly observable) satisfaction variable $\ln(Z)$ and a partition of the real axis into eleven intervals $I_i = (\mu_{i-1}, \mu_i]$ with $-\infty = \mu_0 < \mu_1 < \ldots < \mu_{10} < \mu_{11} = \infty$, such that the respondent responds 'category i' if and only if $\ln(Z) \in I_i$. Hence, if a respondent evaluates his financial situation by '5' it implies that $\mu_5 < \ln(Z) \leq \mu_6$. The parameters μ are unknown and have to be estimated from the responses. The satisfaction variable Z naturally depends on the income y. Alongside that there may be other variables x that determine the response pattern. As an example we consider in this chapter the effect of *family size*, denoted by fs. We cannot assume that everybody with the same personal characteristics (y, x) responds identically: first, because it seems impossible to find an exhaustive list of all explanatory variables x, there will always be *omitted* variables; second, even if it were theoretically possible to make an exhaustive list including all those omitted variables as well, the possibility is remote that the values of all those relevant variables could be measured or collected in the framework of a large-scale survey; third, there may be random influences. In order to account for this necessary incompleteness we introduce the random variable ε that assumes a specific value for each respondent and we postulate a model equation

$$Z = f(y, x; \varepsilon). \tag{2.1}$$

The adoption of this model does not imply that we really believe that individuals are reacting exactly according to this model. It is an *approximating* model, which has to give an *approximate description* of response behavior. The model may be discarded as soon as we find a better one. One should not be dogmatic on that.

[1] We would like to thank the German SOEP organization and its director, Professor Gert Wagner, for making the data available to us.
[2] The BHPS data used in this book were made available through the UK Data Archive. The data were originally collected by the ESRC Research Center on Micro-Social Change at the University of Essex, now incorporated within the Institute for Social and Economic Research. Neither the original collectors of the data nor the Archive bear any responsibility for the analyses or interpretations presented here.

In the econometric literature this problem is traditionally treated by means of the Ordered-Probit (or the related 'Ordered Logit') model (see Maddala 1983; Greene 1991). Some of our readers will not know what Ordered Probit (OP) is. As this method will be frequently used in what follows, we shall explain the method in some detail.

We postulate a *latent* model equation[3]

$$\ln(Z) = \alpha \ln(y) + \beta \ln(fs) + \varepsilon \tag{2.2}$$

where we assume ε to be a standard normal random variable which is not correlated with the variables household income y and family size fs. That is, $E(\varepsilon) = 0$, $\sigma^2(\varepsilon) = 1$, $cov(y, \varepsilon) = cov(fs, \varepsilon) = 0$. Consequently, we have for the expectation

$$\begin{aligned} E(\ln(Z)) &= \alpha \ln(y) + \beta \ln(fs) + E(\varepsilon) \\ &= \alpha \ln(y) + \beta \ln(fs) \end{aligned} \tag{2.3}$$

We see that in this example $\ln(Z)$ is assumed to depend on two explanatory variables: income and family size. Hence, which response category is observed will depend on those variables as well. As not every individual is the same, and we certainly have not included all relevant variables, and, moreover, we are not sure of the functional specification, the log-linear equation (2.2) has been chosen—first, for intuitive reasons; second, because it is frequently used in the literature; and, third, for its econometric convenience. The same holds for the choice of a normal distribution for the random 'error' term ε. In the literature this specification competes with the logistic distribution, but neither the analysis nor its results differ systematically from that of the normal specification. We come back to this later.

The chance that an individual with income y and family size fs responds that he or she is in the ith satisfaction class is

$$\begin{aligned} P(\mu_i < \ln(Z) &= \alpha \ln(y) + \beta \ln(fs) + \varepsilon \leq \mu_{i+1}) \\ &= P(\mu_i - \alpha \ln(y) - \beta \ln(fs) < \varepsilon \leq \mu_{i+1} - \alpha \ln(y) - \beta \ln(fs)) \\ &= N(\mu_{i+1} - \alpha \ln(y) - \beta \ln(fs)) - N(\mu_i - \alpha \ln(y) - \beta \ln(fs)). \end{aligned} \tag{2.4}$$

Here N(.) stands for the standard normal-distribution function. When the yet unknown parameters μ, α and β have been estimated, the chance above may be assessed for each respondent. However, in practice, the first problem is to estimate those parameters. This is performed by the 'maximum-likelihood' (ML) method. Let us assume that we have N individuals, who have the characteristics (y_n, fs_n) $(n = 1, \ldots, N)$. The sample may be succinctly denoted by the observation set $\{(i_n, y_n, fs_n)\}_{n=1}^N$ where i_n stands for the response category answered by individual n. Assuming that the observations are mutually independent, the combined chance or likelihood of the sample is

$$\begin{aligned} L(\mu, \alpha, \beta) = \prod_{n=1}^N [N(\mu_{i_n+1} - \alpha \ln(y_n) - \beta \ln(fs_n)) \\ - N(\mu_{i_n} - \alpha \ln(y_n) - \beta \ln(fs_n)) \end{aligned} \tag{2.5}$$

---

[3] We denote the natural logarithm by ln( ) and the 10-logarithm by log( ).

where $I_{i_n} = (\mu_{i_n}, \mu_{i_n+1}]$ is the response interval corresponding to individual n.

The combined chance of finding this sample is the expression $L(\mu, \alpha, \beta)$, which depends on the unknown parameters μ, α, β. The maximum-likelihood principle says that the most probable values of the unknown parameters are those that *maximize* the chance of the sample we have found in reality. Hence, we maximize the sample likelihood $L(\mu, \alpha, \beta)$ with respect to μ, α, β. In practice, we do not maximize this expression but its logarithm

$$\ln(L(\mu, \alpha, \beta)) = \sum_{n=1}^{N} \ln\left(N(\mu_{i_n+1} - \alpha \ln(y_n) - \beta \ln(fs_n))\right)$$

$$- N(\mu_{i_n} - \alpha \ln(y_n) - \beta \ln(fs_n)))$$

(2.6)

with respect to μ, α, and β. Maximization of the logarithm $\ln(L)$ obviously amounts to the same thing as maximizing L itself.

Equation (2.6) does not include a constant term; say, β_0. We may include such a term by replacing all μ_i's by $(\mu_i - \beta_0)$ and estimating the latter magnitudes. We notice that this β_0 is really unidentified, except if we fix one μ-value beforehand. This is frequently done in software packages where μ_1 is fixed at zero. In what follows we will frequently use such software.

Let us now go on to the empirical analysis. We consider the GSOEP data set, and more precisely the 1997 wave, where we restrict ourselves to the subset of West German workers. Households where no one is working in a paid job are excluded.

In Table 2.1 we tabulate the response percentages for the 11 response categories.

Table 2.1. *Response frequencies for income satisfaction for West German workers, 1997*[4]

Satisfaction categories	Relative frequencies (%)
0	0.00
1	0.30
2	1.05
3	2.74
4	5.34
5	12.31
6	13.60
7	24.46
8	25.62
9	10.03
10	4.55
Number of observations [N]	4,964

[4] We use here a preliminary unauthorized release of the 1997 wave, which slightly differs from the final authorized version. In the final version a few observations are found in category 0 as well.

Table 2.2. *Estimates of three different income-satisfaction equations by ordered probit, Germany, 1997*

Variable	Estimate	t-ratio	Estimate	t-ratio	Estimate	t-ratio
Constant	−3.061	−10.224	−3.093	−10.232	−3.128	−10.319
Ln(household income)	0.734	20.251	0.738	20.113	0.738	20.093
Ln(family size)	−0.223	−6.800	—	—	—	—
Ln(adults)	—	—	−0.223	−6.269	−0.246	−6.751
Ln(children + 1)	—	—	−0.128	−3.680	−0.164	−4.465
Family structure	—	—	—	—	0.070	2.844
*Intercepts**						
μ_0	−∞		−∞		−∞	
μ_1	−∞		−∞		−∞	
μ_2	0		0		0	
μ_3	0.556		0.556		0.557	
μ_4	1.049		1.048		1.049	
μ_5	1.495		1.495		1.496	
μ_6	2.057		2.057		2.058	
μ_7	2.482		2.482		2.483	
μ_8	3.134		3.134		3.136	
μ_9	3.970		3.970		3.972	
μ_{10}	4.617		4.617		4.620	
μ_{11}	+∞		+∞		+∞	
N	4,964		4,964		4,964	
Log likelihood	−9,310		−9,310		−9,306	
Pseudo-R^2	0.020		0.020		0.021	

Note: $^*\mu_1 = -\infty$ because the first response category is empty in this sample.

In Table 2.2 we present *three* versions of the financial-satisfaction equation to be estimated. The first version is the one described by Equation (2.2).

We have two explanatory variables; namely, household income and family size. In the second version we replace *family* size by two variables. We distinguish between children under 16 years of age living at home and other persons living in the household.[5] The latter class will be called 'adults'. In the third specification we add a third variable 'family structure', which equals 0 if the respondent lives alone, 1 if the household has two working adults, and 2 if there are two adults in the household of which only one works. This ordering reflects the idea that household chores are pretty fixed and that they are more easily borne by a family with one person working outside than by a family with two adults in paid employment. The single person or the 'incomplete' family bears the heaviest burden in this respect. The results found in Table 2.2 are as expected and will be discussed in section 2.4.

[5] We add 1 so that we do not get a non-defined logarithm of 0 if the number of children equals 0.

2.3. A METHODOLOGICAL DIGRESSION

In this section we look at some basic methodological issues. Readers who are acquainted with this stuff are advised to skip this section. Before we turn to the economic interpretation of our estimates, the reader who is not acquainted with reading statistical tables may be helped by a few words on how to read these tables, because we will encounter many of them in the pages that follow.

Each equation corresponds with two columns in Table 2.1, the first of which presents the values of the estimates and the second of which gives the t-ratio. The t-ratio is a statistic that gives an idea of the statistical reliability of the estimate. As the estimate is based on a sample, the estimate will vary with the variation in the sample itself. It follows that the estimator has a probability distribution about the estimated value, which is approximately normal (Gaussian) for the large-scale samples we shall study. As the t-ratio is defined as $t = b/s$ where b stands for the value of the estimate and s for an estimate of the standard deviation of the estimator, the estimate becomes sharper the larger the ratio b/s is. In Figure 2.1 we sketch two distributions of estimators.

Both are distributed according to a normal Gauss-curve, but the left distribution is highly concentrated around the estimated value, while the right one is rather dispersed. In other words, the left-hand estimator has a small standard deviation and the right-hand one a rather large standard deviation (spread).

The deviation is best evaluated in relation to the value of the estimator itself, and this is traditionally done by looking at the t-ratio b/s.

When $t > 20$ this implies that the standard deviation of the estimate is $1/20$ of the corresponding value. In the literature we speak of confidence intervals around an estimated value. The conventional two-sided interval is a 2σ interval around the value of the estimate. There is a 95 percent chance that the real parameter value will be found in that interval. When (see Table 2.2 above) the coefficient of household income is estimated at 0.738 and the corresponding t-value at about 20, the corresponding *confidence interval* is

$$((1 - 2^*1/20)(0.738), \ (1 + 2^*1/20)(0.738)) = (0.664, \ 0.812).$$

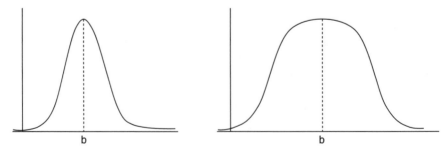

Figure 2.1. *The densities of a sharp and a vague estimator*

We see that this confidence interval does not include the value zero. Hence, we call the estimate *statistically significantly* different from zero at the 95 percent level. It can easily be shown that the estimator is *non*-significant if $-2 < t < 2$, because then the confidence interval would include the value zero. In that case even the sign of the effect cannot be reliably determined.

The (pseudo-)correlation coefficient R^2 (for a definition see McFadden 1974) stands for the quality of the explanation. It may be compared with the R^2 in usual regression analysis. If $R^2 = 100$ percent the explanation is perfect and if it is zero there is no explanation at all. There is a lot of discussion about the value of R^2 as a tool of analysis. Some social scientists, but not micro-econometricians, have the habit of discarding all results without discussion if the R^2 is below 80 percent or so. We will not do that, and we are even against it. It may be good to devote some words to it at the beginning of this study.

In this type of research we are interested in the *structural part* of a relation. The meaning of this term is slightly vague, but we shall take it to be the part of a relation, which we get if we set the error term at zero.

For instance, in the present case the relation to be estimated is

$$\ln(Z) = \alpha \ln(y) + \beta \ln(fs) + cons + \varepsilon, \tag{2.7}$$

where we include a constant.

The structural part is

$$\ln(\hat{Z}) = \alpha \ln(y) + \beta \ln(fs) + cons, \tag{2.8}$$

where the implicitly defined $\ln(\hat{Z})$ is called the *structural* part. After estimating α and β we may calculate a structural prediction $\hat{Z}$ for each individual n with characteristics (y_n, fs_n). The error term is a random term, which is independent of the structural part. Hence, it has a relation neither with the explanatory variables nor with the values of the parameters to be estimated.

There may be many reasons for a small R^2 without the estimates becoming suspect. In this case and in almost all probit-results the explanation in terms of the (pseudo-)R^2 is meagre, which is evidence for the fact that the error term about the expectation plays a relatively strong role. The significance of the structural part shows that there is a strong structural tendency as well. The error term stands also for omitted variables. We surmise that a considerable part of them cannot be observed, as they are individual psychological factors that are difficult to observe and to measure with an acceptable degree of precision. A second reason why the degree of explanation worsens is that we try to explain a continuous variable Z by looking at grouped observations. An a priori coarsening of the data has been applied. It is as if we were looking through glasses that are not precisely fitted to our eyes. A third reason for small R^2s is that we have a very heterogeneous sample, with many observations which is less easy to fit to the observations than a small sample of almost identical observations. In micro-econometrics an R^2 of about 0.10 is not unusual and for probit-type estimation models much lower values are still accepted. Notice also that in time-series data the correlation coefficient is frequently in the order of 90 percent, just because the consecutive observations are highly correlated over time and mostly small in number. The only interesting criterion is whether the estimates of the structural model are significant. If there is a small R^2, it implies that there is a considerable residual variance. It may be that this can be reduced by a better model, but in most cases we have to accept that there is a strong residual random component in human behavior.

2.4. THE ECONOMIC INTERPRETATION

Looking at the *t*-values of Table 2.2 we conclude that all estimates are very 'significant'.

The estimated relation presented in column 1 of Table 2.2 may be written explicitly as

$$\ln(Z) = 0.734 \ln(y) - 0.223 \ln(fs) - 3.061 + \varepsilon. \tag{2.9}$$

We now consider the locus of values of y and fs for which Z is constant, say, $\ln(Z) = c$. This locus is described by the equation

$$0.734 \ln(y) - 0.223 \ln(fs) - 3.061 + \varepsilon = c. \tag{2.10}$$

It describes an indifference curve[6] in $((\ln(y), \ln(fs))$-space with respect to financial satisfaction. The right-hand constant c corresponds to a specific satisfaction level. The same indifference curve is described in (y, fs)-space by the equation

$$e^{\ln(Z)} = Z = y^{0.734} fs^{-0.223} . e^{\varepsilon} = e^c = C. \tag{2.11}$$

These two descriptions are ordinally equivalent, as the latter can be derived from the former by application of the monotonic transform $\varphi(.) = \exp(.)$. We have $C = \exp(c)$.

We sketch the indifference curves for various values of ε and a fixed satisfaction level C in Figure 2.2. Clearly, each individual will have its own value for the disturbance term ε. As ε is assumed to be normally distributed around zero, in 50 percent of the cases $e^{\varepsilon} < 1$, while in the other 50 percent the factor will be larger than 1. The indifference curve with $\varepsilon = 0$ may be seen as a *median* indifference curve for somebody of the type (y, fs). If we take $\varepsilon = 0$ and vary the constant C, we see how the indifference curve changes with varying values of C. This is a second interpretation of Figure 2.2.

Now we see that satisfaction increases with increasing income y and decreases with rising household size fs. Both signs are as expected. A larger household implies that more members have to be supported from the same income, which is concomitant with a reduction in financial satisfaction. However, we do not know by how much satisfaction will change if one of those variables changes. This is because $\ln(Z)$ does not represent satisfaction itself but only *one* monotonous transform of it, and there are many of them.

---

[6] In this case the 'curves' are straight lines. Notice that we do not have to assume optimizing behavior by the individuals in order to identify the indifference curves. They are empirically observed.

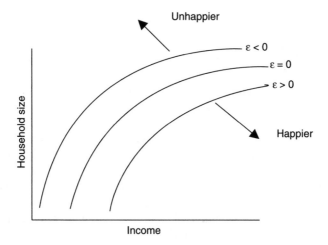

Figure 2.2. *Indifference curves in the (income, household-size) space*

Let us now look at the trade-off between y and fs.

The essential question is the following. If $\ln(fs)$ is increased by $\Delta\ln(fs)$,[7] by how much has $\ln(y)$ to be increased in order to keep the individual at the same satisfaction level? The answer is found by solving for $\Delta\ln(y)$ the equation

$$\begin{aligned}\ln(Z) &= 0.734\{\ln(y) + \Delta\ln(y)\} - 0.223\{\ln(fs) + \Delta\ln(fs)\} \\ &\quad + cons + \varepsilon = 0.734\ln(y) - 0.233\ln(fs) + cons + \varepsilon\end{aligned} \tag{2.12}$$

or

$$0.734\Delta\ln(y) - 0.233\Delta\ln(fs) = 0 \tag{2.13}$$

We see that the solution is found to be

$$\Delta\ln(y) = \frac{0.223}{0.734}\Delta\ln(fs) \tag{2.14}$$

or for infinitesimal changes

$$\frac{d\ln(y)}{d\ln(fs)} = \frac{0.223}{0.734} = 0.304. \tag{2.15}$$

Economists call the logarithmic derivative in (2.15) an *elasticity*. We see that the income household-size elasticity, keeping financial satisfaction constant, equals $0.223/0.734 = 0.304$. As a consequence of the functional double-log specification it is a constant elasticity.

Let us assume that we start at an income level y_0 and a household size of fs_0, and fs increases to fs_1, then we have to multiply the income y_0 by the factor

---

[7] We cast the question in terms of log differences because this is more convenient. A solution in absolute differences would lead to a similar result.

$$y_1/y_0 = (fs_1/fs_0)^{\frac{0.223}{0.734}} = (fs_1/fs_0)^{0.304} \tag{2.16}$$

if at the new income level y_1 financial satisfaction is to stay constant.

This formula leads straightforwardly to a compensation formula to be applied for family allowances. If household size increases from 2 to 4 members, the variable fs increases by a factor of 2. According to the rule, net household income should be multiplied by a factor $2^{0.304} = 1.235$ in order to keep financial satisfaction constant. Given that $0.304 < 1$, we see that each additional child would call for a smaller relative compensation. We observe that this equivalence system is in a certain sense a residual system. Part of the increase is structurally compensated for by the state family-allowance system. Equation (2.16) prescribes how much a household would have to get *on top* of the structural family allowance that is provided by the state. In the ideal case that the state would fully compensate for additional children we would find that no additional compensation would be needed and the exponent would equal zero. (See also Buhmann et al. 1988.)

What is striking in this formula is that the correction factor does not depend on income. Hence, the rich household and the poor household would benefit from the same correction factor. In absolute money amounts the rich household would have to get a much larger compensation than the poor household. In some sense this is not so surprising. Gossen's First Law, which says that the marginal utility of everything decreases when one gets more of it, is generally accepted, even though the empirical verification is impossible, if we assume that utility is non-cardinal. Based on Gossen's Law we feel that rich people should *pay* relatively more taxes than poor households do. This is the basis of every progressive income-taxation system. The same principle would now lead to higher absolute amounts to be *received* for richer families. Nevertheless, for many this will be politically unacceptable. Indeed, it is a question for politics which family-equivalence system will be chosen. Our result provides a benchmark, giving the system that yields *welfare-neutral* family-equivalence scales. If politicians opt for another system for very honourable reasons, they are evidently free to do so. The only point is that such a system is not welfare-neutral anymore. Obviously, the estimated system is not sacrosanct either, since we may introduce other specifications of the equation, as we did in Table 2.2. For comparable results see Buhmann et al. (1988). We present the resulting household-equivalence scale, corresponding to Equation (2.2), in Table 2.3.

The problem of equivalence scales is a politically pressing one. In nearly all economies we find some compensation schedules for large families, either through household size-dependent taxation or through children's benefits.

One of the first researchers who gave attention to the problem is Engel, who formulated the famous law well-known as Engel's Law (1895). The problem took on a political dimension with Rowntree (1941), who tried to develop a scale for comparing poor families with each other, incorporating a correction for different household sizes.

Here we base our approach on a subjective method. This subjective approach to the empirical definition of household-equivalence scales was first developed

Table 2.3. *Household-equivalence scales*
to keep financial satisfaction constant

Household size	Correction factor (%)
1	81
2	100
3	113
4	123
5	132
6	140
7	146
8	152

in Van Praag (1971) and further elaborated in Van Praag and Kapteyn (1973) and Kapteyn and Van Praag (1976). A recent application in Mexico, a less developed country, is provided by Rojas (2007*a*). In the literature we find other methodologies which are apparently less subjective; they are based on the observation of consumption patterns of families.

The simplest method is to define a scale of consumer units out of hand. A famous and frequently used example is the so-called Oxford scale,[8] in which the first adult counts for 1, other adults count for 0.7, and any additional child stands for 0.5. This scale calculates that a couple with two children would stand for $1.0 + 0.7 + 2 \times 0.5 = 2.7$ 'consumer units'. There are clearly economies of scale, but the 'subjective' formula that we estimated above leads to a much flatter scale. From Table 2.3 we would set the ratio at $123/81 = 1.52$. Other objective methods observe the consumption of adults and calculate their absolute value or their relative value as a fraction of household income (see Deaton and Mullbauer 1986). If we use the criterion that this share should be constant over households irrespective of the household size, this leads also to compensations that increase proportionally with income. Pollak and Wales (1979) showed in a short but influential critical note that there are many rather fundamental objections to those objective methods. Given the scope of this study we cannot pay more attention to this fascinating literature. General recent surveys on methodology are found in Whiteford (1985), Browning (1992), Van Praag and Warnaar (1997).

There is one consequence of the specification of our financial-satisfaction index Z or ln (Z) that gives cause for reflection. The index depends negatively on the number of children. As currently households are able to influence their number of children, it suggests that every household should try to reduce the number of children to zero in order to enhance its financial satisfaction. Nevertheless, there are still many households *with* children. There may be three reasons to explain this apparent paradox. First, there is more to life than *financial* satisfaction alone.

[8] This scale has been adopted later on by the OECD after slight modification as their 'official' equivalence scale.

It may be that other aspects of having children weigh positively in one's life and that those aspects more than compensate for the negative effect of children on *financial* satisfaction. A second reason may be that households are myopic; they do not anticipate when deciding to have children that it will affect their future financial satisfaction negatively. A third reason may be that our specification needs improvement. We will come back to it later on.

The second specification in column 3 of Table 2.2 introduces a somewhat more sophisticated household definition. We distinguish between adults and children under sixteen who live in the household. Both household characteristics are separately introduced in the equation as

$$\ln(Z) = \alpha \ln(y) + \beta_1 \ln(adults) + \beta_2 \ln(children + 1) + \varepsilon, \tag{2.17}$$

or

$$\ln(Z) = \alpha \ln(y) + \beta_1 \ln(Ad) + \beta_2 \ln(Ch) + \varepsilon \tag{2.18}$$

for short.[9] We find now as estimate

$$\ln(Z) = 0.738 \ln(y) - 0.223 \ln(Ad) - 0.128 \ln(Ch) - 3.093 + \varepsilon, \tag{2.19}$$

where we drop the t-values, which are (highly) significant.

A household is now defined by two dimensions (Ad, Ch) and the relevant compensation formula is now found by generalizing the previous reasoning. We find

$$y_1/y_0 = (Ad_1/Ad_0)^{\frac{0.223}{0.738}} * (Ch_1/Ch_0)^{\frac{0.128}{0.738}}. \tag{2.20}$$

We also see from this formula that adults carry more weight than children. More precisely, we have a trade-off ratio of $0.128/0.223 = 0.57$. Hence, a doubling of the number of adults from 1 to 2 counts almost twice as heavily as a doubling of children from 1 to 2.

We tabulate this two-dimensional scale in Table 2.4.

Finally, we may derive an equivalence scale from the third specification, in which we take account of the structure of the household as well. Is there one breadwinner or two, or are both non-active; is it a single- or two-parent household?

We see that two-breadwinner families need more than one-breadwinner families. This reflects the fact that there is probably much more home production when only one of the adults is working in a paid job. (See Table 2.5.)

The same equations have been estimated for the British Household Panel Survey. Here we found the following estimates in Table 2.6.

We see that the British coefficient of income is about 0.48, while the German coefficient is about 0.73. The other two coefficients are in both countries of the same order. Therefore, the resulting family-equivalence scale follows an exponential power of $0.223/0.734 = 0.304$ in Germany and a power of $0.237/0.484 = 0.490$ in the UK. The scale appears to be much steeper in the UK than in Germany.

---

[9] We write Ad for adults and Ch for ($children + 1$). The addition by one is used to avoid taking a logarithm of zero.

Table 2.4. *Two-dimensional equivalence scales to correct for (adult, children) differences*[*]

No. of children	No of adults	
	1	2
0	0.670	0.827
1	0.756	0.932
2	0.811	1.000
3	0.853	1.051
4	0.886	1.093
5	0.915	1.128

[*]*Reference*: a household with 2 adults and 2 children.

Table 2.5. *Two-dimensional equivalence scales to correct for (adult, children) differences and household structure*[*]

No. of adults	No. of children				
	0	1	2	3	4
1	0.566	0.660	0.722	0.770	0.809
2, 1 breadwinner	0.783	0.914	1.000	1.066	1.120
2 breadwinners	0.861	1.005	1.099	1.172	1.232

[*]*Reference*: a household with 2 adults, 1 breadwinner, and 2 children, German data set.

Table 2.6. *Estimates of three different income-satisfaction equations by ordered probit, UK, 1997*

Variable	Estimate	*t*-ratio	Estimate	*t*-ratio	Estimate	*t*-ratio
Constant	−1.637	−14.996	−1.686	−15.383	−1.714	−15.639
Ln(household income)	0.484	32.784	0.487	32.256	0.487	32.383
Ln(family size)	−0.237	−8.199	—	—	—	—
Ln(adults)	—	—	−0.220	−6.317	−0.230	−6.583
Ln(children + 1)	—	—	−0.110	−4.197	−0.124	−4.613
Family structure	—	—	—	—	0.047	2.317
Intercepts:						
μ_0	−∞		−∞		−∞	
μ_1	0		0		0	
μ_2	0.499		0.498		0.498	
μ_3	1.015		1.013		1.014	
μ_4	1.622		1.620		1.621	
μ_5	2.386		2.383		2.385	
μ_6	3.223		3.219		3.221	
μ_7	+∞		+∞		+∞	
N	6,298		6,298		6,298	
Log likelihood	−10,904		−10,911		−10,909	
Pseudo-R^2	0.021		0.021		0.021	

Table 2.7. *Household-equivalence scales for the UK and Germany*

Household size	Household-equivalence scales (%)	
	UK	Germany
1	71	81
2	100	100
3	122	113
4	140	124
5	157	132
6	171	140
7	185	146
8	197	152

In Table 2.7 we present the resulting household-equivalence scales for the two countries. Plainly speaking, it implies that additional children in the UK are more expensive than in Germany. The explanation is probably that the family-allowance system and the size of education support is more austere in England than in Germany. Were the government to compensate completely for differences in family size, differences in family size would have no effect on financial satisfaction and the coefficient β would equal zero. It follows that subjective equivalence scales depend on the structure of social security in the specific country.

2.5. IMPLICIT CARDINALIZATION

We saw that ordered-probit analysis yields a valuable instrument for making the ordinal-financial-satisfaction concept tractable. However, we will now probe further. It is frequently stated that the ordered-probit (OP) approach is a solution to the cardinalization problem. Using the OP-tool would imply that we can stay ordinal and that we do not have to accept a specific cardinalization. We remind the reader that satisfaction ln (Z) may be regarded as a utility and cannot be directly measured in an unambiguous way. Our estimates are based on the assumption that: If the respondent belongs to response category i, then there holds

$$\mu_{i-1} < \ln(Z) = \alpha \ln(y) + \beta \ln(fs) + \varepsilon \leq \mu_i. \qquad (2.21)$$

It follows that ln (Z) is 'roughly' cardinalized. We know that ln (Z) lies in a specific interval $(\mu_{i-1}, \mu_i]$. That the cardinalization is 'rough' and not infinitely fine is only because of the practical impossibility of distinguishing between an infinity of adjacent response categories. This cardinalization depends on three factors:

• the choice of the error distribution as normal;

- the fixation of its variance at *one*;
- the choice of the specific structural model.

Hence, we conclude that the ordered-probit model leads to a cardinal-satisfaction concept and that the cardinalization depends on the above more or less arbitrary choice elements.

In order to get a better idea of this cardinalization we specify our last choice in a very special way. We assume that there is no structural part. It follows that in that case $\ln(Z) = \varepsilon$.

In this case we have

$$N(\mu_i; 0, 1) - N(\mu_{i-1}; 0, 1) = P_i \qquad (i = 1, \ldots, k), \qquad (2.22)$$

where P_i is the fraction of respondents belonging to category i. It follows that if there are 10 percent in the first response category then we may calculate μ_1 by solving $N(\mu_1) = 0.10$.[10] If the next category covers another 5 percent, we have $N(\mu_2) = 0.15$, from which we may assess μ_2. It is clear what this would imply if we were able to refine the categories to an infinite number. In that case the population of size N would be ordered according to increasing satisfaction. The order number of a person would be n/N and the corresponding satisfaction would be

$$\ln(Z_n) = N^{-1}(n/N). \qquad (2.23)$$

It is obvious how this would change if we replaced the normal by the logistic or any other continuous distribution function. This remark is not intended to reduce the value of probit approaches to satisfaction analysis. However, the claim that it would not involve any cardinalization cannot be maintained.

2.6. PROBIT-ADAPTED OLS[11]

In the light of the above we may ask ourselves whether we cannot make use of an implicit cardinalization to recast the problem in such a way that it can be tackled by 'ordinary least squares' (OLS). Although Probit is nowadays included as a matter of routine in most standard statistical software packages, we will see later on, when dealing with more complicated multiple-equation models and/or panel data sets, which are conceptually easy to think of, that the Probit formulation will cause technical and computational difficulties.

Therefore, we shall now develop another way to estimate indifference curves. The result will be that we end up with a new method, which appears in most cases to yield roughly the same results as Ordered Probit, but which is much easier to understand, requires much less computing time, and can be much easier generalized to more complex models. The drawback of the method is

---

[10] In the present (German) sample the first response category is empty (see n. 4). It follows that $\mu_1 = -\infty$ as well.

[11] This section has been changed considerably, compared to the 2004 edition.

that it is based on an additional assumption to be stated later on, which is not needed for OP. If the assumption holds, the method is equivalent to OP. We will call that method the POLS-method (Probit OLS).

There is no need to read this section for those who are not fond of statistical technique and formulae. They can straightforwardly switch over to the next section. A summary of the method introduced in this section is given on page 34.

Let us reconsider equation (2.10), which we reproduce here for convenience as

$$0.734 \ln (y) - 0.223 \ln (fs) - 3.061 + \varepsilon = u$$

where u stands for the utility or satisfaction level.

The equation describes the set of 'situations' $(\ln (y), \ln (fs))$ that represent for the individual the same satisfaction level. The individual is indifferent between them. He may choose one or another under the condition that they lie on the same indifference curve. Equation (2.10) is linear in $(\ln (y), \ln (fs))$. For fixed u it describes a line in R^2. If u is varied, we get a whole net of indifference lines on R^2. That net is *dense* as any situation lies at one (and only one) indifference line. We call u the *utility* level associated with the situations on the corresponding indifference line. Those lines are parallel, as the coefficients of the variables (in this case 0.734 and -0.223) do not vary with u. It is mostly assumed that indifference curves are parallel, as otherwise they might intersect, which would imply that one situation is associated with two utility (satisfaction) levels simultaneously. The linearity is just an empirical choice, which may be a rather good approximation. We noticed already that a lot depends on the way in which variables are included. We saw in section 2.4 that, if we do not apply the log-transformations, we will get an indifference curve in (y, fs)-space, which is not straight but curvilinear (see Figure 2.2). Given that more income will be preferred to less income, it follows that a situation lying on a curve with u_2 will be preferred to a situation on u_1, if and only if $u_1 < u_2$. The indifference curves are ordered. However, the utility levels have only ordinal significance. It is a labelling system.

Now we shall generalize the concept. Let us denote 'situations' by vectors x. In the present case we have $x = (\ln (y), \ln (fs))$. If there are more relevant variables needed to describe a situation, say m variables, then the vector x stands for an m-tuple and $x \in R^m$. A linear indifference curve system will now be described by the equation

$$\beta_1 x_1 + \ldots + \beta_m x_m + \beta_0 = \beta' x + \beta_0 = u \tag{2.24}$$

The net of these linear indifference curves may be described by a utility function $U(\beta' x) = U$. When U is fixed at a specific value u, we find a specific indifference curve. When the function $U(\beta' x) = U$ is replaced by $\tilde{U}(x) = \varphi(U(x))$, where $\varphi(.)$ is an increasing monotonic function, the function $\tilde{U}(.)$ still describes the same net of indifference curves. Hence, the term *utility* has no cardinal meaning. The function describes a preference ordering between x's, and there is an infinity of utility functions describing the same geometrical net of indifference curves.

Algebraically, the same line may be described by many equations. For instance, the equations

$$1 = x_1 + 2x_2$$
$$-3 = -3x_1 - 6x_2$$
$$3 = x_1 + 2x_2 + 2$$

describe the same line in R^2.

In order to reduce that ambiguity we introduce the normalized vector $\bar{\beta} = \frac{1}{|\beta|} . \beta$, where $|\beta| = \sqrt{\sum_{j=1}^{m} \beta^2 j}$. We may then write each β as $\lambda . \bar{\beta}$, where $\lambda = |\beta|$. It is obvious that there holds for the substitution ratios $\beta_i/\beta_j = \bar{\beta}_i/\bar{\beta}_j$ as the factor λ cancels out. As the vector describes the (common) slope of the indifference curves it must be estimable from any specification of the utility function. The parameter λ varies with the specific cardinalization of the utility function.

If we assume interpersonal comparability, that is, that individuals who evaluate their satisfaction to be at the same level, either in verbal terms or in numerical grades, are situated on the same indifference curve, we may find such a curve geometrically by plotting the various situations $x^{(1)}, x^{(2)}, \ldots$ in R^2 or R^m. The analogy with the static consumer behaviour model in economics is striking. As Pareto (1909) already demonstrated, the indifference curves in commodity space may be observed. They may be described by a utility function $U(x)$, such that different indifference curves are described by equations $U(x) = u_1, u_2, \ldots$, but that utility function is 'ordinal'. It may be replaced by any monotonic transformation $\tilde{U}(x) = \varphi(U(x))$, which describes the same net of indifference curves.

In real life we encounter the problem that individuals in the same objective situation x will not exactly evaluate their situation in the same way. Therefore, we assume a random term ε. We assume for the response behavior

$$u = \beta'x + \beta_0 + \varepsilon \text{ with } E(\varepsilon) = 0, \ \sigma(\varepsilon) < \infty \tag{2.25}$$

That is, individuals, whose situation is x, will situate themselves on average at the indifference curve $u = \beta'x + \beta_0$.

We include the random term to account for the fact that omitted factors may shift the individual's satisfaction somewhat, so that he or she may be at a somewhat higher or lower indifference curve than predicted. We will employ this idea in the present context.

Let us assume we have a sample $\{(U_n, x_n)\}_{n=1}^{N}$, depicting the objective situation x and their evaluation U for individuals n. That evaluation will be numerical and we assume for the moment it will be on a continuous scale. We might think of a question format where the respondent may express his evaluation U by crossing a point on a continuous interval, e.g. [0, 10]. We do not assign a cardinal interpretation to this evaluation, but we assume that all respondents use the same evaluation system, which implies that it is impossible that two individuals living in the same situation will evaluate their situation by two different numbers, apart from a random error. It is attractive to apply OLS-regression on the equation

$$U_n = \beta' x_n + \beta_0 + \varepsilon_n$$

However, the regression model logically presumes that the numbers u_n cannot be bounded, e.g. between zero and ten. Hence, before regression we will transform the evaluation U by a monotonic transformation $f(.)$ such that $f(U) = u$ can assume all values on the real line $(-\infty, \infty)$. Then we may apply regression and the result will be an estimate $\hat{\beta} = \lambda.\hat{\beta}$. This yields the estimated substitution rates and the slope coefficients of the indifference hyper-planes. For large samples we find the usual statistical properties of the estimator. Especially, we have $\sigma^2(\hat{\beta}) = \lambda^2.\sigma^2(\hat{\hat{\beta}})$. It follows that their two t-values are the same as $\frac{\hat{\beta}}{\sigma(\hat{\beta})} = \frac{\hat{\hat{\beta}}}{\sigma(\hat{\hat{\beta}})}$.

The question is now what transformation $f(.)$ on the ordinal data is desirable. We notice that by assumption the error ε is normally distributed. The expression $\mu_n = \beta' x_n + \epsilon_n$ is a sum of random variables. In most practical examples we use at least eight variables plus the error term. When we use OP and consider a pseudo-sample $\{\bar{u}_n\}$ using the prediction of $\beta' x_n$ and adding a draw $\tilde{\epsilon}_n$ from the N(0,1) distribution, we find that the hypothesis that $\tilde{u}_n$ is normally distributed, cannot be rejected (by Jarques-Bera) in the cases we looked after. Then it implies that the sum $u_n = \beta' x_n + \beta_0 + \varepsilon_n$ is also approximately normally distributed. Hence, it lies then at hand to apply a transformation, such that $f(U_n) = u_n$ is normally distributed. This can be realized by ordering the observations according to u and defining u_n by setting $N(u_n; 0, 1) = \frac{n}{N}$, where $N(.)$ stands for the standard normal distribution function.

As u_n has a conditional distribution, given x_n, we assume that its conditional expectation is $E(u_n; x_n) = \beta' x_n + \beta_0$. The unconditional expectation and variance are by construction $E(u) = 0$ and $\sigma^2(u) = 1$. Applying regression on (2.25)

$$u_n = \beta' x_n + \beta_0 + \varepsilon \tag{2.26}$$

where we assume $E(\varepsilon) = 0, \sigma^2(\varepsilon) < \infty$, we find after normalization $\hat{\beta}$. We notice that the conditions $E(u) = 0$ and $\sigma^2(u) = 1$ are identifying conditions for λ, β_0.

Now there rests still a second nasty problem. Up to now we assumed that satisfactions can be distinguished and observed on an infinitely fine scale.

The practice is that satisfaction levels u are not continuously observed but only in response categories that correspond to intervals $A_1, \ldots, A_k$ that constitute a partition of the real axis. This causes the need for 'discrete statistical analysis' like Ordered Probit or Logit.

In the context we set up above this is not a real problem. In that case the least-squares criterion carries over into

$$\sum_{j=1}^{k} \sum_{n \in S_j} E((x_n' \beta - u_j)^2 | u_j \in A_j) \tag{2.27}$$

where we take the conditional expectation with respect to u_j over the set A_j. We denote the conditional expectation as $E(u_j|u_j \in A_j) = \bar{u}_j$. The first order OLS-conditions become

$$\sum_{j=1}^{k} \sum_{n \in S_j} E(x_n(x'_n \beta - u_j)|u_j \in A_j) =$$

$$\sum_{j=1}^{k} \sum_{n \in S_j} (x_n(x'_n \beta - \bar{u}_j)) = 0 \qquad (2.28)$$

In other words, the unknown u-values are replaced by their conditional expectations.

As we chose for a normal $N(0, 1)$-distribution, it implies that the intervals $A_1, \ldots, A_k$, denoted by $\{(\mu_{j-1}, \mu_j)\}_{j=1}^{k}$, can be easily determined by equalizing the response category frequencies $p_1, \ldots, p_k$ with the theoretical frequencies, that is we solve the system

$$N(\mu_1) = p_1$$
$$N(\mu_2) = p_1 + p_2 \qquad (2.29)$$
$$\ldots$$

for the boundaries μ_j. Now it is easy to determine the conditional expectations $E(u|\mu_{j-1} < u_j \leq \mu_j) = \bar{u}_j$. According to normal distribution theory there holds (see e.g. Maddala 1983: 366)

$$E(u|\mu_{j-1} < u_j \leq \mu_j) = \frac{n(\mu_{j-1}) - n(\mu_j)}{N(\mu_j) - N(\mu_{j-1})} \qquad (2.30)$$

According to the above-described recipe we shall regress $E(u|\mu_{j-1} < u_j \leq \mu_j) = \bar{u}_j$ on the explanatory variables x.

So we may summarize the POLS-method as follows:

1. Calculate the sample fractions $p_1, \ldots p_k$.
2. Calculate the boundaries by solving the system

$$N(\mu_1) = p_1, N(\mu_2) = p_1 + p_2, \ldots \qquad (2.31)$$

3. Calculate the conditional means $E(u|\mu_{i-1} < u_i \leq \mu_i) = \bar{u}_i$. $\qquad (2.32)$
4. Regress the $\bar{u}_{i_n}$ on x_n.

A final question rests. What is the difference with Ordered Probit? The difference is that we assume that the $u_n = \beta' x_n + \varepsilon_n$ will be approximately normally distributed, while the OP-setting makes no assumption on this. Hence, OP is definitely more general than POLS. The test on this empirical equivalence is whether OP and POLS yield statistically different trade-off ratios. In the present context both methods yield the same trade-off ratio of 0.30. The reliability as measured by t-ratios is the same as well. Hence, in this case the assumption is warranted.

Moreover, by specific transformations on the explanatory variables x (e.g. taking logs), we can improve the normality. Numerous estimations on real and simulated data, where POLS and OP have been applied by us side by side, and economic reasoning strongly suggest that in most cases the estimated trade-off ratios (or normalized β's) are approximately the same (that is statistically non-significantly different), and that the reliability, measured by t-ratios, is the same as well. We refer to Table 3.13a, where we compare, as an example, the outcomes of OP and POLS for a multi-variate panel model.

Returning now to the analysis of financial satisfaction we replace the notation by our original notation and we denote

$$\ln(\ddot{Z}_i) = E(\ln(Z|\mu_{i-1} < Z \le \mu_i) = \frac{n(\mu_{i-1}) - n(\mu_i)}{N(\mu_i) - N(\mu_{i-1})}. \tag{2.33}$$

It follows that according to the POLS-method we look at the regression model

$$\ln(\ddot{Z}_{i_n}) = \alpha \ln(y_n) + \beta \ln(fs_n) + cons + \varepsilon_n. \tag{2.34}$$

In Table 2.8 we present the OLS results that correspond to the results from Probit, given in Table 2.2.

Such a comparison shows that the effects as estimated by OP and POLS are indeed almost the same except for a multiplication factor. It follows that the resulting trade-off ratios are almost identical. We also see that the t-ratios, which indicate the reliability or sharpness of the estimates, are virtually identical. The standard deviations are the same except for the multiplication factor. In Table 3.13a, we present another comparison in a panel data context with random fixed effects, where we estimate the same complex relation by OP and by POLS. The similarity of the estimates is striking, but the advantage of POLS is that it performed the estimation of the panel equation in about one minute, while the traditional route via OP required about two hours of computing time.

From now on we call this method 'probit-adapted OLS', or POLS for short. In what follows we shall use this method as an essential building-block for our statistical analysis. It will be seen that many complicated models can be easily handled using POLS. Intuitively, there is also an advantage as we can make use of the classical linear statistical methods, as we will see in the chapters to come.

The POLS approach is computationally much easier than Probit and yields equivalent results. Consequently, we shall mostly use POLS in this study or a cardinal variant to be considered in section 2.8 as an easy shortcut to Probit-type models.

2.7. CARDINAL APPROACH (CP AND COLS)

Now we look at a third method, which makes use of the *cardinal* information in the financial-satisfaction question as well. It is this cardinal information which is neglected by Ordered Probit and POLS. If somebody evaluates his satisfaction level by a '7', it does not imply that his satisfaction is *exactly* equal to 7. For instance, the exact evaluation might be 6.75 or 7.25, but because of the necessary discreteness of the

Table 2.8. *POLS results for the income-satisfaction equations, Germany*

Variable	Effects	t-ratio	Effects	t-ratio	Effects	t-ratio
Constant	−5.475	−19.849	−5.504	−19.663	−5.534	−19.770
Ln(household income)	0.678	19.829	0.681	19.581	0.681	19.584
Ln(family size)	−0.206	−6.624	—	—	—	—
Ln(adults)	—	—	−0.205	−6.122	−0.227	−6.597
Ln(children + 1)	—	—	−0.118	−3.645	−0.152	−4.407
Family structure	—	—	—	—	0.065	2.842
N	4,964		4,964		4,964	—
Adjusted R^2	0.073		0.073		0.075	—

responses we have to round it off to 7. However, it would be very improbable that the exact evaluation was 7.75, for in that case we would have rounded off to 8. More precisely, we assume that if somebody responds '7' his *true* evaluation will be in the interval [6.5, 7.5]. A similar reasoning holds for all other response values. For the extremes we use an obvious modification. The observed value 0 corresponds to the interval [0, 0.5] and the value 10 to [9.5, 10]. If we normalize the scale from [0, 10] to the [0, 1]-interval, the intervals will be [0, 0.05], ..., [0.95, 1].

Let us now assume that the satisfaction U may be explained to a certain extent by a vector of explanatory variables x, including log income. More precisely, we assume

$$U = N(\beta'x + \beta_0; 0, 1) \tag{2.35}$$

where $N(.)$ stands for the (standard) normal-distribution function. We stress that Equation (2.35) is a non-stochastic specification, where the normal distribution function has been chosen only as a handy specification. For estimation purposes we add a random term ε and we assume

$$U = N(\beta'x + \beta_0 + \varepsilon; 0, 1). \tag{2.36}$$

We see that satisfaction is determined by a structural part and a random disturbance ε. We assume the random disturbance ε to be normally distributed with expectation equal to zero. Its variance σ^2 has to be estimated. As usual, we assume that $cov(x, \varepsilon) = 0$. Notice that this model, and especially the specification of Equation (2.36), is an assumption. If another model were to fit the data better, we would have to replace it. However, let us assume it holds.

In that case the chance of response '7' is

$$P[0.65 < U \leq 0.75] = P[N^{-1}(0.65) < \beta'x + \beta_0 + \varepsilon \leq N^{-1}(0.75)]$$
$$= N(u_{0.75} - \beta'x - \beta_0; 0, \sigma) - N(u_{0.65} - \beta'x - \beta_0; 0, \sigma). \tag{2.37}$$

Comparison with Equation (2.4) reveals that the likelihood is equal to the Probit-likelihood except that the unknown μ's are replaced by known normal quantiles u and that σ is not fixed at one, but has to be estimated as well. The β's are estimated by maximizing the log likelihood.

Applying this method to the German data set, we find in Table 2.9 results that are very similar to those in Table 2.2, except for a proportionality factor. We may call this the 'cardinal-probit' (CP) approach in contrast to the 'ordered-probit' (OP) approach. This CP approach looks very much equal to what is called in the literature the 'group-wise' or 'interval-regression method'.

The question is now whether we can develop a cardinal OLS variant of POLS, say COLS, as well.

We may construct a variable $\ln(\ddot{Z})$ by defining for a response category i

$$\ln(\ddot{Z}_i) = E(\ln(Z)|u_{i-1} < \ln(Z) \le u_i), \tag{2.38}$$

where $\ln(Z)$ is N(0,1)-distributed. Application of OLS regression on the observations $\{\ln(\ddot{Z}_{i_n})\}_{n=1}^{n=N}$ yields Table 2.10.

Again we see that the results are very similar. In fact, we see that the trade-off ratios and t-ratios are almost the same in all four approaches OP, POLS, CP, and COLS.

It follows that OP, POLS, CP, and COLS are for practical purposes *equivalent* for the computations of trade-off ratios. The C-versions employ the *cardinal* part of the information as well. The probit versions are computationally more difficult. It follows that if $\ln(\ddot{Z})$, is a linear combination of variables x then the same will hold for $\ln(\ddot{Z})$, where the trade-off ratios will be the same.

Indeed, if we apply regression (to k observations) to find the relation between the 'POLS-Z and the COLS-Z', we find for the German data the regression result

$$\ln(\ddot{Z}) = 0.5359 \ln(\ddot{Z}) + 0.1965$$

with an R^2 of 0.99.

In what follows we prefer COLS or POLS to CP or OP for its computational simplicity.

The implicit cardinalization on which Probit and POLS are based will be called from now on the *frequentist* cardinalization, because it is based on the frequency distribution of satisfaction levels. The cardinalization on which CP and COLS are based will be called the *satisfaction* cardinalization from now on. See also Wolfers (2003) for a similar approach.

2.8. THE INCOME-EVALUATION QUESTION (IEQ)

Finally, let us reconsider the income-evaluation question (IEQ) that we introduced in Chapter 1. The IEQ, first developed by Van Praag (1971), may be seen as a forerunner of the later satisfaction questions. The IEQ has been posed in various countries. Here we are especially interested in comparing the outcomes with previous results derived from income-satisfaction questions. Fortunately, the IEQ was posed in the GSOEP data set in the 1992 and 1997 waves. This gives us the opportunity for a direct comparison between the results based on the financial-satisfaction question and those derived from the IEQ. We utilize the 1997 wave.

Table 2.9. *The financial-satisfaction question estimated by cardinal probit*

Variable	Estimate	t-ratio	Estimate	t-ratio	Estimate	t-ratio
Constant	−2.524	−18.236	−2.536	−18.055	−2.550	−18.159
Ln(household income)	0.342	19.923	0.343	19.652	0.343	19.657
Ln(family size)	−0.102	−6.568	—	—	—	—
Ln(adults)	—	—	−0.101	−6.019	−0.112	−6.480
Ln(children + 1)	—	—	−0.060	−3.697	−0.076	−4.430
Family structure	—	—	—	—	0.032	2.765
Sigma	0.466	94.190	0.466	94.190	0.465	94.184
N	4,964	—	4,964	—	4,964	—
Log likelihood	−9,500	—	−9,500	—	−9,496	—
Pseudo-R^2	0.0198	—	0.0199	—	0.0202	—

Table 2.10. *The financial-satisfaction question estimated by COLS*

Variable	Estimate	t-ratio	Estimate	t-ratio	Estimate	t-ratio
Constant	−2.464	−16.738	−2.477	−16.575	−2.492	−16.678
Ln(household income)	0.354	19.388	0.355	19.123	0.355	19.126
Ln(family size)	−0.108	−6.515	—	—	—	—
Ln(adults)	—	—	−0.107	−5.966	−0.118	−6.427
Ln(children + 1)	—	—	−0.063	−3.669	−0.081	−4.403
Family structure	—	—	—	—	0.034	2.766
N	4,964	—	4,964	—	4,964	—
Adjusted R^2	0.070	—	0.070	—	0.072	—

Our first question is whether the income-evaluation question provides at least as much information as the financial-satisfaction question. Second, we are interested in whether the IEQ provides *more* information than the financial-satisfaction question.

We repeat the question as cited in Chapter 1 (p. 5) in a more recent German version:

Whether you feel an income is good or not so good depends on your personal circumstances and expectations.
In your case would you call your net household income:
a *very low* income if it equalled   DM_____
a *low* income if it equalled   DM_____
an *insufficient* income if it equalled   DM_____
a *sufficient* income if it equalled   DM_____
a *good* income if it equalled   DM_____
a *very good* income if it equalled   DM_____

There are several wordings of this question. First, the number of levels has varied over time between five and nine. When it was first posed in a Belgian survey (Van Praag 1971), nine verbally described levels were used. In Russian surveys (see Ferrer-i-Carbonell and Van Praag 2001) five levels have been used. Second, in the earliest versions (1971) the question was formulated in a bit more complex way as:

Given my present household circumstances, I would consider a monthly household income

below \$ ...	as a very bad income
between \$ ... and \$ ...	as a bad income
between \$ ... and \$ ...	as an insufficient income
between \$ ... and \$ ...	as a sufficient income
between \$ ... and \$ ...	as a good income
above \$ ...	as a very good income.

When introducing this type of question, the IEQ, which requires more response effort from a respondent than the usual income-satisfaction question, survey agencies predicted that the response ratio would be very bad and that if there were a response, the respondents would not have taken this question seriously. It appeared in practice that those questions did have a lower response than usual questions, but not dramatically so. The response may also be incomplete, but the question can still be used if at least *three* levels are filled in. Moreover, the amounts should be ordered in the sense that a good income requires a higher amount than a bad income. Finally, the response is considered to be unrealistic if a *very bad* income is much higher than the respondent's current income or a *very good* income is much less than current income. Such cases represent a small percentage of the response and are rejected for further analysis.

We now analyze the results of the IEQ. Let us denote the answers by $c_1, \ldots, c_6$. For analysis we have two possibilities. The first one is an ordinal analysis, where we consider the separate equations

$$\ln(c_i) = \alpha_i \ln(y) + \beta_i \ln(fs) + \gamma_i + \varepsilon_i \ (i = 1, \ldots, 6). \tag{2.39}$$

These equations may be interpreted as describing indifference lines, corresponding to the levels i. The question is then what these coefficients are and whether these coefficients are equal over the six equations. Regression for the six equations yields Table 2.11. We apply here the 'seemingly unrelated regression' (SUR) model on the GSOEP 1997 data set, where we take into account the correlation between the six disturbances per individual. The estimated correlation matrix is presented in Table 2.12.

For a more extensive ordinal analysis see Van Praag and Van der Sar (1988), where similar results for other data sets were found. Our conclusion is that the coefficients for the separate levels are not equal, but that they follow exactly the same pattern as already found in Van Praag and Van der Sar. At a low level of satisfaction the dependency on own income is considerable at 0.468, and it increases as the level of satisfaction increases up to 0.571 at the highest level of satisfaction. This gives weight to the conjecture that indifference curves are not parallel, although they will intersect at implausible points, say, at income near zero.

The most interesting point is that individuals have different ideas of what represents a 'good' income, a 'sufficient' income, etc. It depends on their own net household income and their household circumstances, in this case characterized by their household size. It shows that evaluations are relative. When $\alpha = 0$, the evaluations would be absolute; that is, independent of current income. When $\alpha = 1$ the evaluation is completely relative. We see from Table 2.11 that we are somewhere in between. The phenomenon of evaluation norms drifting along with rising income has been termed 'preference drift' (see Van Praag 1971). This is similar to an effect discovered independently in the same year by Brickman and Campbell (1971). They called it the 'hedonic-treadmill' effect. Brickman and Campbell found the adaptation effect by laboratory experiments on a small group of individuals without numerically quantifying the effect. Preference drift may be measured by α, the coefficient of $ln(y)$. We notice that preference drift varies per satisfaction level i.

Obviously, preference drift is a puzzling phenomenon. The evaluation of a specific income in combination with a specific household to support should, ideally and according to traditional economic models, not depend on the situation of the evaluator. However, we see that in practice it does depend on the income of the evaluator. It shows most clearly that the notion of 'a good income' is partly relative and psychologically determined. This holds as well for the situation of 'poverty', as we will see later on in this book.

The family-size effect β behaves in just the opposite way. It falls with rising levels of satisfaction.[12] We may stamp the effect of family size as reflecting real needs, while dependency on own income stands for a psychological reference effect. Our findings may then be summarized thus: When individuals become richer, their real needs become less pressing and their norms become more determined by reference effects.

We may calculate for each verbal level i the income amount y_i^* which is evaluated by i for individual n. For that level it holds that

$$\ln (y_i^*) = \alpha_i \ln (y_i^*) + \beta_i \ln (fs_n) + \gamma_i \ (i = 1, \ldots, 6), \tag{2.40}$$

Table 2.11. *Ordinal analysis of the six-level equations of the IEQ*

	C_1		C_2		C_3		C_4		C_5		C_6	
	Effects	*t*-ratio	Effects	*t*-ratio	Effects	*t*-ratio	Effects	*t*-ratio	Effects	*t*-ratio	Effects	*t*-ratio
γ_i	3.499	33.653	3.422	42.488	3.447	46.647	3.558	51.176	3.788	51.033	3.961	41.326
α_i	0.468	35.134	0.507	49.193	0.527	55.774	0.539	60.572	0.550	57.904	0.571	46.534
β_i	0.165	12.870	0.149	14.996	0.141	15.490	0.130	15.144	0.089	9.706	0.056	4.715

Note: System Weighted R^2 0.2318

---

[12] See also Van Praag and Flik (1992) for a comparison with other European data sets.

Table 2.12. *The cross-model error correlation matrix*

	C_1	C_2	C_3	C_4	C_5	C_6
C_1	1	0.906	0.836	0.744	0.611	0.467
C_2	0.906	1	0.963	0.887	0.784	0.630
C_3	0.836	0.963	1	0.951	0.856	0.706
C_4	0.744	0.887	0.951	1	0.917	0.772
C_5	0.611	0.784	0.856	0.917	1	0.899
C_6	0.467	0.630	0.706	0.772	0.899	1

which yields

$$\ln(y_i^*) = \frac{\beta_i \ln(fs_n) + \gamma_i}{1 - \alpha_i} \quad (i = 1, \ldots, 6). \tag{2.41}$$

We notice that the resulting family-size elasticity is $\beta_i/(1 - \alpha_i)$. We also note that the elasticity and the corresponding household-equivalence scale vary with the satisfaction level i. It is tempting to compare these values with the earlier derived elasticities, but we shall postpone that for a few moments.

Now we look at the cardinal concept of the 'individual-welfare function of income' (WFI). Van Praag (1968) argued that financial satisfaction was measurable as a cardinal concept between 0 and 1. At that time it was called utility of money or welfare derived from income. In 1968 this was evidently an almost heretical idea, not in favour with mainstream economics (see e.g. Seidl 1994 for a fierce but belated critique). The approximate relationship was argued to be a log-normal distribution function with parameters μ and σ. In later years Van Praag (1971) and Van Praag and Kapteyn (1973) estimated the μ and σ per individual on the basis of the response to the IEQ. They assumed that the answers $c_1, \ldots, c_i, \ldots c_6$ correspond with satisfaction levels $1/12$, $(2i - 1)/12$ and $11/12$ respectively; this was called the equal-quantile assumption (see Van Praag 1991, 1994 for empirical evidence on this assumption). Moreover, it was assumed that satisfaction $U(c; \mu, \sigma) = \Lambda(c; \mu, \sigma)$ where $\Lambda(c; \mu, \sigma) = N(\ln(c); \mu\sigma)$. The function $\Lambda(.)$ stands for the log-normal distribution function sketched in Figure 1.1. Estimation of μ and σ is possible per individual. We have six or, more generally, k observations per individual and we assume that

$$N\left(\frac{\ln(c_i) - \mu}{\sigma}\right) = \frac{(2i - 1)}{12}. \quad (i = 1, \ldots, 6). \tag{2.42}$$

We estimate the parameters μ and σ for each individual observation n by

$$\hat{\mu}_n = \frac{1}{6}\sum_{i=1}^{6} \ln(c_{in}) \quad \text{and} \quad \hat{\sigma}_n^2 = \frac{1}{5}\sum_{i=1}^{6} \ln(c_{in} - \hat{\mu}_n)^2. \tag{2.43}$$

This is rather similar to our construction of the u's in the CP and COLS approaches outlined above.

Then the estimated $\hat{\mu}_n$ are explained over the sample of N observations by the regression equation

$$\hat{\mu}_n = \alpha \ln(y_n) + \beta \ln(fs_n) + \gamma. \tag{2.44}$$

The regression result for μ is given in Table 2.13. Not unexpectedly, the coefficients are equal to about the average of the six odd-numbered columns in Table 2.11.

Up to now it has proved difficult to explain the σ-variable, which was called by Van Praag (1968, 1971) the 'welfare sensitivity,' to an acceptable extent. It seems to vary over individuals in a random manner. As in many studies, we assume it to be constant over individuals in the same population. We set it as equal to the average over individuals. Hagenaars (1986) found on a multi-country data set that the parameter appears to be related to the log-standard deviation of the income distribution in a country. Her result suggests that the welfare sensitivity σ is higher in more unequal societies. In the present survey (GSOEP 1997) we found $\sigma = 0.453$.

We can now find the evaluation of *own* income y by someone with individual parameters $(\mu(y), \sigma)$. It equals

$$N\left(\frac{(\ln(y) - \mu(y))}{\sigma}\right) = N\left(\frac{(\ln(y) - \alpha \ln(y) - \beta \ln(fs) - \gamma)}{\sigma}\right), \tag{2.45}$$

or, using its ordinal equivalent,

$$\frac{(\ln(y) - \mu)}{\sigma} = \frac{(\ln(y) - \alpha \ln(y) - \beta \ln(fs) - \gamma)}{\sigma}. \tag{2.46}$$

We notice that the IEQ effectively introduces *two* concepts of an individual-welfare function. The first concept is generated by keeping μ constant. It gives a schedule of how individuals evaluate varying (fictitious) income levels from the perspective of their own income, which is kept unchanged at the present level. We call it the 'virtual' or 'short-term' welfare function. It can be estimated for a specific individual by asking the IEQ of that individual.

The second concept is the welfare function according to which individuals with *different* incomes evaluate their *own* income *in reality*. It is an inter-individual

Table 2.13. *OLS regression analysis on the parameter μ of the IEQ*

	M	
	Estimate	*t*-ratio
γ_i	3.611	54.308
α_i	0.527	61.964
β_i	0.121	14.819
N	3,962	—
Adjusted R^2	0.631	—

concept. We call it the 'true' or 'long-term' welfare function. This function has to be derived by using a sample of different individuals. From Equation (2.46) it follows that the *true* welfare function is also log-normal with parameters

$$\left(\frac{\beta \ln fs + \gamma}{1 - \alpha}, \frac{\sigma}{1 - \alpha} \right). \tag{2.47}$$

In Figures 2.3*a* and 2.3*b* we sketch both functions. We see that the true welfare function has a much weaker slope than the virtual. It implies that income changes are *ex ante* perceived as weightier than when they are experienced in reality. In fact, the two concepts correspond to the two concepts of the *decision* and the *experienced* utility function distinguished by Kahneman, Wakker, and Sarin (1997). The virtual welfare function describes the way in which a specific individual evaluates different income levels. It is the perceived *ex ante* relationship between income and welfare on which the individual bases his or her *decisions*. The true welfare function describes how individuals, who experience those incomes themselves, evaluate their incomes in reality.

The welfare function maps incomes on the evaluation range [0, 1]. A second (and easier) way to consider the welfare function is to map the range to the real axis and to consider the function $u(y)$

$$u(y) = [(1 - \alpha). \ln (y) - \beta. \ln (fs) - \gamma]/\sigma. \tag{2.48}$$

The two representations are ordinally equivalent. We call the latter the linear transform. The two representations are sketched in Figures 2.3*a* and 2.3*b*. The short-term version corresponds to $\alpha = 0$. It follows that the short-term *virtual* function is much steeper than the long-term *true* function.

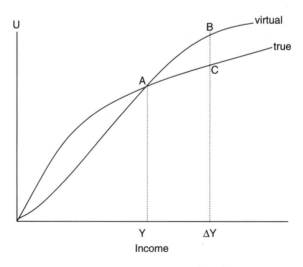

Figure 2.3a. *The virtual and true welfare functions*

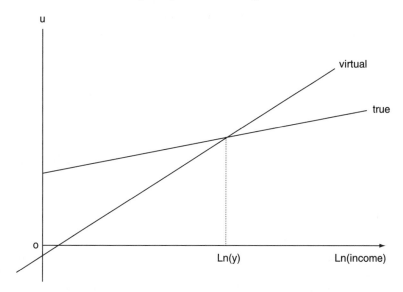

Figure 2.3b. *The virtual and true welfare functions (linear transform)*

The difference between the short- and long-term concepts is best explained by the following simple thought-experiment. Let us assume that somebody with an initial income y gets an income increase of Δy, yielding a new income $y + \Delta y$. Initially the increase will be evaluated by his short-term welfare function yielding an increase from point A to point B in Figure 2.3a. After a while norms will change and this will be reflected in the parameter μ that will increase by α. Δy. Hence, after a first euphoria there will be some disappointment, as the evaluation falls from point B to point C.

This is the so-called preference-drift effect. It is only not there when $\alpha = 0$. If $\alpha = 1$, in the long term an income increase will not yield any increase in satisfaction. The specifications in Table 2.8 we may estimate again for μ, yielding Table 2.14.

Now it is evident that we may also derive family-equivalence scales from our IEQ-estimates. We may derive household-equivalence scales for the individual welfare function by requiring that households with different family sizes fs_0 and fs_1 enjoy an equal welfare level. This implies that incomes are related as

$$y_1/y_0 = (fs_1/fs_0)^{\frac{0.121}{0.473}} = (fs_1/fs_0)^{0.26} \tag{2.49}$$

We notice that this power is 0.26. The comparable figure by the previous methods (OP, etc.) was 0.30.

Now we present the household-equivalence scales for the six levels i, derived from Table 2.11 and those derived from the μ-equation side by side (see Table 2.15). We see that the differences between all subjective scales are rather small.

Van Praag and Flik (1992) derived equivalence scales for various European countries by the same IEQ method. They noticed that the scales in various countries are not the same, reflecting cultural differences and differences in social systems. (See also Hagenaars 1986 and Goedhart et al. 1977.)

Finally, it is interesting to compare the results derived from the IEQ responses with our earlier results in this chapter, based on financial-satisfaction responses (Table 2.3 versus last column of Table 2.15). The resulting trade-offs, derived from the true WFI, and the ratios found earlier are very similar. The additional result that we can derive from the IEQ and which we cannot find from financial-satisfaction questions, which always only refer to current income, is the virtual WFI. As said before the true WFI corresponds to the *experienced* utility function and the virtual WFI to the *decision* utility function.

The true or experienced welfare function for Germany, corresponding to this estimate is

$$U(y) = N(\ln(y); 0.26 \ln(fs) + 7.63, 0.96). \tag{2.50}$$

Comparing this estimate with the experienced welfare function derived from the cardinal-probit approach above, we see that the parameters are not very different.

Comparing (2.36) with (2.50) we see that both are lognormal distribution functions in y, albeit with a different normalization. After all, the 1968 conjecture about the lognormal welfare function still seems realistic.

Table 2.14. *The IEQ estimates for household-equivalence scales, OLS on μ*

Variable	Estimate	t-ratio	Estimate	t-ratio	Estimate	t-ratio
Constant	3.611	54.308	3.572	52.302	3.574	52.309
Ln(household income)	0.527	61.964	0.533	60.667	0.533	60.644
Ln(family size)	0.121	14.819	—	—	—	—
Ln(adults)	—	—	0.090	8.093	0.089	7.958
Ln(children + 1)	—	—	0.096	11.976	0.083	5.355
Family Structure	—	—	—	—	0.011	0.963
N	3,962	—	3,962	—	3,962	—
Adjusted R^2	0.631	—	0.6322	—	0.632	—

Table 2.15. *Household-equivalence scales derived from the IEQ, Germany, 1997 (%)*

Household size	C_1	C_2	C_3	C_4	C_5	C_6	μ
1	81	81	81	82	87	91	84
2	100	100	100	100	100	100	100
3	113	113	113	112	108	105	111
4	124	123	123	122	115	109	119
5	133	132	131	129	120	113	127
6	141	139	139	136	124	115	133
7	147	146	145	142	128	118	138
8	154	152	151	148	131	120	143

2.9. CONCLUSIONS

Let us now summarize the conclusions of this chapter.

1. We found that income satisfaction can be explained by objective factors. This yields trade-off coefficients between family size, income, adults, and children.
2. We found that the ordered-probit method is based on an implicit cardinal-utility assumption.
3. We replaced the ordered-probit method by the method of probit-adjusted ordinary least squares (POLS), as the results in most cases are not significantly different except for a multiplication factor.
4. We found that we can use the cardinal information in financial-satisfaction questions, leading to a cardinal-probit and a cardinal-OLS approach.
5. The frequentist and the cardinalist approach imply two different cardinalizations of satisfaction.
6. The empirical estimates according to those four estimation methods are strongly related and yield (almost) the same trade-off ratios.
7. As the POLS and COLS methods are computationally easier, and (as will emerge in the following pages) have possibilities that cannot be realized by applying ordered Probit, we will use POLS or COLS, even if the Probit road is easily accessible.
8. An earlier method of studying income satisfaction in a quantitative way was developed by Van Praag and Kapteyn (the 'Leyden School'). In this chapter we compared their results derived from the income-evaluation question (IEQ) with results derived from the financial-satisfaction question (FSQ). We found that both methods yield approximately the same trade-off coefficients.
9. The FSQ yields an *experienced* utility function in the terms of Kahneman, Wakker, and Sarin. The IEQ yields a virtual *and* a true individual welfare function, which concepts coincide with Kahneman, Wakker, and Sarin's *decision*-utility and *experienced*-utility functions, respectively. The upshot of this comparison is that almost all results derived by WFI-analysis by or in the spirit of the 'Leyden School' could have been derived by analysis of the FSQ as well.
10. The FSQ is easier to pose to respondents than the IEQ. Moreover, the IEQ format does not seem applicable when we ask for health satisfaction, housing satisfaction, etc., while the FSQ can be used. Hence, the major accent in this study will lie on FSQ-based studies. However, the IEQ yields information on the (*ex ante*) decision-utility function, which the FSQ cannot provide.
11. As older IEQ-based studies are difficult to repeat based on the FSQ, in this study we will present results based on either one of the instruments as being equivalent.

3

Domain Satisfactions

3.1. INTRODUCTION

There is more to life than income. Psychologists distinguish between various *domains of life*. One may be very happy with one's financial situation but very unhappy with one's job or with the time available for leisure. Individuals are able to distinguish various aspects of life and to evaluate them separately in terms of how satisfied they are with respect to each of these aspects. In the German GSOEP data set 6 separate domains are distinguished, while in the comparable British BHPS data set there are 8 separate domains. The similarities and differences in the domains in these two data sets are listed in Table 3.1.

The questions in the GSOEP that provide information about the degree of satisfaction with respect to the separate domains have approximately the following general format (while the particular domain varies: e.g. health, job, etc.):

Please answer by using the following scale in which 0 means totally unhappy and 10 means totally happy:
How satisfied are you with ... (your health, job, ...)

Note that here the respondent is asked to give a numerical evaluation. In older questionnaires we see response categories which are described using verbal labels

Table 3.1. *German and British domains*

German SOEP	British HPS
Job satisfaction	Job satisfaction
Financial satisfaction	Financial satisfaction
Health satisfaction	Health satisfaction
Housing satisfaction	Housing satisfaction
Leisure satisfaction	Leisure satisfaction: amount
—	Leisure satisfaction: use
Environment satisfaction	—
—	Social-life satisfaction
—	Marriage satisfaction
General satisfaction with 'life as a whole'	General satisfaction with 'life as a whole'

This chapter is partly based on Van Praag, Frijters, and Ferrer-i-Carbonell (2003).

like 'bad', 'sufficient', and 'good'. This demonstrates that the well-known opinion agencies that carry out these surveys are confident that this way of putting satisfaction questions can be understood and interpreted similarly by respondents. They speak a common language and their responses are comparable.

It is evident that more domains might have been distinguished. For instance, in the British BHPS leisure satisfaction is split up into two subdimensions; namely, the *amount* of leisure and *use* of leisure time. Moreover, two additional domains are available in the British data set: satisfaction with married life and with social life. The British data set considered does not include a question on satisfaction with the environment.

Both data sets include a question about satisfaction with life as a whole. We shall call that aggregate concept 'general satisfaction' (GS) for short.

In this chapter we shall consider the explanations of the domain satisfactions one by one, and shall compare the German and British outcomes with each other. Note that both data sets are panel data sets. The German set that we consider covers the years 1992–7, while the British set comprises only the three years 1996–8.[1] The variables are not precisely the same in both data sets. A description of the variables used can be found in Appendices 3a and 3b (pp. 78–9 below).

The overall distributions for the evaluation of the various domains are presented in Tables 3.2–3.7.

Table 3.2. *Satisfaction distributions, West German workers 1996 (%)*

	0	1	2	3	4	5	6	7	8	9	10
Job satisfaction	0.80	0.55	1.73	3.04	4.32	10.93	9.96	17.97	27.89	13.73	9.08
Financial satisfaction	0.31	0.33	0.77	1.89	3.46	9.35	10.62	22.19	30.10	13.46	7.53
Health satisfaction	0.68	0.54	2.03	3.59	4.51	12.13	10.11	17.49	26.06	13.25	9.62
Housing satisfaction	0.93	0.50	1.51	2.49	3.50	7.89	7.68	14.85	25.72	17.87	17.06
Leisure satisfaction	1.02	1.33	3.57	5.49	6.32	13.68	11.51	16.86	21.40	10.01	8.81
Environment satisfaction	0.81	0.71	1.78	4.73	6.64	16.95	14.56	22.15	20.29	7.68	3.69
General satisfaction	0.23	0.25	0.71	1.35	2.76	9.72	11.07	23.98	33.51	11.63	4.77

Table 3.3. *Satisfaction distributions, East German workers 1996 (%)*

	0	1	2	3	4	5	6	7	8	9	10
Job satisfaction	0.62	0.72	2.00	4.62	4.26	13.76	10.07	19.31	27.02	10.79	6.83
Financial satisfaction	0.25	0.25	1.41	3.17	4.98	14.38	15.54	25.49	23.73	7.99	2.82
Health satisfaction	0.45	0.25	1.36	4.17	5.58	15.49	10.51	19.91	25.84	11.01	5.43
Housing satisfaction	1.16	0.91	2.37	4.79	5.95	11.86	9.54	15.69	23.26	13.67	10.80
Leisure satisfaction	1.16	2.11	5.33	8.25	8.51	16.91	13.84	16.91	16.51	6.44	4.03
Environment satisfaction	1.56	1.46	4.58	9.00	11.56	20.26	17.40	19.31	11.66	2.46	0.75
General satisfaction	0.30	0.15	0.85	2.82	4.37	16.69	15.43	27.95	24.59	5.23	1.61

[1] The reason for the British data selection is that in the years before 1996 a number of crucial questions were not included. For the Germans, we started in 1992 because by that time the East Germans were supposed to be well integrated into the survey.

Domain Satisfactions

Table 3.4. *Satisfaction distributions, West German non-workers 1996 (%)*

	0	1	2	3	4	5	6	7	8	9	10
Financial satisfaction	0.64	0.92	1.54	3.55	3.91	11.43	9.42	17.44	27.26	13.20	10.68
Health satisfaction	2.71	2.09	4.18	6.05	6.67	14.90	11.19	14.20	20.33	9.62	8.06
Housing satisfaction	0.82	0.65	1.60	2.67	3.29	8.60	6.63	14.17	24.45	16.81	20.32
Leisure satisfaction	0.53	0.90	1.40	2.97	3.84	8.58	7.80	13.60	23.70	14.47	22.21
Environment satisfaction	0.92	1.06	2.21	3.94	6.82	16.30	13.84	21.17	20.61	7.97	5.15
General satisfaction	0.73	0.67	1.56	3.07	3.63	13.65	11.61	19.35	28.53	10.11	7.09

Table 3.5. *Satisfaction distributions, East German non-workers 1996 (%)*

	0	1	2	3	4	5	6	7	8	9	10
Financial satisfaction	0.78	0.57	2.26	4.95	7.14	15.91	13.51	19.73	22.84	7.71	4.60
Health satisfaction	1.97	1.48	4.09	7.19	6.84	21.30	12.91	14.32	18.12	7.05	4.72
Housing satisfaction	1.28	1.07	1.85	4.42	5.49	11.55	9.27	13.47	23.16	13.40	15.04
Leisure satisfaction	0.92	0.71	1.77	3.05	3.26	12.84	9.36	13.76	25.67	12.55	16.10
Environment satisfaction	1.55	1.76	4.52	9.39	11.86	20.82	17.01	16.30	13.06	2.96	0.78
General satisfaction	1.13	0.42	2.04	4.65	5.07	22.06	15.15	19.80	21.28	5.29	3.10

Table 3.6. *Satisfaction distributions, UK, workers 1996 (%)*

	1	2	3	4	5	6	7
Job satisfaction	3.23	4.40	9.11	16.15	25.64	25.51	15.97
Financial satisfaction	4.20	6.52	12.94	21.29	26.75	19.33	8.97
Health satisfaction	1.74	2.72	8.65	14.12	22.41	30.96	19.39
Housing satisfaction	1.97	3.32	7.23	14.79	22.94	29.96	19.80
Leisure-amount satisfaction	3.88	7.94	16.35	19.90	23.96	16.52	11.46
Leisure-use satisfaction	1.98	5.00	10.80	19.48	25.98	22.22	14.54
Social-life satisfaction	1.56	3.77	8.74	17.78	26.95	25.55	15.65
Marriage satisfaction	1.07	1.03	3.13	5.62	9.59	24.60	54.96
General satisfaction	0.70	1.76	5.81	14.30	31.62	34.12	11.69

Table 3.7. *Satisfaction distributions, UK, non-workers, 1996 (%)*

	1	2	3	4	5	6	7
Financial satisfaction	12.59	8.74	13.12	18.59	16.63	14.04	16.30
Health satisfaction	9.11	5.66	11.48	15.16	18.23	20.60	19.76
Housing satisfaction	3.66	3.24	5.25	11.09	15.84	22.85	38.07
Leisure-amount satisfaction	3.29	4.13	7.25	12.94	14.75	17.18	40.46
Leisure-use satisfaction	4.49	4.32	8.92	13.68	18.78	18.62	31.19
Social-life satisfaction	5.54	3.93	8.60	16.37	19.01	20.38	26.17
Marriage satisfaction	1.78	1.34	2.69	4.75	6.67	16.66	66.11
General satisfaction	2.92	3.37	5.88	14.95	22.81	26.87	23.20

From these tables it is obvious that the majority of respondents are fairly satisfied. However, it can also be seen that there are quite a number of respondents who are dissatisfied with their circumstances. For instance, more than 20 percent of West German workers evaluate their job satisfaction (JS) at 5 or less on a scale of 0–10. For UK workers, we find that about 17 percent classify their JS at 3 or less on a scale of 1–7. More generally, we see that each response class is used. Our conclusion is that the responses are sufficiently diverse for us to believe that the response behaviour is credible and not dictated by social-desirability motives. The only issue for which we are not completely sure about the results is the marriage-satisfaction question for the UK sample. The percentages of those questioned found in the highest response class is very high indeed. This may indicate that there was some joint response and hence mutual control by the partners. Nevertheless, we shall assume in the following that all responses reflect the truth.

3.2. SECONDARY ANALYSIS: METHODOLOGICAL CONSIDERATIONS

In this chapter we will propose and estimate a number of equations, which explain the response behavior for each domain. We distinguish between working and non-working respondents, and also between West and East Germany. It follows that we have 24 equations for the German data set and 16 equations for the UK data set. This means that we cannot go into too much detail for each separate equation.

In the previous chapter we looked at financial satisfaction, and we include it again in this chapter, but this time we will use a more complex equation. First, however, we look at the general structure of the relationships that we are trying to estimate and the econometric methodology.

We shall assume a basic equation:

$$\ln(Z) = \beta_1 X_1 + \ldots + \beta_m X_m + \varepsilon. \tag{3.1}$$

The variable to be explained cannot be exactly observed. It is classified as i, where $i = 1, \ldots, I$. The variables X stand for explanatory variables. The question of which variables we will select depends on various factors. First, there must be an intuitive plausibility that they might have some effect on the left-hand side; that is, the response behavior. Second, the data have to be available. A third factor is the frame of reference. For instance, in the previous chapter we explained financial satisfaction by a few variables, while in this chapter we will do this again but with a much greater number of variables. The reason is that in the earlier chapter we were only interested in the household-size effect.

We saw in Chapter 2 that there is more than one way to estimate this type of model. First, there are four ways to estimate the same equation, which yield results that are very similar. The first traditional way is to use ordered probit (OP). In the previous chapter it was shown that OP implies a specific cardinalization of $\ln(Z)$.

Another cardinalization may be based on the fact that respondents are invited to assign numerical evaluations to their satisfactions. Assuming that there is a latent continuous evaluation function on the interval [0, 10], we may postulate that the true satisfaction of somebody who evaluates his satisfaction by 7 on a discrete scale will lie between 6.5 and 7.5. In that case, we get a regression on grouped data where the boundaries of the groups are 0.5, 1.5, ..., 9.5. We call this the 'cardinal-probit approach' (CPA). It is also called 'group-wise regression' in the statistical literature. We saw that there is a one-to-one relationship between the Z values in OP and CPA in the case of financial satisfaction and we will see in this chapter that such a relationship holds for the other domains as well.

A third approach to estimating this model is by assigning to each response category the conditional expectation of $\ln(Z)$, given that it is found in a specific response interval. This is called the probit OLS variant. This trick may also be applied within the cardinal framework. Hence, those conditional expectations are explained by OLS, yielding the POLS or COLS variants. As it is not sensible to apply all four variants, which yield similar answers, in this chapter we use the POLS approach. The reason why we use the conditional expectations is that it fits in very well with the analysis in the next chapter.

Our data sets, at least in this and the next chapter, are panel data. That is, we have N observation units that are followed for T consecutive periods. Hence, each variable has a double index n, t. This makes analysis more difficult, but also more interesting.

First, most variables are not fixed over life. They fluctuate about an average or are perceived by the individual to do so. A famous example is Friedman's (1957) distinction between *permanent* and *transitory* income. The idea is that most individuals n have a steady income level y_n, and that current income may be broken down as $y_{n,t} = y_n. + \Delta y_{n,t}$. The first component is *permanent* income and the second component is *transitory* income. The main thesis is then that both components affect the consumption (or savings) level but that the influence of both is not the same. It follows that we replace the contribution $\beta.y_{n,t}$ in the regression equation by $\beta.y_n. + \gamma.\Delta y_{n,t}$. The first component stands for the permanent income effect and the second term for the transitory income effect. It is obvious that this breakdown can be made for all variables if we have a longitudinal data set. Hence, we will speak, in general, of a breakdown into a *level* effect and a *shock* effect. Obviously, it is not very useful to apply this breakdown with respect to every variable. Some variables do not change over the years at all. It is an empirical matter to decide in which cases the breakdown is worthwhile.

A second important point is the error term. One of the interpretations of the error term is that it stands for omitted variables like semi-fixed psychological characteristics. It is sometimes stated that such omitted variables may be correlated with observed and included explanatory variables. This would imply that the error term is correlated with the explanatory variables, which would lead to an estimation bias in the regression estimates. It is true that if an observed X and an omitted V have a part in common (as a result of correlation) then the regression coefficient of X will differ from the estimate we would find if V were also included in the equation. The variable X takes over the role of V as well. Because of the regression-orthogonality condition, it is only the uncorrelated part of V which is included in the error term. Here we will make the usual assumption that errors and explanatory variables are uncorrelated.

We may assume that there will be a considerable positive correlation between error terms for the same individual over the observation periods. Therefore, we break down the error term into a fixed component ε_n and a variable component $\eta_{n,t}$ and we assume

$$\varepsilon_{n,t} = \varepsilon_{n.} + \eta_{n,t} \tag{3.2}$$

where we assume $E(\varepsilon_{n.}) = 0$ over the observations, and $E(\eta_{n,t}) = 0$ for each n separately. Moreover, we assume that the two components are mutually independent. The correlation coefficient $\rho(\varepsilon_{nt}, \varepsilon_{nt'}) = \rho$ reflects how much is fixed over time. As usual, we assume that both components are normally distributed. This model is called the 'random-effects' model in panel analysis (see e.g. Greene 2000). In fact the error breakdown is analogous to the breakdown of an observed variable into a level and a shock effect. The difference is that for an observed variable we can numerically *observe* the values of both terms, while this is, of course, impossible for the error term. For the error term we have to satisfy ourselves with the stipulation of a statistical structure. After the estimation has been performed it is, of course, possible to calculate residuals $\hat{\varepsilon}$ for each (n, t) observation. Then, we may assess the individual effect by averaging the residuals over the T observations per individual.

3.2.1. Fixed or Random Individual Effects?

There are two approaches to accommodate for the correlation of individual observations over time. The first is the random-effect approach. The second is that of fixed individual effects. In the probit formulation Chamberlain (1980) has shown that the second option is impossible. Das and Van Soest (1999) and Ferrer-i-Carbonell and Frijters (2004) suggest alternatives to include individual fixed effects. However, if we choose the POLS option, that is OLS, both options are feasible. Throughout this study, we choose the random-effects model and we shall now explain why. The difference between the two approaches may be succinctly described by considering the two following model equations:

$$y_{n,t} = \beta x_{n,t} + e_n + \varepsilon_{n,t}$$
$$y_{n,t} = \beta x_{n,t} + \varepsilon_n + \varepsilon_{n,t} . \tag{3.3}$$

In the first equation we introduce an individual-specific non-random fixed effect e_n. In the second equation we have a random effect instead. There are two reasons why we prefer the second version to the first one (see also Mundlak 1978).

In the first model the term e_n is an unknown parameter to be estimated. Hence, if we have 5,000 individuals we would have to estimate 1 extra parameter per individual, adding up to 5,000 extra parameters. Our first objection is that we can hardly call this a parsimonious model. One of the first requirements of a model is that there should only be a few parameters and relationships. If the number of observations is 1 per individual—the situation of a cross-section instead of a longitudinal data set—the model would imply that $e_n = y_n$, and the structural effects β would be zero, but the explanation would be 100 percent. This is the reason why the model is discarded as trivial in the case of cross-section analysis. It is evident that the same objection of parsimony holds for a model when we have longitudinal observations. Our second objection deals with the model structure. In our analysis we allow for the possibility of level (α) and shock (β) effects according to the equation:

$$DS_{n,t} = \alpha X_{n.} + \beta X_{n,t} + \varepsilon_{n.} + \varepsilon_{n,t} \tag{3.4}$$

However, if we replace the random effect by N individual fixed effects e_n to be estimated, it follows that there is no place for a level effect $\alpha X_{n.}$, as the best adaptation is obtained by setting $\alpha = 0$. Hence, it follows that we can only estimate shock effects. We do not think that this is intuitively reasonable, even if the fit becomes better, as in the cross-section case, although not 100 percent. It is possible after estimation to 'calculate' the residuals per individual, and their average over the T observations per individual is an estimate of the random fixed effect per individual.

The basic equation of this chapter reads as:

$$DS_{n,t} = \alpha X_{n.} + \beta X_{n,t} + \varepsilon_{n.} + \varepsilon_{n,t}, \tag{3.5}$$

where $X_{n.}$ stands for the average of $X_{n,t}$ over the T periods considered, and where $\ln(Z)$ is replaced by the specific domain satisfaction variable DS. Notice that we may write $\alpha X_{n.} + \beta X_{n,t} = (\alpha + \beta)X_{n.} + \beta \Delta X_{n,t}$, (see also Mundlak 1978). We shall estimate (3.5) by POLS.

The level effects α are associated with the average or mean values of the variable. So 'mean log-household income' stands for the average over the period while the shock effect is associated with 'log-household income'. The total long-term effect is $(\alpha + \beta)$.

It is feasible to generalize probit analysis to a longitudinal data set. Conceptually it is easy, but in practice rather complex. We ran POLS and OP side-by-side, with STATA, and our conclusion is that, apart from a multiplication factor, there is virtually no systematic difference between the two options (see also Stewart 1983; Van Praag, Frijters, and Ferrer-i-Carbonell 2003). The t-values of the effects and the relative variance attributable to the random effects are almost equal. For the ordered-probit method we have to evaluate many integrals, which can be avoided if we take the POLS road. The difference in computing time is rather spectacular. For the estimation of a typical equation by integration (via STATA) we needed about 2 hours, while it required less than a minute by POLS. We present in

Table 3.13*a* the results for financial satisfaction of West-German workers estimated by OP and by POLS. In the last two columns we present the trade-off coefficients of the relevant variables, normalized such that both norms equal one. We find that after normalization the two estimates are almost equal, while the same holds for the corresponding *t*-values. This is an additional reason to choose the POLS or COLS options throughout. In this chapter we use POLS. But at the end of the chapter in Table 3.25 we give the translation rule from POLS to COLS for each domain.

3.3. SECONDARY ANALYSIS: FINDINGS

Now we shall consider the estimates resulting from the satisfaction equations. From the standpoint of elegance, it would have been nice to use exactly the same functional specification for the German and the UK data or even to combine the data sets into one. We abstained from this ideal for several reasons. First, both sets do not contain the same information. Most conspicuously, the information on health in the German data set is much more sparse than in the UK set. Second, German and British individuals are not identical. Hence, we cannot expect satisfaction to be determined in the same way or by the same variables in the two (or, depending on the definition, three) countries. It follows that there is no convincing reason why the variables would be the same and the coefficients equal, unless we assume that there is some inherent law of identical response behavior. Finally, we mention that we frequently use a log-quadratic specification of the effect of *age*. This entails that the effect of age depends on how old the individual is, and that for a specific domain an increase in age may lead to declining satisfaction up to a certain age, after which individual satisfaction increases with age. The turning point on the age axis, sometimes called minimum or maximum age (depending on the shape of the parabola), is given in the tables (see also Blanchflower and Oswald 2007).

3.3.1. Health Satisfaction

In Table 3.8 we present the health-equation estimates for several specifications. In Health economics, the research based on reported subjective health satisfaction is growing, see, for example, Frijters, Shields, and Haisken-DeNew (2005), Kerkhofs and Lindeboom (1995), and Dolan (2006). We start with the German data set, where we differentiate between four sub-samples: West German workers, East German workers, West German non-workers, and East German non-workers. We apply this differentiation since we feel intuitively that those samples are different and will presumably give different estimates. The data set covers the period 1992–7. Although the two German republics reunited in 1989, it is well known that incomes and conditions of life in general still differ considerably between the two parts of the country. The non-workers are a somewhat non-homogeneous group because they consist of non-working housewives, retired people, the unemployed, students, etc. The common denominator is that they have no income from employment.

Table 3.8. *Health satisfaction, Germany, 1992–1997, POLS individual random effects*

	West workers		East workers		West non-workers		East non-workers	
	Estimate	t-ratio	Estimate	t-ratio	Estimate	t-ratio	Estimate	t-ratio
Constant	-0.985	-1.154	-0.598	-0.441	5.203	7.226	3.454	2.931
Dummy for 1992	0.016	1.140	0.133	6.394	0.001	0.055	0.011	0.381
Dummy for 1993	-0.007	-0.521	0.114	5.342	0.021	1.168	0.051	1.920
Dummy for 1994	-0.001	-0.101	0.047	2.253	-0.004	-0.208	0.023	0.897
Dummy for 1995	-0.001	-0.066	0.044	2.171	-0.001	-0.048	-0.005	-0.189
Dummy for 1996	-0.034	-2.289	0.033	1.513	-0.001	-0.040	0.050	1.792
Ln(age)	0.755	1.564	0.552	0.712	-2.523	-6.292	-1.173	-1.797
(Ln(age))^2	-0.225	-3.310	-0.194	-1.761	0.208	3.778	0.035	0.385
Turning point	5	—	4	—	431	—	2.E + 07	—
Ln(household income)	0.004	0.250	0.037	1.534	-0.001	-0.042	-0.014	-0.413
Ln(years education)	0.122	2.909	0.217	3.072	0.237	4.341	0.292	3.586
Ln(children +1)	0.008	0.514	-0.020	-0.878	0.003	0.143	0.047	1.227
Male	0.081	4.818	0.103	4.264	-0.003	-0.142	0.023	0.726
Living together	-0.012	-0.879	0.008	0.307	0.044	2.489	-0.017	-0.501
Self-employed	0.041	1.707	-0.016	-0.432	—	—	—	—
Ln(Savings))	0.005	2.733	-0.001	-0.428	0.008	2.986	0.003	0.601
Mean (ln(household income))	0.106	3.985	0.017	0.376	0.061	1.957	-0.064	-1.245
Mean (ln(children +1))	0.013	0.499	0.051	1.290	-0.014	-0.408	0.055	0.932
Mean (ln(savings))	0.019	4.406	0.017	2.597	0.020	3.815	0.022	2.667
Standard deviation of individual random effect ε_n	0.643	—	0.596	—	0.700	—	0.659	—
% variance due to ε_n	0.515	—	0.514	—	0.547	—	0.533	—
Number of observations	30,669	—	12,359	—	20,883	—	8,532	—
Number of individuals	8,153	—	3,238	—	6,424	—	2,705	—
R^2:								
Within	0.008	—	0.023	—	0.006	—	0.009	—
Between	0.126	—	0.123	—	0.273	—	0.260	—
Overall	0.083	—	0.089	—	0.191	—	0.172	—

Note: There are dummies for missing variables, which are not included in the table.

The first block presents the influence of general developments over time. We see that health does not systematically vary over time for West Germans. For the eastern part of the population there does seem to be a trend over time. For workers there it seems that the trend is downwards. This might be explained by the fact that conditions seem to have been hardening in the East during those years, while perhaps some of the healthy and young workers emigrated to the western part of the country. For the eastern non-workers, however, we do not find a systematic trend.

As expected, age plays a role. For the workers, health deteriorates with age according to a log parabola with a top at age 5. For the non-workers deterioration with age is also found but the rate of deterioration becomes less pronounced as age increases, with a minimum which is not reached during a human life span. However, contrary to our expectation, the age effects are not always significant. Education has a positive effect. This may be because higher-educated people care better for themselves; a second probable factor is that higher-educated individuals mostly have physically less demanding jobs. The presence of children has no significant effect.

Male workers are significantly healthier than female workers. Western individuals are healthier when they have a higher income. For the East Germans we do not find that pattern. This might have to do with the provision of health care, which might be more egalitarian than in the western part of the country. Finally, the western self-employed are somewhat healthier than employed people.

Health does not seem to be affected by shock variables. It is a long-term condition.

The German figures on health are rather poor, because there is no information in the German data set on the prevalence of diseases and impairments.

In the British data set this information is available. In Tables 3.9 and 3.10 we present two specifications for the whole British data set. In the first specification we only utilize the general information, which we used for the German data set. In the second specification we assume that the subjective impact of a disease or impairment may vary with the age of the individual. Let the dummy variable referring to impairment j be d_j, which equals 1 if the individual suffers from the impairment and 0 otherwise. We include an interaction variable, and we model the effect as $\alpha_{j1}.d_j.ln(age)$. In this way we get age-specific disease effects. Groot (2000) and Cutler and Richardson (1997) used a simpler model, in which the disease effects were assumed to be constant irrespective of age. We will return to this choice in Chapter 9.

We turn first to the first specification, which is roughly comparable with the German estimates, not including specific information on health.

In the first specification we see a strong positive income effect. The effect of having children is negative. Health decreases with age.

In the second specification we see strong negative effects of various diseases. However, we also find as it were a hierarchy of diseases where skin and hearing problems score low and diabetes and heart and chest problems score high. Note that the income effect is halved, which is related to the fact that the occurrence

Table 3.9. *Health satisfaction, UK, 1996–1998, POLS individual random effects*

	Workers		Non-workers	
	Estimate	t-ratio	Estimate	t-ratio
Constant	−0.062	−4.019	8.378	9.504
Dummy for 1996	−0.009	−0.606	−0.017	−0.911
Dummy for 1997	−0.265	−0.440	−0.018	−1.052
Ln(age)	0.014	0.166	−4.622	−9.448
$(Ln(age))^2$	−0.034	−1.518	0.610	9.082
Turning-point	1.227	—	44.158	—
Ln(household income)	−0.096	−3.555	0.003	0.155
Ln(years education)	−0.006	−0.120	−0.004	−0.122
Ln(children + 1)	0.076	3.353	−0.044	−0.500
Gender (male)	−0.010	−0.386	−0.034	−1.221
Living together	0.063	1.963	0.055	1.875
Self-employed	0.011	2.278	—	—
Ln(savings)	−0.180	−2.174	0.009	1.211
Mean (ln(household income))	0.095	1.655	0.003	0.135
Mean (ln(children + 1))	0.018	2.410	0.167	1.790
Mean (ln(adults))	0.879	0.836	0.028	2.351
Standard deviation of individual random effect ε_n	0.834	—	0.837	—
% variance due to ε_n	0.780	—	0.739	—
Number of observations	17,979	—	12,022	—
Number of individuals	7,728	—	5,783	—
R^2:				
Within	0.002	—	0.000	—
Between	0.013	—	0.032	—
Overall	0.011	—	0.024	—

Note: There are dummies for missing variables, which are not included in the table.

of diseases is correlated with income. For all age-dependent effects we see that the disease becomes perceived as more severe as the individual grows older.

It is clear that the information on the occurrence of diseases is still rather restricted. We do not know the degree of affliction. It may be severe or light. Lacking more qualitative information, this is as far as we can go for the moment.

3.3.2. Job Satisfaction

Job satisfaction (JS) is a subject on which much has been written. First, there are the innumerable studies from the field of human resources and personnel;

Table 3.10. *Health satisfaction, UK, explained by disease,*
1996–1998, POLS individual random effects

	Workers		Non-workers	
	Estimate	*t*-ratio	Estimate	*t*-ratio
Constant	3.252	3.295	8.669	10.975
Dummy for 1996	−0.082	−5.351	−0.047	−2.513
Dummy for 1997	−0.019	−1.296	−0.031	−1.817
Ln(age)	−1.561	−2.762	−4.922	−11.192
(Ln(age))^2	0.233	2.911	0.710	11.721
Turning-point	28	—	32	—
Ln(household income)	−0.039	−1.725	0.004	0.196
Ln(years education)	−0.097	−3.843	−0.041	−1.355
Ln(children + 1)	−0.023	−0.448	−0.047	−0.534
Gender (male)	0.010	0.479	−0.055	−2.274
Living together	−0.004	−0.186	0.029	1.115
Self-employed	0.056	1.849	—	—
Ln(savings)	0.011	2.216	0.010	1.247
Problems with arms, legs, hands, feet, back, or neck*Ln(age)	−0.109	−18.596	−0.118	−21.915
Difficulty in seeing*Ln(age)	−0.047	−3.297	−0.044	−5.270
Difficulty in hearing*Ln(age)	−0.039	−3.428	−0.019	−2.599
Skin conditions/allergies*Ln(age)	−0.049	−6.728	−0.020	−2.650
Chest/breathing problems*Ln(age)	−0.112	−13.533	−0.100	−15.146
Heart/blood problems*Ln(age)	−0.113	−12.008	−0.067	−11.218
Problems with stomach/ liver/kidneys*Ln(age)	−0.129	−12.641	−0.089	−11.757
Diabetes*Ln(age)	−0.145	−6.026	−0.087	−6.540
Epilepsy*Ln(age)	−0.142	−3.728	−0.083	−2.995
Migraine or frequent headaches*Ln(age)	−0.070	−8.476	−0.054	−6.333
Other health problems*Ln(age)	−0.163	−14.479	−0.107	−12.527
Mean (ln(household income))	−0.011	−0.366	−0.001	−0.031
Mean (ln(children + 1))	0.074	1.319	0.155	1.665
Mean (ln(adults))	0.009	1.315	0.014	1.230
Standard deviation of individual random effect ε_n	0.736	—	0.666	—
% variance due to ε_n	0.772	—	0.734	—
Number of observations	17,966	—	12,019	—
Number of individuals	7,780	—	5,782	—
R^2:				
Within	0.021	—	0.012	—
Between	0.166	—	0.275	—
Overall	0.126	—	0.221	—

Note: There are dummies for missing variables, which are not included in the table.

second, the subject is central to psychology (of work). However, the approach in that literature differs considerably from ours. Sociologists and a few economists have looked into it. We mention the authors Bender, Donohue, and Heywood (2005), Benz (2005), Clark (1997, 1999, 2000, and 2001), Clark and

Table 3.11. *Job satisfaction Germany, 1992–1997, POLS individual random effects*

	West Workers		East Workers	
	Estimate	t-ratio	Estimate	t-ratio
Constant	3.447	3.459	5.384	3.165
Dummy for 1992	0.101	6.398	0.052	1.791
Dummy for 1993	0.029	1.771	0.107	3.804
Dummy for 1994	0.009	0.573	0.042	1.538
Dummy for 1995	0.014	0.907	0.025	0.961
Dummy for 1996	−0.009	−0.582	0.010	0.400
Ln(age)	−2.883	−5.155	−4.801	−4.921
(Ln(age))^2	0.350	4.423	0.633	4.523
Minimum age	61	—	44	—
Male	−0.060	−1.383	0.030	0.429
Ln(household income)	0.067	3.700	0.066	1.971
Ln(years education)	0.035	0.329	−0.013	−0.068
Ln(adults)	−0.057	−2.821	0.023	0.577
Ln(children + 1)	0.008	0.397	0.002	0.052
Living together	0.008	0.511	−0.018	−0.538
Ln(work income)	0.026	0.571	0.221	2.698
Ln(work income)*Ln(age)	0.013	1.551	−0.010	−0.695
Ln(work income)*Ln(years education)	−0.011	−0.918	−0.008	−0.328
Ln(work income)*male	0.002	0.425	−0.010	−1.152
Self-employed	0.129	4.090	0.185	3.521
Ln(working hours)	−0.015	−0.849	0.021	0.602
Ln(extra money)	0.013	4.444	0.000	0.016
Ln(extra hours)	0.004	0.942	0.013	1.995
Mean (ln(household income))	0.164	5.136	0.175	3.124
Mean (ln(work income))	0.006	0.874	0.030	2.701
Mean (ln(children + 1))	0.030	1.034	0.015	0.297
Mean (ln(adults))	0.025	0.752	−0.074	−1.187
Standard deviation of individual random effect ε_n	0.668	—	0.623	—
% variance due to ε_n	0.471	—	0.406	—
Number of observations	30,084	—	12,122	—
Number of individuals	8,023	—	3,180	—
R^2:				
Within	0.0075	—	0.0068	—
Between	0.0251	—	0.062	—
Overall	0.0198	—	0.0359	—

Note: There are dummies for missing variables, which are not included in the table.

Oswald (1994), Drakopoulos and Theodossiou (1997), Groot and Maassen Van den Brink (1999), Taylor (2006), Vieira and Cabral (2005), and Wottiez and Theeuwes (1998).

Note that for individuals who do not have a job information on JS is obviously absent.

Table 3.11 presents the results for the German workers, again split up into the two sub-samples for West and East German workers.

JS is assumed to depend on age. Since a monotonic relationship seems improbable, we introduce a quadratic relationship in ln(age). We find strong age effects, where satisfaction follows a U-curve. The minimum is reached at age 61 for the West and 44 for the East, after which age JS starts rising with age. The same U-curve effect has been found by Clark and Oswald (1994) and others. Western males are less satisfied than females with their job. For West Germans the number of adults in the household has a negative significant impact on JS.

The role of income with respect to JS is ambiguous. We have to distinguish between the income earned in the job by the respondent, that is the *work income*, and the *household* income. Work income is certainly a dimension of the job: it expresses, to a large extent, how the worker is evaluated by the employer. Given the amount of working hours and the job requirements, the larger the work income is the higher the JS. On the other hand, household income may also influence JS. A larger household income gives each working member of the household more margin to be selective with regard to his or her type of employment, and it also becomes easier to leave an unsatisfactory job if there is additional income in the household. Table 3.11 shows that the coefficient of ln(working income) is 0.026 and non-significant in the West, while it is highly significant and equal to 0.221 in the East. Hence, changes in work income have a strong effect on JS in the East but not in the West. The idea that the effect would vary with age, with education, or with gender could not be substantiated. Self-employed individuals have a markedly higher JS than workers who are employed. This may be because their work is more agreeable, but it may also be that self-employed individuals have a different and more positive attitude to work. Working hours have a non-significant influence on JS. However, the occurrence of overtime seems to have an effect. The same holds for 'extra money'; that is, bonuses, etc.

For the British, the estimated JS equation is presented in Table 3.12.

In the British estimates we also find a strong age component, but there is a striking difference with the Germans. Over most of the lifetime German JS falls, while in the UK JS increases from age 23; in West Germany the minimum is at about age 61, and in East Germany at age 44.

In the British estimates the working income has a strong significant and immediate effect, which decreases with increasing age. JS is strongly affected by whether one lives with a partner. Males are less satisfied with their job than

Domain Satisfactions

Table 3.12. *Job satisfaction UK, 1996–1998, POLS individual random effects*

	Workers	
	Estimate	*t*-ratio
Constant	11.070	9.330
Dummy for 1996	−0.009	−0.574
Dummy for 1997	0.017	1.142
Ln(age)	−7.323	−11.297
$(Ln(age))^2$	1.162	12.556
Minimum age	23	—
Gender (male)	−0.465	−4.159
Ln(household income)	0.029	1.078
Ln(years education)	0.008	0.068
Ln(adults)	−0.089	−1.750
Ln(children + 1)	−0.003	−0.048
Living together	0.128	5.048
Ln(work income)	0.416	4.768
Ln(work income)*Ln(age)	−0.109	−4.989
Ln(work income)*Ln(years education)	−0.014	−0.788
Ln(work income)*male	0.053	3.266
Self-employed	0.143	1.996
Ln(work hours)	−0.031	−1.900
Ln(extra hours)	0.029	3.437
Work at night	−0.119	−1.961
Ln(hours household work)	−0.004	−0.396
Mean (ln(household income))	−0.041	−1.140
Mean (ln(work income))	0.006	0.434
Mean (ln(children + 1))	0.133	2.314
Mean (ln(adults))	0.075	1.212
Standard deviation of individual random effect ε_n	0.766	—
% variance due to ε_n	0.778	—
Number of observations	17,575	—
Number of individuals	7,619	—
R^2:		
Within	0.003	—
Between	0.047	—
Overall	0.038	—

Note: There are dummies for missing variables, which are not included in the table.

females. The dummy for self-employment is strongly positive, which reveals that self-employed individuals derive more JS from their work than employees do.

The number of working hours appears to be important. The number of overtime hours has a significant effect in the sense that more overtime seems to enhance JS. It may be that overtime enhances self-esteem, making the workers feel that they are really needed in their job.

A strong effect is caused by the frequency of non-regular hours like night and weekend shifts.

3.3.3. Financial Satisfaction

For recent examples of research using subjective financial satisfaction questions see Alessie, Crossley, and Hildebrand (2006) and Joo and Grable (2004). The results for the financial-satisfaction (FS) question are shown in Tables 3.13 and 3.14. The curvilinear age effects are very prominent. West German workers reach minimum satisfaction at the age of 44 and east German workers at 54. For non-workers this occurs at age 38 for westerners and 39 for easterners. The quadratic effect may have to do with wage–age profiles and career-pattern differences. It may also result from changing expectations. We might identify it as the *midlife crisis*. At the beginning of life, individuals experience improvements in their life and this leads to rising expectations as to what is 'normal'. At midlife people have had the main improvements and there is a consolidation of circumstances. They do not get large salary increases. This calls for accommodation to reality. If the targets have originally been set too highly, at midlife they are adapted to reality.

The total household-income level effect is 0.396 (= 0.133 + 0.263) for West German workers and 0.421 for Western non-workers. For East German workers it is 0.449 and for eastern non-workers 0.369. Education has a positive impact on FS for westerners but the impact is zero or negative for easterners. This difference probably reflects the different labor-market characteristics and cultures between the two regions. As expected, the number of adults and the number of children living in the household generally have a significantly negative effect on FS, except for the number of children, which is non-significant for eastern workers. The presence of a partner in the household has a positive effect, and male respondents are less content than female respondents. Having savings has a positive effect on FS, as expected.

For the British data we find roughly the same pattern as for the Germans. The dummy for being *self-employed* reveals that the self-employed have much more FS under *ceteris paribus* conditions than employed workers.

In Table 3.13*a* we compare the estimation results of conventional Probit and POLS. We see that, except for the dummy variables, the normed effects in the last two columns are strikingly similar.

3.3.4. Housing Satisfaction

Housing satisfaction (HS) has also been studied by for example, Cuellar, Bastida, and Braccio (2004), Healy (2003), Parkes, Kearns, and Atkinson (2002), and Varady and Carozza (2000). Just as with health, there are two ways in which we can tackle the explanation. The first approach we call the *hedonistic* approach, and the second the *predictive* approach.

First, and this is the most obvious way, we may explain HS by a precise description of the house in which the respondent is living. That is, how many

Table 3.13. *Financial satisfaction, Germany, 1992–1997, POLS individual random effects*

Estimate	West workers Estimate	West workers t-ratio	East workers Estimate	East workers t-ratio	West non-workers Estimate	West non-workers t-ratio	East non-workers Estimate	East non-workers t-ratio
Constant	1.729	1.984	1.529	1.128	8.417	11.294	10.506	8.912
Dummy for 1992	0.214	13.342	−0.074	−2.836	0.079	3.830	−0.230	−6.482
Dummy for 1993	0.105	6.370	0.008	0.302	0.117	5.515	−0.139	−4.154
Dummy for 1994	0.055	3.283	−0.287	−11.168	0.181	8.598	−0.020	−0.622
Dummy for 1995	0.035	2.152	−0.030	−1.173	0.117	5.716	−0.011	−0.353
Dummy for 1996	0.016	0.885	−0.026	−0.952	0.022	0.964	−0.081	−2.286
Ln(age)	−2.854	−5.757	−2.686	−3.474	−6.844	−16.696	−7.258	−11.340
(Ln(age))^2	0.376	5.395	0.336	3.071	0.942	16.764	0.993	11.348
Minimum age	44	—	54	—	38	—	39	—
Ln(household income)	0.133	6.705	0.225	6.463	0.133	5.131	0.212	4.401
Ln(years education)	0.121	2.895	−0.049	−0.738	0.142	2.578	−0.274	−3.525
Ln(adults)	−0.089	−4.195	−0.139	−3.624	−0.014	−0.458	−0.067	−1.129
Ln(children + 1)	−0.039	−1.881	−0.154	−4.349	−0.066	−2.330	−0.088	−1.531
Gender (male)	−0.023	−1.391	−0.041	−1.881	−0.153	−7.216	−0.086	−3.019
Ln(savings)	0.015	6.267	0.017	4.255	0.018	5.285	0.024	4.283
Living together	0.094	4.760	0.169	4.211	0.139	7.178	0.053	1.504
Second earner	−0.015	−0.825	−0.073	−2.290	—	—	—	—
Self-employed	−0.020	−0.787	0.120	3.153	—	—	—	—
Mean (Ln(household income))	0.263	8.204	0.224	4.264	0.288	7.353	0.157	2.364
Mean (Ln(savings))	0.042	9.813	0.032	4.747	0.050	8.875	0.045	5.144
Mean (Ln(children + 1))	−0.065	−2.291	0.042	0.913	−0.128	−3.255	−0.024	−0.343
Mean (Ln(adults))	−0.080	−2.512	−0.153	−2.789	−0.206	−4.812	−0.254	−3.315
Standard deviation of individual random effect ε_n	0.565	—	0.461	—	0.621	—	0.495	—
% variance due to ε_n	0.365	—	0.285	—	0.386	—	0.279	—
Number of observations	30,622	—	12,357	—	20,867	—	8,536	—
Number of individuals	8,148	—	3,236	—	6,419	—	2,699	—
R^2:								
Within	0.015	—	0.035	—	0.011	—	0.037	—
Between	0.115	—	0.136	—	0.181	—	0.201	—
Overall	0.074	—	0.081	—	0.145	—	0.142	—

Note: There are dummies for missing variables, which are not included in the table.

	POLS		Ordered Probit		POLS	OP
	Estimate	t-ratio	Estimate	t-ratio	Norm=1	Norm=1
Constant	1.734	1.990	0.307	13.780		
Dummy for 1992	0.214	13.340	0.312	13.550	0.074	0.073
Dummy for 1993	0.105	6.370	0.249	10.770	0.036	0.074
Dummy for 1994	0.054	3.280	0.220	9.860	0.019	0.059
Dummy for 1995	0.035	2.160	0.293	11.920	0.012	0.052
Dummy for 1996	0.016	0.880			0.005	0.069
Ln(age)	−2.849	−5.750	−4.108	−6.000	−0.980	−0.973
(Ln(age))^2	0.375	5.380	0.544	5.640	0.129	0.129
Minimum age	44		44			
Ln(household income)	0.133	6.710	0.180	6.530	0.046	0.043
Ln(years education)	0.119	2.860	0.173	3.020	0.041	0.041
Ln(adults)	−0.089	−4.190	−0.123	−4.200	−0.030	−0.029
Ln(children + 1)	−0.039	−1.890	−0.057	−2.000	−0.013	−0.014
Gender (male)	−0.023	−1.420	−0.035	−1.550	−0.008	−0.008
Ln(savings)	0.015	6.260	0.020	6.050	0.005	0.005
Living together	0.094	4.750	0.134	4.900	0.032	0.032
Second earner	−0.015	−0.830	−0.017	−0.710	−0.005	−0.004
Mean (Ln(household income))	0.261	8.180	0.361	8.160	0.090	0.085
Mean (Ln(savings))	0.043	9.890	0.059	9.820	0.015	0.014
Mean (Ln(children + 1))	−0.065	−2.290	−0.086	−2.200	−0.022	−0.020
Mean (Ln(adults))	−0.079	−2.480	−0.114	−2.590	−0.027	−0.027
Intercept term 1			−5.617			
Intercept term 2			−5.354			
Intercept term 3			−5.002			
Intercept term 4			−4.588			
Intercept term 5			−4.185			
Intercept term 6			−3.532			
Intercept term 7			−3.056			
Intercept term 8			−2.340			
Intercept term 9			−1.323			
Intercept term 10			−0.561			
Standard deviation of individual random effect ε_π	0.565					
% variance due to ε_π	0.365		0.374			
Number of observations	30,622		30,622			
Number of individuals	8,148					
R^2:						
Within	0.015					
Between	0.115					
Overall	0.074					
Log Likelihood			−56,649.3			

Note: There are dummies for missing variables, which are not included in the table.

Table 3.14. *Financial satisfaction, UK, 1996–1998, POLS individual random effects*

	Workers		Non-workers	
	Estimate	t-ratio	Estimate	t-ratio
Constant	9.176	9.570	14.383	18.295
Dummy for 1996	−0.071	−5.196	−0.115	−6.210
Dummy for 1997	0.005	0.365	−0.044	−2.605
Ln(age)	−7.197	−13.012	−9.672	−22.172
(Ln(age))^2	1.016	13.009	1.371	22.965
Minimum age	35	—	34	—
Ln(household income)	0.245	11.144	0.085	4.306
Ln(years education)	−0.057	−2.405	0.049	1.643
Ln(adults)	−0.109	−2.512	−0.010	−0.147
Ln(children + 1)	−0.120	−2.626	−0.087	−0.999
Gender (male)	−0.025	−1.251	−0.179	−7.356
Ln(savings)	0.054	12.775	0.028	3.670
Living together	0.078	2.475	0.120	4.132
Second earner	0.032	1.199	—	—
Self-employed	0.119	4.281	—	—
Mean (ln(household income))	0.191	6.372	0.191	7.184
Mean (ln(savings))	0.040	6.042	0.104	9.225
Mean (ln(children + 1))	0.086	1.712	0.031	0.329
Mean (ln(adults))	−0.232	−4.307	−0.120	−1.596
Standard deviation of individual random effect ε_n	0.719	—	0.681	—
% variance due to ε_n	0.685	—	0.735	—
Number of observations	17,957	—	12,005	—
Number of individuals	7,770	—	5,775	—
R^2				
Within	0.035	—	0.015	—
Between	0.143	—	0.230	—
Overall	0.119	—	0.187	—

Note: There are dummies for missing variables, which are not included in the table.

rooms it contains, the surface area, the year it was built, in what type of neighborhood it stands, etc. It is obvious that when we fill in those explanatory variables there will be only a marginal role for income and rent or housing cost as an explanation. This is because the quality of the house is strongly correlated with the income and the rent of the respondent. Rich people live in spacious and comfortable, but also expensive, houses, while the poor do not.

A second possibility is to drop the specific housing variables and to explain HS by 'general' variables only, like income, age, and so on. Then it becomes possible to predict the average HS of an individual with reference to the specific characteristics of that individual.

We start with the second, predictive approach. Looking at Tables 3.15 and 3.16 for Germany and the UK respectively, we see that the effects are qualitatively

Table 3.15. *Housing satisfaction (predictive approach), Germany, 1992–1997, POLS individual random effects*

	West workers		East workers		West non-workers		East non-workers	
	Estimate	t-ratio	Estimate	t-ratio	Estimate	t-ratio	Estimate	t-ratio
Constant	2.737	3.137	6.741	4.566	2.546	3.671	4.052	3.550
Dummy for 1992	0.032	2.213	-0.099	-4.018	0.196	11.601	0.083	2.582
Dummy for 1993	0.015	1.011	-0.097	-3.900	0.161	9.236	0.056	1.858
Dummy for 1994	-0.012	-0.781	-0.100	-4.127	0.132	7.672	0.065	2.240
Dummy for 1995	0.023	1.614	-0.055	-2.323	0.082	4.912	0.013	0.441
Dummy for 1996	-0.011	-0.754	-0.048	-2.060	0.018	1.068	-0.005	-0.181
Ln(age)	-3.578	-7.136	-4.386	-5.127	-3.602	-9.362	-3.406	-5.436
(Ln(age))^2	0.535	7.567	0.649	5.320	0.536	10.109	0.498	5.742
Minimum age	28	—	29	—	29	—	31	—
Ln(household income)	0.094	5.623	0.033	1.118	0.059	2.888	-0.029	-0.722
Ln(years education)	-0.032	-0.724	-0.548	-6.855	-0.026	-0.472	-0.389	-4.503
Ln(adults)	-0.118	-6.294	-0.047	-1.335	-0.063	-2.584	0.011	0.219
Ln(children + 1)	-0.055	-3.004	0.020	0.602	-0.022	-0.945	-0.019	-0.373
Gender (male)	-0.056	-3.259	-0.043	-1.602	-0.080	-3.735	-0.040	-1.222
Self-employed	-0.003	-0.136	0.009	0.216	—	—	—	—
Mean (ln(household income))	0.325	10.981	0.191	3.682	0.395	12.155	0.349	5.856
Mean (ln(children + 1))	-0.064	-2.311	-0.010	-0.213	-0.204	-5.692	-0.061	-0.878
Mean (ln(adults))	-0.058	-1.858	-0.018	-0.300	-0.203	-5.223	-0.191	-2.555
Standard deviation of individual random effect ε_n	0.654	—	0.651	—	0.697	—	0.662	—
% variance due to ε_n	0.492	—	0.481	—	0.549	—	0.474	—
Number of observations	30,554	—	12,309	—	20,810	—	8,477	—
Number of individuals	8,143	—	3,232	—	6,393	—	2,681	—
R^2:								
Within	0.0028	—	0.0058	—	0.0089	—	0.0032	—
Between	0.0612	—	0.0385	—	0.1131	—	0.0587	—
Overall	0.041	—	0.0238	—	0.1111	—	0.047	—

Note: There are dummies for missing variables, which are not included in the table.

Table 3.16. *Housing satisfaction (predictive approach), UK, 1996–1998, POLS individual random effects*

	Workers		Non-workers	
	Estimate	*t*-ratio	Estimate	*t*-ratio
Constant	12.176	11.807	9.794	12.297
Dummy for 1996	−0.057	−3.645	0.009	0.459
Dummy for 1997	−0.025	−1.756	−0.003	−0.141
Ln(age)	−8.088	−13.440	−6.555	−14.604
(Ln(age))^2	1.203	14.094	0.992	15.916
Minimum age	29	—	27	—
Ln(household income)	0.044	1.773	−0.011	−0.513
Ln(years education)	−0.072	−2.699	−0.083	−2.501
Ln(adults)	−0.071	−1.449	−0.098	−1.351
Ln(children + 1)	0.069	1.326	0.010	0.109
Gender (male)	−0.077	−3.440	−0.115	−4.276
Self-employed	0.051	1.607	—	—
Mean (ln(household income))	0.124	3.722	0.116	3.984
Mean (ln(children + 1))	−0.124	−2.168	−0.060	−0.593
Mean (ln(adults))	0.103	1.688	0.127	1.540
Standard deviation of individual random effect ε_n	0.812	—	0.767	—
% variance due to ε_n	0.779	—	0.812	—
Number of observations	17,936	—	12,003	—
Number of individuals	7,766	—	5,776	—
R^2:				
Within	0.003	—	0.002	—
Between	0.061	—	0.155	—
Overall	0.046	—	0.121	—

Note: There are dummies for missing variables, which are not included in the table.

similar in both countries. The age effect is U-shaped, reaching a minimum at about age 29. The mean of the household income has a strong positive effect on HS. The number of children and adults has the expected negative effects, implying that HS falls with an increasing number of members of the household. The education effect is negative, although not significantly so for West Germany. We conclude that higher-educated people are more critical of their housing conditions or have higher expectations that cannot be met. Males seem to be less satisfied with their housing than females.

Now we estimate HS for the same countries by means of the hedonistic approach. The results are presented in Tables 3.17 and 3.18. For the German data set we do not have many variables concerning housing. We use two variables; that is, the rent, which is estimated when the house is owned by the

Table 3.17. *Housing satisfaction (hedonistic approach), Germany 1992–1997, POLS individual random effects*

	West workers		East workers		West non-workers		East non-workers	
	Estimate	t-ratio	Estimate	t-ratio	Estimate	t-ratio	Estimate	t-ratio
Constant	4.717	5.494	6.343	4.523	5.953	8.954	5.842	5.771
Dummy for 1992	0.082	5.709	0.090	3.778	0.207	12.202	0.256	8.280
Dummy for 1993	0.055	3.721	0.017	0.686	0.170	9.760	0.155	5.287
Dummy for 1994	0.035	2.384	0.006	0.250	0.148	8.473	0.159	5.389
Dummy for 1995	0.042	2.909	-0.001	-0.051	0.088	5.223	0.051	1.760
Dummy for 1996	0.017	1.202	0.012	0.504	0.029	1.713	0.040	1.394
Ln(age)	-3.841	-7.712	-4.269	-5.160	-4.195	-10.842	-3.946	-6.568
(Ln(age))^2	0.578	8.216	0.627	5.314	0.623	11.679	0.575	6.920
Minimum age	28	—	30	—	29	—	31	—
Ln(years education)	0.076	1.809	-0.440	-6.022	0.098	1.790	-0.360	-4.355
Ln(adults)	-0.118	-6.900	-0.100	-3.166	-0.057	-2.551	-0.084	-1.802
Ln(children + 1)	-0.069	-3.861	-0.014	-0.446	-0.027	-1.198	-0.051	-1.040
Gender (male)	-0.041	-2.402	-0.031	-1.179	-0.093	-4.279	-0.038	-1.210
Self-employed	-0.009	-0.349	-0.037	-0.907	—	—	—	—
Ln(rent)	0.218	26.406	0.270	22.712	0.110	11.420	0.223	14.303
Reforms	0.045	6.372	0.052	5.457	0.026	2.531	0.051	4.031
Mean (ln(children + 1))	-0.065	-2.395	-0.015	-0.313	-0.165	-4.642	-0.012	-0.177
Mean (ln(adults))	0.097	3.546	0.016	0.318	0.057	1.701	0.018	0.293
Standard deviation of individual random effect ε_n	0.650	—	0.622	—	0.703	—	0.627	—
% variance due to ε_n	0.494	—	0.469	—	0.553	—	0.451	—
Number of observations	30,554	—	12,309	—	20,810	—	8,477	—
Number of individuals	8,143	—	3,232	—	6,393	—	2,681	—
R^2:								
Within	0.021	—	0.0481	—	0.0099	—	0.019	—
Between	0.0718	—	0.1078	—	0.0926	—	0.1117	—
Overall	0.0541	—	0.0861	—	0.089	—	0.0863	—

Note: There are dummies for missing variables, which are not included in the table.

Domain Satisfactions

Table 3.18. *Housing satisfaction UK. (hedonistic approach), 1996–1998, POLS individual random effects*

	Workers		Non-workers	
	Estimate	*t*-ratio	Estimate	*t*-ratio
Constant	12.068	12.406	9.120	12.182
Dummy for 1996	−0.033	−2.195	0.019	0.936
Dummy for 1997	−0.008	−0.539	0.012	0.653
Ln(age)	−7.227	−12.965	−5.626	−13.142
(Ln(age))^2	1.057	13.362	0.850	14.301
Minimum age	31	—	27	—
Ln(years education)	−0.079	−3.161	−0.106	−3.347
Ln(adults)	−0.098	−2.197	−0.127	−1.912
Ln(children + 1)	0.059	1.163	0.061	0.635
Gender (male)	−0.072	−3.440	−0.112	−4.408
Self-employed	0.023	0.773	—	—
Number of rooms	0.047	7.293	0.021	2.503
Shortage of space	−0.390	−19.923	−0.412	−14.968
Noise from neighbors	−0.225	−9.305	−0.209	−6.671
Street noise	−0.145	−6.949	−0.138	−5.283
Lack of light	−0.096	−3.306	−0.135	−3.589
Lack of adequate heating	−0.261	−7.798	−0.260	−6.579
Pollution/environmental problems	−0.118	−4.364	−0.087	−2.632
Vandalism or crime	−0.139	−6.765	−0.164	−6.877
House in ownership	0.295	12.711	0.156	5.857
Mean (ln(children + 1))	−0.110	−1.983	−0.045	−0.450
Mean (ln(adults))	0.106	2.011	0.195	2.695
Standard deviation of individual random effect ε_n	0.740	—	0.696	—
% variance due to ε_n	0.761	—	0.806	—
Number of observations	17,940	—	12,014	—
Number of individuals	7,767	—	5,779	—
R^2:				
Within	0.047	—	0.018	—
Between	0.176	—	0.248	—
Overall	0.144	—	0.194	—

Note: There are dummies for missing variables, which are not included in the table.

inhabitant, and the question of whether the house has recently been renovated. This is known from a dummy variable 'reform'. We drop income in this specification. We see that the rent has a strong effect on HS. The other variables have approximately the same effect as in the predictive specification.

For the British hedonistic specification we introduce some specific housing characteristics, such as the (absolute) number of rooms and an ownership dummy. Moreover, we include a variable for 'noise from neighbors' and 'street noise'. Those variables are defined as dummy variables. In this way it is possible to make a housing-quality index. The estimated coefficients speak for themselves. We see, for instance, that 'street noise' carries less weight than 'noise from neighbors'.

3.3.5. Leisure Satisfaction

3.3.5.1. *Leisure satisfaction, German data set*
In the GSOEP data set two kinds of time use, namely working time, and leisure, are identified. Hence, it is possible to distinguish between two independent types of time-spending, the third being equal to household work. Leisure does not include sleeping time, which is set for all at 8. Not unexpectedly, the number of working hours (which is not automatically the complement of leisure!) has a strong negative effect on leisure satisfaction (LS), while the number of hours spent on leisure has a small positive effect. Higher education leads to less LS. The self-employed have much less LS than employed workers. The age effect is again U-shaped, with a minimum at about age 37 for workers and 31 for non-workers. Household income is not a strong factor for LS, but the level effects are always positive. It seems that there is a tendency for people to enjoy their leisure time most when they live alone, which tendency is more pronounced in the West than in the East. The presence of both adults and children has a negative effect on LS, and living together also has a negative effect, although only significantly so for eastern non-workers. Males enjoy their leisure more than females.

3.3.5.2. *Leisure satisfaction, British data set*
For the British data set there are two kinds of LS recorded. The first type of LS has to do with the *amount* of leisure (LS$_A$). The second leisure aspect is the *use* made of the leisure time available (LS$_U$). One may or may not be happy with the quality of the time one has spent on leisure activities. It is obvious that the German concept is an aggregate of the two sub-concepts distinguished in the British data set. Hence, the German and British LS are not comparable. In the British data set there is also information on the third time use component: household work.

Leisure-amount satisfaction
First we consider LS$_A$. As always, we distinguish between workers and non-workers. We expect that for workers the actual amount of leisure time will be most important. Although the coefficient is rather large, it is just on the verge of being significant. Most important is age, with once again a U-curve, with a minimum at age 32. Young people seem to attach decreasing importance to having leisure until the age of 32. After that age they assign an increasing importance to leisure. As expected, the amount of leisure is unimportant for

Table 3.19. *Leisure satisfaction, Germany, 1992–1997, POLS individual random effects*

	West workers		East workers		West non-workers		East non-workers	
	Estimate	t-ratio	Estimate	t-ratio	Estimate	t-ratio	Estimate	t-ratio
Constant	10.183	11.987	12.678	9.748	9.578	14.664	7.028	6.737
Dummy for 1992	0.048	3.349	−0.083	−3.522	0.114	6.522	0.109	3.362
Dummy for 1993	0.066	4.465	−0.043	−1.799	0.055	3.038	0.014	0.461
Dummy for 1994	0.110	7.109	−0.005	−0.222	0.113	6.120	0.020	0.678
Dummy for 1995	0.006	0.449	−0.111	−4.887	0.090	5.193	0.151	5.169
Dummy for 1996	0.097	6.449	0.053	2.253	0.067	3.758	−0.008	−0.282
Ln(age)	−5.340	−11.033	−5.712	−7.626	−5.636	−15.632	−4.504	−7.911
(Ln(age))²	0.742	10.864	0.794	7.431	0.811	16.319	0.655	8.312
Minimum age	37	—	37	—	32	—	31	—
Ln(household income)	0.011	0.583	−0.010	−0.312	0.000	0.019	0.042	0.938
Ln(years education)	−0.076	−1.814	−0.228	−3.359	−0.152	−2.977	−0.246	−3.150
Ln(adults)	−0.036	−1.906	−0.082	−2.407	−0.078	−3.040	−0.068	−1.292
Ln(children + 1)	−0.026	−1.402	−0.044	−1.404	−0.031	−1.286	−0.032	−0.616
Gender (male)	0.170	9.837	0.165	7.128	0.126	6.345	0.074	2.535
Ln(working hours)	−0.251	−17.738	−0.415	−15.212	—	—	—	—
Self-employed	−0.339	−13.707	−0.254	−6.711	—	—	—	—
Ln(leisure time)	0.045	2.096	0.013	0.364	0.008	0.457	0.006	0.168
Ln(leisure time)*Ln(household income)	−0.003	−1.133	0.001	0.288	0.002	0.811	0.001	0.290
Mean (Ln(household income))	0.094	3.247	0.045	0.965	0.072	2.287	0.132	2.325
Mean (Ln(hours of work))	−0.014	−1.489	−0.027	−2.026	—	—	—	—
Mean (Ln(children + 1))	−0.129	−4.775	−0.054	−1.216	−0.180	−5.176	−0.121	−1.808
Mean (Ln(adults))	−0.041	−1.344	0.026	0.496	−0.060	−1.598	−0.237	−3.299
Standard deviation of individual random effect ε_n	0.615	—	0.521	—	0.609	—	0.557	—
% variance due to ε_n	0.463	—	0.393	—	0.460	—	0.378	—
Number of observations	30,569	—	12,323	—	20,804	—	8,528	—
Number of individuals	8,151	—	3,230	—	6,415	—	2,703	—
R^2:								
Within	0.0162	—	0.02	—	0.0101	—	0.0171	—
Between	0.092	—	0.1485	—	0.1506	—	0.1092	—
Overall	0.0686	—	0.1027	—	0.1351	—	0.0926	—

Note: There are dummies for missing variables, which are not included in the table.

Table 3.20. *Leisure-amount UK, 1996–1998, POLS individual random effects*

	Workers		Non-workers	
	Estimate	*t*-ratio	Estimate	*t*-ratio
Constant	10.141	6.316	6.258	2.558
Dummy for 1996	−0.020	−1.364	0.064	3.128
Dummy for 1997	−0.033	−2.443	−0.009	−0.453
Ln(age)	−6.750	−11.615	−4.444	−10.049
$(Ln(age))^2$	0.974	11.814	0.690	11.259
Minimum age	32	—	25	—
Ln(household income)	0.086	0.543	−0.176	−0.534
Ln(years education)	−0.068	−2.700	−0.026	−0.819
Ln(adults)	−0.064	−1.418	−0.122	−1.673
Ln(children + 1)	−0.194	−4.053	−0.157	−1.620
Gender (male)	0.047	2.133	0.129	4.856
Ln(working hours)	−0.080	−3.968	—	—
Self-employed	−0.040	−1.332	—	—
Ln(leisure time)	0.539	1.885	0.012	0.023
Ln(leisure time)*Ln(family income)	−0.026	−0.688	0.041	0.568
Mean (ln(household income))	−0.034	−1.082	0.067	2.339
Mean (ln(hours of work))	−0.069	−3.315	—	—
Mean (ln(children + 1))	−0.056	−1.063	−0.244	−2.382
Mean (ln(adults))	0.177	3.125	0.082	0.996
Standard deviation of individual random effect ε_n	0.768	—	0.720	—
% variance due to ε_n	0.720	—	0.823	—
Number of observations	17,951	—	11,982	—
Number of individuals	7,780	—	5,784	—
R^2:				
Within	0.007	—	0.002	—
Between	0.094	—	0.202	—
Overall	0.075	—	0.170	—

Note: There are dummies for missing variables, which are not included in the table.

non-workers. The number of working hours has a strong negative effect. The more education one has, the less satisfied one is with the amount of leisure. The evaluation of the amount of leisure decreases with the number of children in the household. The interpretation of this effect is that a considerable part of one's 'free time' has to be spent on children; this time use is probably not perceived by many as real leisure. This makes leisure scarce. In this respect, it is interesting that the presence of more adults is, on balance, positively evaluated. This may be because the burdens of childcare can be shared. It also shows that singles are less well-off than (childless) couples. Income as such does not seem to be a relevant factor.

Domain Satisfactions

Table 3.21. *Leisure-use UK, 1996–1998, POLS individual random effects*

	Workers		Non-workers	
	Estimate	*t*-ratio	Estimate	*t*-ratio
Constant	12.254	7.431	9.373	3.822
Dummy for 1996	0.017	1.167	0.061	3.078
Dummy for 1997	−0.011	−0.820	−0.023	−1.285
Ln(age)	−7.740	−12.972	−5.717	−12.456
(Ln(age))^2	1.111	13.125	0.843	13.244
Minimum age	33	—	30	—
Ln(household income)	0.045	0.279	−0.003	−0.010
Ln(years education)	−0.110	−4.286	−0.047	−1.401
Ln(adults)	−0.048	−1.026	−0.083	−1.192
Ln(children + 1)	−0.090	−1.829	−0.076	−0.814
Gender (male)	0.080	3.506	0.061	2.194
Ln(working hours)	0.006	0.309	—	—
Self-employed	−0.018	−0.588	—	—
Ln(leisure time)	0.286	0.973	−0.095	−0.184
Ln(leisure time)*Ln(household income)	−0.012	−0.304	0.009	0.122
Mean (ln(household income))	0.007	0.225	0.016	0.567
Mean (ln(hours of work))	−0.039	−1.805	—	—
Mean (ln(children + 1))	−0.119	−2.176	−0.150	−1.510
Mean (ln(adults))	0.096	1.645	0.171	2.117
Standard deviation of individual random effect ε_n	0.787	—	0.790	—
% variance due to ε_n	0.740	—	0.786	—
Number of observations	17,951	—	11,989	—
Number of individuals	7,781	—	5,786	—
R^2:				
Within	0.002	—	0.003	—
Between	0.064	—	0.106	—
Overall	0.050	—	0.093	—

Note: There are dummies for missing variables, which are not included in the table.

Leisure-use satisfaction

Apart from the now expected U-curve with age, we find that household income has no effect on the evaluation of time use. The number of children has a negative effect. Males are more satisfied with their use of free time than females. The higher one's education, the more dissatisfied one is. This may be because more education implies a wider scope of possibilities and hence an increased feeling that one cannot sufficiently exploit those known possibilities.

The amount of leisure time affects the evaluation of time use positively, although the effect is non-significant.

Table 3.22. Environmental satisfaction, Germany, 1992–1997, POLS individual random effects

	West workers		East workers		West non-workers		East non-workers	
	Estimate	t-ratio	Estimate	t-ratio	Estimate	t-ratio	Estimate	t-ratio
Constant	0.002	0.002	−2.251	−1.765	3.506	5.192	2.970	2.926
Dummy for 1992	0.224	15.155	−0.429	−18.650	0.225	11.992	−0.298	−9.447
Dummy for 1993	0.115	7.823	−0.154	−6.875	0.122	6.550	−0.114	−3.833
Dummy for 1994	0.450	29.016	0.100	4.296	0.455	23.704	0.253	8.424
Dummy for 1995	0.069	4.891	−0.104	−4.799	0.059	3.346	−0.086	−2.995
Dummy for 1996	0.070	4.717	−0.090	−3.902	0.036	1.945	−0.105	−3.562
Ln(age)	−1.037	−2.133	0.724	0.987	−2.614	−6.981	−1.843	−3.252
(Ln(age))^2	0.157	2.296	−0.094	−0.900	0.388	7.572	0.280	3.604
Minimum age	27	—	47	—	29	—	27	—
Ln(household income)	0.051	3.219	0.058	2.225	0.017	0.808	0.000	−0.011
Ln(years education)	−0.059	−1.357	−0.341	−4.759	−0.041	−0.751	−0.254	−3.171
Gender (male)	0.123	7.115	0.095	3.858	−0.032	−1.467	0.060	1.993
Self-employed	−0.020	−0.785	−0.058	−1.490	—	—	—	—
Ln(leisure time)	0.004	2.285	−0.002	−0.675	−0.001	−0.811	−0.007	−2.339
Mean (ln(household income))	0.161	6.106	0.120	2.836	0.094	3.175	0.038	0.761
Mean (ln(leisure time))	0.006	1.721	−0.006	−1.037	0.014	4.264	−0.001	−0.212
Standard deviation of individual random effect ε_n	0.653	—	0.579	—	0.665	—	0.587	—
% variance due to ε_n	0.476	—	0.437	—	0.462	—	0.398	—
Number of observations	30,606	—	12,346	—	20,865	—	8,523	—
Number of individuals	8,145	—	3,235	—	6,417	—	2,697	—
R^2:								
Within	0.051		0.075		0.051		0.067	
Between	0.022		0.042		0.036		0.038	
Overall	0.036		0.050		0.045		0.051	

Note: There are dummies for missing variables, which are not included in the table.

3.3.6. Environmental Satisfaction in Germany

In the German sample there is also a question about satisfaction with the environment. The concrete phrasing of the question is satisfaction with 'environmental conditions in your area'. Therefore, we interpret this as a satisfaction with the local environment, i.e. the quality of the neighbourhood. In the literature there are few studies that analyze the quality of the neighborhood and community by using subjective questions. Examples are Cuellar, Bastida, and Braccio (2004) and Grzeskowiak, Sirgy, and Widgery (2003). We find that household income has a positive effect, which is probably caused by the fact that richer people live in better neighborhoods. However, the same effect is much weaker for non-workers. For East Germans we find a negative effect of increasing education, which is

Table 3.23. *Social-life satisfaction, UK, 1996–1998, POLS individual random effects*

	Workers		Non-workers	
	Estimate	*t*-ratio	Estimate	*t*-ratio
Constant	15.818	14.829	13.354	13.735
Dummy for 1996	−0.009	−0.611	0.041	2.067
Dummy for 1997	−0.067	−4.964	−0.028	−1.524
Ln(age)	−9.598	−16.212	−7.3957	−15.132
(Ln(age))^2	1.351	16.108	1.019	15.200
Minimum age	35	—	38	—
Ln(household income)	0.034	1.600	0.026	1.387
Ln(years education)	−0.101	−3.925	−0.04452	−1.336
Ln(children + 1)	−0.222	−4.625	−0.161	−1.746
Gender (male)	−0.027	−1.182	0.031	1.108
Living together	0.052	2.164	0.140	4.764
Ln(working hours)	0.027	1.338	—	—
Self-employed	0.007	0.242	—	—
Ln(leisure time)	0.098	1.965	−0.169	−2.621
Mean (ln(household income))	0.058	2.042	0.049	1.974
Mean (ln(children + 1))	0.016	0.302	−0.124	−1.257
Mean (ln(hour of work))	−0.010	−0.488	—	—
Standard deviation of individual random effect ε_n	0.804	—	0.795	—
% variance due to ε_n	0.724	—	0.783	—
Number of observations	17,948	—	11,975	—
Number of individuals	7,779	—	5,785	—
R^2:				
Within	0.005	—	0.003	—
Between	0.069	—	0.078	—
Overall	0.054	—	0.062	—

Note: There are dummies for missing variables, which are not included in the table.

conspicuously absent for West Germans. It may be because easterners have less freedom to choose their own type of job. We find the usual age effects. Males have a more positive view on the environment than females. Environmental satisfaction is not asked for in the British data set.

3.3.7. Satisfaction with Social Life in the UK

For the UK, we can construct two very interesting indices, one on satisfaction with social life and the other on the relation with a partner (mostly in marriage). We start with the satisfaction with social life. Table 3.23 shows the results.

There is a strong age pattern. Satisfaction with social relations worsens as one grows older with a minimum at about age 35. This may have to do with the fact that efforts in the age bracket 23–40 are more directed towards family life and establishing a career. After that age, social relations improve with age. Social life deteriorates with an increasing number of children. This reflects the fact that households with children become less externally oriented. We do not find a strong significant effect of household income. Males have slightly less satisfaction from social life than females. Higher education has a negative effect. Living together has a positive effect. Clearly, both partners have their own social network and the social-attraction value of a household increases. However, an alternative explanation may be that a partnership needs fewer social relations because the partners serve each other's needs in this respect.

3.3.8. Marriage

Table 3.24 shows the results for the British marriage satisfaction. The effect of marriage on happiness (or general satisfaction) has interested some economists, such as Stutzer and Frey (2006) who looked at whether happy people get married or married people get happier. Nevertheless the study of marriage satisfaction in economics is fairly unusual. We assume a different age effect for males and females. Although not very significant, this difference is indeed found. It reflects the different impact of aging on the genders. For the female we find a minimum at about age 32, while for the male it is at 21. If this is true, it implies that young women feel that the quality of their marriage is decreasing, while at the same time males believe things are getting better. It would follow that the period in the twenties is an unstable period for marriage as the two partners may have different perceptions of the quality of their marriage. The different quadratic effect for male and female indicates that the age effects for the female are more pronounced (0.600) than for the male (0.275 = 0.600–0.325).

Note that we do not observe couples here. In Chapter 6 we shall try to consider couples as units of observation. Most intriguingly, more household

Table 3.24. *Marriage satisfaction, UK, 1996–1998, POLS individual random effects*

	Workers		Non-workers	
	Estimate	t-ratio	Estimate	t-ratio
Constant	7.596	3.569	0.926	0.532
Dummy for 1996	0.016	0.904	0.006	0.254
Dummy for 1997	−0.003	−0.153	−0.014	−0.657
Ln(age)	−4.141	−3.400	−1.115	−1.130
$(Ln(age))^2$	0.600	3.493	0.231	1.700
Male*Ln(age)	2.472	1.567	1.839	1.263
$Male^*(Ln(age))^2$	−0.325	−1.470	−0.241	−1.222
Minimum age, woman	32	—	11	—
Minimum age, man	21	Max age	1.E+ 15	—
Ln(household income)	−0.067	−2.484	−0.012	−0.447
Ln(years education)	−0.124	−3.679	−0.054	−1.215
Ln(children + 1)	−0.154	−2.616	−0.036	−0.334
Gender (male)	−4.508	−1.611	−3.376	−1.274
Second earner	0.289	10.628	—	—
Ln(hours household work)	0.009	0.706	−0.013	−0.836
Mean (ln(household income))	0.027	0.739	0.057	1.605
Mean (ln(children + 1))	0.021	0.321	−0.063	−0.532
Standard deviation of individual random effect ε_n	0.915	—	0.892	—
% variance due to ε_n	0.580	—	0.610	—
Number of observations	14,142	—	6,924	—
Number of individuals	6,280	—	3,468	—
R^2:				
Within	0.001	—	0.003	—
Between	0.043	—	0.084	—
Overall	0.029	—	0.075	—

Note: There are dummies for missing variables, which are not included in the table.

income is no guarantee of more marital satisfaction. Quite the contrary. The effect of children is strong. We notice, however, that there must be a remarkable difference between the decision utility and the experienced utility of children. When deciding to have children we can assume that the decision utility will be mostly positive. But the experience in reality, that is the negative coefficient, tells a different story. Finally, we observe that males are less satisfied than females and that education also has a negative effect on the perception of marital quality. Interestingly, when there are two breadwinners this affects the marriage quality positively. This is at variance with the traditional view on the role of the housewife.

3.4. THE RELATION BETWEEN POLS AND COLS EFFECT ESTIMATES

With respect to estimation methodology, we saw in Chapter 2 that we may apply ordinal or cardinal ordered probit or their OLS versions. We abbreviated them as OP, CP, POLS, and COLS respectively. In this chapter we have chosen the POLS version, but this choice can be made without loss of generality. Referring to Chapter 2, we may construct for each satisfaction index a u-variable and a Z-variable. The u-variable depends on the *values* in the cardinal questions. The Z-variable assigns a value to each response category which corresponds with, and is determined by, the sample response distribution. Both variables have marginal normal distributions (per assumption), but their expectation and variances are different. However, it is possible to find a linear relation between both, as we have already found empirically in Chapter 2 for financial satisfaction in equation (2.31).

In Table 3.25 we present the same equation for the various domains.

The first line of this table shows that for financial satisfaction we have:

$$Z_{Fin} = 0.536u_{Fin} + 0.196,\tag{3.6}$$

and that for job satisfaction we find similarly:

$$Z_{Job} = 0.567u_{Job} + 0.210.\tag{3.7}$$

The linear relationships are practically perfect, as shown by the R^2. The same holds for the other satisfactions. Let us now assume that there holds

$$u_{Fin} = \beta'_{Fin}x + cons_{Fin}.\tag{3.8}$$

In that case we get

$$Z_{Fin} = 0.536(\beta'_{Fin}x + cons_{Fin}) + 0.196.\tag{3.9}$$

It follows that explanation by operationalizing the satisfaction variables by u- or by Z-variables does not make a difference for the trade-off coefficients. And the same holds for the probit versions.

Table 3.25. *The relation between cardinal and probit POLS*

Domain satisfaction	Slope	t-value	Constant	t-value	R^2
Financial satisfaction	0.536	18.558	0.196	2.713	0.977
Job satisfaction	0.567	16.210	0.210	3.832	0.971
Health satisfaction	0.603	19.564	0.123	2.801	0.980
Housing satisfaction	0.636	16.398	0.343	5.899	0.971
Leisure satisfaction	0.648	23.129	0.183	4.783	0.985
Environment satisfaction	0.529	21.395	−0.016	−0.416	0.983
General satisfaction	0.514	15.434	0.143	2.558	0.968

3.5. CONCLUSION

In this chapter we have considered a number of satisfaction questions, some of which have already been studied by economists, sociologists or psychologists.[2] Here we demonstrated that those satisfactions simply correspond to different dimensions of life. They are similarly structured and may be explained by similar models.

The main conclusion of this chapter may then be formulated as follows:

We may deal with those domain satisfactions (DS) as normal discretely observable variables.

We stress the fact that, just as with traditional variables, these variables may be explained in various ways. We distinguished a predictive and a hedonistic approach. Both approaches have their virtues. It is also obvious that, in general, there is not *one* or *the best* explanation. The explanations of various DS we gave are based on an intuitively plausible choice of available variables. Other researchers will prefer different specifications, depending on their objectives and the data availability. Moreover, it may be that specifications and behavior vary over cultures.

Given the scope of this book, we have not aimed in this chapter at an exhaustive analysis of DS per se.

In the next chapter we will see how we can use the DS in a simultaneous model, in which the DS will serve as explanatory variables in their turn.

APPENDIX 3A: VARIABLES DESCRIPTION FOR GSOEP

In Appendix 3a the variables used for the regressions for the GSOEP that may need clarification are described.

Household income: Net monthly household income in German marks (the same for all the respondents of the same household).
Years of education: For the West this variable is computed according to the GSOEP documentation. For the East we have applied similar conversion rules.
Children + 1: The number of children (+ 1) younger than sixteen in the household.
Adults: The number of adults who live in the household.
Living together: Dummy variable where 1 stands for being married or having a partner living in the household.
Second earner: Dummy variable that takes value 1 if there is more than one earner in the household.
Self-employed: Dummy variable where 1 stands for being self-employed. Non-workers do not have these variables defined.
Work income: The sum of gross wages, gross self-employment income, and gross income from supplementary job(s).

[2] See e.g. Clark and Oswald (1994), DiTella et al. (2001), Frey and Stutzer (2000), McBride (2001), Oswald (1997), Pradhan and Ravallion (2000), Van Praag and Frijters (1999), and Tsou and Liu (2001). Earlier studies include Easterlin (1974), Van Praag (1971), and Van Praag and Kapteyn (1973).

Working hours: Weekly average.

Extra money: The sum of extra working income such as thirteenth or fourteenth month, Christmas bonus, holiday pay, or profit-sharing.

Extra hours: Extra working hours, i.e. overtime hours.

Savings: Amount of money left over each month for major purchases, emergencies, or savings.

Rent: Monthly housing costs, including: rent per month, interest and amortization per month, other costs per month, housing costs per month, maintenance costs previous year (*1/12), and heat and hot water costs previous year (*1/12).

Reforms: Dummy variable that takes value 1 if the respondents or their landlord has made any modernization to the house during the last year.

Leisure time: Hours spent on hobbies and other free time in a typical week (weekdays and Sundays).

APPENDIX 3*B*: VARIABLES DESCRIPTION FOR BHPS

In Appendix 3*b*, the variables used for the regressions for the BHPS that may need clarification are described.

Household income: Net monthly (month before the interview) household income in British pounds (the same for all the respondents of the same household).

Children + 1: The number of children (+ 1) younger than sixteen in the household.

Adults: The number of adults who live in the household.

Living together: Dummy variable where 1 stands for being married or having a partner living in the household.

Second earner: Dummy variable that takes value 1 if there is more than one earner in the household.

Self-employed: Dummy variable where 1 stands for being self-employed. Non-workers do not have these variables defined.

Work income: Labor income last month.

Working hours: Weekly average.

Work at night: Takes value 1 if the respondent usually works night shifts.

Extra hours: Extra working hours, i.e. overtime hours.

Hours household work: Hours per week spent on housework (in an average week).

Savings: That which an individual is able to save on average in a month.

Leisure time: The time left after subtracting working time and household-work time per week.

Number of rooms: Rooms in the house, including bedrooms but excluding kitchens, bathrooms, and any rooms the respondent may let or sublet.

Shortage of space; *noise from neighbors, street noise, lack of light*; *lack of adequate heating, pollution/environmental problems*; and *vandalism or crime*: These variables take value 0 if the respondents consider that their house is not subject to these problems, and 1 otherwise.

House in ownership: This variable takes value 1 if the respondent owns the house where he or she lives.

4

The Aggregation of Satisfactions: General Satisfaction as an Aggregate

4.1. INTRODUCTION

As we pointed out in Chapter 1 we can distinguish various life domains and, on top of that, 'life as a whole'. We may evaluate our satisfaction with respect to these separate domains in numerical terms; similarly, we can evaluate our satisfaction with 'life as a whole'. We call the latter concept 'general satisfaction', or GS for short. We are aware of the fact that some people will express their doubts as to whether it is possible to evaluate the quality of their 'life as a whole'. And even if it is thought possible, some may have reservations about the validity of such answers. However, we observe that thousands of respondents apparently have no difficulty in answering such a question, and that those responses seem to be comparable. Hence, we will accept this as empirical evidence that respondents are able to evaluate their life and that those responses lend themselves to scientific analysis.

General satisfaction can be analyzed like a domain satisfaction (DS), as we did in the previous chapter. We shall start by doing that. A second approach is to consider GS as an aggregate of all the DS. If our satisfaction with respect to one domain increases, this should imply that our GS increases as well under *ceteris paribus* conditions. That means that not only our variable to be explained is a satisfaction but that our explanatory variables are (domain) satisfactions as well. We do not know of this approach in the existing literature. Hence, we are interested not only in the estimated relationship but in the methodology as well.

Moreover, in the British data set there is not only a question on job satisfaction (JS) as such but there are also questions posed with respect to several aspects of the job values; job sub-domains, so to speak. We may then consider JS itself as an aggregate of satisfaction with respect to those separate sub-domains. Hence, in this chapter we apply the aggregating approach to JS as an aggregate of various job sub-domain satisfactions.

This chapter is partly based on Van Praag, Frijters, and Ferrer-i-Carbonell (2003).

General satisfaction is obtained from respondents in a similar way to the domain questions. The only difference is that we ask about satisfaction with 'life as a whole'. The fact that respondents are able to respond to such questions, and that they can evaluate their life on a numerical scale, is evidence for the thesis that such questions may be posed and can be answered by normal individuals. It is obvious that 'life as a whole' is a rather vague concept. The longer you think about its meaning, the vaguer it becomes. Respondents may think of their life today, or during the last year, or even their whole life from birth. Unfortunately, this was not made precise in the questionnaires we are studying, and perhaps it is a question which induces 'too much thinking', resulting in confusion because respondents are likely to have difficulties in responding.

We shall assume that all respondents understand the same thing by the vague term 'quality of life', while acknowledging that this is only true to a certain extent. However, if we are able to explain GS by specific variables, then it is indirect but positive evidence that our assumption is acceptable. If we cannot find a good explanation for GS—however hard we might try—then this still does not mean that respondents give different meanings to the blanket term 'quality of life'. It would only mean that the phenomenon is not explicable by means of the variables we expected would do this. Then, we are in the same position as for any ordinary regression equation, where the dependent variable y is measurable and interpretable in an unambiguous way, but nevertheless not explicable by the independent variables provided. We shall see that GS is explicable, and hence we will utilize the GS question assuming that it is understood in a similar way by all respondents; for in so far as this is not true, the error term will account for that. If we were to reject this assumption in favor of complete agnosticism, we could not analyze the question at all.

When we look at the GS equation it is again possible to deal with it by means of the four methods which we described in Chapter 2 above. We take the POLS road again for reasons which will soon become clear. The other methods yield almost the same results, except for a multiplication factor. Therefore, we will not vex the reader with multiple presentations that are approximately the same.

4.2. THE PREDICTIVE (ORTHODOX) APPROACH

First, we consider an explanation of GS in an orthodox way, where we select a number of directly and objectively measurable variables which might have explanatory value. This analysis is the most common in the happiness economics literature and has been applied to study a large range of interesting and relevant topics. Next to the topics presented in this book, the literature has also looked at whether divorced couples become happier (Gardner and Oswald 2006), the money value of marriage (Blanchflower and Oswald 2004), the effect of unemployment on happiness (Clark and Oswald 1994), the importance of macro-economic variables for an individual's well-being (Alesina, Di Tella, and MacCulloch 2004; Di Tella and MacCulloch 2005; Di Tella, MacCulloch, and Oswald 2001; Di Tella, MacCulloch, and Oswald 2003), and many other interesting topics (Shields and Price 2005).

It has to be understood that many selections have been tried and that we produce only that choice which seems to be intuitively clear, and statistically significant. However, we also include some variables which are non-significant, just to let the reader know that they really were non-significant against our, and probably the reader's, expectations. Moreover, for some variables we include average values over the observation period, which enables us to distinguish between level and shock effects. The estimated equations are presented in Tables 4.1 and 4.2, for Germany and the UK respectively.

The time dummies show a remarkable pattern. West German well-being appears to decline over the period, while East German well-being appears to rise over the same period. This points to a certain convergence of the two parts of the reunited country. It is seen that household income is an important determinant of GS. The economics literature has already seen the first attempts to look at the endogeneity of income by looking at lottery winners (Oswald and Gardner 2007) and at the income increases in former East Germany after the fall of the Wall (Frijters et al. 2005). Other work on the relationship between income and happiness is found in Chapters 7 and 8 of this book, and in Clark, Frijters, and Shields (2006), Easterlin (1995), Frijters, Geishecker, Shields, and Haisken-DeNew (2006), Frijters, Shields, and Haisken-DeNew (2006), and Rojas (2007*b*). The effect of children is ambiguous. The introduction of the interaction term with household income makes the children effect income-dependent. It follows that the total effect of children is negative for low incomes but positive for high incomes. A possible exception is found for West German workers, where all the children effects do not differ significantly from 0.

The age effect is very pronounced. The individual's satisfaction with life decreases until rather late in life. Although we are no psychologists, it is tempting to interpret the phenomenon. We assume that most people start early in life with a set of expectations which set a norm for a happy life. If those satisfactions are fulfilled one feels happy, and if not one feels disappointed. At the beginning of life, when the horizon widens those expectations will even increase. For most people expectations will define a too high aspiration level and this generates disappointment, but it triggers an adaptation process as well. This yields the behavior in which life satisfaction reaches a minimal level in the fifties and increases from then onwards. The effect of savings is small but significant.

For the UK we find a similar but much stronger age effect. The minimum age is reached much earlier than for Germans; that is, in the early thirties. Surprisingly, the effect of income on life satisfaction is negligible in the UK. The other British results are in line with the German ones. The most striking finding is,

Table 4.1. *Predictive explanation of general satisfaction, Germany, 1992–1997, POLS individual random effects*

	West workers		East workers		West non-workers		East non-workers	
	Estimate	t-ratio	Estimate	t-ratio	Estimate	t-ratio	Estimate	t-ratio
Constant	3.234	3.750	3.542	2.650	7.579	9.750	13.620	11.150
Dummy for 1992	0.137	9.830	-0.094	-4.240	0.176	9.440	-0.135	-4.250
Dummy for 1993	0.077	5.380	-0.046	-2.090	0.155	8.090	-0.103	-3.490
Dummy for 1994	0.056	3.770	-0.044	-1.940	0.070	3.560	-0.119	-4.050
Dummy for 1995	0.035	2.550	0.011	0.540	0.058	3.140	-0.066	-2.330
Dummy for 1996	0.009	0.550	0.003	0.130	-0.012	-0.540	-0.045	-1.430
Ln(age)	-2.414	-4.930	-2.921	-3.840	-5.179	-12.100	-8.357	-12.580
(Ln(age))^2	0.298	4.310	0.363	3.360	0.670	11.390	1.123	12.330
Minimum age	57.643	—	56.185	—	47.724	—	41.294	—
Ln(household income)	0.069	3.680	0.172	5.460	0.017	0.670	0.061	1.380
Ln(years education)	-0.034	-0.800	-0.046	-0.670	0.038	0.650	-0.170	-2.070
Ln(children + 1)	-0.100	-0.540	-0.716	-2.360	-0.434	-1.920	-0.718	-1.630
Ln(adults)	-0.036	-2.000	-0.049	-1.560	-0.031	-1.140	-0.025	-0.490
Ln(working hours)	-0.021	-1.500	-0.062	-2.420				
Ln(family income)*Ln(children + 1)	0.012	0.540	0.080	2.150	0.051	1.850	0.103	1.870
Ln(savings)	0.010	4.750	0.021	6.200	0.018	5.990	0.019	3.850
Second earner	-0.028	-1.740	-0.097	-3.520				
Gender	0.009	0.530	0.002	0.090	-0.144	-6.280	-0.081	-2.630
Living together	0.101	5.630	0.176	4.880	0.163	8.550	0.101	2.760
Ln(leisure time)	0.005	3.740	0.002	0.760	0.001	0.800	0.000	-0.080
Mean (ln(family income))	0.142	4.580	0.119	2.360	0.239	6.140	0.159	2.460

Table 4.1. (Contd.)

	West workers		East workers		West non-workers		East non-workers	
	Estimate	t-ratio	Estimate	t-ratio	Estimate	t-ratio	Estimate	t-ratio
Mean (ln(ch + 1))	-0.027	-1.010	0.046	1.080	-0.106	-2.740	-0.129	-1.920
Mean (ln(adults))	0.008	0.260	-0.177	-3.430	-0.116	-2.740	-0.276	-3.760
Mean (ln(savings))	0.037	8.670	0.023	3.450	0.034	6.030	0.037	4.340
Mean (ln(working hours))	-0.019	-2.100	0.008	0.630	—	—	—	—
Standard deviation of individual random effect ε_n	0.643	—	0.549	—	0.735	—	0.620	—
% variance due to ε_n	0.510	—	0.458	—	0.530	—	0.450	—
Number of observations	30,625	—	12,354	—	20,909	—	8,540	—
Number of individuals	8,150	—	32,38	—	6,427	—	2,695	—
R^2:								
Within	0.011	—	0.021	—	0.015	—	0.014	—
Between	0.060	—	0.096	—	0.105	—	0.169	—
Overall	0.046	—	0.067	—	0.086	—	0.1157	—

Note: There are dummies for missing variables, which are not included in the table.

Table 4.2. *Predictive explanation of general satisfaction, UK, 1996–1997, POLS individual random effects*

	Workers		Non-Workers	
	Estimate	*t*-ratio	Estimate	*t*-ratio
Constant	7.740	11.371	6.739	9.784
Dummy for 1996	−0.014	−1.522	0.005	0.373
Dummy for 1997	−0.015	−1.771	−0.018	−1.332
Ln(age)	−4.851	−12.557	−4.409	−12.692
(Ln(age))^2	0.685	12.561	0.641	13.481
Minimum age	34.457	—	31.210	—
Ln(household income)	−0.001	−0.096	0.012	0.838
Ln(years education)	−0.071	−4.496	−0.076	−3.243
Ln(children + 1)	−0.111	−2.251	0.060	0.694
Ln(children + 1)^2	0.017	0.494	0.041	0.853
Ln(adults)	−0.046	−1.595	−0.081	−1.656
Ln(working hours)	−0.030	−2.597	—	—
Ln(family income)* Ln(children + 1)	0.050	1.649	−0.089	−2.322
Ln(savings)	0.010	3.718	0.004	0.664
Second earner	0.012	0.656	—	—
Gender	−0.019	−1.403	−0.076	−3.952
Living together	0.140	6.309	0.149	6.142
Ln(leisure time)	−0.014	−0.680	−0.059	−1.272
Mean (ln(household income)	−0.005	−0.259	−0.023	−1.098
Mean (ln(children + 1))	0.030	0.886	−0.092	−1.353
Mean (ln(adults))	0.044	1.220	0.157	2.775
Mean (ln(savings))	0.012	2.638	0.029	3.387
Mean (ln(working hours))	0.007	0.756	—	—
Standard deviation of individual random effect ε_n	0.471	—	0.526	—
% variance due to ε_n	0.507	—	0.454	—
Number of observations	17,921	—	11,985	—
Number of individuals	7,774	—	5,784	—
R^2:				
Within	0.003	—	0.001	—
Between	0.045	—	0.092	—
Overall	0.034	—	0.073	—

Note: There are dummies for missing variables, which are not included in the table.

however, that most of the variables have a small effect compared to similar effects we found for the domain satisfactions. This may be explained by the fact that although variables may have a sizeable effect on various separate domains, this does not automatically imply a strong effect on the aggregate general satisfaction, because the effects on the domains may be contradictory.

It may also be that a variable has a strong effect on only one of the domains and not on any other. Then, the overall effect is weakened because the specific domain is only one of the channels through which general satisfaction is determined. A final point is that some variables which are intuitively important are not included in this specification; for example, individual health. It is difficult to define one variable which characterizes the health of the individual. Some variables like age and income are predictors of health but their predictive value, as we already saw in the previous chapter, is very low. We need a more comprehensive approach, which takes account of the information collected with respect to the domain satisfactions.

4.3. THE AGGREGATING APPROACH

Now we turn to the second approach, which we call the *aggregating* approach (see also Rojas 2006*a*, and Borooah 2006).

As argued in an intuitive manner in the first chapter, we may view life as an aggregate of various life domains. One may evaluate each domain separately and the results are Domain Satisfactions $DS_1, \ldots, DS_k$.

Hence, we may assume a model equation of the type:

$$GS = GS(DS_1, \ldots, DS_k). \tag{4.1}$$

For instance, we might think of a linear aggregate:

$$GS = \alpha_1 DS_1 + \ldots + \alpha_k DS_k. \tag{4.2}$$

This is precisely what we will do where we operationalize the DS_j variables $(j = 1, \ldots, k)$ by their conditional expectations, as we did for the POLS estimation in Chapter 3. We define:

$$\ddot{DS}_j = E(\ln(DS_j) \mid \mu_{j,\,i-1} < DS_j \leq \mu_{j,\,i}) = \frac{n(\mu_{j,\,i-1}) - n(\mu_{j,\,i})}{N(\mu_{j,\,i}) - N(\mu_{j,\,i-1})}. \tag{4.3}$$

We see here the enormous advantage of choosing the POLS approach. We can deal (again) with satisfactions as ordinary variables. If we had stuck with the ordered-probit approach, it would have been quite problematic as to how to operationalize the explanatory variables in this model. It would involve $(k + 1)$ - dimensional normal orthant probabilities, which do not lend themselves to large-scale statistical computations as a matter of routine. Another econometric approach would be via 'simulated-moments' methods (see Hajivassiliou and Ruud 1994; Gourieroux and Monfort 1995; Eggink, Hop, and Van Praag 1994), which are, in practice, also unfeasible at the scale at which we would need them.

Hence, our basic model will be of the type:

$$GS_{n,\,t} = \alpha_{1,\,0}\,\overline{DS}_{1n} + \ldots + \alpha_{k,\,0}\,\overline{DS}_{kn} + \alpha_{1,\,1}\ddot{DS}_{1,\,n,\,t} + \ldots$$
$$+ \alpha_{k,\,1}\,\ddot{DS}_{k,\,n,\,t} + \beta.Z_n + \gamma.X_{n,\,t} + \varepsilon_n + \eta_{n,\,t} \tag{4.4}$$

In this equation we explain GS by the domain satisfactions and by a mysterious variable Z, which we shall describe in a moment. We leave the possibility open of including some other variables X. Moreover, we add the averages over the observation periods in order to distinguish between *level* and *shock* effects, and we do likewise for the error term by introducing individual random effects.

Let us now explain the Z-variable. When we considered the DS equations in the previous chapter we observed that the DS could not be fully explained by the observed variables. There may be some psychological traits (e.g. optimism vs. pessimism) that codetermine satisfactions but that cannot be, or at least are not, observed in the present samples. Those omitted variables are part of the regression error term. More specifically, if we assume them to be stable traits over time, they will be part of the individual random effect $\varepsilon_{j,\ n}$ (see Equation 3.5).

When we consider all DS together, we may assume that they are all influenced by the *same* psychological traits, albeit to varying extents. But if that is assumed it follows, almost as a matter of course, that the $\varepsilon_{j,\ n}$ for different domains, say for j and j', will be correlated. Indeed, after the six German (or the eight British) domain equations have been estimated, it is possible to calculate the residuals on the basis of the estimated structural equations. We consider the British case, where we have eight domain equations which are estimated by:

$$\ddot{D}\ddot{S}_{jnt}(x) = \hat{\gamma}'_j X_{jnt} + \hat{\varepsilon}_{jnt} \ (j = 1, \ \ldots, 8). \tag{4.5}$$

The $\hat{\gamma}_j$ stands for the vector of estimated parameters in the jth domain equation, and the vector X_j for the selection of explanatory variables for the jth domain. Then, we find the calculated residuals $\hat{\varepsilon}_{jnt} = \hat{\varepsilon}_{jn} + \hat{\eta}_{jnt}$ $(j = 1, \ \ldots, 6)$. Averaging those calculated residuals per individual over time, for individual n and domain j, we find an estimate of the individual effect $\hat{\varepsilon}_{jn}$, because the average of the second term over time tends to 0 per individual. Then, it is possible to estimate the covariance of the fixed effects for *two* domains as:

$$\text{cov}(\varepsilon_{j.}, \varepsilon_{j'.}) = \frac{1}{N} \sum_1^N \hat{\varepsilon}_{jn.} \cdot \hat{\varepsilon}_{j'n.} \tag{4.6}$$

We present the (8*8) variance/correlation matrix for the British married workers. The diagonal cells present the variances and the off-diagonal cells the correlation coefficients. It is evident that the correlations between the fixed effects are considerable.

If there is a common psychological trait in these fixed effects, this must show up in a common variable that is responsible for the sizeable correlation between the fixed effects.

This component is isolated by application of a principal-components[1] analysis on the fixed-effect covariance matrix. We do indeed find that the first

---

[1] Unfortunately, it is beyond the scope of this study to explain principal-components analysis to the reader. For an elementary explanation see Dhrymes (1970).

Table 4.3. *Domain error variance/correlation matrix, British individuals with job and married*

	Job satisfaction	Financial satisfaction	Housing satisfaction	Health satisfaction	Leisure-use satisfaction	Leisure-amount satisfaction	Social-life satisfaction	Marriage satisfaction
Job satisfaction	0.625	—	—	—	—	—	—	—
Financial satisfaction	0.395	0.655	—	—	—	—	—	—
Housing satisfaction	0.279	0.355	0.667	—	—	—	—	—
Health satisfaction	0.292	0.357	0.251	0.858	—	—	—	—
Leisure-use satisfaction	0.335	0.345	0.290	0.335	0.719	—	—	—
Leisure-amount satisfaction	0.351	0.335	0.263	0.290	0.676	0.742	—	—
Social-life satisfaction	0.411	0.370	0.313	0.341	0.681	0.609	0.663	—
Marriage satisfaction	0.226	0.208	0.243	0.200	0.287	0.263	0.328	0.797

principal component explains more than 50 percent of the total variance in the error/covariance matrix. Consider for individual n that his individual effect vector $\varepsilon_{n.} = (\varepsilon_{1n.}, \ldots, \varepsilon_{8n.})$. Introducing a new coordinate system with the principal components as coordinate axes, we may rewrite each individual effect vector in terms of the new coordinate system as $\varepsilon_{n.} = (v_{\{1n.\}}, \ldots, v_{8n.})$. Here the number $v_{1n.}$ is the loading with respect to the first principal component, which we identify with the latent psychological trait. This number is denoted as Z_n. In this way we have succeeded in isolating (part of) the latent psychological trait.

Considering Equation (4.4), we now see that it is very likely that the common psychological trait which codetermines the domain satisfactions DS will affect GS, the evaluation of 'life as a whole', as well. For GS too this common trait will be included in the error term. Naive estimation by regression of Equation (4.4) will lead to biased results in this case. We have the situation that econometricians call an *endogeneity bias* (see Greene 2000).

We speak of an 'endogeneity bias' if the error term in the regression equation is correlated with one or more of the explanatory variables in that equation. The fundamental OLS assumption is that there is no correlation and in that case the estimates of the regression coefficients are unbiased. That is, the only reason why the estimate for a specific sample may differ from the population parameter is that the specific sample is not completely representative for the underlying population distribution. This is because the sample is a random selection out of the population. If the sample size tends to infinity, the estimated value will tend to the population value. In the case of endogeneity bias this will not be the case. However, we have now isolated and assessed this common trait as the variable Z. It follows that if we add Z as an additional explanatory variable to the equation we make the omitted variable visible. It is no longer included in the error term and the endogeneity bias is discarded.

In Tables 4.4 and 4.5 we present our estimates of Equation (4.4) for the four German sub-samples and the two British sub-samples respectively. For the British, the selection of the various DS differs from the German selection. It is obvious that respondents who are unmarried or do not live with a partner cannot answer the question about marital satisfaction. Therefore, we include a dummy variable for non-married, which is 0 when the respondent is married or living with a partner, and which equals 1 for a single respondent.

The estimation results are fascinating. We see that GS can indeed be regarded as an aggregate of all the separate DS. Each domain makes its specific contribution to the aggregate. It is very interesting to see that almost all domain effects are significant. The Z-variable, which stands for the common omitted trait, is significant only for a few cases. The correlation coefficients are surprisingly high, especially when compared with the traditional explanation, as presented in Table 4.3. Intuitively, this can be explained as follows. There is a two-layer model, which can be sketched as in figure 4.1:

Table 4.4. *German general satisfaction explained, 1992–1997, POLS individual random effects*

	West workers		East workers		West non-workers		East non-workers	
	Estimate	t-ratio	Estimate	t-ratio	Estimate	t-ratio	Estimate	t-ratio
Constant	0.051	4.697	−0.036	−1.950	0.021	1.369	−0.111	−4.798
Dummy for 1992	0.065	5.382	−0.092	−4.991	0.093	5.552	−0.153	−5.810
Dummy for 1993	0.037	3.079	−0.071	−3.841	0.077	4.626	−0.115	−4.443
Dummy for 1994	0.001	0.120	−0.013	−0.709	−0.027	−1.592	−0.138	−5.369
Dummy for 1995	0.015	1.247	0.019	1.028	−0.002	−0.131	−0.071	−2.769
Dummy for 1996	0.002	0.171	−0.004	−0.227	−0.015	−0.959	−0.049	−1.955
Job satisfaction	0.138	23.452	0.145	17.701	—	—	—	—
Financial satisfaction	0.128	22.669	0.154	18.166	0.125	17.008	0.142	12.681
Housing satisfaction	0.072	11.677	0.077	8.497	0.083	8.994	0.099	7.615
Health satisfaction	0.169	25.419	0.108	10.175	0.245	28.066	0.190	13.441
Leisure satisfaction	0.061	9.937	0.036	3.905	0.076	8.730	0.074	5.909
Environment satisfaction	0.044	7.453	0.044	4.798	0.056	7.074	0.028	2.307
Mean (job satisfaction)	0.063	3.835	0.047	2.167	—	—	—	—
Mean (financial satisfaction)	0.235	15.593	0.243	10.142	0.380	18.251	0.341	11.499
Mean (house satisfaction)	−0.012	−0.919	−0.042	−2.271	0.003	0.212	−0.032	−1.524
Mean (health satisfaction)	0.088	7.276	0.087	4.789	0.113	8.654	0.057	2.753
Mean (leisure satisfaction)	0.021	0.967	0.036	1.389	−0.017	−1.115	0.112	4.662
Mean (environment satisfaction)	−0.010	−0.706	0.037	1.632	−0.146	−4.463	−0.029	−0.567
First component	−0.070	−1.630	−0.063	−1.038	−0.193	−3.384	−0.076	−0.798
Standard deviation of individual random effect ε_n	0.362	—	0.342	—	0.446	—	0.430	—
% variance due to ε_n	0.284	—	0.279	—	0.324	—	0.307	—
Number of observations	29,636	—	11,941	—	20,427	—	8,335	—
Number of individuals	7,995	—	3,157	—	6,353	—	2,651	—
R^2:								
Within	0.170	—	0.153	—	0.137	—	0.116	—
Between	0.567	—	0.519	—	0.536	—	0.470	—
Overall	0.464	—	0.413	—	0.464	—	0.405	—

Table 4.5. *British general satisfaction explained, 1996–1998,*
POLS individual random effects

	Workers		Non-Workers	
	Estimate	*t*-ratio	Estimate	*t*-ratio
Constant	−0.887	−126.015	−0.908	−85.739
Dummy for 1996	−0.001	−0.139	−0.018	−1.498
Dummy for 1997	−0.009	−1.137	−0.012	−1.021
Job satisfaction	0.067	11.899	—	—
Financial satisfaction	0.075	11.810	0.037	3.864
Housing satisfaction	0.019	3.447	0.055	6.458
Health satisfaction	0.066	12.085	0.096	10.132
Leisure-use satisfaction	0.103	15.057	0.134	12.589
Leisure-amount satisfaction	0.032	4.729	0.057	5.842
Marriage satisfaction	0.054	9.524	0.046	4.141
Social-life satisfaction	0.086	12.779	0.143	14.135
Mean (job satisfaction)	0.046	3.700	—	—
Mean (financial satisfaction)	−0.011	−0.919	0.050	4.013
Mean (housing satisfaction)	0.022	2.621	0.002	0.166
Mean (health satisfaction)	0.035	2.300	0.071	5.603
Mean (leisure-use satisfaction)	0.007	0.389	0.103	5.698
Mean (leisure-amount satisfaction)	0.003	0.166	−0.082	−5.225
Mean (marriage satisfaction)	0.017	2.212	0.022	1.600
Mean (social-life satisfaction)	0.030	2.897	0.044	3.126
First component	−0.019	−0.437	−0.149	−4.917
Dummy for non-married	−0.024	−2.567	−0.047	−3.955
Standard deviation of individual random effect ε_n	0.254	—	0.254	—
% variance due to ε_n	0.279	—	0.203	—
Number of observations	17,310	—	11,578	—
Number of individuals	7,580	—	5,717	—
R^2:				
Within	0.206	—	0.230	—
Between	0.555	—	0.588	—
Overall	0.478	—	0.531	—

and is summarized as:

Objective variables → Domain satisfactions → General satisfaction

It is obvious, therefore, that we get a more detailed and more accurate description when we concentrate on the second arrow in the sequence than when we try to cover the two stages in one equation.

Figure 4.1. *The two-layer model*

It is explicitly observed that it also emerges from these tables that general satisfaction (GS) should not be treated as identical to financial satisfaction (FS). Although this observation looks rather trivial in the present context, we should not forget that in the economic literature up to recently as a rule no sharp distinction is made between the two concepts. But now it appears that maximization of FS must lead to different results than maximization of GS.

The estimated effects are seemingly much smaller for the British samples than for the German samples. However, we have to realize that the number of explanatory variables is different and that the number of distinct response categories is 11 in the German data set and 7 in that of the UK. Given that we find similar results for each of the six different sub-samples distinguished, it follows that we have ample evidence that this method can be used and will lead to approximately the same results for any western data sets. Although we do not have evidence for non-western countries, we conjecture that we will also find the same kinds of results for other populations.

Again, we may distinguish between the shock and the level effects. For instance, for West German workers the shock effect of FS is 0.128, while the level effect is 0.363 (0.128 + 0.235). We present the corresponding level effects in Tables 4.6. and 4.7.

The fact that we find a shock and a level effect indicates that there is a dynamic adaptation process working over time. Hence, the immediate impact of a change in x_t is the shock effect and 1/6 of the impact of a change of the average. The ratio $0.128/0.363 + (\frac{1}{6} \times 0.235)/(0.363) = 0.35 + 0.11 = 0.46$ may be interpreted as the fraction of a change which is immediately absorbed. If the change in x_t is permanent, the remaining fraction of 54 percent is absorbed over the remaining five years of the adaptation period. If the change was incidental, in the next five years the effect will peter out to 11 percent, after which the effect suddenly drops to 0. Similar estimates of the adaptation process can be made for the temporal impact of other variables. We notice that there is not *one* adaptation process but that the process differs per variable. It is obvious that this modelling of the adaptation process is rather crude. This is because we assumed the Mundlak model, in which unweighted averages over time are used. It would be fascinating to estimate the time weights more

Table 4.6. *Level effects for the German data set*

	West German workers	East German workers	West German non-workers	East German non-workers
Job satisfaction	0.202	0.191	—	—
Financial satisfaction	0.363	0.397	0.505	0.483
Housing satisfaction	0.060	0.035	0.086	0.067
Health satisfaction	0.257	0.194	0.357	0.246
Leisure satisfaction	0.082	0.072	0.059	0.186
Environment satisfaction	0.035	0.081	−0.091	−0.001

Table 4.7. *Level effects for the British data set*

	Workers	Non-workers
Job satisfaction	0.112	—
Financial satisfaction	0.064	0.087
Housing satisfaction	0.041	0.057
Health satisfaction	0.102	0.166
Leisure-use satisfaction	0.109	0.237
Leisure-amount satisfaction	0.036	−0.025
Marriage satisfaction	0.071	0.068
Social-life satisfaction	0.116	0.187

precisely, but this is outside the scope of this chapter. We shall describe a more modest attempt to estimate these 'memory weights' in Chapter 7.

From the same tables we can derive the trade-offs between domains. For, just as we can calculate trade-off coefficients between objective variables, we can also calculate trade-off ratios between domains from the estimated GS equation. For example, if we assume that job satisfaction (JS) is reduced by ΔJS, by what amount do we have to increase FS in order that GS remains at the same level? For the West German workers this boils down to solving the equation:

$$-0.202\Delta JS + 0.363\Delta FS = 0. \tag{4.7}$$

This yields:

$$\Delta FS = \frac{0.202}{0.363}\Delta JS. \tag{4.8}$$

The trade-off ratio is (0.202/0.363), which is about 0.55. At first sight we may consider this calculation of trade-offs between satisfactions as rather esoteric. However, if we realize that FS in its turn depends on income and that an increase in FS may be generated by a specific increase in income, we see that a decrease (or increase) in JS may be translated into a monetary equivalent. We will make extensive use of those trade-offs in some of the chapters that follow.

In fact, the GS equation makes the various DS that figure in that equation comparable with each other. We see, for example, that we may construct a hierarchy of domains. For West German workers financial satisfaction scores highest, followed by health satisfaction. Then we get job, leisure, and housing satisfaction, in that order. Environment satisfaction scores lowest.

We also see that this hierarchy and even the numerical order of those ratios is rather similar over the German subgroups. For the UK, satisfaction with health scores higher than satisfaction with finance; while satisfaction with social life scores the highest of all for British workers. We remind the reader that a question on satisfaction with social life and one on marriage were not asked in the German survey.

In order to evaluate the status of 'non-married' against the status of being 'married'[2] we compare the addition of the dummy variable 'non-married' with the addition of a marriage. The level effect of a marriage is 0.071 (see Table 4.7). As the non-married effect equals −0.024 (see Table 4.5) it follows that the non-married-status is equivalent to a marriage that yields a marriage satisfaction of −(0.024/0.071) = −0.34. This is, so to speak, the threshold value for divorce.

4.4. A BREAKDOWN OF JOB SATISFACTION

It is evident that the use of the aggregation model discussed above is one example of the breakdown of a satisfaction (in this case general satisfaction) into its constituent satisfaction components. Thus, it creates the possibility of a 'calculus of satisfactions'.

The same methodology can also be used to break down each of the domain satisfactions. For we can distinguish various aspects of a domain, and we are able to express our satisfaction with respect to those aspects separately. We might call those aspects *sub-domains.*

In the UK data set we find the opportunity to apply the technique to the domain of job satisfaction (JS). The questionnaire contains a question with respect to 'job satisfaction as a whole', but alongside it there are satisfaction questions posed with respect to several aspects of the job.[3] Again there are 7 satisfaction levels specified. The aspects are: promotion prospects, total pay, relations with supervisor, job security, opportunity to take initiative, satisfaction with the work itself and with the hours worked. We now re-estimate the regression for JS, where we specify the equation as an aggregate of those sub-domain satisfactions as follows:

$$JS = \alpha_1 JSPROM + \alpha_2 JSPAY + \alpha_3 JSBOSS + \alpha_4 JSSECUR$$
$$+ \alpha_5 JSINIT + \alpha_6 JSWORK + \alpha_7 JSHOURS + \beta.Z_{JS} \ldots \tag{4.9}$$

---

[2] We do not distinguish between the status of being legally married and any other status of permanent partnership.

[3] Some of the sub-domain job-satisfaction questions were not posed after 1997.

Table 4.8. *The seven job sub-domain equations, UK, 1996–1997, POLS individual random effects*

	Satisfaction with promotion		Satisfaction with pay		Satisfaction with supervisor		Satisfaction with job security	
	Estimate	t-ratio	Estimate	t-ratio	Estimate	t-ratio	Estimate	t-ratio
Constant	7.941	6.296	3.880	3.840	6.559	6.013	6.915	6.670
Dummy for 1996	0.017	1.098	−0.006	−0.413	0.002	0.100	−0.001	−0.066
Ln(working income)	0.060	2.105	0.089	6.530	−0.145	−5.510	−0.032	−2.388
Ln(age)	−4.524	−6.056	−2.339	−3.946	−3.275	−5.060	−3.651	−6.004
(Ln(age))^2	0.660	6.200	0.345	4.104	0.481	5.232	0.512	5.942
Minimum age	30.765	—	29.730	—	30.093	—	35.277	—
Ln(working hours)	−0.035	−1.043	−0.071	−2.842	−0.073	−2.372	−0.007	−0.287
Ln(extra hours)	0.035	2.394	0.040	2.976	0.048	3.246	0.016	1.221
Work at night	−0.161	−2.165	−0.025	−0.368	−0.091	−1.305	−0.220	−3.239
Gender (male)	−0.131	−4.801	−0.117	−4.924	−0.045	−1.787	−0.150	−6.198
Self-employed	—	—	0.404	4.758	—	—	−0.134	−1.579
Ln(years education)	−0.114	−3.403	−0.034	−1.147	−0.042	−1.327	−0.075	−2.473
Mean (Ln work income)	0.006	0.233	0.076	4.645	0.043	1.853	0.018	1.088
Mean (working hours)	−0.093	−2.281	−0.214	−7.318	0.003	0.091	−0.034	−1.142
Mean (overtime)	0.036	1.735	−0.048	−2.575	−0.040	−2.007	0.028	1.486
Standard deviation of individual random effect ε_n	0.744	—	0.714	—	0.647	—	0.741	—
% variance due to ε_n	0.555	—	0.521	—	0.426	—	0.546	—
Number of observations	8,784	—	11,615	—	10,095	—	11,522	—
Number of individuals	5,547	—	6,972	—	6,154	—	6,923	—
R^2:								
Within	0.004	—	0.010	—	0.002	—	0.001	—
Between	0.020	—	0.048	—	0.036	—	0.023	—
Overall	0.019	—	0.042	—	0.028	—	0.019	—

Table 4.8. (Contd.)

	Satisfaction with initiative		Satisfaction with work itself		Satisfaction with hours worked	
	Estimate	t-ratio	Estimate	t-ratio	Estimate	t-ratio
Constant	0.252	0.250	1.949	1.925	3.677	3.707
Dummy for 1996	0.006	0.412	0.016	1.159	0.013	0.981
Ln(working income)	-0.018	-1.340	0.001	0.067	-0.004	-0.310
Ln(age)	-0.360	-0.609	-1.388	-2.338	-1.630	-2.802
(Ln(age))^2	0.085	1.012	0.245	2.906	0.249	3.019
Minimum age	8.369	—	17.089	—	26.429	—
Ln(working hours)	0.001	0.025	-0.038	-1.515	-0.099	-4.000
Ln(extra hours)	0.054	3.998	0.024	1.760	-0.059	-4.386
Work at night	-0.050	-0.751	-0.237	-3.511	0.003	0.039
Gender (male)	-0.064	-2.706	-0.124	-5.197	-0.088	-3.792
Self-employed	0.254	3.002	0.080	0.945	-0.003	-0.037
Ln(years education)	-0.023	-0.780	-0.003	-0.100	-0.112	-3.816
Mean (Ln work income)	0.022	1.369	0.001	0.056	0.011	0.676
Mean (working hours)	-0.033	-1.116	-0.007	-0.229	-0.085	-2.921
Standard deviation of individual random effect ε_n	0.007	0.397	0.022	1.179	-0.111	-5.944
% variance due to ε_n	0.706	—	0.717	—	0.690	—
	0.509	—	0.521	—	0.501	—
Number of observations	11,629	—	11,659	—	11,656	—
Number of individuals	6,972	—	6,986	—	6,985	—
R^2:						
Within	0.007		0.006		0.002	
Between	0.042		0.033		0.073	
Overall	0.037		0.028		0.062	

Note: There are dummies for missing variables, which are not included in the table.

Table 4.9. *Job satisfaction explained by job sub-domain satisfactions, UK, 1996–1997, POLS with individual random effects*

	Estimate	t-ratio
Constant	−0.201	−17.150
Dummy for 1996	−0.042	−3.142
Satisfaction with promotion	0.128	6.995
Satisfaction with pay	0.098	6.073
Satisfaction with supervisor	0.164	10.389
Satisfaction with job security	0.124	7.557
Satisfaction with initiative	0.017	0.987
Satisfaction with work itself	0.224	13.231
Satisfaction with hours worked	0.119	7.436
Mean (satisfaction with promotion)	0.020	0.638
Mean (satisfaction with pay)	0.081	3.982
Mean (satisfaction with supervisor)	0.007	0.259
Mean (satisfaction with job security)	−0.006	−0.246
Mean (satisfaction with initiative)	0.029	0.930
Mean (satisfaction with work itself)	0.052	1.259
Mean (satisfaction with hours worked)	0.024	1.150
First component	−0.166	−1.902
Self-employed	0.192	6.029
Standard deviation of individual random effect ε_n	0.493	—
% variance due to ε_n	0.374	—
Number of observations	9,842	—
Number of individuals	6,172	—
R^2:		
Within	0.242	—
Between	0.507	—
Overall	0.482	—

Table 4.10. *Level effects of various job aspects on job satisfaction*

Satisfaction with promotion	0.148
Satisfaction with pay	0.179
Satisfaction with supervisor	0.171
Satisfaction with job security	0.118
Satisfaction with initiative	0.046
Satisfaction with work itself	0.276
Satisfaction with hours worked	0.143

We then specify JS sub-domains analogously to the procedure in Chapter 3. We do the same for self-employed individuals, where we add a dummy variable for 'self-employed'. Note that for a self-employed worker the relations with the boss and promotion prospects are irrelevant. They are replaced by one dummy variable, which equals 1 when the respondent is self-employed and is 0 otherwise.

The sub-domain questions in Table 4.8 are very interesting. We see that the higher the income, the less satisfied workers are with their supervision and with their job security. Age presents the now familiar log-parabolic pattern. Males are less satisfied than females, and the self-employed are more satisfied with their situation than employed workers.

The second equation, presented in Table 4.9, shows that it is possible to break down JS in terms of satisfaction levels with respect to its various sub-domains. The level effects are given in Table 4.10.

We see that the content of the work itself has the greatest weight, followed by pay. The quality of supervision also appears to be quite important.

4.5. CONCLUSION

In this chapter we have developed the satisfaction aggregation model. We have shown that we can distinguish various domain levels, which lead to a two- or three-layer model. First, we looked at the level of general satisfaction with 'life as a whole'. It was shown that we could explain it by the satisfaction levels with respect to the separate domains. In the second half of the chapter we applied the same method to job satisfaction, and were able to explain satisfaction by various sub-domains or aspects of the job domain. It follows that we may combine the two models, and hence get a three-layer model.

The most important point of this chapter is that we can deal with the various satisfactions as if they were observed numerical variables, which can be used in econometric one- and multiple-equation(s) models. This opens up new avenues for the 'econometrics of feelings'.

Clearly, we have to see the present attempt as a first endeavor. There is certainly considerable room for improvement. For instance, the model structure could be further refined with respect to causality. Also, this type of research very much depends on the available data. There is no rich source of data available, although it is growing substantially in recent times (see Diener 2006).

In the following chapters we will use the developed model rather selectively. We will concentrate on specific aspects and equations, basing our material partly on older work.

5

Political Satisfaction

5.1. INTRODUCTION

In the previous pages we considered the individual's satisfaction with his or her personal circumstances. We distinguished a number of 'domains of life', like health, finance, and employment. With respect to each domain the individual can express satisfaction either in verbal terms like 'bad' or 'excellent' or by evaluating the degree of satisfaction on a numerical scale from 0 to 10 or alternatively from 1 to 7. We estimated equations of the type

$$DS_i = \beta_i x + \varepsilon_i \tag{5.1}$$

where the first part may be called the structural part, while the residual ε stands for individual factors and errors. We found stable and significant estimates for the structural parts, but the degree of explanation was mostly minor, indicating that individual non-measured factors must be quite important.

In Chapter 4 we extended this type of analysis by introducing a structural multi-equation model. We considered the question on the individual's satisfaction with 'life as a whole', called general satisfaction (or GS for short), and we found that GS could in turn be explained by the domain satisfactions DS.

The estimates of this system as shown in the previous chapter are very satisfactory. In the same Chapter 4 we considered job satisfaction as an aggregate of various sub-domain satisfactions like pay, hours, and work content. This led to a three-layer model.

In this chapter we will apply the same model to *political* satisfactions. The level of someone's political satisfaction may be derived by asking an individual how satisfied he or she is with the government. Say the answer is political satisfaction *PS*. Then we may try to explain *PS directly* by objective variables x. Another road, which we will take here, is to distinguish political sub-domain satisfactions PDS. The PDS are explained by objective variables x. In its turn we may see political satisfaction as one of the determinants of general satisfaction, next to the other life domains. We sketch this structure in Figure 5.1.

This chapter is partly based on the MA thesis by Chris Van Klaveren (Univ. of Amsterdam: 2002) and Van Klaveren, Maassen Van de Brink, and Van Praag (2002). We are grateful to Chris and Henriette for their permission to include results in this monograph.

In this chapter we shall estimate this structure for a Dutch cross-section data set. To avoid boring the reader, we shall focus on the lowest channel from x to GS in Figure 5.1.

Figure 5.1. *A three-layer structure*

5.2. THE DATA SET

Ours is a large cross-section data set which has been collected in a rather unorthodox way; namely, via Dutch dailies. We must say something now about the nature of our data set.

In the Netherlands there is still a rather diversified daily press, which may be split up into three segments. The first segment is that of about six national daily journals, comparable to *The Times* and *The Guardian* in the UK or the *New York Times* and the *Washington Post* in the USA. Apart from giving news and opinions they also have a more or less outspoken political color. They do not focus on regional and local news. They are distributed on a subscription basis throughout the country.

The second segment of the Dutch daily press consists of regional dailies. They do not have a political color. They are distributed on a subscription basis within a specific region or city. Most of those approximately twenty-three regional dailies were in 2001 united in the Associated Press Services (in Dutch abbreviated as GPD). This is a joint production facility, which produces most of the copy on the national and international news items; that copy is shared by all the GPD members. Whilst keeping their independence and their own owners, this practice allows the members to benefit from the scale economies of a large newspaper. Each GPD member adds to these national and international pages its own pages on local and regional news. The collective readership in terms of subscriptions consists of about 2.2 million households. The GPD newspapers are typically read by most households in the country. The more educated and/or politically conscious individuals have a national daily, frequently as a second subscription. The third segment consists of the dailies which are distributed in trains and metros. They are for free and their financial backbone comes from advertisements.

In 1983 Van Praag and Hagenaars were contacted by the GPD with the idea of putting a survey questionnaire in a Saturday issue of all the member journals. This was done for the first time in 1983 and then repeated in 1984, 1991, 1998, and 2001. It is evident that the endeavor was considered a success by both parties involved. Obviously, some questions may be posed. What are the advantages and disadvantages of such a sampling procedure?

As the questionnaires could be sent off anonymously and there was no way of finding out the identity of the respondents, one can assume that more—and more intimate—questions could be asked in such a questionnaire than in a face-to-face interview or a non-anonymous questionnaire. Moreover, one can ask a lot in such a questionnaire. In the last survey more than a thousand items were combined. As the time taken to fill out such a questionnaire may vary from half an hour to two hours, it is obvious that the response rate is low. It is in the order of 2 percent. There is also no possibility of reminding potential respondents, as their names are unknown. However, given the total readership, a response rate of 2 percent means about 40,000 respondents, which is clearly a gigantic number. To limit the cost of data entry, about 50 percent of the received questionnaires are utilized. So the sizes of the actual samples used varied between 7,500 and 15,000. It is always difficult to evaluate the representativity of such surveys. There are always difficult groups: individuals who on principle do not cooperate in any survey, people who cannot read or write, and, in this special case, individuals with no GPD subscription. However, various tests have shown that the GPD samples, after some reweighting, are fully representative of the Dutch population—except for the ethnic minorities, a growing group in the Netherlands. The data sets have also been used for government-commissioned research on sociopolitical issues. In this chapter our primary interest is not of course in fully representative results but in the development of new theories and models. For this objective the GPD questionnaires are a wonderful playground.

For the academic partners in this project the advantage was to get hold of a very large survey at practically no cost, where the contents of the questionnaire could be selected by the designers at will. This provided the opportunity to put a number of questions which were considered as 'non-validated' by established but less-adventurous fellow-researchers. Most of those questions led to innovative research, and a remarkable number of those questions were subsequently taken over into 'official' surveys in the Netherlands and abroad. Moreover, in the eighties there was practically no possibility for Dutch academic economic researchers to get hold of large data sets, unless commissioned by themselves. Overscrupulous privacy regulations, moreover, meant that the availability of data sets could not be compared with that in the USA or the Scandinavian countries. However, in those latter surveys we did not find the kind of subjective questions we were interested in.[1] There were some, mostly sociological, surveys, but these did not even include a simple question on income; that being

---

[1] In the 1980s Van Praag and Kapteyn devoted a considerable effort to trying to convince American agencies and other organizers of surveys to include a very few questions like the IEQ, but to no avail. This was also a question of political opportunism, as it could have led to unsolicited results with respect to the USA poverty line. (See also Ch. 15.)

considered irrelevant to sociological research. In the GPD questionnaires a host of questions were posed. Although the questionnaires changed over the years, there is a fairly constant core on the objective circumstances of the respondent, of his or her partner, and on the household and its composition, labor, health, and finance. Moreover, there are many 'subjective questions', which were included at a time when for nearly all mainstream economists it was anathema to attach any significance to such 'bad psychology'.

For the commercial partners, the members of the GPD, the advantage was to get actual information at very low cost *plus* a primary data analysis by the academic partners. As the survey was so large each regional daily had a sub-sample of about 600–1,000 respondents. So it became possible to extract a lot of information at the regional level as well. The information was transformed into unique copy for the participating journals. In the questionnaire issued in November 2001, a number of questions were posed with respect to aspects of government policy. We reproduce the question module in Table 5.1, where N stands for the number of respondents to each specific question and where the columns 1–5 give the response percentages to each response category. In the last column we find the average response levels, rescaled on a [0, 10]-scale.

Obviously, this 41-item module could itself be the subject of a whole research volume. In the present framework we will devote a few words to the questions, because they have to be interpreted in the context of Dutch politics at the end of 2001. It is amazing how dissatisfied the respondents were with respect to a number of public issues, including privatization policies, the 24-hour economy, etc. Remember, however, that the upcoming May 2002 elections were by any standards the most surprising of Dutch post-war history, culminating in the murder of Pim Fortuyn, who created in three months a political party, the List Pim Fortuyn (LPF), which managed to emerge as the second party of the country, even though its leader was already killed before the election day. So the dissatisfactions seen in this table were all too real. It should also be observed that at the time of the survey there was no political campaign running and Dr. Fortuyn's ideas were not yet disseminated on a wide scale. These are genuine dissatisfactions, not generated by Dr. Fortuyn.

The political sub-domains we distinguish in this study are a subset of the list of forty-one issues above.

Our first variable to be explained is 'satisfaction with the government', which we identify as the political-satisfaction (PS) variable introduced before. We try to explain it by political-domain satisfactions (PDS), for which we take a subset from the list above.

The distributions of 'satisfaction with the government' in the population and within some sub-groups of the population are given in Table 5.2. The values in Table 5.2 show that approximately 40 percent of the respondents feel satisfied with the government. However, it is obvious that the opinions gather around being 'indifferent about the government' indicating that it is useful to examine the levels of government satisfaction of certain subgroups. The values in Table

Table 5.1. *Satisfaction with current Dutch situation (September 2001)*

N	Domain	1	2	3	4	5*	Average
14328	Our government (cabinet–Kok)	5.67	17.09	36.93	36.97	3.34	6.30
14103	The parliamentary system in the Netherlands	2.49	9.85	29.19	48.39	10.09	7.08
13763	The proportional voting system	1.74	6.21	27.44	50.62	13.99	7.38
13075	Privatization policy with respect to education (DS1)	17.78	40.35	31.03	9.66	1.18	4.72
13651	Privatization policy with respect to health care (DS2)	26.86	43.54	21.27	7.28	1.04	4.24
13936	Possibility to have a say in important decisions (DS3)	18.00	34.44	30.13	14.75	2.68	4.99
13991	National environmental policy	9.68	29.62	44.13	16.19	0.88	5.41
13924	Municipal environmental policy (DS4)	8.68	25.95	46.66	17.83	0.88	5.53
13874	Municipal parking policy	14.24	25.90	34.03	23.05	2.78	5.48
13930	Municipal traffic policy	14.21	28.34	36.53	19.48	1.45	5.31
13047	National employment policy (DS5)	3.31	11.91	54.22	29.04	1.52	6.27
13895	Policy with respect to shopping hours (DS6)	7.53	20.94	37.96	30.68	2.90	6.01
13795	Policy on the 24-hour economy (DS7)	31.97	30.19	23.17	11.92	2.75	4.47
12331	Elementary education (DS8)	6.99	23.53	43.18	24.60	1.70	5.81
12069	Intermediate education (DS9)	6.74	25.44	44.78	21.64	1.41	5.71
11682	Vocational education (DS10)	6.23	21.39	47.19	23.52	1.66	5.86
11233	University education (DS11)	4.31	15.22	48.86	29.13	2.47	6.20
13346	Policy on old-age pensions (DS12)	7.22	24.15	41.65	25.24	1.73	5.80
12908	Policy on Schiphol (national airport at Amsterdam) (DS13)	10.37	27.90	40.85	19.15	1.73	5.48
13538	National policy on railways (DS14)	30.62	46.14	18.56	4.18	0.51	3.96
12687	National policy on social assistance (DS16)	11.18	28.99	47.66	11.32	0.86	5.23
12851	Policy on labor-disability benefits	12.63	33.53	42.35	10.82	0.66	5.07
13758	National policy on health care (DS17)	20.88	41.22	27.14	10.17	0.59	4.57
13449	National policy towards farmers	20.88	33.01	32.11	12.11	1.89	4.82
13892	Our queen	6.10	7.52	32.74	39.28	14.36	6.97
13575	Maxima (future bride of)	6.48	6.38	34.53	37.65	14.95	6.96

Table 5.1. *(Contd.)*

N	Domain	1	2	3	4	5*	Average
13606	Willem Alexander (Crown Prince)	6.28	7.23	34.46	39.31	12.71	6.90
13869	Fight against fraud in social security	23.12	41.03	25.53	9.16	1.15	4.48
13823	Fight against corruption	33.70	42.51	17.29	5.66	0.84	3.95
12381	Promotion of workers' interests by trade unions	6.02	16.02	53.86	22.17	1.93	5.96
11599	Employees' council	4.91	15.29	55.65	22.25	1.89	6.02
12922	Fight against fraud at the stock exchange	24.24	35.96	30.53	8.25	1.02	4.52
13604	Policy with respect to integration of immigrants and asylum-seekers (DS18)	29.26	40.14	23.95	5.99	0.66	4.17
13426	Policy with respect to participation of immigrants and asylum-seekers in the labor market (DS19)	26.06	42.34	25.86	4.90	0.84	4.24
13830	Admission policy of asylum-seekers (DS20)	35.24	36.27	21.80	6.03	0.66	4.01
13406	Admission policy on immigrants (DS21)	28.00	30.96	31.36	8.77	0.90	4.47
13917	Policy with respect to the euro (DS22)	8.53	10.74	38.24	36.52	5.96	6.41
13481	Policy with respect to expansion of the European Union (DS23)	10.41	20.53	42.24	24.00	2.83	5.77
13147	Policy of the European Commission (DS24)	13.85	29.57	43.31	12.08	1.19	5.14
13600	Policy with respect to dispatching Dutch soldiers on UN peace missions (DS25)	7.96	13.76	44.67	30.45	3.15	6.14
13653	The Dutch role in the United Nations (DS26)	4.67	14.81	47.07	30.10	3.35	6.25

* 1 = very dissatisfied; 2 = dissatisfied; 3 = not satisfied, not dissatisfied; 4 = satisfied; 5 = very satisfied.

5.2 show the descriptive statistics of political satisfaction divided into three subgroups: age, education, and the employment status of the respondent.[2] Respondents who are older than 56 tend to be less satisfied with the government. Older people are in poorer health and on average have a lower income (Frey and Stutzer 2002*a/b*). If individuals are dissatisfied about specific-domain policy issues, like health care and income, then it can be argued that older individuals

---

[2] A differentiation according to number of children or gender did not provide interesting results.

Table 5.2. *Satisfaction with the government divided into subgroups on a five-point scale*

	General	Age			Education			Working	
		16–36	36–56	Above 56	Lower	Middle	Upper	No	Yes
Very unsatisfied	5.67	3.12	4.70	7.46	7.35	5.70	4.59	9.68	4.44
	813	*52*	*313*	*448*	*269*	*238*	*293*	*15*	*382*
Unsatisfied	17.09	14.59	15.06	20.04	19.13	18.11	15.17	32.26	15.30
	2,449	*243*	*1,002*	*1,204*	*700*	*756*	*968*	*50*	*1,316*
Indifferent	36.93	36.13	36.17	37.99	38.62	37.53	35.60	28.39	35.96
	5,291	*602*	*2,407*	*2,282*	*1,413*	*1,567*	*2,271*	*44*	*3,094*
Satisfied	36.97	42.98	40.41	31.50	31.40	35.45	41.29	25.81	40.66
	478	*716*	*2,689*	*1,892*	*1,149*	*1,480*	*2,634*	*40*	*3,498*
Very satisfied	3.34	3.18	3.67	3.01	3.50	3.21	3.34	3.87	3.64
	—	*53*	*244*	*181*	*128*	*134*	*213*	*6*	*313*
Average	—	3.29	3.23	3.03	3.05	3.12	3.24	2.82	3.24
	—	*1,666*	*6,655*	*6,007*	*3,659*	*4,175*	*6,379*	*155*	*8,603*

Note: Table 5.2 gives the relative frequencies, with the number of observations printed in italics below them.

who experience the most 'pain' are likely to be the ones who are the most dissatisfied with the government.

Higher-educated individuals tend to be more satisfied with the government. Higher education levels lead to higher income levels. First, higher-educated individuals more often work for the government, which possibly makes them more satisfied with the government than others. Alternatively, the government has mainly focused on individuals with a higher income; for example, by lowering the top income-tax tariff from 72 to 52 percent in eight years. An additional reason is that lower-educated individuals have to compete on the labor market with immigrants and asylum-seekers, which may have a negative influence on general political satisfaction. Individuals who are working are on average more satisfied with the government than those who are not working.

The PDS were chosen with a view to the political reality in the Netherlands. Respondents had to have an opinion or had to be able to formulate an opinion easily. Nevertheless, as political debate was rather lively in the survey period, we feel that we were able to select a rather broad variety of issues, which cover a fairly complete spectrum of government policy. We shall now briefly elaborate on some of the items, keeping in mind that we consider the 2001 situation before the September 11 disaster.

1. The Prime minister in 2001 was Wim Kok, who headed the so-called 'purple coalition'—a mixture of socialists and conservatives. The Christian Democratic Party, which was a steady member of the government from 1900 to 1994, did not participate during the period 1994–2002.
2. Nearly all of the education system is regulated and controlled by the government, with 95–100 percent state support. There is a lot of discontent with the system and a belief that more private initiative, in one form or another, would improve the quality of the system.
3. The same holds for the health-care system.

4. There are many opportunities to participate in political decision processes, especially at the local level. The consequence is seen as much delay in the taking of decisions. Moreover, many feel that they can participate but that they do not have real influence in the end.

5. Many citizens believe that the policy towards the unemployed is too weak, in the sense that many are supported by unemployment benefits and do not have much incentive to look for a job, while at the same time there is a considerable unmatched demand for labor.

6. Closure times have recently been extended, so that some shops open on Sundays or stay open until 10p.m. Small shops in particular do not like this liberalization.

7. Considerable deregulation had recently been realized with respect to all kinds of trade and industry aimed at the ideal of a 24-hour economy.

8. There is state pension provision on a pay-as-you-go system and a 'funded pillar' based on pension savings by individuals. As in many countries, the aging problem raises the fear that future pensions will be trimmed.

9. Amsterdam's one really national airport creates a lot of environmental damage and traffic jams in the Amsterdam area. Discussion centres around whether the airport should be continuously expanded or contained at its present size.

10. National railways are in the process of privatization, with a reduction in state support. The service level is a source of national distress.

11. Social assistance is debated in the same way as unemployment.

12. As the number of disabled is put at about 20 percent of the active labor force, there is doubt as to whether all of these are really disabled or whether this is just unemployment in disguise. The regulations for disability benefits are better than those for unemployment benefits.

13. Policy regarding immigration and asylum-seekers is very liberal, resulting in a great minority of not sufficiently integrated and frequently illegal immigrants.

5.3. POLITICAL DOMAIN SATISFACTIONS EXPLAINED

Following the same path as in Chapter 3 we shall first try to explain the political-domain satisfactions. We do this by the COLS method. We have already explained that the COLS method yields the same effects as the probit approach and that choosing cardinalization, which the respondents provide, we extract not only the ordinal but also the cardinal information. As expected, the estimation results for the three alternative methods described in Chapter 2 did not differ significantly from those presented here, except for a proportionality factor.

We regroup the domains in related fields. In the questionnaire we used a different order, and this was intentional. When domains from the different fields are supplied in one block after another, we expect that the respondent will assume a certain consistency in answering. For instance, if we were to ask about attitudes to privatization with respect to health care, education, public transport, etc. one after another, the respondent would see this as a general question about whether state services should be privatized or not. This would lead to a kind of willed consistency between answers on the part of the respondent, who in reality has no uniform attitude towards privatization, which he judges as positive for one sector and negative for another. Therefore we mix the privatization questions over the fields instead of putting them in one block.

We see from Table 5.3 that older individuals are much more critical of the education system than younger respondents and that the respondent's level of education has only a minor effect on this. However, the more children the respondent has, the more positive he or she becomes about the primary education system. The R^2's are invariably low. The main impression is that much of the critique on the Dutch education system comes from individuals who are not in direct contact with that system. This is a surprising result, as many 2001 press publications suggested an emergency situation. This may be the opinion of professionals (teachers, school administrators and politicians), but fortunately it does not seem to be the uniform opinion of the respondents.

The next block deals with health care and social security (Table 5.4). We find that the imminent threat of privatization of the health care system is felt more severely by older people. This is understandable, as older people are more in need of health care or at least run higher health risks than younger individuals. City inhabitants are more negative than respondents living outside the cities, reflecting the dire scarcity in cities, where it is sometimes very difficult to find a general practitioner or to get home care, etc. The more income respondents have, the more positive they are about privatization tendencies. This may be explained by the fact that the more income one has the more market power one has.

The next four satisfactions do not deal with a tendency but with the evaluation of the current situation with respect to the care of the elderly, social security, the level of social benefits, and the situation of the health care system. We see a strong age effect for the level of social benefits and health-care; the elderly are more negative, which is not surprising.

In Table 5.5 we look at the opinions with respect to immigration and asylum policy. The main result is that there is a strong negative age effect, while more education leads to a more positive attitude towards immigrants and asylum-seekers.

In Table 5.6 we look at some international aspects. We see that there is a good feeling about the then (2001) imminent introduction of the Euro despite some prophets of doom. The attitude becomes more positive if one is male, married, and better educated. Finally, richer people are more positive. With respect to the expansion of the European Union we see that respondents in work are much more positive than individuals with no work or who have retired. Older individuals are less sympathetic to the expansion. The way in which the European Commission acts is not appreciated by older respondents. The same holds for the evaluation of the participation of the Dutch army in international peace-keeping missions and the way in which the Netherlands participate in the UN. This is an expression of the fact that older and poorer people tend to be less internationally oriented than younger individuals.

Table 5.3. *Estimation results–education*

Explanatory variables	Privatization (DS$_1$)	Primary (DS$_8$)	General (DS$_9$)	Vocational	
				Lower/Intermediate (DS$_{10}$)	Higher (DS$_{11}$)
Gender (male)	−0.022	−0.021	−0.044	−0.083	−0.028
	−1.750	*−1.640*	*−3.430*	*−6.520*	*−2.110*
Marital status	0.002	0.073	0.054	0.054	0.035
	0.120	*5.350*	*3.860*	*3.860*	*2.430*
Log(ch. + 1)	0.007	0.044	0.008	0.016	0.024
	0.480	*2.880*	*0.520*	*0.990*	*1.430*
Log(age)	0.951	1.601	1.311	1.381	0.578
	3.720	*6.510*	*5.200*	*5.440*	*2.170*
(Log(age))^2	−1.073	−1.823	−1.467	−1.564	−0.670
	−3.900	*−6.870*	*−5.400*	*−5.700*	*−2.330*
Education	−0.017	−0.009	−0.035	−0.005	0.031
	−1.340	*−0.720*	*−2.730*	*−0.350*	*2.350*
Log(monthly wage)	0.039	−0.004	0.011	0.032	0.022
	2.520	*−0.260*	*0.690*	*2.030*	*1.290*
Living in the city	0.000	−0.009	−0.021	−0.015	0.021
	0.030	*−0.780*	*−1.740*	*−1.220*	*1.670*
Living in the countryside	0.016	0.062	0.047	0.045	0.009
	1.230	*4.880*	*3.580*	*3.420*	*0.660*
Employed	0.023	0.028	0.004	0.025	0.082
	0.980	*1.130*	*0.160*	*1.030*	*3.010*
Constant	−0.087	−0.061	−0.042	−0.071	−0.022
	−3.700	*−2.620*	*−1.770*	*−2.960*	*−0.890*
Number of observations	6,955	6,718	6,587	6,467	6,183
R^2	0.006	0.024	0.015	0.0222	0.0082

Note: t-statistics are printed in italics.

Table 5.4. *Estimation results—health care and social security*

Explanatory variables	Dependent Variable				
	Health care privatization (DS_2)	Pension funds (DS_{12})	Social security (DS_{15})	Benefits levels (DS_{16})	National health (DS_{17})
Gender (male)	-0.021	-0.039	-0.043	0.0252	0.0279
	-1.7	*-3.18*	*-3.33*	*2.07*	*2.26*
Marital status	-0.011	0.03	0.07	0.066	0.0074
	-0.79	*2.33*	*5.07*	*5.1*	*0.56*
Log(ch. + 1)	0.029	0.057	-0.037	-0.0077	0.036
	1.87	*3.82*	*-2.4*	*-0.52*	*2.41*
Log(age)	0.559	-1.262	-0.488	-0.1024	-1.0389
	2.15	*-5.02*	*-1.83*	*-0.4*	*-4.08*
(Log(age))^2	-0.765	1.314	0.507	0.0752	0.8951
	-2.73	*4.86*	*1.77*	*0.28*	*3.27*
Education	-0.045	0.107	0.042	0.1063	0.0564
	-3.51	*8.63*	*3.2*	*8.69*	*4.51*
Log(monthly wage)	0.007	0.072	0.014	-0.0373	-0.0231
	0.42	*4.59*	*0.83*	*-2.43*	*-1.48*
Living in the city	-0.017	-0.013	-0.035	-0.0119	0.0326
	-1.38	*-1.08*	*-2.89*	*-1.03*	*2.77*
Living in the countryside	-0.013	0.008	0.033	0.0125	0.0216
	-0.97	*0.62*	*2.35*	*0.97*	*1.66*
Employed	-0.038	0.018	0.017	0.0541	0.0537
	-1.65	*0.73*	*0.72*	*2.59*	*2.48*
Constant	-0.109	-0.08	-0.026	-0.0455	-0.0495
	-4.59	*-3.53*	*-1.09*	*-2.01*	*-2.15*
Number of observations	7,144	6,870	6,794	6,862	7,188
R^2	0.022	0.023	0.01	0.0183	0.048

Note: t-statistics are printed in italics.

Table 5.5. *Estimation results—immigrants and asylum seekers*

Explanatory variables		Dependent variable (DS)		
	Nationalization (DS$_{18}$)	Labour market (DS$_{19}$)	Immigration policy	
			Asylum-seekers (DS$_{20}$)	Immigrants (DS$_{21}$)
Gender (male)	−0.073	−0.005	−0.085	−0.0708
	−5.78	*−0.36*	*−7.11*	*−5.87*
Marital status	0.021	0.011	0.008	0.0079
	1.53	*0.79*	*0.64*	*0.61*
Log(ch. + 1)	−0.011	−0.01	−0.03	−0.0026
	−0.73	*−0.64*	*−2.07*	*−0.180.18*
Log(age)	1.181	1.526	0.157	0.4378
	4.55	*5.78*	*0.63*	*1.81*
(Log(age))^2	−1.254	−1.651	−0.155	−0.4603
	−4.5	*−5.81*	*−0.58*	*−1.77*
Education	0.056	0.085	0.141	0.1099
	4.35	*6.46*	*11.53*	*8.91*
Log(monthly wage)	−0.031	−0.051	−0.027	−0.0297
	−1.96	*−3.12*	*−1.81*	*−1.95*
Living in the city	0.036	0.038	0.042	0.044
	3.01	*3.13*	*3.69*	*3.8*
Living in the countryside	0.016	0.002	0.027	0.0552
	1.2	*0.11*	*2.12*	*4.39*
Employed	0.068	0.033	0.047	0.0654
	3.13	*1.32*	*2.19*	*3.16*
Constant	−0.103	−0.109	−0.05	−0.0859
	−4.4	*−4.5*	*−2.23*	*−3.8*
Number of observations	7,267	7,154	7,393	7,266
R^2	0.016	0.017	0.034	0.0255

Note: t-statistics are printed in italics.

Table 5.6. *Estimation results–international issues*

Explanatory variables	Dependent variable				
	euro (DS$_{22}$)	Eu (DS$_{23}$)	EC (DS$_{24}$)	Use of Dutch soldiers (DS$_{25}$)	Dutch role in UN (DS$_{26}$)
Gender (male)	0.077	−0.042	−0.148	0.116	0.0396
	6.14	*−3.34*	*−11.75*	*9.45*	*3.1*
Marital status	0.046	−0.002	0.012	0.0128	0.0481
	3.4	*−0.13*	*0.88*	*0.98*	*3.51*
Log(ch. + 1)	0.012	0.037	−0.012	0.0203	0.022
	0.77	*2.46*	*−0.75*	*1.36*	*1.41*
Log(age)	−0.443	−0.489	−0.217	−0.8217	−1.973
	−1.77	*−1.98*	*−0.87*	*−3.27*	*−7.55*
(Log(age))^2	0.474	0.468	0.13	0.7998	2.0134
	1.75	*1.76*	*0.48*	*2.96*	*7.17*
Education	0.146	0.069	0.056	0.1285	0.1205
	11.41	*5.49*	*4.42*	*10.32*	*9.3*
Log(monthly wage)	0.096	0.078	0.023	0.0323	0.0585
	6.17	*4.93*	*1.46*	*2.1*	*3.63*
Living in the city	0.014	0.009	0.025	−0.0311	−0.0128
	1.2	*0.73*	*2.06*	*−2.66*	*−1.05*
Living in the countryside	0.032	−0.019	0.029	0.0345	0.0377
	2.47	*−1.45*	*2.22*	*2.65*	*2.77*
Employed	0.038	0.118	0.019	0.0673	0.0791
	1.76	*5.11*	*0.85*	*2.66*	*3.36*
Constant	−0.011	−0.039	−0.1	0.0189	0.0689
	−0.45	*−1.68*	*−4.32*	*0.83*	*2.9*
N	7,435	7,104	6,958	7,141	7,159
R^2	0.041	0.017	0.046	0.0406	0.0352

Note: *t*-statistics are printed in italics.

Table 5.7. *Estimation results—environment, employment, participation on important issues, economic flexibility and transportation*

Explanatory variables	Dependent variable					
	Participation (DS$_3$)	Environment policy (DS$_4$)	Employment policy (DS$_5$)	Shop closing times (DS$_6$)	24-hour economy (DS$_7$)	Schiphol Airport (DS$_{13}$)
Gender (male)	-0.110	0.001	0.035	-0.108	0.049	0.006
	-8.930	*0.110*	*2.850*	*-8.770*	*3.900*	*0.440*
Marital status	0.063	0.036	0.001	-0.019	-0.048	0.073
	4.740	*2.780*	*0.110*	*-1.400*	*-3.590*	*5.390*
Log(ch. + 1)	0.002	0.058	0.009	-0.022	-0.029	-0.016
	0.110	*3.950*	*0.610*	*-1.450*	*-1.890*	*-1.000*
Log(age)	-0.430	-1.128	0.269	0.264	-0.445	-0.763
	-1.740	*-4.530*	*0.990*	*1.060*	*-1.770*	*-2.940*
(Log(age))^2	0.428	1.092	-0.437	-0.273	0.373	0.754
	1.610	*4.070*	*-1.500*	*-1.020*	*1.380*	*2.690*
Education	0.096	0.057	0.026	0.047	0.053	0.050
	7.680	*4.640*	*2.030*	*3.690*	*4.170*	*3.860*
Log(monthly wage)	0.046	0.044	0.078	-0.002	0.086	0.037
	2.930	*2.830*	*4.900*	*-0.110*	*5.470*	*2.290*
Living in the city	0.020	0.005	-0.047	-0.015	-0.007	-0.020
	1.710	*0.390*	*-3.970*	*-1.290*	*-0.560*	*-1.670*
Living in the countryside	0.036	-0.009	0.010	0.002	-0.054	0.012
	2.830	*-0.690*	*0.740*	*0.130*	*-4.120*	*0.850*
Employed	0.091	0.034	0.085	-0.023	-0.023	0.048
	3.940	*1.560*	*3.810*	*-1.050*	*-1.030*	*2.050*
Constant	-0.025	-0.010	-0.093	0.006	-0.007	-0.023
	-1.090	*-0.420*	*-3.920*	*0.260*	*-0.310*	*-0.990*
N	7,411	7,366	7,164	7,535	7,520	6,900
R^2	0.0285	0.0179	0.0276	0.017	0.0315	0.0127

Note: *t*-statistics are printed in italics.

The last block we consider deals with satisfaction with participation in important issues, environment policy, employment policy, shop closing times, the 24-hour economy, Schiphol airport, and the railways. Results are presented in Table 5.7.

We see here the by-now familiar negative age effect, which may be partly explained by the nature of the party coalition in September 2001, which had a mildly progressive color, as a part of which many older people did not recognize themselves in it. Respondents living in the countryside are less satisfied with the environmental policy and more content with the railways.

Summarizing these results we see that we may explain political-domain satisfactions simply as individual domains. The explanation is rather meagre, but this is certainly partly the result of the discretization into five classes of the variable to be explained. The explanations we found are intuitively plausible, although not spectacular. It is perhaps possible to improve the explanation by ad hoc selections of explanatory variables for each domain. However, in the context of this chapter we have to limit ourselves and we do not try to do that. It is obvious that the structural parts are heavily correlated to age and income.

5.4. POLITICAL SATISFACTION

As in Chapter 4, we now assume that the satisfactions with respect to the political sub-domains are aggregated in the overall satisfaction with government policy. Hence, we assume an equation of the type

$$PS_n = \beta_1 PDS_{1, n} + \ldots + \beta_{26} PDS_{26, n} + \gamma Z_n + \varepsilon_n. \qquad (5.2)$$

As in Chapter 4, we include a variable Z, which is the first principal component of the (26×26) covariance matrix of the 26 political sub-domains we distinguish. This variable is included in order to correct for a potential endogeneity bias.

In Table 5.8 we present the estimate of this equation, where each PDS has been rescaled by dividing it by its population standard deviation. The resulting regression coefficients are the so-called standardized regression coefficients. This operation does not alter the *t*-values. However, as we did not know whether there would be a strong variation between the variances of the PDS we standardized in order to get a better comparability of the effects. All explanatory variables have a standard deviation equal to 1. We can order the various sub-domains according to importance. Some specific PDS, which appeared to be highly correlated, are replaced by their average.[3] The item referring to the railways was dropped, as it yielded non-interpretable results. This may have to do with the fact that many respondents do not use the railways themselves but express an opinion. The question seems not to be understood in the same way by everybody.

---

[3] We defined them as follows: 'mean privatization' $= (DS_1 + DS_2)/2$; 'mean education' $= (DS_8 + DS_9 + DS_{10} + DS_{11})/4$; 'mean immigration' $= (DS_{18} + DS_{19} + DS_{20} + DS_{21})/4$; 'mean international' $= (DS_{22} + DS_{23} + DS_{24} + DS_{25} + DS_{26})/5$.

Table 5.8. *Estimation results—general political satisfaction (standardized)*

Satisfaction with respect to:		Satisfaction with respect to:	
Mean privatization	0.079***	Social security	−0.003
	4.31		−0.170
Participation in important issues	0.108***	Amount of social benefit	−0.004
	7.42		−0.21
Environment policy	0.082***	Our national health	0.109***
	5.67		6.66
Employment policy	0.113***	Mean education	0.035
	7.99		1.37
Shop closing time	0.083***	Mean immigration	0.106***
	6.10		4.18
24-hour economy	0.065***	Mean international issues	0.155***
	5.01		6.79
Pension funds	0.013	Endogeneity correction variable	−0.077
	0.84		−1.04
Schiphol airport	0.022	Constant	0.038
	1.46		2.86
N	4,856		—
R²	0.244		—

Note: *** = significant at 1% level; *t*-statistics are printed in italics.

From this table it appears that the main determinants of political satisfaction are the attitude to privatization, the perceived participation possibilities in political decision making, environment policy, employment, national health, immigration, and international issues. It is rather remarkable that international issues are the most important determinant. We notice that the Z-variable is non-significant in this equation.

5.5. THE RELATION BETWEEN POLITICAL SATISFACTION AND GENERAL SATISFACTION

Finally, we are interested in the way in which political satisfaction fits into the general-satisfaction equation. Therefore, we regressed (by COLS) general satisfaction with life (GS) on the domain satisfactions in the GPD survey. The selection in the GPD survey is not identical with that in the German or British survey which we considered in Chapters 3 and 4. The estimates with standardized coefficients are presented in Table 5.9.

As expected, we find similar results to those in Chapter 4. The novelty is that political satisfaction is included as well. Although it is relatively less important than the individual domains distinguished, the political dimension is certainly not negligible. It seems that the relative importance of the domains in the

Table 5.9. *General satisfaction in the*
Netherlands explained by five life domains and
political satisfaction

Variable	Effect	t-value
Political satisfaction	0.068	6.00
Job satisfaction	0.219	11.98
Financial satisfaction	0.217	12.74
Housing satisfaction	0.169	10.07
Health satisfaction	0.263	13.65
Leisure satisfaction	0.235	14.12
Z	−0.390	−7.47
Constant	−0.008	−0.75
N	6,820	—
R^2	0.1875	—

Netherlands differs somewhat from the trade-off ratios in the UK or Germany. It is remarkable that leisure satisfaction scores exactly as high as health satisfaction, while in the other two countries the contribution of leisure is modest. This may have to do with the fact that the Dutch in 2001 were very much leisure-oriented. It is a matter of fact that leisure, both amount and use gets disproportionate attention in the Dutch press and in everyday life. That housing satisfaction scores high in Table 5.9 may have to do with the particular situation of the Dutch housing market. Since the end of World War II there has been a tremendous housing shortage, and this may have made the Dutch relatively housing-conscious.

5.6. CONCLUSION

The main conclusions of this chapter can be summarized as follows:

The 'satisfaction-calculus' methodology that we developed in Chapters 3 and 4 appears to be applicable in the public domain as well. We find that political satisfaction, that is satisfaction with the government, may be broken down with respect to a number of satisfactions with political aspects; that is, political sub-domains. Moreover, we find that political satisfaction is a non-negligible component of general satisfaction with life as a whole. It implies that there is a trade-off between more and less political satisfaction and satisfaction with respect to the individual domains. The method is applied here to Dutch data. It would be very interesting to apply the same method to countries where there are fewer political liberties; for example, with respect to freedom of speech.

6

Males, Females, and Households

6.1. INTRODUCTION

In this chapter we will look for gender differences in satisfactions. The relevant question is whether males and females have a different perception of their situation, resulting in different levels of satisfaction even when their objective situation is the same. We saw before that satisfaction levels may be partly explained by a structural model. If those structural models differ gender-wise, it implies that the structural satisfaction derived from a specific situation x would differ between male and female.

The literature on satisfaction has only incorporated gender as a 'dummy' but has not looked at the relation between the satisfaction level of husband and wife. Moreover, existing literature has mainly focused on general satisfaction and has not looked systematically at the domain satisfaction differences. In the existing literature gender differences are usually found to be small. Women are, in general, more frequently depressed and experience more negative emotions than men, but are not consistently unhappier. Diener et al. (1998) explain this by suggesting that even if women experience negative emotions more often, they also experience more positive emotions, so that these balance out. The empirical evidence using satisfaction questions seems contradictory. Some studies find women to be happier (see e.g. Gerdtham and Johannesson 2001) and others find men to be happier (see e.g. Clark and Oswald 1994; Theodossiou 1998), but the difference tends to be small. We have already looked at gender differences in domain satisfactions in Chapter 3. There, for instance, we found for Germany that women are in general more satisfied, except with regard to leisure satisfaction.

In the British and German household panels, satisfaction questions were posed to all adults in a specific household. This implies that we are able to compare the well-being of the husband and wife in the same household. In this way we can disentangle whether there are systematic differences between husband's and wife's satisfactions. First, we study whether the reported satisfaction levels differ between man and woman. Second, we estimate the satisfaction equations to see whether there are structural differences; that is, whether the influence of the objective situation on subjective happiness differs between man and woman. Finally, we analyse the statistical relation between the error terms of the two partners to see whether the unobservable variables of both partners are correlated; that is, whether there is a common error term for both members of the household. Plug and Van Praag (1998) considered the structural differences between males and females in the same household when comparing responses of husband and wife to the income-evaluation question.

This chapter is structured as follows. In Section 6.2 we introduce the model and the estimation method. In Section 6.3 we present and discuss the estimation results for males and females. In Section 6.4 we look at the correlation between the unobservables of partners. In Section 6.5 we draw our conclusions.

6.2. MODEL AND ESTIMATION

We now consider a straightforward generalization of the model introduced in Chapters 3 and 4. For simplicity we shall consider only traditional households, with a husband, denoted by M, and a wife, denoted by F. Homosexual partnerships are excluded.[1] Moreover, and for simplicity, we shall restrict ourselves to a cross-section analysis of the 1998 wave of the British Household Panel Survey.

We have for each household two joint observations: (DS_M, GS_M, X_M) and (DS_F, GS_F, X_F). There are for each individual 8 domain satisfactions. Hence, we end up with the following 16 equations:

$$DS_M = \alpha_M X_M + \varepsilon_H + \varepsilon_M$$
$$DS_F = \alpha_F X_F + \varepsilon_H + \varepsilon_F.$$

(6.1)

The male domain satisfactions DS_M are explained by the male's individual characteristics (X_M) and the female satisfactions DS_F by the female's characteristics (X_F). The error term of the male and female DS equations is divided into two independent error components. One term represents the unobservable and random factors that are equal for male and female in the same household, ε_H. A second component is specific to the male and female and is represented by ε_M and ε_F respectively. The three error vectors are assumed to be mutually independent, to have zero expectations, and to have covariance matrices $\sum_H, \sum_M, \sum_F$. It is fairly evident how this would have to be changed were we to take into account several waves simultaneously. As we do not focus on the time aspect here, we do not operationalize this extension. We denote $\tilde{\varepsilon}_M = (\varepsilon_H + \varepsilon_M), \tilde{\varepsilon}_F = (\varepsilon_H + \varepsilon_F)$.

The sixteen equations are estimated separately by COLS. We then compare the corresponding coefficients α_M and α_F to see whether there are structural differences between males and females.

We will then proceed by estimating the joint covariance matrix of the sixteen errors $(\varepsilon_H + \varepsilon_M, \varepsilon_H + \varepsilon_F)$ by means of the calculated residuals. The covariance matrix is denoted by

[1] In the data set there are 12 homosexual partnerships out of the 3,281 couples.

$$\begin{bmatrix} \tilde{\sum}_{MM} & \tilde{\sum}_{MF} \\ \tilde{\sum}_{FM} & \tilde{\sum}_{FF} \end{bmatrix}.$$

(6.2)

We have, in view of our assumptions on the errors,

$$\tilde{\sum}_{MM} = \sum_{M} + \sum_{H}$$
$$\tilde{\sum}_{FF} = \sum_{F} + \sum_{H}$$
$$\tilde{\sum}_{MF} = \sum_{H}$$
$$\tilde{\sum}_{FM} = \sum_{H}.$$

(6.3)

In theory, the last two sub-matrices should be symmetric matrices as well, since they are estimates of the covariance matrix of ε_H. In the sample context this holds approximately. We estimate $\sum_H$ by setting

$$\hat{\sum}_{H} = \frac{1}{2}\left(\tilde{\sum}_{MF} + \tilde{\sum}'_{FM}\right).$$

(6.4)

Then, the other two matrices $\sum_M$ and $\sum_F$ may be found by subtraction. By looking at the errors of the sixteen equations we are able to disentangle whether both partners in the household have some unobservable characteristics in common. In other words, we find whether $\hat{\sum}_H$ contributes substantially to the total matrices $\tilde{\sum}_{MM}$ and $\tilde{\sum}_{FF}$.

After estimating the covariances of the error components it would be possible to perform a second-round estimation, where the joint covariance matrix would be used in a SUR procedure. Given the large number of observations and the consistency of OLS, we abstained from doing that.

Finally, we proceed to estimate the general-satisfaction equations for males and females. Here, we follow the same procedure as in Chapter 4. The main characteristics of this estimation are: (1) general satisfaction is seen as an aggregate of the domain satisfactions; (2) a term Z_M, Z_F is incorporated into the equation so as to account for correlation between the unobservables of GS (ε_{GH}; ε_{GM}; ε_{GF}) and the DS (see Ch. 4 for details). For individuals who do not work we set job satisfaction at 0. At the same time, we create a dummy variable called 'no job' (NJ) that takes the value 1 if the individual does not work and the value 0 otherwise. The two GS equations are

$$GS_M = \beta_M DS_M + \beta_{MJ} NJ + \gamma_M Z_M + \varepsilon_{G,H} + \varepsilon_{G,M}$$
$$GS_F = \beta_F DS_F + \beta_{FJ} NJ + \gamma_F Z_F + \varepsilon_{G,H} + \varepsilon_{G,F}.$$

(6.5)

Summarizing, we are interested in:

• the satisfactions of the two genders;

- the difference in satisfaction between the two partners in the same household;
- whether the differences $\alpha_M - \alpha_F$ and $\beta_M - \beta_F$ are statistically different from zero;
- the covariance and correlation between the errors of the satisfactions of the two partners in the household.

6.3. DOMAIN AND GENERAL SATISFACTION DIFFERENCES BETWEEN MALE AND FEMALE

We start by looking at some descriptive statistics of the data. In order to make the numbers easier to interpret, we transform all (British) satisfaction answers from the (1, 7) scale to a (0, 10) scale. The average satisfaction values for female and male are presented in Table 6.1.

From Table 6.1 we can conclude that there is not much difference in the average satisfaction levels between males and females. In general, females are somewhat more satisfied than males except with respect to health, leisure-use, marriage, and social life satisfactions.

Next we consider the differences between males and females *within* the same household. We conclude that there are no significant differences either. The larger differences are found for health, leisure-use and -amount, and job satisfactions. The smaller differences are for marriage, housing, and financial satisfactions, in that order. The next relevant question is to ask whether these small differences in answers result from small differences in the objective situation (X_M and X_F) or from differences in the 'psychological mechanism' that translates the objective situation into subjectively perceived satisfactions. In other words, whether there are structural differences between men and women.

Next we explore these structural differences between males and females. For that, we estimate the eight domain equations for male and female separately. The results are presented in Tables 6.2–6.9. We notice that these equations are

Table 6.1. *Average satisfactions of males and females*

	Male	Female
Job satisfaction	6.76	6.95
Financial satisfaction	5.95	6.16
Housing satisfaction	7.43	7.50
Health satisfaction	6.92	6.77
Leisure-use satisfaction	6.63	6.48
Leisure-amount satisfaction	6.26	6.32
Marriage satisfaction	9.05	8.83
Social-life satisfaction	6.77	6.74
General satisfaction	7.25	7.36

Table 6.2. *Financial satisfaction*

	Female			Male			Difference of estimates
	Estimates	t-value	Standardized estimates	Estimates	t-value	Standardized estimates	
Intercept	11.141	6.444	—	12.013	6.491	—	0.344
Ln(age)	−7.926	−8.022	−2.744	−8.111	−7.851	−2.742	−0.130
(Ln(age))^2	1.131	8.438	2.915	1.124	8.150	2.874	−0.039
Minimum age	33.239	—	—	36.948	—	—	—
Ln(monthly household net income)	0.438	18.062	0.305	0.393	16.277	0.274	−1.310
Ln(years education)	−0.024	−0.667	−0.011	0.051	1.174	0.019	1.328
Dummy for missing education	−0.322	−1.319	−0.021	0.293	1.233	0.020	1.805
Ln(adults)	−0.454	−6.295	−0.101	−0.471	−6.698	−0.105	−0.170
Ln(children + 1)	−0.044	−0.424	−0.023	0.020	0.201	0.011	0.444
(Ln(children + 1))^2	0.004	0.051	0.003	−0.086	−1.116	−0.057	−0.817
Turning point children	233	—	—	1.125	—	—	—
Ln(savings)	0.000	4.962	0.073	0.000	7.713	0.113	2.206
Dummy for missing savings	0.330	4.453	0.065	0.189	2.895	0.041	−1.429
N	3,194	—	—	3,079	—	—	—
Adjusted R^2	0.137	—	—	0.141	—	—	—

estimated on only one wave of the BHPS. Therefore, we do not distinguish between permanent and transitory effects as we did in Chapter 3.

The structure of these tables is as follows: The first column gives the estimated coefficients for the female and the second column gives the corresponding t-values. The distribution of some of the explanatory variables differs between males and females and thus it is a bit difficult to compare the male and female coefficients. Therefore, the third column of these tables presents the 'standardized'[2] effects. The fourth, fifth, and sixth columns present the numbers for the male. In the last column we consider the difference $(\alpha_M - \alpha_F)/\sqrt{\sigma_M^2 + \sigma_F^2}$. The denominator represents the two variances of the male and female coefficients. If the absolute value of this difference is more than 1.96, the difference is considered to be significant at the 5 percent level.[3]

Financial Satisfaction
The financial domain is remarkably similar for both sexes. The only significant difference is with respect to the savings coefficient, which is larger for males than for females.

Job Satisfaction
The differences between men and women regarding influences on job satisfaction are significant for various coefficients. The age effect for females is much less pronounced than for males and it reaches a minimum at a younger age than for males. The minimum for men is at the age of 37, and for females at 29. The salary received for working has a positive significant effect on the males' satisfaction, while it is non-significant for the females. The same holds for the number of hours of overtime worked: it is a positive factor for males and it is non-significant for females. The effect for males is puzzling. We think that overtime hours probably reflect other job characteristics and effects, such as the status of the job, the fact that a person feels more needed if overtime is required, and that men who like their job are not against working longer hours.

We saw that, compared to other domains, job satisfaction presented relatively large differences between men and women. In view of the results presented in Table 6.3 we can conclude that these differences result from differences both in the objective situation and in the subjective perception of reality.

---

[2] The effect is standardized by multiplying the original coefficient by the standard deviation of the corresponding X-variable. This transformation has no repercussions for statistical significance tests.

[3] Notice that the denominator would be different if we had applied a SUR procedure. As there would be a positive correlation between the two estimators, the denominator would be smaller and hence the significance would be more easily reached. The positive correlation stems from the fact that the errors of male and female in one household are positively correlated (see Table 6.14).

Table 6.3. *Job satisfaction*

	Female			Male			Difference of estimates
	Estimates	t-value	Standardized estimates	Estimates	t-value	Standardized estimates	
Intercept	8.431	2.987	—	17.740	6.070	—	2.291
Ln(monthly household net income)	0.003	0.079	0.002	0.017	0.395	0.010	0.240
Ln(age)	−4.561	−2.804	−1.321	−10.152	−6.168	−2.828	−2.416
(Ln(age))^2	0.675	2.990	1.413	1.401	6.228	2.867	2.276
Minimum age	29.257	—	—	37.433	—	—	
Ln(years education)	0.012	0.278	0.005	0.022	0.430	0.009	0.154
Dummy for missing education	−0.363	−1.050	−0.020	0.259	1.009	0.020	1.444
Ln(monthly working income)	−0.020	−0.861	−0.027	0.079	2.289	0.100	2.384
Dummy for missing working income	0.042	0.184	0.006	0.336	0.859	0.049	0.652
Ln(working hours)	−0.037	−1.109	−0.032	0.048	1.230	0.036	1.656
Dummy for missing working hours	−0.561	−2.110	−0.100	0.374	1.490	0.063	2.557
Ln(overtime hours)	−0.009	−0.423	−0.008	0.062	3.702	0.070	2.634
Dummy for missing overtime hours	0.237	3.365	0.075	0.308	5.976	0.122	0.805
Night shift	−0.176	−1.343	−0.024	0.004	0.036	0.001	1.019
Dummy for missing work time	−0.121	−0.454	−0.020	−0.716	−1.957	−0.107	−1.316
Ln(household-work hours)	0.015	0.503	0.011	−0.002	−0.125	−0.002	−0.486
Dummy for missing household work	0.155	0.702	0.013	−0.303	−1.518	−0.026	−1.540
Ln(children + 1)	0.000	0.006	0.000	0.068	1.848	0.036	1.212
Ln(adults)	−0.085	−0.979	−0.020	0.013	0.161	0.003	0.820
N	1,997			2,198			—
Adjusted R^2	0.027			0.038			—

Housing Satisfaction
The estimated coefficients for housing satisfaction show no significant differences between men and women.

Health Satisfaction
For health satisfaction we see two significant differences. First, the employment situation has a greater positive impact on health for males than for females. The direction of the causality is, however, unclear: Does working have a positive influence on health? Or are healthy men more likely to work? Second, the negative influence of 'heart and blood problems' on the male's health satisfaction appears to be much stronger than on the health of the female.

The differences between the health-satisfaction answers of both partners are relatively large when compared to differences on other domain satisfactions. This difference cannot be explained by the two significant differences in coefficients alone; it probably depends on the differences in the objective health situations of male and female.

Leisure Satisfaction
Satisfaction answers in the areas of leisure use and leisure amount present, together with job and health satisfaction, the largest differences between spouses in the same household. These relatively large differences could be explained both by the differences in the objective variables influencing leisure-use and -amount satisfactions and by the differences in the regression coefficients. Tables 6.6 and 6.7 show that there are indeed some significant differences in the coefficients of the regressions, which probably explain the different answers for male and female.

For leisure-use satisfaction we find significant differences between males and females. The presence and number of children in the household affect satisfaction with leisure-use negatively for both genders. The burden, however, appears to be much heavier for women than for men. The number of leisure hours has a much stronger positive effect for men than for women. In contrast, the number of hours worked has a strong negative effect on leisure-use for women and no effect for males. We remind the reader here that we distinguish between three different categories of time use: work, leisure, and household work.

For satisfaction with the amount of leisure we see again that the negative effect that children have on leisure-amount satisfaction is much larger for women than for men. The age effect is also significantly different for leisure-amount satisfaction: men have a more pronounced age effect and they reach their minimum level of satisfaction at an older age; that is, 33, as 25 opposed to women.

Table 6.4. *Housing satisfaction*

	Female			Male			Difference of estimates
	Estimates	t-value	Standardized estimates	Estimates	t-value	Standardized estimates	
Intercept	5.917	3.347	—	5.615	2.990	—	−0.117
Ln(age)	−3.810	−3.778	−1.320	−3.472	−3.317	−1.174	0.233
(Ln(age))^2	23.595	—	—	24.342	—	—	—
Minimum age	0.603	4.385	1.554	0.544	3.864	1.391	−0.299
Ln(monthly household net income)	0.128	5.145	0.089	0.107	4.339	0.075	−0.600
Ln(years education)	−0.074	−2.061	−0.033	−0.068	−1.618	−0.026	0.124
Dummy for missing education	−0.221	−0.912	−0.014	−0.426	−1.857	−0.029	−0.616
Ln (adults)	−0.145	−2.038	−0.032	−0.250	−3.695	−0.056	−1.064
Ln(children + 1)	−0.100	−2.944	−0.052	−0.121	−3.877	−0.063	−0.462
Employed	0.032	0.868	0.015	0.077	1.763	0.035	0.804
N	3,194	—	—	3,076	—	—	—
Adjusted R^2	0.092	—	—	0.087	—	—	—

Table 6.5. Health satisfaction

	Female			Male			Difference of estimates
	Estimates	t-value	Standardized estimates	Estimates	t-value	Standardized estimates	
Intercept	6.845	3.993	—	10.515	5.484	—	1.427
Ln(age)	−3.342	−3.408	−1.1581	−5.321	−4.968	−1.797	−1.363
(Ln(age))^2	0.474	3.526	1.222	0.741	5.127	1.893	1.354
Minimum age	34.061	—	—	36.299	—	—	—
Ln(monthly household net income)	−0.013	−0.537	−0.009	−0.038	−1.511	−0.027	−0.726
Ln(children + 1)	0.022	0.681	0.011	−0.018	−0.571	−0.010	−0.886
Ln(years education)	−0.025	−0.715	−0.011	−0.021	−0.487	−0.008	0.075
Dummy for missing education	0.129	0.546	0.008	0.183	0.774	0.012	0.160
Ln(savings)	0.000	1.565	0.022	0.000	0.689	0.010	−0.552
Employed	0.115	3.191	0.056	0.287	6.126	0.130	2.903
Dummy for missing savings	0.043	0.595	0.008	−0.072	−1.115	−0.016	−1.189
Problems with arms, legs, hands, feet, back, or neck	−0.505	−14.754	−0.228	−0.467	−13.842	−0.209	0.800
Difficulty in seeing	−0.197	−2.698	−0.039	−0.296	−3.909	−0.057	−0.937
Difficulty in hearing	−0.020	−0.314	−0.005	−0.018	−0.364	−0.005	0.026
Skin conditions/allergies	−0.141	−3.594	−0.052	−0.052	−1.090	−0.016	1.452
Heart/blood problems	−0.233	−5.316	−0.081	−0.437	−10.120	−0.158	−3.325
Problems with stomach/liver/kidneys	−0.419	−7.999	−0.115	−0.492	−8.807	−0.128	−0.963
Diabetes	−0.433	−4.502	−0.065	−0.228	−2.644	−0.038	1.583
Anxiety, depression, or bad nerves	−0.601	−12.123	−0.178	−0.538	−7.520	−0.111	0.728
Alcohol- or drug-related problems	−0.963	−2.399	−0.034	−0.465	−1.850	−0.026	1.051
Epilepsy	−0.646	−4.263	−0.060	−0.435	−2.644	−0.037	0.945
Migraine or frequent headaches	−0.185	−4.426	−0.064	−0.141	−2.223	−0.032	0.585
Other health problems	−0.632	−11.115	−0.158	−0.630	−8.891	−0.127	0.022
N	3,186	—	—	3,074	—	—	—
Adjusted R^2	0.251	—	—	0.246	—	—	—

Table 6.6. *Leisure-use satisfaction*

	Female			Male			Difference of estimates
	Estimates	t-value	Standardized estimates	Estimates	t-value	Standardized estimates	
Intercept	5.679	2.993	—	9.597	4.575	—	1.385
Ln(age)	−3.194	−3.016	−1.106	−5.953	−5.226	−2.011	−1.774
(Ln(age))^2	0.496	3.437	1.279	0.865	5.643	2.209	1.750
Minimum age	24.983	—	—	31.258	—	—	—
Ln(monthly household net income)	0.064	2.412	0.044	0.009	0.345	0.007	−1.438
Ln(adults)	−0.295	−3.928	−0.065	−0.112	−1.520	−0.025	1.739
Ln(children + 1)	−0.302	−8.193	−0.159	−0.142	−4.174	−0.074	3.200
Ln(years education)	−0.092	−2.435	−0.041	−0.105	−2.322	−0.040	−0.234
Dummy for missing education	−0.371	−1.463	−0.024	−0.458	−1.837	−0.031	−0.245
Ln(leisure hours)	0.054	0.888	0.017	0.301	3.750	0.092	2.441
Ln(working hours)	−0.116	−3.439	−0.190	−0.006	−0.140	−0.010	1.988
Dummy for missing working hours	−0.371	−2.663	−0.181	−0.154	−0.862	−0.070	0.956
Employed	−0.024	−0.226	−0.011	0.098	0.853	0.044	0.784
N	3,190	—	—	3,075	—	—	—
Adjusted R^2	0.112	—	—	0.092	—	—	—

Table 6.7. *Leisure-amount satisfaction*

	Female			Male			Difference of estimates
	Estimates	t-value	Standardized estimates	Estimates	t-value	Standardized estimates	
Intercept	6.379	3.381	—	11.784	5.530	—	1.899
Ln(age)	−4.037	−3.836	−1.398	−7.354	−6.354	−2.483	−2.120
(Ln(age))²	0.620	4.325	1.599	1.050	6.744	2.681	2.029
Minimum age	25.882	—	—	33.177	—	—	—
Ln(adults in the household)	−0.246	−3.304	−0.055	−0.063	−0.842	−0.014	1.738
Ln(children + 1)	−0.343	−9.343	−0.181	−0.150	−4.353	−0.079	3.826
Ln(years education)	−0.046	−1.235	−0.020	−0.012	−0.270	−0.005	0.570
Dummy for missing education	−0.330	−1.311	−0.021	−0.110	−0.437	−0.007	0.616
Ln(leisure hours)	0.228	3.738	0.070	0.413	5.067	0.126	1.817
Ln(working hours)	−0.141	−4.198	−0.231	−0.080	−1.792	−0.136	1.096
Dummy for missing working hours	−0.183	−1.321	−0.089	−0.258	−1.424	−0.117	−0.331
Employed	0.097	0.938	0.047	−0.197	−1.684	−0.089	−1.882
N	3,192			3,071			—
Adjusted R²	0.189			0.218			—

Social-Life Satisfaction

For social-life satisfaction, we see that an increase in the net household income has a strong positive effect for the female but no significant effect for the male. It may be that the higher income makes it possible to have daily help, to mechanize the household work, or to get childcare. All these things give the female more free time for social life. The number of children and adults in the household reduces the female's social-life satisfaction considerably, while this effect is not found for the male.

Marriage Satisfaction

We find that marriage satisfaction is again U-shaped with age, where the age profile for the female is somewhat (but not significantly) more pronounced than for the male. Both genders have their minimum at the same age of 36. The only significant difference between man and woman is with respect to education. The more education the man has, the less satisfied he is with his marriage. For the female this effect is not found.

Marriage-satisfaction answers present the smallest differences between males and females in the same household. Moreover, the coefficients do not seem to differ considerably between male and female, and the objective circumstances are fairly identical. It is also evident that marriage is evaluated highest of the domains. This may be partly caused by its social desirability and partly by the fact that marriage partners may talk about their answers.

General Satisfaction

Finally we turn to general satisfaction. Note that the 'no-job' dummy equals 1 when job satisfaction is set to 0. Thus, the impact on general satisfaction of the fact that a male does not work is equal to $(0^*0.126) + (1^*0.051) = 0.051$, which is larger than the average male contribution of job satisfaction; namely,[4] $(0.43^*0.126) + (0^*0.051) = 0.07$. The results show that if a male has a job-satisfaction level below the average, this male would achieve a higher general-satisfaction level by not working.

Table 6.10 shows that the aggregation weights for males and females do not significantly differ. We find that leisure use and social life are the main determinants of general satisfaction, both for the husband and the wife. This is similar to the results found for the Netherlands (Chapter 5). Comparison with Germany is impossible due to the difference in domain definitions. For females these two are followed by job, marriage, and health satisfactions, in that order. For males it is health, then job, then marriage satisfactions. Financial, housing, and leisure-amount levels are, for both genders, less important for general satisfaction.

---

[4] The average male satisfaction on a 0–10 scale corresponds to almost 7, which equals 0.43 when transformed by COLS.

Table 6.8. *Social-life satisfaction*

	Female			Male			Difference of estimates
	Estimates	t-value	Standardized estimates	Estimates	t-value	Standardized estimates	
Intercept	7.524	4.091	—	9.855	4.984	—	0.863
Ln(age)	−4.445	−4.332	−1.538	−5.628	−5.243	−1.902	−0.797
(Ln(age))^2	0.645	4.610	1.661	0.804	5.570	2.056	0.793
Minimum age	31.390	—	—	33.073	—	—	—
Ln(monthly household net income)	0.100	3.895	0.069	0.014	0.560	0.010	−2.362
Ln(children + 1)	−0.254	−7.113	−0.134	−0.168	−5.258	−0.088	1.787
Ln(adults)	−0.217	−2.989	−0.048	0.004	0.056	0.001	2.204
Ln(years education)	−0.008	−0.232	−0.004	−0.036	−0.835	−0.014	−0.485
Dummy for missing education	−0.310	−1.267	−0.020	0.067	0.287	0.005	1.114
Ln(leisure hours)	0.036	0.607	0.011	0.096	1.272	0.029	0.626
Ln(working hours)	−0.013	−0.401	−0.021	0.007	0.175	0.012	0.386
Dummy for missing working hours	−0.115	−0.855	−0.056	−0.170	−1.012	−0.077	−0.257
Employed	0.040	0.400	0.020	0.067	0.622	0.031	0.183
N	3,184	—	—	3,073	—	—	—
Adjusted R^2	0.072	—	—	0.060	—	—	—

Table 6.9. *Marriage satisfaction*

	Female			Male			Difference of estimates
	Estimates	t-value	Standardized estimates	Estimates	t-value	Standardized estimates	
Intercept	7.392	4.827	—	6.449	4.403	—	-0.445
Ln(age)	-3.248	-3.718	-1.120	-2.489	-3.052	-0.838	0.635
(Ln(age))^2	0.452	3.781	1.160	0.348	3.175	0.885	-0.643
Minimum age	36.339	—	—	35.852	—	—	—
Ln(monthly household net income)	-0.032	-1.390	-0.022	-0.043	-2.248	-0.030	-0.384
Ln(children + 1)	-0.251	-2.795	-0.132	-0.218	-2.760	-0.114	0.271
Ln(adults)	0.073	1.070	0.049	0.083	1.369	0.055	0.113
Ln(years education)	-0.010	-0.328	-0.005	-0.103	-3.069	-0.039	-2.018
Dummy for missing education	-0.270	-1.277	-0.017	-0.214	-1.156	-0.014	0.199
Household with 2 earners	0.049	1.222	0.022	0.003	0.117	0.002	-0.931
Ln(household-work hours)	0.009	0.463	0.007	0.002	0.205	0.002	-0.282
Dummy for missing household work	-0.193	-1.518	-0.021	0.079	0.607	0.007	1.496
N	3,168	—	—	3,048	—	—	—
Adjusted R^2	0.033	—	—	0.042	—	—	—

Table 6.10. *General satisfaction*

	Female			Male			Difference of estimates
	Estimates	t-value	Standardized estimates	Estimates	t-value	Standardized estimates	
Intercept	0.094	4.427	—	0.066	1.895	—	−0.693
Job satisfaction	0.163	9.446	0.118	0.126	8.352	0.092	−1.604
Financial satisfaction	0.086	7.513	0.073	0.092	7.608	0.078	0.365
Housing satisfaction	0.045	3.241	0.036	0.077	6.139	0.061	1.727
Health satisfaction	0.118	10.266	0.105	0.141	11.869	0.127	1.436
Leisure-use satisfaction	0.175	11.374	0.151	0.197	11.921	0.170	0.988
Leisure-amount satisfaction	0.015	1.189	0.014	0.025	1.803	0.024	0.529
Marriage satisfaction	0.133	9.071	0.083	0.120	8.136	0.075	−0.640
Social-life satisfaction	0.170	10.752	0.136	0.190	10.892	0.152	0.828
No job	0.080	3.447	0.035	0.051	2.300	0.023	−0.890
Z	0.057	3.895	0.055	−0.017	−0.916	−0.024	−3.151
N	3,022	—	—	3,022	—	—	—
Adjusted R^2	0.563	—	—	0.561	—	—	—

6.4. COVARIANCE BETWEEN SATISFACTIONS OF THE TWO PARTNERS IN THE HOUSEHOLD

In this section we examine the correlation and covariance structure of the error terms of the males and females as described by Equations (6.2)–(6.4). First, we look at the variances and covariances of the error terms for male, female, and household for each domain satisfaction. The results are presented in Table 6.11.

Table 6.11 shows that, for example, the variance of the error term of the male financial-satisfaction equation is 0.618 and the corresponding figure for the female is 0.671. The covariance between both error terms is the variance of the household unobservables (see Equation 6.4). These variances are presented in the third column—for financial satisfaction it equals 0.234. The last two columns present the percentage that the pure male and female error terms represent as a percentage of the total error terms, $\dfrac{\sigma^2(\varepsilon_M)}{\sigma^2(\varepsilon_{M+H})}, \dfrac{\sigma^2(\varepsilon_F)}{\sigma^2(\varepsilon_{F+H})}$. Table 6.11 shows that the pure individual error terms (male or female) are more important than the common error (ε_H). The household common unobservables represent at most about 40 percent of the total error term. For financial, housing, and marriage satisfaction the household common-error component is the largest. These are also the domain satisfactions for which the differences between partners are the smallest.

Second, we look at the total covariance matrix of the error terms. Table 6.12 shows the covariance matrix of the error terms for males and Table 6.13 for females. The tables show that there is indeed a correlation between the error terms of the domain satisfactions. The male and female covariance matrices look very similar. For example, the covariance between the error term of males' financial satisfaction and male housing satisfaction is 0.207. For females this is 0.239.

Table 6.14 shows the covariance matrix between male and female for all domain satisfactions. We see that there is a mild positive correlation for all domains between husband and wife. The average correlation coefficient is about 0.16.

6.5. CONCLUSION

The main findings of this chapter can now be summarized as follows: First, that the structural differences between males and females with respect to satisfaction analysis are not very large and mainly non-significant. This, together with the fact that a large number of objective characteristics are common to all members of the household, leads to the fact that differences in answers to subjective questions are very similar between male and female in the same household. This is especially true for satisfactions with respect to housing, financial, and marriage as compared to health, leisure, and job satisfactions. Second, that the error correlations between husband and wife are not very

Table 6.11. *Variances error terms, domain satisfactions*

	$\sigma^2(\epsilon_M) + \sigma^2(\epsilon_H)$	$\sigma^2(\epsilon_F) + \sigma^2(\epsilon_H)$	**Var(H)**	$\% \frac{\sigma^2(\epsilon_M)}{\sigma^2(\epsilon_M)+\sigma^2(\epsilon_H)}$	$\% \frac{\sigma^2(\epsilon_F)}{\sigma^2(\epsilon_F)+\sigma^2(\epsilon_H)}$
Financial satisfaction	0.618	0.671	0.234	0.622	0.651
Health satisfaction	0.605	0.625	0.036	0.941	0.943
Job satisfaction	0.302	0.303	0.024	0.920	0.920
House satisfaction	0.577	0.658	0.249	0.568	0.622
Leisure-use satisfaction	0.677	0.719	0.139	0.795	0.807
Leisure-amount satisfaction	0.697	0.711	0.121	0.827	0.830
Social-life satisfaction	0.602	0.672	0.157	0.739	0.767
Marriage satisfaction	0.375	0.502	0.143	0.620	0.716

Table 6.12. *Covariance matrix of error terms, male*

	General satisfaction	Financial satisfaction	Health satisfaction	Job satisfaction	Housing satisfaction	Leisure-use satisfaction	Leisure-amount satisfaction	Social-life satisfaction	Marriage satisfaction
General satisfaction	0.195	−0.003	−0.007	−0.005	−0.001	−0.001	−0.003	−0.001	−0.001
Financial satisfaction	−0.003	0.618	0.192	0.100	0.207	0.230	0.205	0.238	0.080
Health satisfaction	−0.007	0.192	0.605	0.085	0.157	0.211	0.158	0.214	0.086
Job satisfaction	−0.005	0.100	0.085	0.302	0.064	0.077	0.077	0.116	0.060
Housing satisfaction	−0.001	0.207	0.157	0.064	0.577	0.206	0.180	0.203	0.112
Leisure-use satisfaction	−0.001	0.230	0.211	0.077	0.206	0.677	0.435	0.434	0.126
Leisure-amount satisfaction	−0.003	0.205	0.158	0.077	0.180	0.435	0.697	0.369	0.118
Social-life satisfaction	−0.001	0.238	0.214	0.116	0.203	0.434	0.369	0.602	0.146
Marriage satisfaction	−0.001	0.080	0.086	0.060	0.112	0.126	0.118	0.146	0.375

Table 6.13. *Covariance matrix of error terms, female*

	General satisfaction	Financial satisfaction	Health satisfaction	Job satisfaction	Housing satisfaction	Leisure-use satisfaction	Leisure-amount satisfaction	Social-life satisfaction	Marriage satisfaction
General satisfaction	0.217	−0.002	−0.007	−0.002	0.001	0.001	0.002	0.001	0.000
Financial satisfaction	−0.002	0.671	0.180	0.052	0.239	0.220	0.223	0.244	0.128
Health satisfaction	−0.007	0.180	0.625	0.056	0.133	0.177	0.168	0.170	0.085
Job satisfaction	−0.002	0.052	0.056	0.303	0.067	0.066	0.070	0.083	0.065
Housing satisfaction	0.001	0.239	0.133	0.067	0.658	0.197	0.178	0.204	0.143
Leisure-use satisfaction	0.001	0.220	0.177	0.066	0.197	0.719	0.534	0.489	0.178
Leisure-amount satisfaction	0.002	0.223	0.168	0.070	0.178	0.534	0.711	0.441	0.163
Social-life satisfaction	0.001	0.244	0.170	0.083	0.204	0.489	0.441	0.672	0.199
Marriage satisfaction	0.000	0.128	0.085	0.065	0.143	0.178	0.163	0.199	0.502

Table 6.14. *Covariance matrix of error terms, household*

Male → Female ↓	General satisfaction	Financial satisfaction	Health satisfaction	Job satisfaction	Housing satisfaction	Leisure-use satisfaction	Leisure-amount satisfaction	Social-life satisfaction	Marriage satisfaction
General satisfaction	0.011	0.009	0.015	0.003	0.001	0.016	0.006	0.009	0.010
Financial satisfaction	0.009	0.234	0.035	0.013	0.092	0.094	0.083	0.104	0.042
Health satisfaction	0.015	0.035	0.036	0.000	0.029	0.048	0.048	0.054	0.022
Job satisfaction	0.003	0.013	0.000	0.024	0.013	0.020	0.017	0.025	0.014
Housing satisfaction	0.001	0.092	0.029	0.013	0.249	0.066	0.062	0.070	0.038
Leisure-use satisfaction	0.016	0.094	0.048	0.020	0.066	0.139	0.109	0.134	0.048
Leisure-amount satisfaction	0.006	0.083	0.048	0.017	0.062	0.109	0.121	0.108	0.044
Social-life satisfaction	0.009	0.104	0.054	0.025	0.070	0.134	0.108	0.157	0.053
Marriage satisfaction	0.010	0.042	0.022	0.014	0.038	0.048	0.044	0.053	0.143

strong. This means that the unobservables relate mostly to individual circumstances and not to characteristics that are common to both members of the household. The structural parts are strongly correlated, as most partners will have a similar background with respect to variables such as age and education. Third, that the correlation between the error terms of the different domain satisfactions for males and females must not be underestimated. This means that the unobservable characteristics that influence one domain satisfaction are correlated with the ones that influence another domain satisfaction. For example, a male's optimism is bound to affect all domain satisfactions.

These results may be evaluated as not spectacular and to be expected. For data-collection purposes, however, the results seem quite valuable. They imply that for most households it does not make much difference whether we interview the husband or the wife with respect to some domain satisfaction. Therefore, we may conceive of something as satisfaction of the household as such. Not because we propose a composite concept, say household utility or wellbeing, but because we observe that there is a strong correlation between husband and wife with respect to most satisfactions. This means that while data collectors should still ask both partners about, for example, their health and job satisfaction, they would not need to ask both of them about other domains, such as housing, financial, and marriage satisfactions.

7

The Impact of Past and Future on Present Satisfaction

7.1. INTRODUCTION

We saw in the preceding chapters that financial satisfaction does not only depend on income but on other intervening variables as well. In fact, present satisfaction is based on a norm of what is 'bad', 'sufficient', or 'good'. Such norms not only depend on the present situation, but also on what we have experienced in the past and on what we expect to experience in the future (Camerer and Loewenstein 2004; Elster and Loewenstein 1992; Helson 1947). This implies that the individual's current satisfaction will depend on his or her past experiences and expected future. In this chapter we shall try to operationalize this idea (for other attempts see Burchardt 2005, Easterlin 2005, and Senik 2006). We start with the memory part of the subject.

Contrary to what we might think, the memory process is still not well understood by psychologists (see e.g. Kahneman 1999; Stone, Shiffman, and DeVries 1999; Loewenstein and Prelec 1991; Frederick, Loewenstein, and O'Donoghue 2002). Hence, we feel free to expound our own ideas, however fragmentary, on the subject.

In the previous pages we considered satisfaction functions with respect to several domains. Some domains could be described rather precisely. For instance, the financial situation is characterized by some objectively measurable variables like income y and some intervening variables x. For a specific situation (y, x) the corresponding financial satisfaction is then $U = F(y; x)$. We may consider the function $F(. ; x)$ as the *norm*, by which a financial situation y is evaluated. Other domains like marriage or social life are difficult to describe by objectively measurable variables, although we are able to express our satisfaction U with reference to those domains on a numerical scale. In this chapter we will restrict ourselves, therefore, to an empirical application with respect to financial satisfaction.

If we assume that past income influences present satisfaction norms, this implies that our log-income history $\{y(t)\}_{t=-\infty}^{t=0}$ should be included as an argument in our present satisfaction function. If we assume that other historical variables z are also relevant, they should be included as well. Then our relevant history would be $\{y(t), z(t)\}_{t=-\infty}^{t=0}$. Now the first question is what the relevant history variables are. The answer may be different depending on the domain. For instance, past

This chapter is partly based on Van Praag and Van Weeren (1988).

income will be a relevant variable for financial satisfaction, but probably it will not be directly relevant for evaluating one's marriage. The operationalization of a *history* in terms of objectively measurable variables is not easy. That is another reason for restricting ourselves to *financial* satisfaction.

It may be that each period-income in the past has its own influence on present norms, but it seems more probable that the history can be represented by one or a few summary measures. Let us assume that the impact of history on a norm may be summarized by one or a few parameters, which we denote by $\mu(\{y(t)\}_{t=-\infty}^{t=0})$. The μ may stand for a parameter vector. It implies that we assume that our satisfaction function (or *norm*) reads $U = F(y; x, \mu)$, where x depends only on current variables and μ depends on the history.

The next question is then how the parameter μ is generated by past history.

Usually we have a continuous profile in which $y(t)$ evolves along a smooth path over time with possibly moderate random fluctuations. This is typically the case for an income flow. In that case it seems appropriate to assume that a memory-weighted average of the income flow $\mu = \sum_{-\infty}^{0} w_t y_t$ is the representative for past experiences, where w stands for a specific weighting pattern over time. It stands to reason that the weighting of incomes a long time back becomes negligible. We call $\{w_t\}_{-\infty}^{0}$ the *memory-weighting* distribution, where we assume that weights add up to 1. In the literature it is frequently assumed that such a distribution is exponential and that it is the same for everybody. In this study we will not make those assumptions. The main objective of this chapter will be to *estimate* that weighting pattern.

An assumption that is frequently made (although not explicitly mentioned) is that the memory-weighting distribution would be the same irrespective of the life domain we have in mind. However, a moment of reflection tells us that the norms to evaluate the content of your daily newspaper are much less dependent on what you experienced a month ago than your financial situation a month ago on evaluating your present financial situation. In short, the memory distribution and the time horizon may vary with the life domain. It is an empirical question whether they do or not.

An interesting characteristic is the half-life value of a memory-weighting distribution. It is a handy indicator of memory decay. We define that value as the median $t_{-\frac{1}{2}}$ such that $\sum_{t_{-1/2}}^{0} w_t = \frac{1}{2}$. For instance, if the half value is reached at one month back we may typify the memory span as short, while we may call it long if the half value is five years. Obviously, what is long and short will depend on the life domain in question and the personal characteristics of the individual. For instance, we may assume that an adolescent has a lower half value than an adult.

Endogenous memory weights

There is another type of remembering which is frequently the subject of psychological investigations. We shall not take this as our point of departure, but this model is important enough to mention; we call it *endogenous remembering*. There we distinguish between less and more important life events. Say a specific event has taken place three years ago. Whether we still have it in our memory now depends on the impact the life event had on us. For instance, if it was a dinner in a restaurant with our spouse, there is a good chance that we will have forgotten it by now, if eating out is more or less of a routine for us. However, if that dinner happened to be our first meeting, there is a higher chance that we will still remember it three years later and even twenty years later. In this approach the weight has less to do with the time period elapsed, since the event took place, than with the importance y of the event y_t. The weight pattern over time becomes *endogenous*.

At specific (mostly random) moments $t_1, \ldots, t_k$ a specific rare event takes place. This may be a special pain inflicted, a temporary disease, falling in love, a prize in a lottery, a substantial promotion. The specific domain descriptor y is constant, say zero, except for a few discrete moments or periods, when it takes the values $y_{t_1}, \ldots, y_{t_k}$. In those cases it may be argued that the exception, say $\mu = \max(y_{t_1}, \ldots, y_{t_k})$, becomes the measuring rod for evaluating new rare events. The peaks in the past determine the norms in the present. Although we do not ignore the existence of this type of memory nor its practical importance for the understanding of human psychology, it seems to be less important for the explanation of the genesis of everyday norms, which are not shaped by a few impressive life events but by everyday practice (see Kahneman 1999).

In what follows we shall only consider the memory process of the first kind, which we might call *exogenous* weighting.

Extension to the future
A fairly natural extension is that norms are also partly determined by what one anticipates of the future. For instance, if you expect your income to increase in the future your satisfaction with current income will be lower than if you expect your income to fall in the future. Similarly, if your health is expected to deteriorate in the future you evaluate your present health higher than if you expect it to remain at the same level in the foreseeable future.

Therefore, we suggest that the memory-weighting distribution should be extended to a memory *and* anticipation weighting distribution $\{w_t\}_{t=-\infty}^{t=\infty}$ and we assume that the parameter μ is of the type $\sum_{-\infty}^{\infty} w_t y_t$.

Then, we may consider two half-value periods $t_{-1/2}$ and $t_{1/2}$, where the latter period refers to the future. Moreover, it may be helpful to distinguish between the total weights, we assign to the past, the present, and the future, defined as

$$W_p = \sum_{-\infty}^{-1} w_t.$$

$$W_c = w_0$$

$$W_f = \sum_{1}^{\infty} w_t$$

respectively.

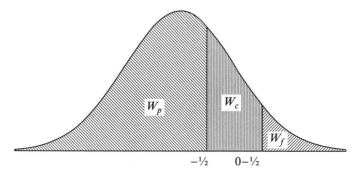

Figure 7.1. *A time–weight density function*

A natural continuous generalization is based on a time-weight density function (see Fig. 7.1). We define $W_p = \int_{-\infty}^{-\frac{1}{2}} w(t)dt$, $W_c = \int_{-\frac{1}{2}}^{\frac{1}{2}} w(t)dt$, and $W_f = \int_{\frac{1}{2}}^{\infty} w(t)dt$.

7.2. THE MODEL AND ITS OPERATIONALIZATION

In this chapter we return to the IEQ already introduced in Section 2.8. We found that individuals evaluated income levels according to a log-normal function $U = N(\ln y; \mu, \sigma)$. We saw that we can distinguish between two concepts of an individual welfare function: the *virtual* WFI according to which *one* individual evaluates *all* levels, and the *true* WFI which describes how different individuals evaluate their *own* actual income. We also stressed that the first concept is comparable to a *decision* utility function and the second one to an *experienced* utility function in the sense of Kahneman, Wakker, and Sarin (1997). The virtual welfare function can be seen as representing an individual norm on what is a 'bad' or a 'good' income. The true WFI may be interpreted as a 'social' norm. It is a synthetic concept, derived from individual norms, but not an individual norm itself. Hence, to find out more on the genesis of an individual norm we prefer the analysis of the virtual WFI to that of the 'true' WFI.

We saw in Chapter 2 that the answers by individual n on the IEQ may be modelled and explained by the equation

$$\ln(c_{in}) = \alpha_i \ln(y_n) + \beta_i \ln(fs_n) + \gamma_i + \varepsilon_{in} \qquad (i = 1, \ldots, 6), \qquad (7.1)$$

and that their average μ is explained in the same way by

$$\mu_n = \alpha \ln(y_n) + \beta \ln(fs_n) + \gamma + \varepsilon_n \qquad (7.2)$$

Those equations give a foothold for the model suggested earlier. The responses c_i describe the norm on income. Assuming that past incomes and anticipated future incomes determine the norm as well, we replace present income by a sequence of annual incomes and we write

$$\ln(c_i) = \alpha_i \sum_{-\infty}^{\infty} w_t \ln(y_t) + \beta_i \ln(fs) + \gamma_i + \varepsilon_i \qquad (i = 1, \ldots, 6). \qquad (7.3)$$

Hence, we assume that present norms with respect to what presents a 'good' or 'bad' income are not anchored on current income alone but rather on a weighted average of past, present, and anticipated income levels. It stands to reason that the observed income sequence is finite and that in practice we have to truncate the time series. If the weights vanish fairly quickly, it seems acceptable to truncate after a few years. A similar approach may be tried on μ. Although the c_i's are correlated, they provide more information than their average μ.

Hence, our basic model will be the six-equation system above, where we assume that coefficients are equation-specific except for the time weights w_t.

The data set which we use stems from the German Socio-Economic Panel (1997). In the 1997 wave an IEQ module was included. Moreover, we know from the panel the incomes for the years 1992–2000. Hence, if we truncate the income sequence to five years back and three years in the future, we may use this data set to estimate the system above and more specifically the w_t's. The year 1997 is then equated with $t = 0$. There are in practice various methods of operationalization. The first problem that arises is with the sequence of future incomes $\{y_t\}_1^\infty$. The researcher knows those incomes in retrospect, because the data set he observes stems from 2001. However, in 1997 the individual who answered the IEQ did not know his future income, but he based his norm on a prediction of his future income. Hence, there are two options. Either we take the future incomes as the real ones, which we have in the data set, or we replace them by predicted future incomes. We choose the latter option.

In fact, we can also question how far actual past net household incomes determine the norms. Incomes always include a random element: windfall profits, etc.; many people do not even know their exact monthly net income, because it fluctuates from month to month, even for individuals with an essentially fixed income like civil servants. We assume that the past income levels which determine the evaluation of present income are not the real ones, but a smoothed out version of them, where random fluctuations from year to year are ignored. We assume that norms, which are typically long-term ingrained standards, are determined by a *structural* income level and its *structural* development out of the past into the future. If we opt for predicted incomes we have to estimate an earnings profile for each individual. So we come to the distinction into four options as described in Table 7.1 below.

Table 7.1. *Four ways to operationalize past and future incomes*

	Real values	Structural values
Past income		X
Future income		X

We prefer the second column of Table 7.1 both for the past and the future. For the structural option we estimate an individual net-household-earnings profile by the equation

$$\ln(y_{n,t}) = \alpha_0 + \alpha_1 GEN + \alpha_2 \ln age + \alpha_3 \{\ln(age)\}^2 + \alpha_4 LEDU +$$
$$+ \alpha_5 \, EARN1 \, TG + \alpha_6 \, EARN1 \, NTG + \ldots + \alpha_7 self + \qquad (7.4)$$
$$+ \alpha_8 \, NONWORK + \alpha_t \, time + \varepsilon_n + \varepsilon_{nt},$$

where we use the answers of the main breadwinner, that is, the one who has the largest individual income in the household. We assume that log–(net-household) income is a quadratic function of log–age, which determines the earnings profile over the lifetime. The number of income earners in the household, the education level and gender(GEN) of the respondent, and the answer on the question whether he or she lives in steady partnership are assumed to be income determinants. The variable LEDU stands for the logarithm of the years of formal education. The dummy variable EARN1 TG equals 1 if there is one breadwinner and there are two adults living in partnership. This is the traditional household. The dummy EARN1 NTG stands for the single earner not living with a partner. The two-earner household is taken as the reference. Moreover, we add terms for those who are self-employed or not working. Finally, we add time dummies to account for inflation and growth over the years. It is evident that specific individuals will not have 'average' incomes. Some individuals will be 'structurally' 10 percent above the average profile while others are structurally 5 percent below the profile. This results from specific individual traits, which we cannot observe directly. Hence, these are part of the error term. That is why we split the error term into an individual random effect ε_n and the usual error term ε_{nt}. The individual random effect can be estimated per individual by averaging the estimated residuals per individual over the years. The average of ε_{nt} is zero, while the individual effect is constant over time per individual. This yields an estimate of the individual random effect $\hat{\varepsilon}_n$. The predicted log–income per individual in each year is now assessed by filling in his or her individual characteristics *plus* ε_n.

The estimation of the weight pattern poses similar problems. We may estimate the weights directly from Equation (7.4). That is, each w_t is estimated separately. However, it seems an attractive supposition that the weighting pattern itself does not remain the same over life, but that it changes with age. For instance, we may assume that individuals at the beginning of life and when they near retirement age are more past-oriented and that they are more future-oriented during the active stage of life. The length of the time horizon, in a sense to be exactly defined later on, may vary in a similar way. This suggests the estimation of age-specific weights. It is clear that even further refinements with respect to other individual characteristics than age are conceivable as well. It appeared impossible to include all these refinements without any a priori functional specification of the weight distribution. We specify the weights according to a mass distribution over time. The weights are then defined by

$$w_t = F\left(t + \frac{1}{2}; \gamma_\tau\right) - F\left(t - \frac{1}{2}; \gamma_\tau\right) \quad (t = \ldots, -1, 0, 1, \ldots), \qquad (7.5)$$

where $F(.)$ stands for a distribution function and γ_τ stands for a parameter vector. The distribution is defined on the real axis $(-\infty, \infty)$, where the point zero corresponds to the present moment in time. The choice of the distribution is not a trivial problem. Memory weighting is frequently studied in and outside the economic context. There the weights are only stretched over the real half-axis $(0, \infty)$ where a positive value t corresponds to 't years back'. The most popular specification is then the exponential specification where $F(t) = 1 - e^{-\gamma t}$ $(t \in (0, \infty), \gamma > 0)$. The corresponding density function is $f(t) = \gamma e^{-\gamma t}$, as sketched in Figure 7.2.

The discrete analogue is described by the weights

$$w_t = (e^{-\gamma(t-\frac{1}{2})} - e^{-\gamma(t+\frac{1}{2})}),$$

with a trivial modification for the first weight w_0. The interesting point is that the ratio between two adjacent weights is constant

$$w_t/w_{t-1} = e^{-\gamma}.$$

Hence, the memory decay is described by a geometric sequence with a ratio $e^{-\gamma}$. The value of γ is unknown. There are many different estimates of γ varying from 0.02 to more than 1. Notice that the value can only be interpreted given a specific unit of time. For instance, a γ value of 0.05 per month is equivalent to 0.60 per year. Although this exponential choice is nearly always made in the literature—its similarity to special physical phenomena and to the economic discounting mechanism is obvious—it is not at all evident why the pattern should be exponential. It describes a very fast pattern of decay. In recent literature it is sometimes suggested that memory weighting should be described by a

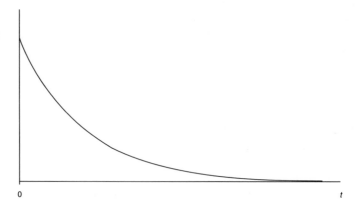

Figure 7.2. *Exponential memory-discount function*

hyperbolic density function. Its distribution function is $F(t) = 1 - t^{-\gamma} (t \in (1, \infty), \gamma > 0)$. In that case the separate weights are $w_t = \gamma((t - \frac{1}{2})^{-\gamma} - (t + \frac{1}{2})^{-\gamma})$. Those weights decrease at a rate which is 'time-dependent'. The weights become particularly small when t becomes large, but the ratio between two succeeding weights tends to 1. If we calculate the discount weights assuming an exponential model, while in reality the discounting is performed hyperbolically, the implicit discount rate over longer time horizons is lower than the implicit discount rate over shorter time horizons (see Frederick, Lowenstein, and O'Donoghue 2002, p. 360). This is conform to an experiment by Thaler (1981), who asked subjects to specify the amount of money they would require in one month/one year/ten years from now to make them indifferent to receiving \$15 now. The implicit annual discount rates were 345 percent, 120 percent and 19 percent, respectively. Van Praag (1968, ch. 6) also suggested a hyperbolic discount function.

A similar model is used for the impact of the future, in which a positive value t corresponds to 't years in the future'. This exponential model is routinely used in financial economics and savings theory. An amount of \$100 now is equivalent to an amount of $(1 - r)$. \$100 one year from now and $(1 - r)^2$. \$100 two years from now, where γ is set as equal to the market interest rate r.

The problem we face now is that we have to describe the memory and anticipation weighting *simultaneously* by one distribution over the real axis $(-\infty, \infty)$. Although in theory any mass distribution may be suggested, there are in practice only a few which seem attractive. The first option might be the two-sided exponential, which we define by its density function

$$f(t) = \begin{cases} \delta \gamma_p e^{-\gamma_p(-t)}, & \text{if } t \leq 0 \\ (1 - \delta)\gamma_f e^{-\gamma_f(t)}, & \text{if } t > 0 \\ \gamma_p, \gamma_f > 0; \delta \in [0, 1]. \end{cases} \tag{7.6}$$

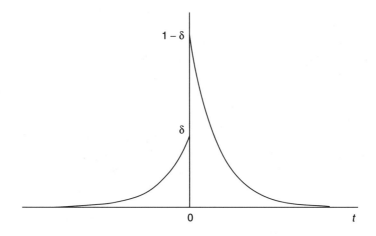

Figure 7.3. *A double-exponential time-discount function*

This specification, which may be seen as a direct generalization of the previous two exponential specifications, which are merged, is not very attractive because at the present moment $t = 0$ the density is not continuous. The left and right branches both tend to infinity. Why should the present have such an exclusive position? Moreover, both the left and right branches exhibit exponential decay, albeit with different decay rates γ_p and γ_f respectively. The parameter δ gives the possibility that the weights on the past and on the future may differ. All in all the distribution has three parameters. If we doubt the idea that the 'joint' has to be at $t = 0$, which is indeed not obvious at all, we would need a fourth shift parameter. In short, what we need is a flexible, everywhere continuous, and differentiable mass distribution, defined on the whole real time axis. The choice will always be in some sense arbitrary as long as we have no empirical experience with a widely accepted function. It seems to us that this is the first time[1] that the problem has been posed in this form. Hence, we do not have a literature we can draw upon and we have to make our own choice.

As it covers the whole real axis, we choose a normal distribution function $N(t; \mu_\tau, \sigma_\tau)$. The normal is well known to be symmetric around μ_τ. If $\mu_\tau = 0$, it implies that the weight distribution is symmetric around the present $t = 0$. If $\mu_\tau > 0$, it implies that the individual puts less weight on the past than on the future, as $N(0; \mu_\tau, \sigma_\tau) < N(\mu_\tau; \mu_\tau, \sigma_\tau) = \frac{1}{2}$, where $N(0; \mu_\tau, \sigma_\tau)$ is the accumulated weight before the present moment. We call such an individual *future-oriented*. We will call μ_τ the *time focus* of the individual. If it is negative the individual is called *past-oriented*. In a similar way we may consider the second parameter σ_τ. We call it the individual's *time span*. This parameter determines the shape of the density function around μ_τ. If σ_τ tends to zero, the weight distribution becomes more and more concentrated about μ_τ and will ultimately tend to a point mass at the point μ_τ. Let $\mu_\tau = 0$, then the weight[2] $N(\sigma_\tau; 0, \sigma_\tau) - N(0; 0, \sigma_\tau) = 34.13$ percent. So if an individual has a $\sigma_\tau = 1$, it follows that 34 percent of the total time weight lies in the first year ahead and that another 34 percent lies in the past year. However, if $\sigma_\tau = 0.5$ we find that 34 percent of the total time weight lies in the time-span of the coming half year and another 34 percent in the last six months. Hence, it seems that for the second individual time runs twice as fast as for the first individual. Let us inversely assume that the real distribution remains the same but that the unit of time is changed from a year into a month. In that case the individual who has $\sigma_\tau = 1$, if we reckon in terms of years, will have $\sigma_\tau = 12$ when we reckon in months.

It is well known that individuals perceive the flow of time as varying. Some individuals have the impression at the end of the year that the speed of time has been fast, while others perceive the same year as having elapsed very slowly. Obviously, this is a *subjective* perception of the *velocity of time*. The same holds for one individual who is comparing the experienced lengths of two years, say, when he

[1] With the exception of Van Praag and Van Weeren (1988), on which this chapter is based.
[2] According to standard tables of the normal distribution.

was twenty and when he was fifty years old. Although the years have the same objective length, most individuals in the middle of life will have the idea that a year when one was young took longer than in middle age. Hence, we can consider the time span σ_τ, or rather $1/\sigma_\tau$, as a measure of the subjectively perceived *velocity* of time. If σ_τ decreases, the velocity of time increases. In the limiting case that σ_τ tends to zero, the velocity of time tends to infinity. Any moment other than the present moment will lie in the distant past or future and will have no effect on present income satisfaction. Such a person lives in the moment.

The same analysis with respect to the role of σ_τ holds when we assume that the time focus μ_τ is unequal to zero. In the limiting case that σ_τ tends to zero but $\mu_\tau < 0$, the individual lives with fixed norms (with respect to financial satisfaction), where the norms have been fixed at a date μ_τ years ago.

Given these interpretations of μ_τ and σ_τ, it stands to reason that these parameters will differ between individuals, as most individuals have different time perceptions.

We assume that the parameters will (at least) depend on *age* and we postulate

$$\mu_\tau = \gamma_{\mu,\,0} + \gamma_{\mu,\,1} age + \gamma_{\mu,\,2} age^2$$
$$\ln(\sigma_\tau) = \gamma_{\sigma,\,0} + \gamma_{\sigma,\,1} age + \gamma_{\sigma,\,2} age^2. \tag{7.7}$$

The discrete weights are now operationalized as

$$w_t = N(t + \tfrac{1}{2}; \mu_\tau, \sigma_\tau) - N(t - \tfrac{1}{2}; \mu_\tau, \sigma_\tau) \quad (t = \ldots, -1, 0, 1, \ldots). \tag{7.8}$$

In practice, t will be bounded from below and above at $t_{min}(< 0)$ and $t_{max}(> 0)$. We define for the outer weights

$$w_{t_{min}} = N(t_{min} + \tfrac{1}{2}; \mu_\tau, \sigma_\tau)$$

$$w_{t_{max}} = 1 - N(t_{max} - \tfrac{1}{2}; \mu_\tau, \sigma_\tau).$$

In the next section we will present the estimates of this model.

7.3. THE MODEL ESTIMATED

The model sketched above will now be estimated. Our objective is to estimate equation (7.3) in which we have added some dummy and interaction variables. The variables to be explained are the six levels $c_i(i = 1, \ldots, 6)$. As the errors between the six equations are correlated according to our findings in Chapter 2, we could enhance the efficiency by applying a SUR approach. However, as our model is non-linear and the number of observations is very large, we do not utilize this SUR option. This may mean that the reliability of the estimates is somewhat overrated. It does not hamper the consistency of the estimates. Notice that each of the six equations has its own coefficients except for the memory and anticipation weights that are shared.

Table 7.2. *The household-earnings function, West Germany*

	Estimate	Standard deviation
Gender	−0.022	0.005
Constant	−1.021	0.234
Ln(age)	3.999	0.126
(Ln(age))^2	−0.496	0.017
Ln(education)	0.635	0.010
1 breadwinner with partner	−0.209	0.005
1 breadwinner without partner	−0.642	0.006
Self-employed	0.091	0.008
Not working	−0.201	0.006
1992	−0.104	0.009
1993	−0.069	0.009
1994	−0.051	0.009
1995	−0.035	0.008
1996	−0.016	0.008
1998	0.0076	0.008
1999	0.028	0.008
2000	0.043	0.007
N	44.490	—
R^2	0.456	—

We start by estimating equation (7.4), which describes the life-household earning profile for the population of West German workers.

The results are presented in Table 7.2.

We see that there is a pronounced age pattern with a top at age 56. The one-earner household has about 20 percent less and the one-earner household with only one adult has about 64 percent less. The latter type is the single person or the 'incomplete' family. Being self-employed pays somewhat more, and the household where the main breadwinner does not have a paid job earns about 20 percent less. The income elasticity with respect to years of education is 0.635.

We explained in the previous section that we could distinguish between four options when estimating equation (7.3). The first choice to be made is whether we use free weights or parametric weights. The second choice is whether to use the observed incomes or the incomes as smoothed out by the earnings equation. With respect to the first choice we did not find attractive outcomes when we left the weights free. In our view this is because the weights are not the same for every individual but depend on age. Hence, we would have to estimate weights w_t(age) for each t (see equations 7.7 and 7.8). We considered that too formidable a task. We do not reproduce the outcomes for the free-weights case, because they were not interesting.

With respect to the second choice option, observed or smoothed-out incomes, our results are less clear. However, as we assume that the norm on income is based on remembered incomes, we think that a smoothing-out pattern is imposed on incomes by the individual. For anticipated incomes there is still less reason to use the real income values, which are not known to the individual at present (but only to the researcher with hindsight). The first six lines present the estimates of Equation (7.7). These estimates are the main subject of this chapter. The other lines refer to the constant and the family-size effect, which we assume to be dependent on the response level ('bad', 'good', etc.). We include them not so much because we are interested in them here, as to get a correct specification. As we estimate six equations we specify the coefficients as $\alpha_i = \alpha_1 + \Delta\alpha_i$ for $(i = 2, \ldots, 6)$. In the first-level block we present the α_1 and in the following

Table 7.3. *The memory and anticipation weighting system*

	West German workers 1997		Dutch households 1979	
	Estimate	Standard deviation	Estimate	Standard deviation
μ_τ-equation constant	−10.5531	1.2345	−4.5736	0.3242
Age	0.4906	0.0653	0.2039	0.0134
Age^2	−0.0055	0.0008	−0.0021	0.0001
σ_τ-equation constant	2.6622	0.8640	3.7730	0.2944
Age	−0.1076	0.0419	−0.1450	0.0130
Age^2	0.0014	0.0005	0.0014	0.0001
First-level constant	3.5150	0.1526	3.79	0.15
Ln(family size +1)	0.1981	0.0132	0.11	0.01
Ln(income)	0.4686	0.0188	0.56	0.02
Second-level constant	−0.3464	0.2120	−0.40	0.22
Ln(family size +1)	−0.0271	0.0182	−0.01	0.01
Ln(income)	0.0707	0.0261	0.05	0.02
Third-level constant	−0.4166	0.2118	−0.72	0.22
Ln(family size +1)	−0.0255	0.0183	−0.02	0.02
Ln(income)	0.0999	0.0261	0.10	0.02
Fourth-level constant	−0.4624	0.2096	−0.94	0.22
Ln(family size +1)	−0.0363	0.0181	−0.03	0.02
Ln(income)	0.1294	0.0258	0.14	0.02
Fifth-level constant	−0.6884	0.2095	−1.23	0.22
Ln(family size +1)	−0.1026	0.0248	−0.06	0.02
Ln(income)	0.1947	0.0258	0.19	0.02
Sixth-level constant	−0.9780	0.2118	−1.42	0.22
Ln(family size +1)	−0.1455	0.0184	−0.08	0.02
Ln(income)	0.2706	0.0261	0.23	0.02
N	8,482(resp.)	—	598(indiv.)	—
R^2	—	0.73	—	0.75

Note: Since we drew on past research for the 1979 data set, it was impossible for us to retrieve the data and to streamline the table. Therefore, the number of decimal points is taken over from the original 1988 publication. The number of observations in the 1979 data set refers to the number of individuals involved. The earlier study is not based on a panel data set. The earnings function is estimated on the basis of a cross-section. A more detailed description of this Dutch data set, which is part of a data set of several European countries, can be found in Hagenaar (1986).

blocks we present the increments $\Delta\alpha_i$. In the third and fourth columns we present similar estimates for a sample of Dutch households, collected in 1979. The latter results are borrowed from Van Praag and Van Weeren (1988).

Let us now look at the time-weighting system of the German sample. First, we observe that all coefficients are significant. However, we have to be honest. In this type of 'soft' observations one may expect and indeed one finds a number of outliers, in the sense that tails of the distribution of residuals are too fat for a normal distribution. Hence, we applied a kind of 'robust regression'. After a first round we discarded the observations for which the relative residuals $\left|\dfrac{\varepsilon^2}{S^{(2)}}\right|$, where the denominator stands for the residual variance, exceed a number α. We found in practice that this worked well when we set $\alpha = 0.5$. For less restrictive bounds we found nonsensical and/or non-significant estimates. As a consequence we have removed about 10 percent of the observations. This procedure may strike the reader as a bit arbitrary, and we cannot ignore that. However, the primary assumption that errors would be normally distributed also contains an element of arbitrariness. The modern literature on robust estimation actually stems from that recognition. It is acknowledged that 'errors' do not follow an exact normal distribution, and hence that the estimated errors are not completely normally distributed but contain 'outliers'. This leads to a modification of the weighting process, where some squared residuals are assigned a greater influence than others. The idea is that outliers have smaller influence or no influence at all. Our way of handling outliers has to be seen in that tradition. The problem of identifying outliers is to some extent a value judgement. We do not want to remove too many observations, but we also do not like to have a lot of outliers. We chose the above procedure, which led to stable and plausible estimates and a removal of about 10 percent of the observations. Observations correspond in this context to the six levels of the IEQ. So each individual stands for six observations if the IEQ has been filled out completely. Most of the removed observations refer to the extremes; that is, the first and sixth levels of the IEQ. It is intuitively plausible that these levels yield the most inaccurate responses. This is because many individuals regard 'excellent' or 'very bad' as levels that are very remote from their present position, and consequently they are less able to give realistic estimates of those income levels.

Graphs of μ_τ and σ_τ as function of age for the West German data are depicted in Figures 7.4*a* and 7.4*b* below.

The time focus μ_τ appears to vary with age. The top of the parabola is found at the age of about 44 years and the maximum value of μ_τ equals about half a year. This implies that individuals at the age of 44 are future-oriented. Their time focus is about six months ahead. We see that σ_τ varies with age as well. Its minimum is reached at the age of 41. As we interpret $1/\sigma_\tau$ as the subjectively perceived *velocity of time* of the individual it implies that the velocity of time increases with age up to about the age of 41, after which it falls again. We illustrate this behavior by the graphs of μ_τ and σ_τ as functions of *age*.

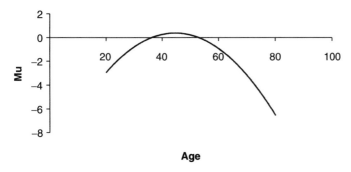

Figure 7.4a. *Behavior of* μ_τ *as a function of age*

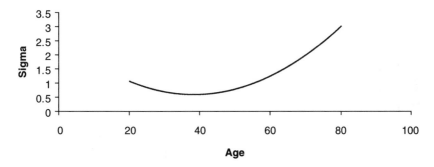

Figure 7.4b. *Behavior of* σ_τ *as a function of age*

It is now interesting to look at how the weight-density function looks for three representative ages; 25, 45, and 65. We see that for a 25-year-old financial satisfaction norms are largely determined by past experiences. For somebody of 45 we find that norms are derived for a good part from anticipations about the future. The velocity of time is relatively high. For the elderly, norms are based on the past and the velocity of time slows down. It is really surprising how much the older Dutch results resemble the German ones. Qualitatively we have about the same time-weighting pattern.

In Table 7.4 we present the resulting estimates for the weights on past, present, and future and the two half-value times. We see that, at the beginning of life the weight on the past (70%) and present (13%) together is large and the weight assigned to the future–more than half a year ahead–is consequently small (17%). The future half-value time is about a year and a half. As people grow older the weight distribution shifts to the future. After midlife (45) the weight on the future is even greater than on the past. When the age of 53 has been reached, the process is reversed. If we interpret σ as a measure for the relevant time horizon, we see that the time horizon decreases until 41

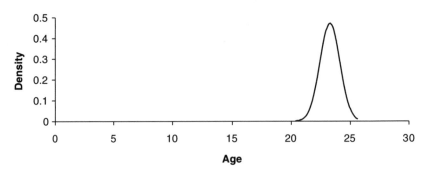

Figure 7.5a. *Time-density function for an individual of 25 years of age*

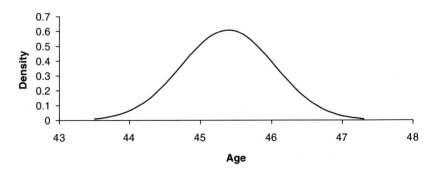

Figure 7.5b. *Time-density function for an individual of 45 years of age*

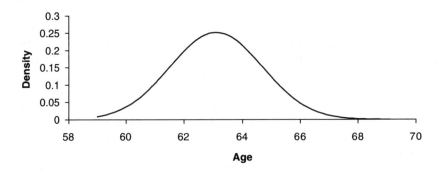

Figure 7.5c. *Time-density function for an individual of 65 years of age*

Table 7.4. *Weights on past, present and future and half-value times for various ages*

age	μ_τ	σ_τ	$t_{-\frac{1}{2}}$	W_p	W_c	W_f	$t_{\frac{1}{2}}$	r_{subj}
25	−1.7322	2.2965	−2.60	0.7042	0.1303	0.1655	1.45	1.541
35	−0.1328	1.7855	−1.58	0.4185	0.2200	0.3615	1.50	0.042
45	0.3644	1.8269	−1.46	0.3181	0.2115	0.4704	1.68	−0.109
55	−0.2407	2.4599	−2.07	0.4580	0.1603	0.3817	1.91	0.040
65	−1.9480	4.3591	−4.05	0.6301	0.0827	0.2872	2.69	0.103
75	−4.7576	10.1659	−9.20	0.6623	0.0352	0.3025	5.72	0.046
85	−8.6694	31.2002	−24.88	0.6033	0.0123	0.3844	18.47	0.009

and increases thereafter. At the age of 85 it is seen to have become very large indeed. This is a very interesting result, as it shows that the memory and anticipation process differs with age. We see as well that the bulk of the weight lies in the future from the age of 36 to approximately 53.

We may now ask whether there are more variables, which may be influencing the memory process. We tried two variables which could have that effect. The first is gender and the second is education (in years). We modified Equation (7.7) as

$$\mu_\tau = (\gamma_{\mu, 0} + \gamma_{\mu, 0}^M MALE) + \gamma_{\mu, 1} age + \gamma_{\mu, 2} age^2$$
$$\ln(\sigma_\tau) = (\gamma_{\sigma, 0} + \gamma_{\sigma, 0}^M MALE) + \gamma_{\sigma, 1} age + \gamma_{\sigma, 2} age^2. \tag{7.9}$$

The dummy MALE is 1 if the respondent is a male. A similar specification is used to include the variable EDU, the years of formal education.

$$\mu_\tau = (\gamma_{\mu, 0} + \gamma_{\mu, 0}^E EDU) + \gamma_{\mu, 1} age + \gamma_{\mu, 2} age^2$$
$$\ln(\sigma_\tau) = (\gamma_{\sigma, 0} + \gamma_{\sigma, 0}^E EDU) + \gamma_{\sigma, 1} age + \gamma_{\sigma, 2} age^2. \tag{7.10}$$

The results are presented in Table 7.5. We only show the time-weighting parameters. The other estimates hardly changed at all.

From Table 7.5 it appears that the influence of gender is very significant. Males seem to be more past-oriented than females, while their time span is considerably larger, and consequently their velocity of time much lower than that of females.

The effect of education cannot be ignored either. We see that individuals with higher education are more future-oriented and that their time span σ_τ is somewhat higher. Notice that education is defined in calendar years. Hence, the effect of an additional year is quite considerable.

7.4. APPLICATIONS

An income reduction
In this section we apply the previous findings to the question of what the desirable smoothing-out or adaptation pattern should be when someone loses

Table 7.5a/b. *The gender- and education-specific memory and anticipation parameters, West Germany, 1997*

(a) Gender-dependent weights			(b) Education-dependent weights		
	Estimate	Standard deviation		Estimate	Standard deviation
μ_τ-equation constant	−10.9228	1.2520	Constant	−11.8058	1.2939
Age	0.5350	0.0661	Age	0.4847	0.0647
Age^2	−0.0061	0.0008	Age^2	−0.0053	0.0008
Male	−0.7321	0.1562	Education	0.1088	0.0389
σ_τ-equation constant	3.2002	0.8904	Constant	1.6273	0.8882
Age linear	−0.1441	0.0435	Age	−0.1119	0.0417
Age^2	0.0018	0.0005	Age^2	0.0014	0.0005
Male	0.2791	0.1246	Education	0.0899	0.0225

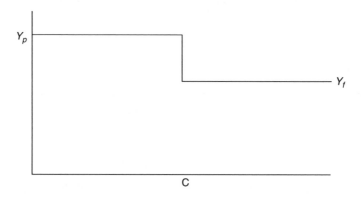

Figure 7.6. *A downward fall in income*

his or her job and consequently becomes dependent on social assistance (cf. Clark, Frijters, and Shields 2006). Let us consider a simple log-income profile, where income is constant over the past and equals the present log-income, $y_p = y_0$, and the individual faces a lower income y_f in the future. This is sketched in Figure 7.6.

In the stationary case, ignoring for convenience other variables, we have

$$c_i = \beta_i + \alpha y. \tag{7.11}$$

The norm for what constitutes a log income c_i corresponding with an (ordinal) welfare level i depends on a utility index β_i and an income-dependent scale factor $\alpha.y$. Obviously, the index β_i increases with the utility level i. For the income the individual currently has there holds

$$y = \beta_{\bar{i}} + \alpha y, \tag{7.12}$$

where $\beta_{\bar{i}}$ stands for the value of the utility index corresponding to the income level y. We may rewrite that ordinal utility index as

$$u(c; y) = c - \alpha y. \tag{7.13}$$

In the present case, where we take account of a dependence on the income flow, realized in the past and expected for the future, we may write

$$u(c; \tilde{y}) = c - \alpha \tilde{y}$$
$$= c - \alpha \sum_{-\infty}^{\infty} w_t y_t, \tag{7.14}$$

where $\tilde{y}$ is the weighted average income.

At the moment when income drops from a higher level y_p to a lower level y_f the evaluation of an amount c will become

$$u(c; \tilde{y}(0)) = c - \alpha \sum_{-\infty}^{0} w_t y_p - \alpha \sum_{0}^{\infty} w_t y_f. \tag{7.15}$$

If we assume that the time weights follow a normal distribution such that

$$\sum_{-\infty}^{0} w_t = N(0; \mu_\tau, \sigma_\tau), \quad \sum_{0}^{\infty} w_t = 1 - N(0; \mu_\tau, \sigma_\tau), \tag{7.16}$$

we find that

$$u(c; \tilde{y}(0)) = c - \alpha y_f - \alpha(y_p - y_f)N(0; \mu_\tau, \sigma_\tau), \tag{7.17}$$

and, more generally, if a period t has elapsed after the downfall we have

$$u(c; \tilde{y}(t)) = c - \alpha y_f - \alpha(y_p - y_f)N(-t; \mu_\tau, \sigma_\tau). \tag{7.18}$$

This process is evidently none other than a gradual shifting of the norm. When t tends to infinity the third term tends to zero and we have adopted the new norm. Notice that the speed of the adaptation process depends on σ_τ. If it is large, i.e. the time velocity is low, the adaptation will take much more time. This implies for the evaluation of the new income

$$u(y_f; \tilde{y}(t)) = y_f - \alpha y_f - \alpha(y_p - y_f)N(-t; \mu_\tau, \sigma_\tau). \tag{7.19}$$

The time path is depicted in Figure 7.7.

It follows that, although the final evaluation will be $u(y_f; y_f) = y_f - \alpha y_f$, the individual will temporarily endure more hardship because of the last term in the equation above. The additional hardship depends on the proportional size of the income reduction, the size of the preference drift α, and the time period

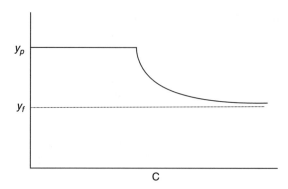

Figure 7.7. *Adaptation path to the new welfare level*

that has elapsed since the income loss. We repeat that the velocity of the adaptation depends on σ_τ.

It follows then that we look for a way to eliminate the additional hardship by adapting the individual gradually to the new, lower income level. The obvious adaptation path is

$$y(t) = y_f + \alpha(y_p - y_f)N(-t; \mu_\tau, \sigma_\tau). \tag{7.20}$$

The unfortunate individual who has been condemned to a low income y_f gets a temporary addition, which tends eventually to zero. It mitigates the pain and it tends ultimately to y_f. Notice that this is an ordinal analysis, because $u(.)$ may be replaced by any monotonic transform. We see that the suggested path depends on μ_τ, σ_τ, both of which depend on the *age* of the individual concerned. As it is impossible to implement exactly in reality an age-differentiated practical policy, we take an average value of μ_τ, σ_τ, or we use a specific path for youth, for midlife, and for seniors. For practical reasons the continuous path has to be replaced by a stepwise adaptation profile.

Increasing Wage Profiles and/or Inflation
A second subject for which the findings of this chapter are valuable is the following: In many modern economies it is taken for granted that there is an annual productivity growth of 1, 2, or 3 percent. If future and past incomes influence our present satisfaction with income, this implies that this growth rate, say δ, must have an impact on the evaluation of incomes and on the perception of income inequality.

We assume that the log-earning profile over life is

$$y_t(age; \delta) = y_0(age) + [f(age + t) - f(age)] + \delta.t. \tag{7.21}$$

Here *age* stands for the present age and $y_0(age)$ for current income. Notice that a reduction of 10 percent in $y_0(age)$ is equivalent to a permanent approximate reduction of 10 percent of the earnings profile. At the present moment $t = 0$. The second term describes how income develops as a function of age. The third term reflects the annual productivity growth. It follows then that

$$u(c; \bar{y}) = c - \alpha y_0 - \alpha \sum_{-\infty}^{\infty} w_t[f(age + t) - f(age) + \delta.t]$$

$$= c - \alpha y_0 - \alpha g(age) - \alpha.\delta.\mu_\tau(age).$$

(7.22)

where $g(.)$ is implicitly defined.

For the evaluation of y_0 we find

$$u(y_0; \bar{y}) = (1 - \alpha)y_0 - \alpha g(age) - \alpha.\delta.\mu_\tau(age).$$

(7.23)

The function $g(.)$ describes the effect of the individual career, while the term $\delta.\mu_\tau$ reflects the effect of the general productivity growth.[3] If we replace c by y_0 we get the evaluation of current income. We see that δ has an effect. The direction of that effect depends on the sign of $\mu_\tau(age)$. Hence, the effect differs with age. As we saw in Figure 7.4a, $\mu_\tau(age)$ has a parabolic behavior. It starts as negative, rises above the *age* axis in midlife, and falls again after a certain age. Hence, we may distinguish three periods in life: youth, midlife, aging. It follows that an increasing wage profile ($\delta > 0$) leads to more satisfaction for young and old, but to less satisfaction with current income for individuals in midlife.

We also see that there is a trade-off between the level of $y_0(age)$ and growth. More precisely, if δ increases to $\delta + \Delta\delta$ we have to change $y_0(age)$ into $y_0(age) + \Delta y_0$ according to the equation

$$(1 - \alpha)y_0 - \alpha.\delta.\mu_\tau(age) = (1 - \alpha)(y_0 + \Delta y_0) - \alpha.(\delta + \Delta\delta).\mu_\tau(age)$$

(7.24)

from which we derive the trade-off ratio

$$\Delta y_0 = \frac{\alpha.\mu_\tau(age)}{(1 - \alpha)} \Delta\delta.$$

(7.25)

So we find that a specific income y_0 at $\delta = 0$ is equivalent to an income $y_0(\delta)$ at growth rate δ. Again the impact of the growth (or inflation) rate on different age brackets differs. If we have a specific income distribution $\{y_n(0)\}_{n=1}^{N}$ with a prevailing growth rate of $\delta = 0$, then there is a utility-equivalent distribution $\{y_n(\delta)\}_{n=1}^{N}$ when a growth rate $\delta > 0$ prevails. If we look at the skewness of the income distribution, which we measure by the variance of log incomes, it follows that if we take a set of utility-equivalent distributions we find a log variance, which depends on the prevailing δ, say $\sigma^2(\delta)$. As the impact of δ depends on the age distribution of the population concerned, we cannot find an analytic expression for $\sigma^2(\delta)$. However, we can calculate $\sigma^2(\delta)$ for a specific

---

[3] We substitute the approximate identity $\mu_\tau = \sum_{t=-\infty}^{+\infty} w_t.t$.

Table 7.6. *The log variance of utility-equivalent income distributions for various values of* δ

δ %	$\sigma^2(\delta)$
−30	0.164
−20	0.155
−10	0.156
−5	0.161
0	0.169
5	0.179
10	0.192
20	0.227
30	0.272

population, for which we take a 1981 sample of the Dutch population. The results are recorded in Table 7.6.

From Table 7.6 it is clear that skewness is more tolerable in a growing economy than in a contracting economy. We stress that this result is found for the Dutch age–income distribution in 1981, and it may be that things are different in other populations.

7.5. CONCLUSION

The present results are certainly promising. They are evidence that we can define the time-weighting process in a quantitative way, where there is no essential caesura between the influence of the past remembered and the future anticipated. Obviously, if we were to use our findings to describe, e.g., the individual's savings or investment decisions, where we use subjective discounting we could use the time-weighting system, but truncated to the positive half-axis.

As an application we looked at the situation of an impending reduction in social-security benefits. Given different graduation patterns, the way in which the gradual phasing-in will do smallest harm to the individual who is subjected to the reduction is sought. It can also be used to calculate the impact of inflation or steady wage growth on income evaluation and the perception of income differences over time. It may in addition be employed to compare income distributions with different rates of inflation or productivity growth in terms of their log variance. It is also possible to give operational meaning to the psychological concept of the velocity of time.

In theory, it seems possible to generalize this approach to other domains of life. The problem is then how to characterize *history* and *the future* with respect to domains other than income. What observable variables characterize health, leisure, job, etc.? And how can we predict their future behavior? Although we consider that this novel approach yields promising results for financial satisfaction and the corresponding time-weighting process, a great deal of data collection and thought will be needed to apply this method of reasoning to other domains of life. However, the fact that the approach yields fairly stable, intuitively plausible, and replicable results invites further research.

More generally, the results, which have been derived with a minimum of theory and primitive assumptions and with a maximum of empirical measurement, show clearly that the perception of time is subjectively determined. There is no theoretical reason in our opinion why it should be described by an exponential density function. Although we do not claim that the normal distribution we employ is necessarily the best approximation, our results demonstrate the normal-density function to be a very credible candidate. The steepness of the tails shows that the idea of replacing the subjective discount rate by a market interest rate in the order of 4 percent per year does not seem very realistic.

When we recall that the interest rate r for an exponential weight-density function $f(t) = re^{-rt}$ is equal to $r = -\dfrac{d\ln(f)}{dt}$, then the comparable subjective interest rate, denoted by r_{subj}, would be

$$r_{subj} = -\frac{d}{dt}\ln(e^{-\frac{(t-\mu_\tau)^2}{2\sigma_\tau^2}}) = \frac{(t-\mu_\tau)}{\sigma_\tau^2}. \tag{7.26}$$

It follows that the subjective interest rate is not constant but time-dependent. In the last column of Table 7.4 (p. 153) we listed the values of r_{subj} at various ages at time $t = 0$. We note that when $\mu_\tau > 0$ we will have for a short period in the near future $r_{subj} < 0$. That means that the individual is not impatient but initially patient. There is negative time preference, a phenomenon which has been empirically demonstrated by Loewenstein and Prelec (1991). We see a huge impatience at the age of 25. At the other ages the instantaneous subjective interest rate is rather moderate. For the age of 45 we find even a mild negative time preference. We repeat, however, that this subjective interest rate is not constant over the period ahead. The rate increases with t.

For the future we see several tasks ahead. We see applications of this model to savings and investment behavior. It may also be applied to get some idea of the impact of past and anticipated inflation and adaptation processes to new income levels. We will not dwell on those applications. A beginning may be found in Van Praag and Van Weeren (1988) and in this chapter. Apart from repeating and refining this research we hope that it can be extended to other domains of life. Moreover, there is of course a need for cooperation with psychologists, because time perception has a lot of psychological aspects. It is very probable that psychological research using methods from behavioral psychology may greatly improve our understanding. Our source of information—large general surveys—has the important advantage of being a cheap means of collecting information, but, on the other hand, fine-tuned small-scale research seems indispensable to achieving greater insight into the memory and anticipation mechanisms.

8

The Influence of the Reference
Group on our Norms

8.1. INTRODUCTION

One of the essential concepts in sociology is that of the reference group. Loosely speaking, the basic idea is that our norms and our behavior are strongly influenced by what other people think and do. Some individuals will have more influence on us than others. The group of individuals who have a lot of influence on us we call our *social reference group*.

It is clear that the concept is of the utmost importance to understanding the formation of norms and the interaction of people in society. In practice, however, it is very difficult to give operational meaning to the concept. In fact, we believe that the theory and even more the operationalization of the theory is in its infancy. In this chapter we try to add a few building blocks without any pretence at having brought our knowledge very much farther.

Although the concept of the reference group originates in sociology it is now also increasingly considered and studied in economics. We mention, for example, Clark and Oswald (1996), Duesenberry (1949), Easterlin (1974, 1995), Frank (1985), Kahneman, Krueger, Schkade, Schwarz, and Stone (2006), and Veblen (1909). We abstain from giving a complete survey of the abundant sociological and economic literature. More information can be found in Senik (2005) and Clark, Frijters, and Shields (2006).

In this chapter we will restrict ourselves to the effect on norms, and neglect actual behavior, although we might say that the acceptance of a norm as such is a mode of behavior.

8.2. STRAIGHTFORWARD APPROACHES

Ferrer-i-Carbonell (2005) considers reference effects in the German GSOEP data set, where she studies the general-satisfaction question (for a similar approach see Luttmer 2005). She explains GS by an ordered-probit specification and she adds an extra explanatory variable. She starts to define the reference groups for each individual in the sample. A distinction is made between fifty subgroups on the basis of a division into five education categories, five age brackets, and two regions (West and East). For each subgroup the average log-income y_{ref} is defined. Notice that the groups are a priori defined and that *within* each group all members carry the same weight. This is usual in most studies (cf. Van de Stadt et al. 1985, Easterlin 1995, 2001, McBride 2001, Persky and Tam 1990). There are several ways to include the reference variable. Ferrer-i-Carbonell considers three variants. The first is to add y_{ref} as an additional variable. The hypothesis is then that it should get a negative sign, reflecting the human trait that you are less satisfied with your situation when all your 'neighbors' are better off than yourself. Obviously 'life as a whole' includes more than your financial situation, but it is clear that your neighbor's financial situation is an important correlate of your satisfaction with 'life as a whole'. Moreover, it is one of the life aspects which is relatively easier to recognize than the health or marriage situation of your neighbor.

In the second variant Ferrer-i-Carbonell considers the influence of the gap between one's own income and the reference income $y - y_{ref}$. It may be surmised that the influence of this gap is much less pronounced when you are on the 'right side', that is $y > y_{ref}$, than when you are on the 'wrong side' of y_{ref}. Given the approximate log-normality of the subgroup income distributions, y_{ref} is approximately median log income of the reference group's income distribution. We can translate the 'right side' by the upper 50 per cent and the 'wrong side' by the lower 50 percent of the income distribution. We do not present here the estimation results with respect to the other explanatory variables, which do not differ significantly from the results presented in Chapter 4. We present in Table 8.1 only the effects which are relevant in the context of the subject of this chapter; that is, reference groups. The results in Table 8.1 are derived from the German GSOEP data set over the period 1992–7.

The results in Table 8.1 confirm the expectations. The effect (-0.226) of the reference group's average income is firmly negative and of the same order as the transitory income effect (0.248). The permanent effect (0.456) is unchanged. The second specification shows that there is indeed asymmetry, in the sense

Table 8.1. *Reference income effects on individual life satisfaction, Germany*

	Benchmark		First specification		Second specification	
	Estimate	*t*-value	Estimate	*t*-value	Estimate	*t*-value
Family income	0.248	16.67	0.248	16.80	0.100	1.49
y_{ref}	—	—	−0.226	−3.47	—	—
$y - y_{ref}$ when rich	—	—	—	—	0.079	1.17
$y - y_{ref}$ when poor	—	—	—	—	−0.189	−2.83
Mean family income	0.449	15.69	0.456	16.07	0.463	16.07
Pseudo-R^2	0.080	—	0.080	—	0.080	—

Source: Ferrer-i-Carbonell (2005).

that the income gap causes the individual more pain if he or she is on the 'wrong' side, whilst a positive gap is a cause for less celebration if one is on the 'right' side. The idea that income is purely relative in the sense that if everybody were to get the same increase life satisfaction would not increase appears to be too simple. The combined effect of the total income effect (0.449 + 0.248) on the one hand and the reference effect (−0.226) is still firmly positive (0.471).

Stutzer (2004), in a similar study, considers a variable, 'income aspirations', which is defined as the fourth level c_4 (sufficient) in the six-level income-evaluation question (IEQ). We note that the norm, which is studied by Stutzer, is definitely narrower than 'life as a whole'. His database is a large sample of Swiss households, collected by Leu, Burri, and Priester (1997). As we already saw in Chapter 2 the levels $c_i(i = 1, \ldots, k)$ in the IEQ may be considered as 'norms', and the same holds for their average μ. Now Stutzer considers the idea that c_4 may be explained by the usual variables *and* the average log income in the (Swiss) municipality where the individual is living. Stutzer identifies the Swiss municipality as the reference group of the individual and the average log-household income in that municipality as the reference income y_{ref}. We note that 490 municipalities are distinguished, which guarantees a considerable variation in the reference income y_{ref}. He comes up with the results in Table 8.2, where again we reproduce only the effects that are relevant in this context.

In the first specification a significant preference drift is found of about 0.4, completely in line with the Leyden results, but alongside it Stutzer finds, indeed, that the average income in the municipality in which one lives has a significant effect on income aspiration. The reference effect, which was earlier termed 'reference drift' by Kapteyn and Van Praag, is about 0.2. In a very old similar study (based on joint work with Kapteyn and Van Herwaarden) Van Praag (1976) reported an even higher reference drift, of 0.3. In Stutzer's second

Table 8.2. *The effect of the reference group on income aspirations where again we reproduce only the effects that are relevant in this context*

Variable	Estimate	t-value	Estimate	t-value	Estimate	t-value	Estimate	t-value
Ln(household income)	0.404	25.47	0.403	25.46	0.404	25.57	—	—
Ln(y_{ref})	0.188	5.57	0.119	2.18	—	—	—	—
Rich*contact	—	—	0.109	1.91	—	—	—	—
Rich	—	—	—	—	0.483	5.83	0.201	1.53
Rich*contact	—	—	—	—	—	—	0.442	3.04
Contact with neighbors	—	—	−0.018	−1.46	—	—	−0.020	−1.57
R^2	0.573	—	0.574	—	0.573	—	0.575	—
N	4,554	—	—	—	—	—	—	—

Source: Stutzer (2004).

specification a variable 'contact with neighbors' is introduced. It is a simple dummy variable which equals 1 if the respondent says that he has contact with his neighbors. Stutzer hypothesizes that an individual with social contacts will have a greater reference drift. He operationalizes the variable 'social contacts' by asking whether the respondent has contacts with his neighbors.

Another variable is the percentage of 'rich' people in the population of the respondent's community, where 'rich' is defined as having more than $46,900 in 1997. This gives the variable 'rich'. Indeed, the reference income effect is doubled for the rich with contacts. The last two columns give comparable results.

A third and much earlier study we consider in this section is that by the late Aldi Hagenaars (1985) (also given in Hagenaars and Van Praag 1985). The norm is here two-dimensional. The first dimension is the μ of the income evaluation question, which is very similar to the income-aspiration variable c_4 studied by Stutzer. The second dimension is the σ^2 of the IWF (see Ch. 2, p. 41). The data set considered is a rather large international household survey (13, 132 observations) which was carried out for EUROSTAT in 1979. It covers Belgium, Denmark, France, (West) Germany, Ireland, Italy, the Netherlands, and the United Kingdom. Here an attempt was made to explain the two welfare parameters on the basis that each respondent would use the population of his or her country as his or her reference group, in which each co-citizen weighs equally.

We found then the following equation for μ:

$$\mu = 1.410 + 0.574 \ln(y) + 0.224\,\mu_y + 0.712\,\sigma_y + 0.085 \ln(fs)$$

$$(0.175)\ (0.005) \qquad (0.017) \qquad (0.046) \qquad (0.005) \qquad\qquad (8.1)$$

$$(R^2 = 0.616;\ N = 13{,}132;\ \text{standard deviations in parentheses}).$$

The variable μ_y is the average log income in the country of the respondent and σ_y is the standard deviation of log incomes. This equation is a highly interesting result. It shows that there is a considerable reference drift, almost equal to the values found by Ferrer-i-Carbonell and Stutzer. It implies that a fraction of 0.574 + 0.224 = 0.798 'leaks away' if everybody in the country gets the same income increase. It follows that income increases or material welfare increases are not very powerful instruments for increasing financial satisfaction. The additional term σ_y is motivated, as it is assumed that inequality in the reference group will make individuals more aware of higher incomes and hence make people less satisfied with the same income. This is a strong argument for a levelling of incomes within a country.

The picture is made more complex by the second equation, where σ is explained as well.

If μ is the individual's reference income, which he identifies with 'halfway up', one possibility might be

$$\sigma^2 = a.(\ln(y) - \mu)^2 + (1 - a)\frac{1}{N}\sum_n (\ln(y_n) - \mu_y + \mu_y - \mu)^2$$

$$= a.(\ln(y) - \mu)^2 + (1 - a)\frac{1}{N}\sum_n (\ln(y_n) - \mu_y)^2 + (1 - a)(\mu_y - \mu)^2, \tag{8.2}$$

where a stands for the discrete weight the individuals assign to themselves, and consequently the weight given to others in the country is $(1 - a)$.

Hagenaars reports the following estimate:

$$\sigma^2 = 0.116 + 0.191\sigma_y^2 + 0.210(\ln(y) - \mu)^2 + 0.053(\mu_y - \mu)^2$$

$$(0.009) \quad (0.033) \qquad (0.007) \qquad\qquad (0.006)$$

$$(R^2 = 0.078; \text{ number of observations} = 13{,}132;$$

standard deviations in parentheses). $\tag{8.3}$

This equation is also very significant; the R^2 is low. This equation does not satisfy the restrictions on the coefficients set above; for instance, the coefficient of σ_y^2 does not equal that of $(\mu_y - \mu)^2$. Hence, this attractive idea is too simple. However, the interesting point of this equation is that the slope of the welfare function, that is the welfare sensitivity, depends on the income inequality within a country. The more skewed the income distribution, the higher the awareness of income differences as reflected by σ. The third term reflects the difference between the individual's norm and the average income in society, where we notice from Chapter 2 that $U(e^\mu) = 0.5$, if one accepts the cardinal interpretation. The second term depends on the distance between the individual's own income and what he or she considers to be necessary to reach the level 0.5 on a $(0-1)$ scale.

If we stick to the cardinal interpretation of the welfare function, we find for its linear transform when we substitute Equations (8.1) and (8.3)

$$\frac{\ln(y) - \mu}{\sigma} = \frac{\ln(y) - 1.410 - 0.574\ln(y) - 0.224\mu_y - 0.712\sigma_y - 0.085\ln(fs)}{(0.116 + 0.191\sigma_y^2 + 0.053(\mu_y - \mu)^2 + 0.210(\ln(y) - \mu)^2)^{\frac{1}{2}}}. \tag{8.4}$$

We see that the income distribution throughout the country plays a role in people's happiness, at least in so far as income is a determinant of happiness. Although in our view Equation (8.4) is not a definite result on which to build political statements, we see from this equation that individual welfare does not necessarily decrease with the reduction of income inequality.

The results quoted here are based on ideas on reference groups developed in Leyden over the period 1976–85. Theories have changed over the years, but without any definitive result. The key assumption (see also Ch. 1), which was called by Kapteyn (1977) the preference-formation assumption, is that the individual's welfare function of income is actually identical to the society's income distribution as it is perceived by that individual. The perception process includes reference weighting and weighting over past experiences and future anticipations (see Ch. 7). Literature on this can be found in, among others, Van Praag (1976), Kapteyn (1977), Kapteyn, Van Praag, and Van Herwaarden (1978), and Van Praag, Kapteyn, and Van Herwaarden (1979). In Kapteyn and Van Herwaarden (1980) we find a fascinating application of these ideas, as they argue that the welfare functions of individuals are interdependent and hence an optimal income distribution has to take this fact into account.

Up to this point we took for granted that we know the reference group of an individual, namely the reference group is *exogenously* defined. Ideally, the empirical and theoretical analysis should have to take into account the fact that in reality the reference group is *endogenously* determined (see Falk and Knell 2004). Individuals may have different weights w_n, and probably many individuals have even a zero weight. That is, they have no influence at all. It is obvious that the definition of a reference group is not that easy. The first complication is to define who is in the reference group; that is, where its border lies. Strictly speaking, the whole of society is our reference group or even the whole world, but most individuals will carry negligible weight. This is not very helpful. In practice, we might say that our reference group is a subset R of the society N, consisting of the individuals with non-zero weights. Additionally, we observe that not every individual in our reference group needs to have the same weight, where we normalize in such a way that the weights add up to 1. More exactly, the reference group should be defined as a weight distribution $\{p_n\}_{n \in N}$ over the society N, assigning reference weights to individuals n in society. Thus, the first sociological problem would be to estimate this weight distribution.[1]

It is not even self-evident that the individual has *one* reference group. An individual may live in two or more worlds. For instance, in one's job environment one may use different norms and compare oneself with other people than in one's family life, ethnic community, or hobbies. So we can conceive of different reference groups, depending on the aspect of life we are considering.

In the next section we consider in more detail the so-called *social-filter* theory. It is an attempt to estimate the reference group of individuals, in which we shall restrict ourselves (as before) to norms with respect to financial satisfaction.

8.3. SOCIAL FILTER THEORY

Another approach to tackling the problem of reference groups is initiated in Van Praag (1981) and Van Praag and Spit (1982). The present exposition, however, will draw on Van der Sar (1991) and Van Praag and Van der Sar (1991).

---

[1] We can formulate this more elegantly by using the mathematical concept of a measure space. We consider a reference measure distribution defined on the society N (see Kapteyn, Van Praag, and Van Herwaarden 1978).

Social-filter theory starts from the same idea as Kapteyn's preference-formation hypothesis. The WFI is the distribution function of the perceived income distribution in society. That is, an income level y is evaluated by 0.4 on a (0, 1) scale if the individual believes that 40 percent of society earns less. As each individual has his or her own personal perception of the income distribution, it follows that each person has his or her own individual welfare function of income $U_n(y)$. Let us denote the distribution function of the objective income distribution by $U(y)$. We denote the corresponding density functions by $u_n(y)$ and $u(y)$ respectively. If individual perception conformed to reality, then we would have

$$u_n(y) \equiv u(y). \tag{8.5}$$

Let us consider now a small income bracket $[y - \frac{1}{2}\Delta y, \, y + \frac{1}{2}\Delta y]$ and let us have recourse to a frequency interpretation. The real fraction of income earners in this bracket is $u(y)\Delta y$. The fraction of those that are *perceived* by individual n to be in this bracket is $u_n(y)\Delta y$. It is now interesting to look at the ratio of the two fractions, which we denote by ϕ_n; that is,

$$\phi_n(y) \equiv \frac{u_n(y)}{u(y)}. \tag{8.6}$$

If $\phi_n(y) = 0$, it implies that the income bracket around y does not play a role in the perception of individual n. If the ratio equals 2, the individuals in that bracket are counted double, etc. We call ϕ_n the *social-filter function*. It describes how an individual filters reality and derives his or her own perception of it. The respondent shows us his or her frame of reference with respect to income by assigning weights to all members of society. We notice that the filter function is not a probability density function. It may take any form, except for the condition that the integral $\int_0^\infty \phi_n(y)u(y)dy = 1$, as $U_n(.)$ is a distribution function.

What would such a function ϕ look like? We sketch some examples in Figure 8.1*a–c*.

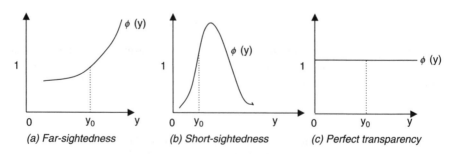

(a) Far-sightedness   (b) Short-sightedness   (c) Perfect transparency

Figure 8.1. *Three social-filter profiles*

Let y_0 stand for the income of the individual. In the picture in the middle (Fig. 8.1b) we see somebody who assigns more weight than 1 to people nearby on the income axis and much less than 1 to people far away on the income axis. The maximum weight may be assigned to the individual's 'own kind', but it is somewhat more probable that he or she assigns disproportionate value to the individuals with a somewhat higher income than him- or herself and somewhat less weight to people below. Two other cases, which we include for completeness, are also sketched. The filter function is exactly equal to 1. This amounts to a completely transparent society. The 'far-sighted' curve corresponds to people who assign more weight to a person, the farther he or she is up the income ladder.

Let us now try to operationalize this idea using a suitable and fairly realistic specification.

Again let us assume that the WFI is fairly well approximated by a log-normal distribution function; that is, $U_n(y) = N(\ln(y); \mu_n, \sigma_n)$. Let us assume as well that the income distribution in society is given by the log-normal distribution function $U(y) = N(\ln(y); \mu_y, \sigma_y)$. Applying the identity (8.6) we get the identity

$$\phi_n(y) \equiv \frac{\sigma_y}{\sigma_n} \exp\left(-\frac{1}{2}\left(\frac{\ln(y) - \mu_n}{\sigma_n}\right)^2 + \frac{1}{2}\left(\frac{\ln(y) - \mu_y}{\sigma_y}\right)^2\right) \quad (8.7)$$

or

$$\ln(\phi_n(y)) \equiv -\frac{(\ln(y) - \mu_n)^2}{2.\sigma_n^2} + \frac{(\ln(y) - \mu_y)^2}{2.\sigma_y^2} + C \quad (8.8)$$

where C stands for a constant. We may rewrite the quadratic term in the exponential by completing the square as

$$
-\frac{1}{2}\left(\frac{1}{\sigma_n^2} - \frac{1}{\sigma_y^2}\right)\left[\ln(y) - \frac{-\mu_n/\sigma_n^2 + \mu_y/\sigma_y^2}{-1/\sigma_n^2 + 1/\sigma_y^2}\right]^2 +
$$
$$
+ \left(\frac{1}{\sigma_n^2} - \frac{1}{\sigma_y^2}\right)\left[\frac{\mu_n/\sigma_n^2 - \mu_y/\sigma_y^2}{1/\sigma_n^2 - 1/\sigma_y^2}\right]^2 + \frac{\mu_n^2/\sigma_n^2 - \mu_y^2/\sigma_y^2}{1/\sigma_n^2 - 1/\sigma_y^2}. \quad (8.9)
$$

The second and third term are constants and we denote their sum by C_n. Now we define the auxiliary parameter μ_n^* by

$$\mu_n^* = \frac{-\mu_n/\sigma_n^2 + \mu_y/\sigma_y^2}{-1/\sigma_n^2 + 1/\sigma_y^2}. \quad (8.10)$$

Hence, the filter function is easily identified. Its logarithm is a quadratic polynomial in $\ln(y)$. Individuals with the same value of ϕ_n have equal social weight in the eyes of individual n. After some rewriting and defining $q_n^s = \sigma_n^2/\sigma_y^2$ we find

$$\phi_n(y) = \frac{\sigma_y}{\sigma_n} \exp\left(-\frac{1}{2} \frac{(1/q_n^2 - 1)}{\sigma_y^2} (\ln(y) - \mu_n^*)^2 + C_n\right). \tag{8.11}$$

We see that ϕ_n reaches a maximum at $\ln(y) = \mu_n^*$ if $q_{n^2} < 1$. We call μ_n^* the *social focal point* of individual n. It implies that individual n assigns a maximum weight to individuals with log income μ_n^*.

We call $q_n^2 = \sigma_n^2/\sigma_y^2$ the (degree of) *social myopia* (parameter). In general, it is found that $q < 1$. It is clear that we use the optical analogy of focal point and myopia intentionally.

It is easily shown that μ_n may be seen as a weighted average of the social focal point and the median of the objective income distribution. The less myopic the individual is, the larger q_n^2, the more his or her μ_n will tend to the μ_y of the objective distribution. We have

$$\mu_n = (1 - q_n^2)\mu_n^* + q_n^2 \mu_y. \tag{8.12}$$

Let us assume that the focal point is own income *plus* a percentage. More precisely, let us assume

$$\mu_n^* = \ln(y_c) + \delta_0. \tag{8.13}$$

We know also from our empirical observations that the individual's μ_n depends on current income via the preference-drift term β_1. Combining (8.12) with (8.13) we find then an *individualized* preference-drift coefficient

$$\beta_{1n} = (1 - q_n^2) = 1 - \frac{\sigma_n^2}{\sigma_y^2}. \tag{8.14}$$

This gives a clear possibility of testing the theory. A large preference drift would be synonymous with a small myopia factor q_n^2. A β_1 of 0.6 would imply a myopia factor of 0.4. As the ratio $q_n^2 = (\sigma_n^2/\sigma_y^2)$ is known, this can be checked, and it holds approximately. Van der Sar (1991) estimated this model for a small American data set collected by Steven Dubnoff in the Boston area (Van Praag et al. 1988). Now we need to explain μ_n^* and $q_n^2 = (\sigma_n^2/\sigma_y^2)$. Explanation of the latter variable is evidently also an attempt to explain σ_n^2. The difference from earlier attempts (see e.g. Hagenaars 1985) is that we estimate the equations for μ_n^* and σ_n^2 simultaneously. As we shall see the quality of the explanation is not much improved, but the significant results are interesting nevertheless.

The model is specified as follows:

$$\begin{aligned}
\ln(c_{in}) &= \beta_{1n}\mu_n + \sigma_n u_i + \varepsilon_{in} \\
&= (1 - q_n^2)\mu_n^* + q_n^2 \mu_y + q_n \sigma_y u_i + \varepsilon_{in}
\end{aligned} \tag{8.15}$$

$$(i = 1, \ldots, 6; n = 1, \ldots, N),$$

where we assume

Table 8.3a/b. *Estimation of the social-filter model, Boston sample*

	Focal point	Standard deviation		Myopia factor	Standard deviation
Constant	$\delta_0 = -5.39$	0.65	Constant	$\gamma_0 = -1.00$	0.15
Income	$\delta_1 = 1.52$	0.06	Schooling	$\gamma_1 = 0.22$	0.05
Family size	$\delta_2 = 0.26$	0.03	Experience	$\gamma_2 = -0.05$	0.01
N	448				
R^2	0.77				
	a			*b*	

$$\mu_n^* = \delta_0 + \delta_1 \ln y_n + \delta_2 \ln fs_n \tag{8.16}$$

and

$$q_n^2 = \exp(\gamma_0) sc_n^{\gamma_1} pex_n^{\gamma_2}. \tag{8.17}$$

The parameters δ and γ have to be estimated.

Equation (8.15) describes the six responses by individual n, where we substituted Equations (8.12) and (8.14). In (8.16) we specify an equation for the social focal point, while (8.17) specifies the myopia factor. The variable sc stands for the years of schooling and pex for potential years of labor market experience, where we define pex as $(age - sc - 6)$. Minimization of the sum of squared errors in (8.15) with respect to δ_0, δ_1, δ_2 and γ_0, γ_2, and γ_2 yields the results presented in Table 8.3, derived from Van der Sar (1991).

We notice that $\delta_1 = 1.52$ and not 1, as assumed for convenience in (8.13).

We see that the myopia factor varies positively (0.22) with schooling, which implies that better-educated persons have a wider reference group. With increasing age and settledness in the labor market the social horizon narrows and the myopia increases. The focal point has a strong relation to income.

As the empirical estimates presented above were derived from a rather specific and small data set we repeated the analysis on wave 1997 of the GSOEP, where

Table 8.4a/b. *Estimation of the social-filter model, standard deviation Germany, 1997, workers and non-workers*

	Focal point	Standard deviation		Myopia factor	Standard deviation
Constant	$\delta_0 = -9.08$	0.49	Constant	$\gamma_0 = -0.26$	0.04
Income	$\delta_1 = 1.99$	0.06	Ln(school)	$\gamma_1 = 0.06$	0.03
Family size	$\delta_2 = 0.47$	0.02	Ln(age)	$\gamma_2 = -0.07$	0.02
N	4,107	—	—	—	—
R^2	0.64	—	—	—	—
	a			*b*	

Table 8.5a/b. *Estimation of a more complex social-filter model, Germany, 1997, workers and non-workers*

	Focal point	Standard deviation		Myopia factor	Standard deviation
Constant	−9.52	0.51	Constant	−0.47	0.05
Ln(income)	2.10	0.06	Ln(education)	0.08	0.03
Ln(family size)	0.28	0.02	Ln(age)	0.05	0.03
Ln(child)	0.17	0.03	Civil servant	−0.10	0.02
Ln(age)	−0.09	0.03	Worker	0.02	0.01
			Self-employed	0.10	0.02
			Non-working (< 65)	0.10	0.01
			Gender	0.02	0.01
N	4,107				
R^2	0.65				
	a			*b*	

we used only the responses of the 4,150 western workers. The estimation convergence of this non-linear model is rapid, but it is difficult to get significant effects on q. We employed a specification which differs somewhat from that of Van der Sar. We used the model

$$\mu_n^* = \delta_0 + \delta_1 \ln y_n + \delta_2 \ln fs_n$$
$$q_n^2 = \exp(\gamma_0) lsc^{\gamma_1} lage^{\gamma_2} \tag{8.18}$$

where *lsc* stands for the *logarithm* of the years spent in regular education and where *lage* stands for the *logarithm* of age.

It appears that the results of Tables 8.3 and 8.4 do not differ that much from each other, if we take into account that the schooling variable is logged for the German data and that the experience variable has been replaced by the logged age variable. We find that schooling again has a reducing effect on social myopia, while aging makes individuals more myopic, socially speaking. In Table 8.5 we present one of the many alternative, more complex, specifications which we tried.

This specification shows that other variables may be added with sensible effects. All effects are significant at the 5 percent level, except the age effect, which is nearly significant. It seems that the focal point increases with more family members and that there is an additional children effect. The focal point slightly decreases with age. The more interesting effects are with respect to myopia. It appears that a civil servant is more myopic than a worker and that a self-employed person is less myopic than both. We differentiate between non-workers under and over 65. Not surprisingly, the younger one is less myopic than the older one. However, we find it quite surprising that the young non-worker is less myopic than the worker. It might be that a number of the non-workers under 65 have a working experience and, as they are non-working at the time, they live, so to speak, in two worlds: that of the unemployed, early retired, and disabled, and that of their earlier working environment. The differentiation between non-workers under and over 65 may be the cause of the non-significance of the age effect in contrast to the negative effect in Table 8.4. Finally, the male is slightly less myopic than the female.

8.4. SOCIAL REFERENCE SPACES

We may interpret $\exp(\phi)$ as a weight function on the income axis. The relative weight, which somebody with income y has in the reference group of individual n, is given by its logarithm

$$\ln(\phi_n(y)) \equiv -\frac{1}{2}\ln(q_n^2) + \frac{(1/q_n^2 - 1)}{2.\sigma_y^2}(\ln(y) - \mu_n^*)^2. \tag{8.19}$$

In order to make explicit that it is a weight system we define the social weight function

$$w(y; y_n) = \phi_n(y). \tag{8.20}$$

The Weight Assigned by Myself to Others
We assume that n has a reference group of individuals, which is described by a reference-weight distribution over society. The reference-weight distribution over society is described by its density function $w(y; y_n, lsc_n, lage_n).u(y)$. Individuals carrying a large share of the total reference weight are important to n, while individuals with a weight equal to zero or nearly zero are very unimportant for n. The weight $w(y_i; y_n)^2$ is the relative weight which individual n assigns to an individual i with income y_i. Notice that the anonymous i is only characterized by his or her income, while the known observer is characterized by $(y_n, lsc_n, lage_n)$. One may call it also the *relative influence* which the unknown i exerts on n, as expressed in n's evaluation of income. As already observed, the integral $\int_0^\infty w(y; y_n)u(y)dy = 1$; hence, the weights add up to 1. A second interpretation is of course that the average weight of the average individual in society is 1. Hence, if the weight function is larger than 1, the individual i has more than average influence on n. The fact that $w = w(y; y_n, lsc_n, lage_n)$ shows that w depends on more variables than y_n only. Which variables these are depends on the empirical specification. We use the simple specification of Table 8.3. It is well known that income y is approximately described as a function of schooling and working experience. We have an *earnings function* y (*lsc, lage*). It has to be understood that such a relation is always an approximate one. We may

---

[2] We write simply n or y_n instead of $(y_n, lsc_n, lage_n)$ if there is no cause for confusion.

add more explanatory variables and an error term to make it complete. However, let us assume that the earnings function is an exact description. Then we can write

$$w = w(y(lsc, lage); y_n, lsc_n, lage_n).$$ (8.21)

The weights in this latter specification are made dependent on age and schooling but no longer on income. Social types are then described by two social characteristics; namely, age and schooling. Let us define n's own weight as

$$w(y(lsc_n, lage_n); y_n, lsc_n, lage_n) = w_n$$ (8.22)

where we substitute the earnings function for n as well. Consider now the set of individuals in the $(lsc, lage)$ space which satisfy

$$w(y(lsc, lage); y_n, lsc_n, lage_n) = w_n.$$ (8.23)

The last equation describes the locus of all people with varying lsc and $lage$ values who carry the same social weight for individual n. It is, so to speak, his or her 'own class'. Notice, however, that in this situation where 'others' are described by just one characteristic, that is their income y, (8.23) describes just the equal-earnings curve of individual n.

Let us conceive of a society N where every member n is completely characterized by two social characteristics or dimensions: schooling and age. In that case we may interpret (8.23) as a *social contour* line in N. In fact, by replacing w_n with an arbitrary w we can define another social contour line, which corresponds to a class to which individual n him- or herself does not belong. By varying w we can cover the whole society with a net of social contour lines. We notice that these nets of contour lines differ for each individual or rather in the last specification with each social type, defined by the characteristics $(lsc, lage)$. The interesting point is not that we find contour lines, which are just the equal-earning curves in this simple case. The new point is that we can attach to each curve a social reference weight w. This implies that each social type has its own reference-weight system. We notice that the total weight carried by a contour line is found by multiplying the weight w per individual by the number of people on that line. It is obvious that we may refine this approach by adding more social characteristics. The main drawback of this method is that it is based on income norms and that social classes are characterized by income and income only to begin with. It is only by the trick of replacing an income level y by a curve defined by the *earnings function* $y(lsc, lage)$ that we can derive the social contour curve. A much better way to do this would be to consider the objective $(y, lsc, lage)$ distribution in N and to compare this with a subjectively perceived $(y, lsc, lage)$ distribution. As we do not have those figures and we do not see any easy way of getting information about this, we do not pursue this line any further.

Let us now divide the German working population according to age brackets into $A_1 =$ (under 25), $A_2 =$ (25, 45), $A_3 =$ (45, 65), $A_4 =$ (above 65), with corresponding population shares p_1, p_2, p_3, p_4 and sizes N_1, N_2, N_3, N_4. The reference weight that an individual n assigns to a person i with an income y_i is then $w(y_i; y_n, lsc_n, lage_n)$. Let i belong to a group A_k with group size N_k. Then, the average individual reference weight assigned by n to individuals i belonging to A_k is

$$\overline{w}(A_k; y_n, lsc_n, lage_n) = \frac{1}{N_k} \sum_{i \in A_k} w(y_i; y_n, lsc_n, lage_n). \tag{8.24}$$

In that case we may define the reference weight of bracket A_k in the eyes of n as

$$W(A_k; y_n, lsc_n, lage_n) = p_k \overline{w}_n(A_k), \quad (i = 1, 2, 3, 4), \tag{8.25}$$

where we multiply the average social weight of the individuals in bracket A_k by their numerical share p_k in the population. If we have a division of the population, we have

$$\sum_{k=1}^{4} W(A_k; y_n, lsc_n, lage_n) = 1. \tag{8.26}$$

We may interpret the terms in (8.25) as describing a mass distribution over the age brackets. The individual's weight distribution over the brackets, including his own, is interesting. However, now we can also look at the average reference weight distribution over the age brackets in the eyes of all individuals in bracket A_j, or, for short, 'in the eyes of bracket A_j'. Therefore, we look at the weight distributions of all individuals in the same bracket A_j and average those individual weight distributions. We define the reference weight distribution over age brackets as seen by bracket A_j as

$$W(A_k; A_j) = \frac{1}{N_j} \sum_{n \in A_j} W(A_k; y_n, lsc_n, lage_n) \quad (i = 1, 2, 3, 4). \tag{8.27}$$

In Table 8.6a we present those distributions for the four age brackets distinguished.

Table 8.6a. *Reference-weight distributions over age brackets as seen by heads of German households in different age brackets*

Age bracket	Under 25	25–45	45–65	Over 65
Under 25	0.11883	0.37876	0.26960	0.23282
25–45	0.04278	0.45044	0.31955	0.18724
45–65	0.04352	0.44884	0.32392	0.18372
over 65	0.07326	0.40839	0.28929	0.22905
Population shares	0.034	0.461	0.334	0.171

We see that the individuals under the age of 25 assign a reference weight of 11.8 percent to their own bracket, 37.8 percent to the age bracket [25, 45], and so on. To interpret these shares we have to compare them with the objective numbers in the population. The population share of the bracket [under 25] is only 3.4 percent, which is very small. This is because in the German sample individuals under sixteen are not counted as respondents. The reference weight per individual in that bracket is then $(0.118/0.034) = 3.471$. This shows that young individuals assign more than three times as much weight to their peer group as to an average member of the population. For the other age brackets the reference shares are more or less proportional to their objective population shares.

This leads to the conclusion that if we look for *one* dimension to describe a reference group, *age* would not be a suitable candidate. This does not imply that age might not be informative in a context with more dimensions, but this would be hard to tabulate. Within the scope of this chapter we do not look at more-dimensional reference groups.

We also looked at single-variable groups based on 'years of education', 'family size', 'net monthly household income', and 'type of worker'. Our conclusion is that most reference-weight distributions which are defined on the basis of only one dimension yield weight distributions which do not differ very much from the objective population shares. This may result from the choice of only one dimension or the fact that we have averaged opinions and that we use too coarsely defined groups. We found serious differences between the population shares and the reference weight distributions for incidental cases. For instance, 'single-person households' assign a reference weight to their own group of 50.7 percent, while their population share is only 22.1 percent.

A good differentiator is 'net monthly family income'. We found the information in Table 8.6*b*.

We see that individuals in the lowest brackets give about 4 times as much weight to their own bracket as on average. They underweight high income brackets by a factor of more than 1/20. For individuals in the high-

Table 8.6*b*. *Reference-weight distributions over income brackets as seen by heads of German households in different income brackets*

Income bracket in DM 1997 ($\approx$ 0.5 €)	Under 2,000	2,001–3,500	3,501–5,500	Over 5,501
Under 2,000	0.67320	0.24550	0.07330	0.00801
2,001–3,500	0.28499	0.40633	0.25448	0.05420
3,501–5,500	0.10930	0.35463	0.39262	0.14345
Over 5,501	0.03738	0.23087	0.43407	0.29768
Population shares	0.143	0.323	0.361	0.173

income bracket the distortion is less dramatic but still considerable, with corresponding factors of about 4 and 1.6 respectively. The reason that income is a much better differentiator than the other variables we tried is that the underlying model is based on the difference between the objective and the subjective income distribution. The latter is identical with the individual income-evaluation function. The other variables like *age* are only interesting in the present context in so far as they are correlated with individual income.

The Weight Assigned to Myself by Others

Up to now we have considered how an individual or a population subgroup attaches social weight to other individuals or subgroups, including the group to which each belongs. The inverse question is what is our *social weight* in the eyes of others?

We may see $w(y_i; y_n)$ as the *reference* weight which an individual n with income y_n assigns to an individual i with income y_i The distribution over all i describes the reference weight distribution of individual n over his or her reference group. Then $w(y_n; y_i)$ is the *social* weight which is assigned by i to n. Adding all the social weights of n yields an idea of the social importance which society assigns to n. Notice that *reference* weights and *social* weights are generally not the same. For instance, let us assume that i stands for the Queen of the Netherlands and n for a normal citizen. Then the reference weight of the Queen is likely to be non-zero for almost every Dutch individual n, but the social weight of n is likely to be nil in the eyes of the Queen.

Let us now assume again that the population is divided into the age brackets A_k with sizes $N_k (k = 1, 2, 3, 4)$. Then, we may define

$$\bar{w}(y_n; A_k) = \frac{1}{N_k} \sum_{i \in A_k} w(y_n; y_i; lsc_i, lage_i) \tag{8.28}$$

as the average reference weight which members of A_k attach to individual n. If we want to know what the average reference weight attached by the whole society N to individual n is, we find for the average

$$\bar{w}(y_n; N) = \sum_{k=1} p_k \frac{1}{N_k} \sum_{i \in A_k} w(y_n; y_i; lsc_i, lage_i). \tag{8.29}$$

When n belongs to the group A_j we also can find the social weight of the group A_j in the society N. It equals

$$W(A_j, N) = p_j \frac{1}{N_j} \sum_{n \in A_j} \bar{w}(y_n; N) = p_j \frac{1}{N_j} \sum_{n \in A_j} \sum_{k=1}^{4} p_k \frac{1}{N_k} \sum_{i \in A_k} w(y_n; y_i, lsc_i, lage_i). \tag{8.30}$$

We see that $W(A_j, N)$ is written as the objective population share times a correction factor, which is larger than 1 if the group is evaluated as having

Table 8.7a-e. *Social-weight distribution over age, education, family-size, income, and type-of-worker brackets for the German population*

Age	Under 25	25–45	45–65	Over 65
Social weights	0.05112	0.43998	0.31392	0.19498
Population shares	0.034	0.461	0.334	0.171

a

Education	<= 12 years	13–16 years	16 years >
Social weights	0.76740	0.14332	0.08928
Population shares	0.737	0.155	0.108

b

Family size	1	2	3	4	5 or more
Social weights	0.29614	0.30483	0.18114	0.14896	0.06893
Population shares	0.221	0.321	0.201	0.175	0.082

c

Income (DM 1997)	< 2,000	2,000–3,500	3,501–5,500	5,500 >
Social weights	0.23921	0.33189	0.30721	0.12169
Population shares	0.143	0.323	0.361	0.173

d

Type of worker	Civil servant	Blue/white collar	Self-employed	Non-worker < 65	Non-worker > 65
Social weights	0.04465	0.47937	0.05093	0.23678	0.18828
Population shares	0.055	0.521	0.057	0.203	0.164

e

more social weight than average, and smaller than 1 if the group is less important than average.

In Table 8.7 we give the social-weight distributions for the age brackets, the education brackets, the family-size brackets, the income brackets, and the brackets defined by the type of worker.

Let us now return to the social-filter function in (8.11). The function does not reach its minimum in y_n but in n's social focal point μ_n^*. As the focal point is mostly not one's own position, this implies that individuals do not give most weight to their own type but to others. Using Equation. (8.11) as estimated in Table 8.3 we get the following figure in $\ln(y)$-space. We see that most individuals position their focal point upwards, while poor people put the focal point downwards, from themselves. The point of 'self-centeredness' is found at the

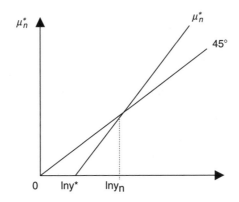

Figure 8.2. *The social focal point as a function of income*

intersection point with the 45° line. Van der Sar calculated for the American sample (1983) that this point would lie at $15,962 per year for a family with two children. For a couple without children it lay at $35,446. It is very remarkable that family size would have such an impact on the reference-weighting system. We reproduce Figure 11.1 from Van der Sar (1983).

For the West German workers' (1997) sample the 'self-centeredness' point was found at a monthly household income of DM 6,923 for families with two children.

A consequence of this asymmetry of the social-filter function is that individuals do not assign equal weight to each other. Therefore, it is not a proper distance function in the mathematical sense. However, from a sociological point of view this makes the function more realistic and attractive. The asymmetry implies that there may be individuals or social types, say n and m, such that $w_m(n) = 1$ and $w_n(m) = 100$. An example is again the relation between the Dutch queen and her citizens. Many citizens may see the Queen as a role model, while she herself is not influenced at all by many of her citizens. The same may hold even more strongly for the United Kingdom.

8.5. DISCUSSION

It is obvious that we can point to a lot of shortcomings in this draft of social-filter theory. The first point is that the preference-formation hypothesis is a critical building-block, where we assume that the evaluation function reflects a subjective perception of an objective distribution. As the individual's perception procedure may be compared to looking through an optical lens, he or she looks at society with a certain myopia, concentrating on a specific focal point. The result is a 'filtered' perception.

The second point of critique may be the functional specifications. They yield elegant formulae, but do they reflect reality? We think that they are fair approximations. However, for other functional specifications the same theoretical model may be implemented and estimated.

The third point to be considered is that this model depends on income evaluation. Income is an important but partial aspect of satisfaction with life as a whole. Is it enough to get an idea of someone's reference group? We do not know, but we doubt it. As we said earlier, it may be that individuals have several reference groups for several domains or dimensions of life. An obvious generalization which we shall try to develop in the future is a more-dimensional approach. For a first attempt in that direction see Van Praag and Spit (1982).

An alternative approach to the operationalization of the reference-group concept may be to investigate 'who imitates whose behavior'. For instance, if Mr. Jones likes to play golf and Mr. Smith sees Mr. Jones as a role model, then he will play golf as well. In practice, this approach is difficult to implement. What are the behavioral aspects that are 'reference-loaded' and how can we find who is the initiator and who the imitator over the course of time? Although we see this imitation approach as a valid approach as well, we consider the present approach superior, being more general and easier to operationalize. In a sense we may see one's norms as behavior as well.

9

Health and Subjective Well-being

9.1. INTRODUCTION

It is well known that in all western economies health costs are soaring. Medical technology is improving and provides us with new therapies. The costs of those new therapies are considerable. In view of this tendency there is a need for cost–benefit analysis, or some other evaluation method, such as cost-effectiveness. What are the costs of a therapy and what is the resulting benefit? If we knew that the therapy would cost $10,000 per year but that the benefit would have a value of $20,000, there would be a case for making the therapy available, and—most essential in that respect—for including the therapy in the health-insurance policy. It is fairly easy to assess the cost of a therapy but it is more difficult to assess the benefits. When the individual works in a paid job, one of the benefits of a therapy will consist in the productivity gain of the individual, and this can be measured in money terms. This is a good measure for choosing between becoming registered disabled, and hence becoming eligible for a disability benefit, or applying the therapy, where we assume that the therapy will reduce or even remove the work disability. However, for individuals who are not part of the workforce, for example the retired, this would have dismal consequences. Even if they are cured, they will not be 'productive' any more. It demonstrates that the benefit of a therapy consists of more components; there is also a component which we may describe as enhancing of the quality of life per year and/or increasing the life expectancy. The latter benefit is also called *intangible benefits*. In fact, those benefits are mainly perceptible as health improvements. The problem is how to assign to them monetary values. In this chapter we will make an attempt to do that. First, we will explain the novel method we propose and present some empirical results. Then we will have a look at the solutions presented in the health-economics literature and make the link with our ideas. Finally, we will make a comparative evaluation.

As shown in Chapter 2, we can employ the utility function for estimating trade-offs between income and other variables that play a role in our evaluation of well-being. In Chapter 2 we considered the example of family size.

This chapter is based on Ferrer-i-Carbonell and Van Praag (2002) and Van Praag and Ferrer-i-Carbonell (2002).

We investigated the impact of having children on financial satisfaction. We assume there that financial satisfaction U depends on two variables, income y and family size fs, that is, $U = U(y, fs)$. Then, we can compensate for an increase in the family size by Δfs by an income increase Δy by solving the equation $U(y + \Delta y, fs + \Delta fs) = U(y, fs)$ for Δy. We can interpret the money amount Δy as the subjective cost or shadow cost of the family extension Δfs.

As we already saw in Chapter 2 this finding can be used for the construction of a family-allowance system which is *welfare-neutral*. We call it 'welfare-neutral' because if households are compensated for an additional family member, usually their additional child, according to this system their welfare remains constant. It should be made explicit that we do not state that the welfare-neutral system is politically optimal. As we saw in Chapter 2, the specification that we use would imply a family allowance that is a fixed percentage of income, irrespective of whether the household is poor or rich. The rich would get a larger family allowance than the poor in absolute money amounts. Politically this may be unacceptable. However, this does not reduce the significance of the welfare-neutral system as a measuring-rod by which we can evaluate family-allowance systems.

Now we shall generalize this method. Let there be other variables x that have an impact on well-being or welfare. This can be checked when we try to estimate $U = U(y, x)$. If x has a significant effect, we may apply the method just described and assess the subjective cost of a change in the variable x. In this chapter we will apply the method to the occurrence of chronic diseases. Let x be a dummy variable[1] which equals 1 if the individual has a specific disease, such as diabetes, and which equals 0, if the individual is healthy. In that case, the difference $U(y, 0) - U(y, 1)$ stands for the utility loss resulting from having diabetes. This loss may vary with varying incomes y. We may calculate the disease shadow cost Δy by solving the equation $U(y + \Delta y, 1) = U(y, 0)$ for Δy. This last term is known in economics as the compensating income. We notice that this compensation does not depend on a cardinality assumption. If we replace U by a monotonic transform $\tilde{U} = \varphi(U(y, x))$, we end up with the same compensation Δy. Van den Berg and Ferrer-i-Carbonell (2007) use this method to find the monetary value of informal care.

9.2. METHODOLOGY AND SATISFACTION ESTIMATES

In Chapters 3 and 4 we estimated a comprehensive 'two-layer'-model for Germany and the UK. Domain satisfactions were explained by objectively measurable variables and in their turn domain satisfactions (*DS*) explained general satisfaction (*GS*); that is, satisfaction with 'life as a whole'. In Chapter 3

---

[1] It would be preferable for the severity of the disease to be reflected on a continuous scale instead of by a 0–1 variable, but, as our data sets do not contain severity measures, we can't adopt that refinement.

the health satisfaction of the British was assumed to depend on the interaction term between illnesses and age. In other words, the effect of illnesses on health satisfaction was assumed to be age-dependent. In this chapter we will re-estimate the health-satisfaction equation for the British data set (1996–8), assuming that the impact of an illness on health satisfaction is not age-dependent. Thus, the regression includes dummy variables, where the value 1 indicates that one suffers from the specific disease. This is the obvious road. If we were to make the effects of diseases age-dependent, as in Table 3.10, the intangible costs would be age-dependent, as well. For the sake of explanation, we here take simple dummies. We present the dummy effects in Table 9.1, in which we estimate the health-satisfaction equation by POLS as in Chapter 3. Surprisingly, illness information is absent in the German SOEP. Hence, we restrict ourselves mainly to the British data.

It can be seen that all diseases have strong negative effects on health. The question is now what is the impact of a chronic disease on general satisfaction. In Chapter 4 we found that general satisfaction may be seen as an aggregate of domain satisfactions. Leaving out some auxiliary variables like the Z-variable, the equation looks like this:

$$GS = \alpha_1 DS_1 + \ldots + \alpha_k DS_k. \tag{9.1}$$

Let us assume that DS_1 stands for the health domain satisfaction. From Table 9.1 it appears that DS_1 may be written as

$$DS_1 = \gamma_1 d_1 + \ldots + \gamma_k d_m + \beta' x, \tag{9.2}$$

where we take the specification without age–disease interactions and the d's stand for the disease dummy variables. The part $\beta' x$ stands for the contribution of the other variables, which are irrelevant in this context. Hence, it follows that the impact of an illness dummy i on GS is $\alpha_1 \gamma_i d_i$. This is the welfare loss caused by the health loss. If we want to compensate for it in terms of money, we have to calculate the effect of income on general satisfaction. Now we have seen that there are various channels through which an income change affects GS. In the first place we have an income effect through financial satisfaction, but the income level influences other domain satisfactions as well. Let us write the effect of income on the various domains j as $\beta_{jy} ln(y)$, then the effect of an income change $\Delta ln(y)$ on the domain satisfaction will be $\beta_{jy} \Delta ln(y)$. Hence, the effect via domain j on GS will be $\alpha_j \beta_{jy} \Delta ln(y)$. If we add the effects on GS for all the domains together, we get the total income effect, which equals $\sum_{j=1}^{k} \alpha_j \beta_{jy} \Delta ln(y)$. Hence, it follows that the monetary compensation for a disease i is found by solving the equation

$$\sum_{j=1}^{k} \alpha_j \beta_{jy} \Delta ln(y) = -\alpha_1 \gamma_i d_i \tag{9.3}$$

Table 9.1. *Health satisfaction, workers, UK, 1996–1998,*
POLS individual random effects

	Workers	
	Estimate	t-ratio
Constant	2.927	2.978
Dummy for 1996	−0.083	−5.388
Dummy for 1997	−0.019	−1.323
Ln(age)	−1.307	−2.323
(Ln(age))^2	0.189	2.368
Age turning point	32	—
Ln(family income)	−0.040	−1.766
Ln(years education)	−0.096	−3.825
Ln(children +1)	−0.023	−0.443
Gender (male)	0.008	0.386
Living together	−0.003	−0.118
Self-employed	0.056	1.857
Ln(savings)	0.011	2.213
Problems with arms, legs, hands, feet, back, or neck	−0.409	−18.921
Difficulty in seeing	−0.169	−3.269
Difficulty in hearing	−0.153	−3.534
Skin conditions/allergies	−0.172	−6.647
Chest/breathing problems	−0.398	−13.544
Heart/blood problems	−0.436	−12.204
Problems with stomach/liver/kidneys	−0.493	−13.141
Diabetes	−0.562	−6.232
Epilepsy	−0.517	−3.818
Migraine or frequent headaches	−0.249	−8.397
Other health problems	−0.603	−14.515
Mean (ln(family income))	−0.011	−0.369
Mean (ln(children + 1))	0.073	1.297
Mean (ln(adults))	0.009	1.320
Standard deviation of individual random effect, ε_n	0.734	—
Error standard deviation	0.772	—
% variance due to ε_n	0.474	—
Number of observations	17,966	—
Number of individuals	7,780	—
R^2:		
Within	0.021	—
Between	0.169	—
Overall	0.128	—

Note: There are dummies for missing variables, which are not included in the table.

for $\Delta ln(y)$. This is approximately equal to the percentage by which income has to be increased to neutralize the health loss. Notice that the solution $\Delta ln(y)$ for the equation

$$\sum_{j=1}^{k} \alpha_j \beta_{jy} \, \Delta ln(y) = \alpha_1 \gamma_i d_i \qquad (9.4)$$

where we drop the minus sign yields the *equivalent* income decrease. That is, having the disease i is equivalent to a proportional income reduction of $exp(\alpha_1 \gamma_i d_i / \sum_{j=1}^{k} \alpha_j \beta_{jy})$.

The above-presented specification is the most simple one we can think of. However, why should a disease only affect your health satisfaction? In fact, we found that having a disease will significantly affect satisfaction with respect to other domains. Only for housing and marriage satisfaction we did not find significant effects. After re-estimation with POLS and including the illness dummies, we found the information in Table 9.2a–e. We see that, for instance, 'depression' and 'problems with arms, etc.' affect job satisfaction and financial satisfaction in a way which cannot be ignored. If we include those 'other-channels' effects and look for an overall monetary compensation, we can find this compensation $\Delta ln(y)$ by generalization of the formula above to

$$\sum_{j=1}^{k} \alpha_j \beta_{jy} \, \Delta ln(y) = \sum_{j=1}^{k} \alpha_j \gamma_{ji} d_i \qquad (9.5)$$

where we add at the right-hand side the health losses over all k domains. The coefficient γ_{ji} stands for the effect of disease i on the jth domain satisfaction. It is obvious that we can generalize this approach still further by looking at the case in which an individual suffers from several diseases simultaneously. In that case the above formula is replaced by

$$\sum_{j=1}^{k} \alpha_j \beta_{jy} \, \Delta ln(y) = \sum_{i=1}^{m} \sum_{j=1}^{k} \alpha_j \gamma_{ji} d_i, \qquad (9.6)$$

where we sum over the diseases i as well. We notice that these effects are log-additive. Hence, we get for the proportional increase in y

$$exp(\Delta ln(y)) = exp \left[\frac{\sum_{i=1}^{m} \sum_{j=1}^{k} \alpha_j \gamma_{ji} d_i}{\sum_{j=1}^{k} \alpha_j \beta_{jy}} \right] \qquad (9.7)$$

Table 9.2a. *Job satisfaction, UK, 1996–1998, POLS individual random effects*

	Estimate	t-ratio
Constant	11.362	9.865
Dummy for 1996	−0.019	−1.214
Dummy for 1997	0.009	0.648
Ln(household income)	0.055	1.853
Ln(age)	−7.158	−10.700
(Ln(age))^2	1.052	11.139
Living together	0.167	4.514
Gender (male)	−0.121	−4.434
Ln(years education)	−0.084	−3.278
Ln(work income)	0.014	1.104
Ln(working hours)	0.007	0.348
Ln(extra hours)	0.042	3.876
Self-employed	0.163	2.293
Ln(desired hours)	0.218	11.093
Work at night	−0.125	−2.092
Second earner in the household	−0.042	−1.395
Ln(hours household work)	−0.027	−1.788
Ln(children + 1)	0.249	1.010
Ln(children + 1)^2	0.053	0.944
Ln(adults)	−0.113	−2.235
Ln(children + 1)*income	−0.043	−1.422
Ln(children + 1)*living together	0.027	0.523
Problems with arms, legs, hands, feet, back, or neck	−0.130	−5.918
Difficulty in seeing	−0.073	−1.390
Difficulty in hearing	−0.032	−0.732
Skin conditions/allergies	−0.025	−0.934
Chest/breathing problems	−0.049	−1.647
Heart/blood problems	−0.040	−1.098
Problems with stomach/liver/kidneys	−0.102	−2.677
Diabetes	0.070	0.752
Depression	−0.341	−9.152
Alcohol or drug-related problems	−0.122	−0.673
Epilepsy	0.114	0.840
Migraine or frequent headaches	−0.060	−2.006
Other health problems	−0.047	−1.126
Mean (ln(household income))	−0.031	−0.849
Mean (ln(children + 1))	0.100	1.736
Mean (ln(adults))	0.057	0.932
Mean (ln(work income))	0.000	−0.031
Mean(working hours)	0.004	0.170
Mean(overtime)	0.011	0.629
Mean(desired hours)	0.208	6.289
Mean(household work)	0.043	2.128
Standard deviation of individual random effect, ε_n	0.743	—
Error standard deviation	0.772	—
% variance due to ε_n	0.481	—
Number of observations	17,563	—
Number of individuals	7,617	—

[handwritten margin note: One of largest effects → pointing to "Depression"]

Table 9.2a. *(Contd.)*

R^2:		
Within	0.019	—
Between	0.089	—
Overall	0.074	—

Note: There are dummies for missing variables, which are not included in the table.

Table 9.2b. *Financial satisfaction, workers, UK, 1996–1998,*
POLS individual random effects

	Estimate	*t*-ratio
Constant	9.499	9.934
Dummy for 1996	−0.078	−5.673
Dummy for 1997	0.002	0.180
Ln(age)	−7.289	−13.161
(Ln(age))^2	1.037	13.242
Gender (male)	−0.049	−2.477
Ln(household income)	0.237	9.837
Ln(years education)	−0.053	−2.284
Ln(adults)	−0.111	−2.543
Ln(children + 1)	−0.279	−1.277
Ln(children + 1)^2	−0.039	−0.790
Ln(children + 1)*income	0.026	0.979
Ln(savings)	0.054	12.756
Living together	0.079	2.524
Second earner in the household	0.027	1.012
Self-employed	0.118	4.272
Problems with arms, legs, hands, feet, back, or neck	−0.122	−6.236
Difficulty in seeing	−0.072	−1.550
Difficulty in hearing	−0.053	−1.352
Skin conditions/allergies	−0.037	−1.579
Chest/breathing problems	−0.082	−3.065
Heart/blood problems	−0.121	−3.715
Problems with stomach/liver/kidneys	−0.112	−3.290
Diabetes	−0.023	−0.273
Depression	−0.296	−8.971
Alcohol or drug-related problems	−0.113	−0.738
Epilepsy	0.029	0.228
Migraine or frequent headaches	−0.050	−1.872
Other health problems	−0.090	−2.404
Mean (ln(household income))	0.177	5.926
Mean (ln(children + 1))	0.083	1.631
Mean (ln(adults))	−0.232	−4.326
Mean (ln(savings))	0.036	5.500
Standard deviation of individual random effect, ε_n	0.706	—
Error standard deviation	0.684	—
% variance due to ε_n	0.516	—

Table 9.2b. *(Contd.)*

	Estimate	*t*-ratio
Number of observations	17,944	—
Number of individuals	7,768	—
R^2:		
Within	0.037	—
Between	0.164	—
Overall	0.1357	—

Note: There are dummies for missing variables, which are not included in the table.

Table 9.2c. *Leisure–use satisfaction, workers, UK, 1996–1998, POLS individual random effects*

	Estimate	*t*-ratio
Constant	13.100	12.253
Dummy for 1996	0.010	0.672
Dummy for 1997	−0.013	−0.937
Ln(age)	−7.651	−12.506
$(\text{Ln(age)})^2$	1.103	12.752
Ln(household income)	−0.004	−0.180
Ln(adults)	−0.045	−0.966
Ln(children + 1)	−0.230	−3.095
$\text{Ln(children + 1)}^2$	0.139	2.592
Gender (male)	0.057	2.535
Ln(years education)	−0.106	−4.172
Living together	−0.013	−0.541
Ln(working hours)	−0.009	−0.436
Ln(leisure time)	0.105	3.047
Problems with arms, legs, hands, feet, back, or neck	−0.087	−4.085
Difficulty in seeing	−0.094	−1.877
Difficulty in hearing	−0.077	−1.800
Skin conditions/allergies	−0.037	−1.429
Chest/breathing problems	−0.038	−1.313
Heart/blood problems	−0.031	−0.877
Problems with stomach/liver/kidneys	−0.125	−3.377
Diabetes	0.108	1.181
Depression	−0.310	−8.634
Alcohol or drug related problems	−0.568	−3.446
Epilepsy	−0.052	−0.382
Migraine or frequent headaches	−0.097	−3.327
Other health problems	−0.028	−0.695
Mean (ln(household income))	−0.008	−0.244
Mean (ln(children + 1))	−0.151	−2.746
Mean (ln(adults))	0.096	1.660
Mean(ln(working hours))	−0.043	−2.014
Standard deviation of individual random effect, ε_n	0.772	—
Error standard deviation	0.739	—
% variance due to ε_n	0.522	—

Table 9.2c. *(Contd.)*

Number of observations	17,938	—
Number of individuals	7,779	—
R^2:		
Within	0.003	—
Between	0.087	—
Overall	0.066	—

Note: There are dummies for missing variables, which are not included in the table.

Table 9.2d. *Leisure–amount satisfaction workers, UK, 1996–1998, POLS individual random effects*

	Estimate	*t*-ratio
Constant	11.558	8.662
Dummy for 1996	−0.026	−1.777
Dummy for 1997	−0.034	−2.561
Ln(age)	−6.719	−11.232
$(Ln(age))^2$	0.972	11.494
Ln(household income)	−0.006	−0.054
Ln(adults)	−0.065	−1.427
Ln(children + 1)	−0.286	−3.952
Ln(children + 1)^2	0.089	1.704
Gender (male)	0.029	1.324
Ln(years education)	−0.065	−2.619
Living together	−0.007	−0.303
Ln(working hours)	−0.100	−5.192
Ln(leisure time)	0.250	1.264
Ln(leisure time)*ln(income)	−0.004	−0.158
Problems with arms, legs, hands, feet, back, or neck	−0.094	−4.550
Difficulty in seeing	−0.071	−1.443
Difficulty in hearing	−0.074	−1.757
Skin conditions/allergies	−0.029	−1.161
Chest/breathing problems	−0.011	−0.373
Heart/blood problems	0.021	0.597
Problems with stomach/liver/kidneys	−0.092	−2.567
Diabetes	0.118	1.333
Depression	−0.237	−6.780
Alcohol or drug related problems	−0.445	−2.770
Epilepsy	−0.024	−0.183
Migraine or frequent headaches	−0.087	−3.063
Other health problems	−0.050	−1.277
Mean (ln(household income))	−0.046	−1.457
Mean (ln(children + 1))	−0.078	−1.451
Mean (ln(adults))	0.177	3.129
Mean (ln(working hours))	−0.072	−3.428

Table 9.2d. *(Contd.)*

	Estimate	*t*-ratio
Standard deviation of individual random effect, ε_n	0.758	—
Error standard deviation	0.720	—
% variance due to ε_n	0.526	—
Number of observations	17,938	—
Number of individuals	7,778	—
R^2:		
Within	0.0079	—
Between	0.1081	—
Overall	0.0854	—

Note: There are dummies for missing variables, which are not included in the table.

Table 9.2e. *Social-life satisfaction, workers, UK, 1996–1998,*
POLS individual random effects

	Estimate	*t*-ratio
Constant	15.504	14.381
Dummy for 1996	−0.015	−1.037
Dummy for 1997	−0.068	−5.035
Ln(age)	−9.030	−14.549
$(Ln(age))^2$	1.281	14.597
Ln(household income)	0.034	1.460
Ln(adults)	−0.362	−4.939
Ln(children + 1)	0.139	2.590
Ln(children + 1)^2	−0.017	−0.369
Gender (male)	−0.069	−2.776
Ln(years education)	−0.086	−3.391
Ln(leisure time)	0.026	0.704
Second earner in the household	0.030	1.042
Living together	0.018	0.523
Ln(hours household work)	−0.019	−1.724
Ln(working hours)	0.013	0.628
Problems with arms, legs, hands, feet, back, or neck	−0.059	−2.829
Difficulty in seeing	−0.139	−2.792
Difficulty in hearing	−0.130	−3.059
Skin conditions/allergies	−0.060	−2.384
Chest/breathing problems	−0.046	−1.599
Heart/blood problems	−0.076	−2.173
Problems with stomach/liver/kidneys	−0.148	−4.037
Diabetes	0.057	0.629
Depression	−0.376	−10.594
Alcohol or drug related problems	−0.396	−2.428
Epilepsy	−0.006	−0.046
Migraine or frequent headaches	−0.088	−3.048
Other health problems	−0.066	−1.663
Mean (ln(household income))	0.005	0.168
Mean (ln(children + 1))	−0.014	−0.265

Table 9.2e. *(Contd.)*

Mean (ln(adults))	0.124	2.159
Mean (ln(working hours))	−0.015	−0.713
Standard deviation of individual random effect, ε_n	0.785	—
Error standard deviation	0.723	—
% variance due to ε_n	0.541	—
Number of observations	17,935	—
Number of individuals	7,777	—
R^2:		
Within	0.008	—
Between	0.097	—
Overall	0.0746	—

Note: There are dummies for missing variables, which are not included in the table.

It follows that if somebody suffers from two diseases the compensation will be the product of the two separate compensation factors.

9.3. MONETARY VALUATION OF ILLNESSES

On the basis of the formulae presented in Section 9.2 and the coefficients found in Chapters 3 and 4 and Tables 9.1–9.2e of this chapter, we calculate in Table 9.3 the equivalent income losses for several diseases for British married workers. We do this in two ways. First, we assume that the disease only has an effect through health satisfaction. Second, we take the broad view and use the multi-channel approach. It stands to reason that the equivalent income in the

Table 9.3. *Equivalent income correction factors for various diseases*

Disease	British married workers (health-only approach)	British married workers (comprehensive approach)	German workers (British parameters)
Problems with arms, legs, hands, feet, back, or neck	0.777	0.984	0.334
Difficulty in seeing	0.462	0.946	0.155
Difficulty in hearing	0.429	0.911	0.141
Skin conditions, allergies	0.468	0.820	0.158
Chest, breathing problems	0.767	0.951	0.327
Heart blood problems	0.798	0.965	0.352
Problems with stomach/liver kidneys	0.836	0.994	0.387
Diabetes	0.873	0.747	0.428
Epilepsy	0.850	0.891	0.402
Migraine or frequent headaches	0.599	0.947	0.219

What about depression?

latter case must be larger than in the former case. Finally, we calculate the equivalent income for West German workers according to the simple version, where we assumed that the dummy effects were equal to the effects on British workers as we estimated them in Table 9.1. In Table 9.3 we present the different equivalent income correction factors.

We see from Table 9.3 that the effects of health impediments in terms of equivalent income losses are, especially for the British, very considerable. For instance, for 'problems with arms, legs, hands, feet, back or neck' we find that the equivalent income loss is 77.7 percent. The income-compensation factor would have to be $(1/0.223 - 1) \approx 3$ in order to compensate for the intangible costs of the handicap. If we include the effects on the other domains as well, the compensation needed increases to about forty-nine times the present income. If we assumed that our British dummy effects would hold in Germany as well, we might plug them into the German model estimates as given in Chapters 3 and 4. This gives us for the simple equivalent-income method the factors presented in the third column of Table 9.3. For Germany the equivalent-income compensations are much lower than the corresponding figures for the British (see Ferrer-i-Carbonell and Van Praag 2002).

9.4. DISCUSSION OF THE METHOD

The first question that arises is whether these costs, which may amount to very considerable sums indeed in terms of current income, are credible. In order to understand why the estimates in our view are not outrageous, we have to consider the question in the spirit of Becker's 'full-income' concept. That income concept is the sum of earned income plus the value of leisure hours evaluated at the market wage. So if one is normally only working for 8 hours per day, full income would be 3 times as high. It shows that the value of leisure is quite high. But because we do not have to buy it in the market we often do not realize that it is a formidable income in kind. It also makes clear that the value of a life as a whole may be much more than just the actual income or rather the capitalized value of money income. In this context the same holds for human capital in general, of which one's health is one important dimension. You may consider 1 year in good health as the annual interest on your health capital. The money value of that interest seems to be of the same order as your earned income. Consider your earning capital on the basis of a net income of $30,000 a year. On the basis of a 5 percent discount rate and a compensation factor of 4 it would imply a capitalized value of $2,400,000 value ($\frac{4}{0.05}*30.10^3$), where we assume for convenience that life expectancy is infinite. The value of one's health capital would be of the same order. For older persons we would assume a smaller life expectancy. We used here a market discount rate, but there is reason to assume a subjective time discount rate and there is evidence that this rate is much higher, say 20 percent or more per year

If we apply such a higher subjective time discount rate, the value of $2,400,000 would shrink to $600,000.

Notice that according to this model the value of health would be proportional to current income. Hence, diseases would require higher absolute compensations in money for rich people than for poor individuals in order to yield *equivalent* compensations. Whether we want that or not is a political decision. Obviously, we may also use the capitalized value of the health improvement to compare it with the cost of the therapy in order to evaluate the costs and benefits of the therapy. We notice that the total benefits are likely to be underestimated, as productivity gains are not included here. The same may hold for the benefits to family members caused by the improved health of the individual; for, if one member of the household is in bad health, it will probably affect the well-being of the other household members as well.

The present method is not interesting only for the choice of health policies, but also for medical-damage insurance compensations. Although our estimates look pretty high, they resemble the results of American litigation cases brought to court. Nevertheless, we find the factors, at least for the British sample, very high. For some diseases we find an equivalent income loss of about 100 percent. If we assume that individuals with no income are completely unhappy, which is implied by our model in Chapters 3 and 4, this would mean that such disease-inflicted individuals would be extremely unhappy due to their disease. The high ratios may also reflect the fundamental truth that money is never sufficient to compensate for lack of health. Hence, a monetary compensation will never be enough.

There are more mundane specification problems, which, at the present stage, we were unable to solve in a satisfactory way. First, the diseases are quite summarily described in our data set. We have no idea about the severity of most diseases. Hence, we have to be content with 0 – 1 variables. The second point is that our functional specifications may not be fine enough to describe extreme cases. A third point may concern the income definition. We think it rather remarkable that the effect of income on well-being is much higher in Germany than in the UK. If we discard the possibility that the British character differs significantly from the German, this would imply that the income definition might be different from that used in Germany. It is well known that measurement errors in explanatory variables reduce the absolute values of the corresponding regression coefficients. We have the feeling that the income coefficient in financial satisfaction and the effect of financial satisfaction on general satisfaction in particular may be underestimated from the British data set at our disposal. These are the coefficients that play an important role, because they figure in the denominator in the formulae above. The conclusion is that we would not advise the use of the coefficients which we found in this first research endeavor in practice, but rather consider this research as a pilot study. It shows that this method can be utilized in practice, but that the model should be refined on the basis of data sets which provide more detailed information, especially on the health situation of the respondents.

9.5. OTHER METHODS IN THE HEALTH ECONOMICS LITERATURE

In order to evaluate this method and to see it in its proper perspective we will now briefly describe some other (established) methods. Evidently, we cannot exhaust the broad literature.

As we saw above, there are two basic steps. The first one is to identify and to evaluate a health change caused by a medical intervention or application of a therapy. Say the original health situation is H_0 which is evaluated by its utility $U(H_0)$ and the situation 'after' is H_1 with utility $U(H_1)$. The second step is to value this change in terms of money. In the sections above we have developed and empirically operationalized a method which does this twofold job.

In the literature, which is vast, several other methods have been developed for both tasks. However, in most cases they focus on one of the above; that is, either on the establishment of a health-utility function or on assigning a money value to health changes.

We start by considering briefly the proposals in the literature for defining and measuring health-utility functions. In this context we abstain from giving numerous references but we base ourselves on Drummond et al. (1997) and the *Handbook for Health Economics* by Culyer and Newhouse (2000) as up-to-date references. See also Dolan and Tsuchiya (2005), Dolan, Peasgood, and White (2006), and Tsuchiya and Dolan (2005).

Let us assume that the health situation can be described by a variable or a vector H. Then, we assume that there is a cardinal utility function $U(.)$ which evaluates health situations. Nearly always this utility function is scaled between 0 and 1, where perfect health is evaluated by 1 and the situation of death and all situations worse than death are evaluated by 0.

Frequently an intervention will not only change the health level or quality but also the life expectancy, say from T_0 to T_1. In that case we have to assign a time index to the health profile and we can evaluate the change from (H_0, T_0) to (H_1, T_1) by $\sum_{t=1}^{T_1} q_t U(H_1) - \sum_{t=1}^{T_0} q_t U(H_0)$, where q stands for a time weight or discount factor. In that case we can have a health improvement by an improvement in quality, an increase in life expectancy, and an increase in both dimensions simultaneously. Here we neglect the time aspect and focus on the quality aspect.

The problem is how to evaluate health situations by a utility function $U(H)$. How do we construct such a cardinal utility function? In the literature we do not find a uniformly accepted solution. There are various suggested methods.

The Standard Gamble (SG) method
The first method is the Standard Gamble (SG) method. We have a specific health situation H and we offer a respondent a gamble with chance p on being in perfect health and a chance on death. We might think of a specific operation

with a chance $(1 - p)$ on instantaneous death. We ask the respondent for which value of p he or she is indifferent between H and the offered gamble. Assuming that the respondent deals with this problem according to the Von Neumann-Morgenstern model, this question is tantamount to solving $U(H)$ from the equation

$$U(H) = (1 - p)U(death) + pU(completely\ healthy) = p. \qquad (9.8)$$

This is an extremely easy method, but there are some major problems attached to it.

First, it assumes Von Neumann-Morgenstern behavior, which is debated in the literature (see e.g. Kahneman and Tversky 1979 and their prospect theory). Second, it is well known that different individuals have different attitudes to risk which are reflected in individual parameters in their utility function. Say, $U_i(H) = U(H; \gamma_i)$. Hence, it is very likely that you will find different answers from different individuals. This does not make the method invalid, but it implies that we should account for those individual differences, and that is not easy. We would for instance find that a 25-year-old would have a different utility function from a '65-year-old', and hence would evaluate the objective health changes differently. A third objection, which is still more basic, deals with the fact that the choice situation is handled on the basis of a *decision utility* function in the sense of Kahneman, Wakker, and Sarin (1997). This is a problem if the evaluation of health situations depends on the health situation, say H_0, of the evaluator. Then a health situation H is evaluated by $U(H; H_0)$. It is well known from adaptation theory that individuals adapt to their situation. For instance, a mobile person may deem the situation of being immobile as worthless; however, if he or she is in such a situation for some time the individual will adapt and learn to live with the new situation. The reference or anchor point has changed (cf. the preference drift model). It implies that the respondent solves

$$U(H; H_0) = (1 - p)U(death) + pU(completely\ healthy) = p. \qquad (9.9)$$

This is unfortunate to say the least. It implies that the response on this SG would differ between healthy respondents and respondents who are in situation H; that is, actual patients. And in that case we face the dilemma of whether the health change should be evaluated according to the feelings of the patient or according to the evaluation of the healthy citizen. The SG method seems only acceptable for policy if it were to be based on an experienced utility function.

This would suggest as a proxy solution that the SG is not posed to laymen but to medics, who may be supposed to know all the health situations involved and who may have an objective evaluation function in their mind. However, if we base our evaluation of health differences on the evaluation made by doctors, we introduce a paternalistic element and, moreover, even among doctors opinions are not uniform but differ widely. Finally, the attraction of the SG method was exactly that we could base our work on the opinions of citizens and patients instead of on the opinions of the medical profession, which are not necessarily representative of the population as a whole.

The Time Trade-off (TTO) Method

The TTO method resembles the SG method to some degree and it suffers accordingly from the same shortcomings. Now the offer is to live for T years in imperfect health H or to live for $T_0 < T$ years in perfect health H_0 with $U(H_0) = 1$ by definition. The question is how many years in perfect health are equivalent to a longer life in imperfect health. If we assume that health over lifetime is evaluated by an additive utility function over life $\sum_{t=1}^{T} U(H_t)$, the TTO question implies the solution of the equation

$$T.U(H) = T_0 \tag{9.10}$$

which yields $U(H) = T_0/T$. Again a very simple solution, but it hangs very much on the additive definition of the utility function. For instance, when we assume a subjective time-discount process such that the utility function looks like $\sum_{t=1}^{T} \rho^t U(H_t)$, where ρ stands for the subjective time discount rate, it is obvious that the solution of the previous equation becomes

$$U(H) = \frac{\sum_{t=1}^{T_0} \rho^t}{\sum_{t=1}^{T} \rho^t} \tag{9.11}$$

It follows that the estimated health utility function, when operationalized in this way, depends not only on H but also on the subjective time discount rate ρ, which may and probably will vary between individuals. Moreover, the same objections as against the SG method may be raised with respect to the TTO method. We mention only that it is also based on an *ex ante* approach; that is, on a decision utility function.

The VAS method

Finally, we consider the visible-attitude-scale method. In this case individuals are asked to evaluate a specific health situation either by a numerical grade on a (0, 10)-scale or by positioning the health situation under consideration on a bounded interval scale, where the end points represent death and perfect health. It is obvious that this method is much simpler than the thought-experiments required by SG or TTO. The answers are not affected by differences in attitudes to risk or time-discounting. It still suffers from the anchor problem, and the method will result in a *decision* utility function according to which several health situations are evaluated. We saw already that decision utility functions are not a direct basis for producing a health utility function which can be used for policy. However, in this case it is conceivable to use the method for producing an experienced utility function as well. For this we have to ask each individual to evaluate his or her *own* health situation only. If we again write the decision utility function as $U(H; H_0)$ the utility experienced is $U(H_0; H_0)$ and it is this utility which is measured by VAS applied to the *own* situation. Hence, if we have a sample of respondents with varying and known health situations H and we derive evaluations $U(H; H) = \tilde{U}(H)$ the latter function can be interpreted as the *experienced* utility function we look for.

In fact, this last procedure looks very similar to the health-satisfaction question, and the outcome resembles our domain-satisfaction value for health. In the next section we shall see how similar it exactly is.

But first, let us briefly look at the second step. Let us assume we have a utility measure by means of which it is possible to evaluate a utility difference between H_0 and H_1 as $U(H_0) - U(H_1)$. The unit with which we are measuring is utility or, as it is frequently called, a quality-adjusted life year (QALY). The latter term refers to the unit of a year of life in perfect health, and obviously $U(H)$ is the value of a year living in health situation H. Now the question which is relevant for comparisons between various policies is whether we can assign a monetary value to a QALY? For if we can do that we can evaluate the money value of a difference $\sum_{t=1}^{T_1} q_t U(H_1) - \sum_{t=1}^{T_0} q_t U(H_0)$.

In the literature there are roughly two methods proposed. The first method is to assign an amount to a QALY unit which is decided by intuition and political acceptability. For instance, in American literature (see e.g. Cutler and Richardson 1997, 1998) the value is frequently put at $100,000. This value is chosen somewhat arbitrarily. Mostly, no difference is made between rich and poor people, between young and old people, or between people with a lot of dependants and singles. It seems to us that the main charm of this choice is its simplicity. However, the choice is not without consequences. If we try to evaluate the value of a therapy which costs $20,000 and the health improvement is 0.21 QALY, it is clear that the therapy will lead to a 'profit in money' of $1,000, while at a choice of the QALY-value of $90,000 the application would cause a 'loss in money' of $2,100. It follows that the choice of the money value of a QALY is quite crucial in terms of political decision-making.

The second way in which money values are assigned is by means of contingent valuation (CV) surveys (see e.g. Diener, O'Brien, and Gafni 1998 and Luchini, Protière, and Moatti 2003). In such a survey (see Luchini et al.) 'vignettes' are presented of the type

	Breast cancer
Proposed service	New treatment for poor diagnosis
Concerned population	Women aged 45–70
Outcomes	3 additional years' survival for 3 women out of 200 new cases, where 27 other women already get 3 more years.

The question is then how much individuals are willing to pay for the availability of such treatment. Undoubtedly this method gives some insight into the value individuals attach to the proposed service. Adding up the individual responses we get some idea of the money value the society attaches to this treatment. However, there are a lot of questions which have to be solved before such a method becomes generally acceptable. The first problem is clearly that the responses will vary per responding individual. Whether the individual is a male or a female obviously makes a difference. Are there cases of breast cancer in the family of the respondent? What is the age of the respondent? etc. What is the effect of the wording, description, and framing of the issue under consideration? What is the difference between willingness to pay and willingness to accept? The reader can easily think of other discussion points. The method of contingent valuation is frequently used for the evaluation of choices for the solution of environmental problems. Although the method is accepted by some, others are very critical. We refer to Hausman (1993), who gathered a number of critical reviews of aspects of the method. In this context we are not considering this method in depth. Personally we agree with most of the arguments presented in Hausman (1993). Although the approach has steadily improved, the main points of critique are not solved yet.

9.6. A SIMPLE OPERATIONALIZATION OF THE QALY CONCEPT

Given the above summary it is evident that the question of how to evaluate the health quality of life is far from resolved. Therefore, we would like to return to the health-satisfaction question already considered above. In our opinion this is a natural basis for the definition of health quality and consequently of QALY measurement.

If an individual evaluates his or her health at 7 on a 0–10 scale, this means that his or her health is less than perfect and the difference from perfect health is 3. We have asked the individual to give a cardinal judgement and there is no reason to interpret it in a more prudent, that is ordinal, way. We quote Cutler and Richardson (1997: 252), who state: 'this method is preferable to the others in the literature because it is straightforward for people to answer, it is based on individual, not expert opinion'. Indeed, the question looks for an experienced (health) utility function. Hence, if we pose the question to individuals of whom we know their health, it is possible to link various health situations with their subjective evaluation in terms of health quality.

Health utility is here operationalized by means of the following health-satisfaction question:

How dissatisfied or satisfied are you with your health?

In the British Household Panel Survey individuals are asked to give a categorical answer from 1 to 7, where 1 stands for 'not satisfied at all', and 7 for 'completely satisfied'. We call the answer to this question the individual's health satisfaction (HS). Health satisfaction (HS) is the observed discrete-valued counterpart of an individual continuous health utility function U(h), which is not continuously observable. It is assumed that U can take values on a bounded interval $[a, b]$. In the BHPS module this is the interval $[1, 7]$. Without loss of generality, we may rescale to the $[0, 1]$-interval. This means that the $[1, 7]$ interval is mapped, by a linear transformation, onto $[0, 1]$. The seven response categories stand for intervals on the continuous scale. It stands to reason that a discretely valued response of 5 signals that the underlying value of U has to be found in the interval $(4.5, 5.5]$. For, if H equalled 4.25, the respondent would round it off to 4 instead of to 5 or 3. Similarly, a response of 1 stands for an H value in the interval $[1.0, 1.5]$ and a response of 7 for an H value in the interval $(6.5, 7.0]$. After rescaling the $[1, 7]$-scale on to the $[0, 1]$-scale, the interval $[1.0, 1.5]$ is mapped to $[0, \frac{0.5}{6}]$, the interval $(1.5, 2.5]$ to $[\frac{0.5}{6}, \frac{1.5}{6}]$, and so on. We denote this partition of the $[0, 1]$-interval as $\{(U_{i-1}, U_i)\}_{i=1}^{i=7}$.

Our first aim is to explain the variable U by means of some individual characteristics, such as age, education and income, and by the occurrence of chronic diseases. In the BHPS, as we saw (Table 9.1), we can distinguish 13 diseases and impairments, which correspond to 13 dummy variables. The dummy variables take the value 1 if the respondent has the disease and are 0 otherwise. In order to account for omitted or unobservable variables, random influences, and errors, a normally distributed error ε with mean zero and variance equal to σ^2 is added. The theoretical relation between the individual's health utility function and individual characteristics is then specified by us as

$$U = N(\beta'x + \varepsilon) \qquad (9.12)$$

where the function $N(.)$ stands for the standard normal-distribution function, x for a vector of explanatory variables, and β for an effect vector to be estimated. We assume that ε is not correlated with x. The unknown variance σ^2 will have to be estimated as well. Clearly, we may ask at this point: How do you know that this normal distribution function is the relation we are looking for? The answer must be that we do not. Just as in empirical regression analysis, where we approximate a relationship between a dependent variable y and a number of independent variables x by a linear regression equation $y = \beta'x + \varepsilon$, we conjecture or postulate here that the above relation is appropriate to model the relation between the x and the U values. The reason for choosing a linear relationship in regression analysis is mostly not very convincing. The main reason is that the linear specification is simple and tractable. If there are serious non-linearities, they may be repaired by taking non-linear transforms of the x's like square roots, logs, or exponentials. Here the main point is that the answer U has to be bounded by 0 and 1. This calls for a distribution function, defined on the real axis. The normal distribution function is then the most appropriate function. There is no dogma behind this choice. It is a question of empirical fit whether the normal distribution function is the best choice. However, there are not many tractable distribution functions, defined on the real axis, which can compete. We may think of the logistic curve. Then, we would have to replace the normal quantiles u by their logistic analogues, and the estimation procedure runs similarly. It may also be questioned whether the random ε is normally distributed or whether it follows another distribution, such as the logistic. However, it is well known that the results from both specifications do not differ much, except for a proportionality factor.

The likelihood of the sample is found by realizing that

$$P(U_{i-1} < H \leq U_i) = P(u_{i-1} < N^{-1}(H) \leq u_i)$$

$$= P\left(u_{i-1} < \frac{\beta' x + \varepsilon}{\sigma} \leq u_i\right) \tag{9.13}$$

$$= N\left(\frac{u_i - \beta' x}{\sigma}\right) - N\left(\frac{u_{i-1} - \beta' x}{\sigma}\right),$$

where the u's are quantiles of the normal distribution, defined by $u_1 = N^{-1}(U_1)$, $u_2 = N^{-1}(U_2)$, ... Equation (9.12) is estimated. Table 9.4 presents the estimation results for three different specifications of Equation (9.12) by means of the COLS method (grouped data regression) (see Greene 1991; ch. 21 and Chapter 2 of this book). This model is very similar to the ordered-probit model, except that the intercept terms u_i are known. As argued in Chapter 2 we cannot here use ordered probit, because we make explicit use of the cardinal information supplied by the respondent.

We present various versions of the health equation in Table 9.4. In the first specification health satisfaction HS is explained only by various socio-economic and demographic variables, such as age, income, education, family size, and employment status. In the second specification the dummies for illnesses are added. In the third and last specification interaction terms between the illnesses and age are included so as to make the illness effects age-specific. The last specification is, to the best of our knowledge, estimated for the first time.

Let us start with the simplest explanation in which no information about the diseases is used. The first two columns of Table 9.4 show the results.

Age is included in logarithms, as we believe the effects to be non-linear. Additionally, the variable ln(age) is introduced in squared form. The reason for this is to explore whether the effect of age is non log-linear. The first specification shows that the age effects are not significant. Health satisfaction falls monotonically with age (see also Deaton and Paxson 1998). Health satisfaction is positively and significantly correlated with income. The positive correlation between income and health has been extensively discussed in the literature (see e.g. Smith 1999; Deaton and Paxson 1998). Males are slightly more satisfied with their health than females. The coefficient for education is negative but

Table 9.4. *Health-satisfaction equations, total sample, UK, 1998, COLS*

	Estimate	t-ratio	Estimate	t-ratio	Estimate	t-ratio
Intercept term	-1.265	1.736	2.721	4.162	2.221	3.353
Ln(age)	-0.427	-1.033	-1.107	-2.974	-0.712	-1.880
(Ln(age))^2	0.027	0.480	0.175	3.405	0.114	2.162
Minimum	25.59	—	24	—	23	—
Ln(income last month)	0.076	6.047	0.010	0.867	0.001	0.093
Ln(children + 1)	0.173	2.396	0.054	0.856	0.055	0.882
Ln^2(children + 1)	-0.104	-1.841	-0.033	-0.666	-0.030	-0.625
Maximum	2.30	—	2.28	—	2.47	—
Gender (male)	0.061	3.052	-0.035	-1.924	-0.033	-1.838
Ln(years education)	-0.023	-0.985	-0.038	-1.823	-0.046	-2.278
Missing education	-0.275	-2.168	-0.267	-2.411	-0.302	-2.767
Living together	0.016	0.655	-0.011	-0.494	-0.009	-0.437
Problems with arms, legs, hands, feet, back, or neck	—	—	-0.509	-24.052	-0.491	-23.478
Difficulty in seeing	—	—	-0.238	-5.654	-0.225	-5.434
Difficulty in hearing	—	—	-0.094	-2.844	-0.076	-2.343
Skin conditions/allergies	—	—	-0.137	-5.236	-0.099	-3.843
Heart/blood problems	—	—	-0.378	-14.029	-1.448	-4.345
Problems with stomach/liver/kidney	—	—	-0.520	-15.691	-2.032	-6.197
Diabetes	—	—	-0.401	-7.299	-1.591	-2.740
Anxiety, depression, or bad nerves	—	—	-0.670	-20.024	-0.644	-19.487
Alcohol or drug-related problems	—	—	-0.854	-6.353	-0.798	-6.010
Epilepsy	—	—	-0.584	-5.975	-0.555	-5.764
Migraine or frequent headaches	—	—	-0.155	-5.090	-0.141	-4.681
Other health problems	—	—	-0.624	-16.281	-1.561	-4.296
Chest/breathing problems*ln(age)	—	—	—	—	-0.103	-15.348
Heart/blood problems*ln(age)	—	—	—	—	0.270	3.287
Problems with stomach/liver/kidneys*ln(age)	—	—	—	—	0.395	4.717
Diabetes*ln(age)	—	—	—	—	0.300	2.086
Others*ln(age)	—	—	—	—	0.246	2.634
Sigma	0.976	115.215	0.848	115.192	0.834	115.185
Log likelihood	-18,362.5	—	-17,101	—	-16,962	—
Number of individuals	10,385	—	10,385	—	10,385	—

One pt greater effect on health satisfaction

non-significant. The negative correlation between education and health satisfaction has also been found by Groot (2000) and Kerkhofs and Lindeboom (1995). The number of children in the household is also included in logarithms and in squared logs so as to find whether there is a turning-point effect. We find, indeed, that, healthwise, having children seems to be a mixed blessing, with an optimum number around two children.

The results for the second specification are shown in the third and fourth columns of Table 9.4 (see also Table 3.10). It is seen that the explanation changes considerably when we introduce dummies for specific diseases. The first thing that emerges is age becoming significant. Moreover, the quadratic specification of age shows that age now has a positive effect on health from the age of 23 years onward. Thus, the inclusion of the dummies for illnesses changes the age coefficient from negative to positive for most of life. This may be explained by the fact that the date of incidence of most illnesses is correlated with age. Thus, the variable age in the first specification is picking up the effect of the illnesses. Income and children, on the contrary, become now insignificant. The gender effect is now reversed. Education becomes more negative and significant. The disease coefficients are all significant and negative. Using this, we can derive a hierarchy of diseases according to the magnitude of their effects on individual health satisfaction. Notice that we have to bear in mind that illnesses are not differentiated by degree of severity. Therefore, an illness that can be found in various very different degrees will have a coefficient that depends on the frequency distribution of the degree of severity in the sample.

The results of the third specification are presented in the fifth and six columns of Table 9.4. This specification includes interaction terms between illnesses and age, so that the question of whether the impact of the illness on health satisfaction is age-dependent or not can be explored. The reasons for this are two: (1) The degree of severity of an illness may vary with age. This

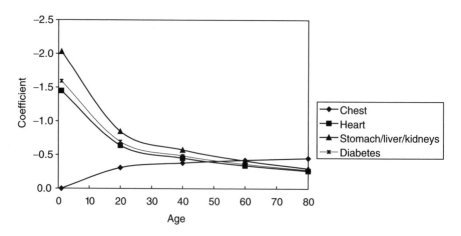

Figure 9.1. *Age-dependent effects of various illnesses and impediments*

seems to be the case for 'chest and breath problems', the effect of which on HS increases with age as shown in Table 9.4. (2) Even if the illness becomes objectively more severe with age, the individual may subjectively perceive it differently. The reasons can be diverse: people may adapt to an illness; older individuals may require less from their body than younger individuals; and older individuals may get other disorders as well, such that their original illness becomes only one of several complaints. These reasons could be the explanation for the positive age coefficients found for 'heart and blood problems', 'problems with the stomach, liver, and kidneys', and 'diabetes'. For the other 9 omitted impediments and illnesses we did not find a marked age-dependency. Figure 9.1 displays the age pattern for various illnesses and shows that health losses decrease with age except for the 'chest and breath problems'.

9.7. QALY ESTIMATES OF HEALTH LOSSES

In Table 9.5 we present the estimation results in which the evaluation of health is specified as a function of individual characteristics, including disease dummies. From the estimated model we now derive the predicted health utility

$$\hat{H} = N(\hat{\beta}'x). \qquad (9.14)$$

Although prediction for individuals would be rather inaccurate, for the assessment of the *average* health of a population we can use this expression, as the random errors will cancel out.

Then, one can define the *absolute* health-utility change when moving from one health status (1) to another health status (2). Assuming that status (1) stands for having none of the specified diseases or impairments, we define the absolute health loss by

$$\text{Absolute loss} = \hat{H}(1) - \hat{H}(2) \qquad (9.15)$$

Similarly, the *relative* health-utility loss is defined as

$$\text{Relative loss} = \frac{\hat{H}(1) - \hat{H}(2)}{\hat{H}(1)} \qquad (9.16)$$

Using the above formulae, we present the absolute and relative health-utility losses for all discerned illnesses for a representative individual of 30 and for one of 60. The results are presented in Table 9.5. As a representative individual we take an individual who shares all characteristics with the sample mean, except that he or she does not suffer from any illness.[2] Evidently, age is not set at the sample average but at 30 or 60 years old in order to assess the impact of diseases at various ages.

---

[2] The sample mean in 1998 for income is £1,642 (UK) per month, around 11 years of education, and about 40 years old.

Table 9.5. *Health losses caused by various diseases*

	Absolute health loss		Relative health loss	
	30	60	30	60
Average health for individuals without specified diseases	0.840	0.862	—	—
Problems with arms, legs, hands, feet, back, or neck	0.147	0.137	0.175	0.159
Difficulty in seeing	0.061	0.056	0.073	0.065
Difficulty in hearing	0.019	0.017	0.023	0.020
Skin conditions/allergies	0.025	0.023	0.030	0.027
Chest/breathing problems	0.100	0.114	0.119	0.132
Heart/blood problems	0.161	0.089	0.192	0.103
Stomach/liver/kidneys	0.219	0.111	0.261	0.129
Diabetes	0.176	0.096	0.210	0.111
Anxiety, depression, or bad nerves	0.203	0.190	0.242	0.220
Alcohol or drug-related problems	0.262	0.247	0.312	0.287
Epilepsy	0.170	0.158	0.202	0.183
Migraine or frequent headaches	0.037	0.033	0.044	0.038
Other health problems	0.234	0.158	0.279	0.183

Table 9.6. *Health utility sample averages*

	Total	Male	Female	<30	30–60	>=60
Average predicted health utility (U)	0.7164	0.7311	0.7040	0.7628	0.7195	0.6540
Health utility (U) loss	0.1349	0.1152	0.1514	0.0769	0.1292	0.2170
N	10,385	4,737	5,648	2,762	5,300	2,323

Table 9.5 shows that an individual of 30 years old with none of the diseases asked about in the BHPS has an average health utility of 0.840 on a [0, 1] scale. For somebody of 60 with none of the specified diseases this is even slightly higher,[3] being 0.862. An individual of 30 with problems with his or her 'arms, legs, hands, feet, back, or neck' will in general incur an absolute loss of 0.147 in health utility. This is equivalent to a relative loss of 17.5 percent. Evidently, these are average figures, standing for individuals with completely different degrees of severity of the handicap. Table 9.5 shows that for all diseases except for each individual we calculate its predicted health utility given its personal and household characteristics. . . .

[3] This unexpected result is caused by the fact that young and old have different utility functions, the old individuals having fewer requirements than the young.

Let us now look at the health utility for the sample averages. The first column of Table 9.6 shows the average predicted actual health utility for all respondents. In other words, for each individual we calculate its predicted health utility given their personal and household characteristics and the actual presence of one or various illnesses. The average predicted health utility for the whole population is about 0.72. The average health-utility loss for the population caused by the fact that individuals in the sample suffer from one or more illnesses equals 0.1349. Average predicted health falls with increasing age from 0.76 to 0.65. This is not caused by increasing age per se but by the fact that older people have more of the (specified) diseases. Females have a lower health utility than males. The average health utility loss caused by the illnesses, shown in the second row of Table 9.6, also depends on the sub-sample. For the total sample the health utility is reduced, as a result of illnesses, by more than 18 percent (0.13/0.71). This percentage is about 30 percent for individuals older than 60.

9.8. DISCUSSION

Above we presented a rather ambitious alternative to the usual QALY definitions. As we pointed out before there is no accepted methodology in the literature. In the last resort the definition is a matter of subjective preferences, as there is no natural concept of QALY simply waiting to be defined and measured.

One way is to assess 'quality of life' according to expert medical opinion. When the assessment is done by (medical) experts, they will of course express their own opinions and use their own value-system. Whether this value-system is actually representative of the very heterogeneous population they are representing is questionable. Given the diversity of human beings, old and young, with widely differing value-systems, we believe the task is simply impossible. A second way to assess health quality is to base the assessment on the valuations of individuals of their own *experienced* health situation. In our view the subjective approach is the most appropriate way to get insight into the health perception of individuals. This can be done in more or less sophisticated ways; for example, by TTO or SG analyses on the one hand, or by a simple health-satisfaction question (HSQ) on the other, as we propose here. Both approaches have their own pros and cons. The HSQ approach has the advantage that we can gather large and representative data sets at low cost. Given the setting of this question in a large multi-purpose questionnaire, the chance of influencing the response by 'framing' and the creation of a bias seems to be negligible.

Another objection which is sometimes made is that a status of 'perfect health' is not the same objective situation for a 25-year-old as for somebody who is 70. This is clearly true. However, does it matter in this context? We are interested in how individuals evaluate their own health situation and we take it for granted that if two individuals evaluate their health by the same number (on the same scale) they feel equally satisfied with their health, even if their objective health situations differ.

The health-utility losses caused by various physical handicaps and illnesses are measured by means of individual self-ratings of health, as provided by the health-satisfaction question in the British Household Panel Survey. The health losses appear to be considerable and to vary over the distinct diseases. It is seen that the effect of an illness on health may vary with the age of the individual. Therefore, interaction terms between illnesses and age are introduced in this study. Indeed, for some diseases we did find a considerable age-dependency. For instance, a 30-year-old individual suffering from diabetes appears to experience a health-utility loss of 0.176, while this is only 0.096 if the individual is 60 years old. It is obvious that this can be extended to other characteristics such as gender and job situation. The health-utility losses differentiated by age have a clear implication for the cost-effectiveness analysis of therapies, as the effectiveness of the therapy depends on the individual health-utility gain derived from it. It is obvious that this measurement could be much improved if differentiation according to the severity of the disease were possible. For that, a more refined data set is needed.

Recently, Cutler and Richardson (1997) analyzed the HSQ in an American data set. Later on, Groot (2000) replicated their analysis on the same British data we are using. Superficially their method resembles ours. However, the methods are different. The methodological difference between those contributions and ours is that they do not use the cardinal information which is supplied by the response behavior. They do not specify the interval bounds U_i but consider them to be unknown. Those bounds are estimated by the ordered-probit method simultaneously with the effect vector β, which we denote by $\beta^{(CR)}$ for short. The estimated bounds are denoted by $\mu_0, \mu_1, \ldots, \mu_6, \mu_7$, where the extreme bounds are equal to $-\infty$ and $+\infty$. The result is an estimated health index $(\beta^{(CR)})'x$, which is not bounded between 0 and 1, but which may assume any positive or negative value. Its scaling depends on the health distribution in the sample considered. The higher the value is, the higher the *probability* of good health. In order to scale the index between 0 and 1 they define a truncated health-utility index by

$$H^{(CR)} = \beta^{(CR)}x/(\mu_6 - \mu_1) \qquad \text{if } \mu_1 < \beta^{(CR)}x \leq \mu_6$$
$$H^{(CR)} = 0 \qquad \text{if } \beta^{(CR)}x \leq \mu_1$$
$$H^{(CR)} = 1 \qquad \text{if } \mu_6 < \beta^{(CR)}x.$$

Hence, Cutler and Richardson assume that health is constant and equal to 0 for all respondents in the lowest response category and constant and equal to 1 for all respondents in the highest response category. It follows that this index

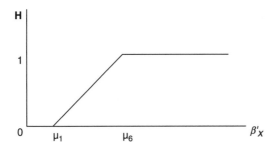

Figure 9.2. *The linear health curve according to Cutler and Richardson*

cannot differentiate between health situations *within* the extreme response categories. The outer bounds, that is the values μ_1 and μ_6, are defined by the fractions of respondents found in the outer response classes. The linearity in the middle range is also questionable. According to the logic of this model we would expect a spline function with nodes at $\mu_1, \ldots, \mu_6$. It implies that the slope would change per interval $[\mu_{i-1}, \mu_i]$. However, the most important critique of this definition is that the μ-values are defined by the sample distribution. Hence, different samples will yield different μ-values and outer bounds (the anchors). Hence, the Cutler–Richardson index values between different samples cannot be compared. In our method we do not need a scaling device as we use the cardinal information supplied by the respondents themselves.

We are aware of the fact that the operationalization of health utility remains a difficult methodological problem. The following 'criteria' seem relevant for a methodological evaluation: How does the index differentiate between health situations? Is it easy to operationalize the index, and does it yield comparable and repeatable results? What are the costs of implementing the index on a large scale? Our proposal obviously scores quite high on these criteria.

We have also to keep the objective in mind. If we want to assess the health of a specific individual we should have a much more accurate instrument than the one we develop here. Our approach seems useful to evaluate the health situations of populations and population subgroups and the impact of specific illnesses and handicaps on population health. Other more problem-oriented surveys are needed to trace the effect of illnesses and possible therapies in more detail.

9.9. CONCLUSION

In this chapter we have investigated whether it is possible to trace the effect of specific diseases on health and indirectly on the quality of life as a whole. We found that this is indeed quite possible. This gave rise to two applications.

First, using the satisfaction model developed in Chapter 4, we could assess money values equivalent to the losses in well-being caused by the incidence of specific diseases. These estimates may be used as one of the ingredients for cost–benefit analyses, as they indicate the money value of 'intangible costs' caused by diseases. We might clearly extend this model by looking at the effect of the disease of one spouse on the well-being of the other spouse to get an idea of the intangible costs inflicted on a healthy spouse by his or her non-healthy partner. Then we would get the intangible costs inflicted on the house-hold. We abstained from doing this here.

Second, we exploited the health-satisfaction question on its own to construct a new QALY concept. The attraction of this method is that it leads to an intuitively plausible concept and that it is extremely easy and cheap to collect the basic data for it. We repeat that the results are based on a data set which is not rich on health information, but it is very likely that the method, when replicated on a data set with more patients whose health situation is described in more detail, may lead to a very valuable method of health assessment. Evidently, we should have the opportunity to compare the behavior of various QALY measures on the same sample of individuals.

In fact, the methods developed in this chapter must be applicable in other contexts as well. This will be the subject of the three following chapters.

The Effects of Climate on Welfare and Well-Being—External Effects

10.1. INTRODUCTION

In the previous chapter we investigated the effect of chronic diseases on satisfaction with life as a whole. We were then able to estimate trade-off ratios between those diseases and income, or, in other words, the shadow prices of various diseases.

It is rather obvious that, at least in theory, the same approach can be used for the assessment of the impact of many other exogenous variables as well. In the next two chapters we consider two examples. In this chapter we look at the effect of climate on welfare and well-being. This chapter sets the stage for a general method for the assessment of *external effects*. For non-economists this concept needs some explanation. An individual's situation may be described by two types of variables, say y and x, and, accordingly, the individual's well-being is evaluated by an evaluation function $U(y; x)$. The first variables are variables which the individual may change by purchasing goods and services, choosing another job, and so on. The second class consists of variables that cannot be influenced by the individual but that affect his or her well-being as well. The climate is an obvious example. In fact, it would be preferable to speak of external *factors* instead of external *effects*. However, the subject was first studied within the framework of industries that pollute their environment and hence damage the living environment of others. Here we can indicate an agent that generates an external effect from which others are suffering. The question is then how the disadvantage for the passive party should be evaluated and whether he or she can be compensated for the damage. In the present framework we use the word in a wider context, where no specific generator can be identified and where the external effect cannot be stopped.

When one is looking for climate effects it stands to reason that one must have observations from regions with different climates. It follows that we can only use data sets which refer to large countries or which cover a sufficient variety of small countries. There are not many data sets which allow for those possibilities. A second conceptual problem is that the definition of climate is not as simple as one might expect.

At the moment there is a growing awareness of climate as a major dimension and determinant of our natural environment. This evidently springs from the insight that mankind is able to change the climate nationally or worldwide and that such a change can have an impact on individuals, households, and the cost of living, not to speak of the whole ecosystem. There is an 'intangible cost' associated with such changes and there is a need for an assessment method for such costs.

Similarly, as before we can distinguish between the 'decision-utility' and the 'experienced-utility' approach. In this chapter we shall look at experienced utility throughout.

There are various ways in which climate may affect our life. First, prices may vary with the climate. Grapes will cost less in Italy than in Norway. It may also be that our needs vary with the climate. For instance, we need more and more expensive clothing in a cold climate than in a warm climate.

Apart from these effects, which we hope to discover when studying financial satisfaction, it may be that climate affects such other life domains as our health satisfaction, job satisfaction, and finally satisfaction with life as a whole.

When thinking about climate we have to realize that climate is not a one-dimensional concept. We have the variables rain, hours sunshine, average temperature, windiness, etc. Hence, the definition of climate as such is already a problem. Let us start by assuming a vector C of climate variables.

In this chapter we will report on two earlier studies (Van Praag 1988 and Frijters and Van Praag 1998). The first deals with data collected in the European Community in 1979. Here we consider how financial satisfaction and household costs are affected by climate. In the second study a Russian data set was analyzed in which the effect of climate on household costs and on general satisfaction was considered. Although no new calculations have been done, this chapter does not repeat the earlier papers completely, as, with the benefit of hindsight, we will give the results some new interpretations.

There are only a very few studies on the effect of climate on individual welfare or well-being, and we do not know of studies which are genuinely comparable to ours.

10.2. THE EFFECT OF CLIMATE ON HOUSEHOLD COST

Before we look at the climate effect we have to make sure what we mean by 'household costs'. Let us assume that the household has an income y and that one evaluates this income by a financial satisfaction function $U(y; x)$ where x stands for a vector of intervening variables. If we use the more traditional economic terminology, we call $U(.)$ the (indirect) utility function of income. Let us specify a specific welfare level by U_0, then we can calculate the household cost c which is required to realize that welfare level U_0 by solving the equation

$$U(c; x) = U_0 \tag{10.1}$$

for *c*. We call the function $c = c(U, x)$ the *household-cost function*. We notice that costs increase when we aspire to a higher utility level, and that household costs may depend on a vector of 'other variables'. In traditional economic analysis the vector *x* is replaced by the price vector *p*. If we know the function, we may then look at the effect of price changes on the household costs. We may then look at the ratio $c(U_0, p + \Delta p)/c(U_0, p)$ which gives the percentage decrease or increase in *c* which is needed to compensate for the price change from *p* to $p + \Delta p$. This ratio is a price index. Notice that this price index depends on the specification of the utility function and that it depends on the utility level U_0. The latter property is rather annoying. When politicians or citizens look at the changes in the price level, in general no differentiation is made between rich and poor people. It is assumed that the change of price level, as reflected by the price index, is the same for every citizen. It is obvious that this is possible if and only if $c = c(U, p) = \tilde{c}(U).I(p)$. Then the cost effect will not depend on *U* as

$$c(U_0, p + \Delta p)/c(U_0, p) = I(p + \Delta p)/I(p). \tag{10.2}$$

In that case we speak of a *homothetic* utility function. This property is frequently assumed in the literature in order to get a general price index.

Instead of the price vector *p* we can also put in its place the household size *fs*, and this is in fact what we did in Chapter 2, where we derived a family-equivalence scale.

In a similar way we may set for *x* the climate vector *C* and we will get a climate-equivalence scale. It is evident that we can also use a combination of prices, household structure, climate, etc.

The concept of household costs does not depend on a specific cardinalization of utility. Whether we attach a cardinal meaning to the value *U* or only an ordinal interpretation does not matter.

We can interpret $U(\Delta)$ as a decision utility function or as an experienced utility function. In the first case household costs are the costs we *expect to be needed* in order to reach the level *U*; in the second case they are the household costs needed *in reality* in order to reach the level *U*.

There are two ways in which climate can affect household costs. The first is via direct needs. It is quite probable that living in a harsh climate requires more expenditures to reach a specific satisfaction level than living in a mild climate. The second influence is more indirect. Climate can have an effect on prices. We may think of vegetables and meat and of production costs, where heating and transport are elements. Ideally, we would model the price vector as $p(p_0, C)$, where p_0 is a reference price vector. Then, household costs in order to reach utility level U_0 would be $c = c(U; p(p_0, C), C)$, where climate would affect household costs in two ways: through prices and directly. As we do not have information on prices, we shall look at a more simple specification; namely, $c = c(U; x)$. We can consider this as a reduced form, in which the two climate effects are aggregated and cannot be distinguished from each other. This implies that we can identify the climate effect, but that we cannot distinguish how much stems from climate-dependent *price* changes and how much from climate-induced differences in *needs*.

10.3. THE EFFECT OF CLIMATE ON HOUSEHOLD COSTS MEASURED BY INCOME EVALUATION

One of the few data sets we know of in which the income-evaluation question (IEQ; see Ch. 2) was posed simultaneously to inhabitants in several European countries, is a survey carried out in 1979. It was commissioned by the European Community and designed by Van Praag and Hagenaars. It is described extensively in Van Praag, Hagenaars, and Van Weeren (1982) and in Hagenaars (1986).

In the framework of the first European poverty study in which attention was given to the concept of 'subjective' poverty (see Ch. 15), the IEQ was posed to about 9,000 households in the Netherlands, the UK, Denmark, France, Belgium, Italy, Germany, and Ireland. An obvious way to test the effect of climate is then to look at whether climate has an effect on the parameter μ in the individual welfare function (see section 2.8).

We recall that the IEQ asks for income amounts $c_1, \ldots, c_6$, which may be called 'bad income', 'sufficient income', 'good income', etc. The parameter μ stands for the average of the log amounts.

The main problem is how we define the climate variable. As a matter of fact, up to now there is not *one* climate variable in the literature which is considered to represent climate as such. Therefore, we decided to use several variables simultaneously. In this European context many variables do not differ that much by country. The climate variables are not precisely known per individual, as the individual's location is only known by region and climatic variables are not registered by locality but only by region. Hence, we split Western Europe into 90 different regions, for which we could find a number of climate statistics. We ended up with the explanatory variables TEMP standing for the average annual temperature in centigrades, HUM standing for average humidity in percentages, and PREC standing for the precipitation in millimeters per year. We specified the equation

$$\ln(c_i) = (\beta_0^{(i)} + \beta_{0j}^{(i)}) + (\beta_1^{(i)} + \beta_{1j}^{(i)}) \ln(fs) + (\beta_2^{(i)} + \beta_{2j}^{(i)}) \ln(y_c) + \ldots$$
$$+ \gamma_1^{(i)} \ln(TEMP) + \gamma_2^{(i)} \ln(HUM) + \gamma_3^{(i)} \ln(PREC), \tag{10.3}$$

in which we added interaction terms for each country j in order to allow for the fact that effects may differ by country and level (c_i) in aspects other than climate as well. We found the usual differences[1] in β for the levels (c_i). The level differences for the climate variables were negligible. Hence, we reproduce our Table 10.1 from Van Praag (1988), where we have taken the average of the six-level equations (μ).

---

[1] See Ch. 2, Table 2.11.

Table 10.1. *The μ-equation estimated for Western Europe*

	Intercept	Log(fs)	Log(y)
The Netherlands (reference)	6.94	0.11	0.57
	(0.36)	(0.01)	(0.01)
UK	0.63	0.02	−0.08
	(0.23)	(0.02)	(0.02)
Denmark	−1.55	0.00	0.16
	(0.19)	(0.02)	(0.01)
France	0.42	−0.05	−0.02
	(0.18)	(0.02)	(0.02)
Belgium	0.31	0.00	−0.03
	(0.24)	(0.02)	(0.02)
Italy	1.30	0.03	−0.14
	(0.19)	(0.02)	(0.02)
Germany	−0.40	−0.01	0.03
	(0.21)	(0.02)	(0.02)
Ireland	0.45	0.06	−0.06
	(0.19)	(0.02)	(0.02)
Log(TEMP)	−0.15	—	—
	(0.03)	—	—
Log(HUM)	−0.41	—	—
	(0.06)	—	—
Log(PREC)	−0.10	—	—
	(0.01)	—	—
N	13,428	—	—
R^2	0.6548	—	—

Note: The Netherlands is taken as the reference. The other entries correspond to dummy coefficients. So the family-size elasticity in the UK is 0.11 + 0.02. Standard deviations are presented in parentheses. The estimates of the intercepts are based on the official exchange rates to the Dutch guilder of October 1979. For this particular problem involving only *slope* coefficients it is in fact not necessary to express the money amounts in one common currency unit.

The first thing which is striking is that the slope coefficients do not differ very much between the various countries. For most interaction coefficients we see that they do not differ statistically from zero. The second point is, evidently, that the three climate variables have a significant influence. In reality their effect will be even higher, as we only measured the climate variables regionally and not at the individual level. Consequently, they are ridden with measurement error.

More precisely, we find that the same income is evaluated higher the higher the temperature, the higher the humidity, and the more rain that falls. With respect to the interpretation of those coefficients we have to keep in mind that climate variables at a specific site are correlated. For instance, rain in Western Europe is correlated with lower temperatures.

We conclude that we may interpret

$$C = 0.15 \ln (TEMP) + 0.40 \ln (HUM) + 0.10 \ln (PREC) \tag{10.4}$$

as the log climate index for the *ex ante* utility function. The true climate index $m(C)$ is found by multiplying C by the multiplier $1/(1 - \beta_2 - \beta_{2j})$ and setting

$$m(TEMP, HUM, PREC) = \exp\left(\frac{1}{1 - \beta_2 - \beta_{2j}}(C - C^{(R)})\right), \tag{10.5}$$

where $C^{(R)}$ stands for the value of C in the reference country. In Table 10.1 this is The Netherlands. As the denominator varies per country we would get country-specific climate indices. This is not very helpful. As the values do not vary that much over countries, we take here an approximate average which amounts to $\beta_2 + \beta_{2j} = 0.5$. When we do that, it is possible to characterize any European site in terms of the three climate variables and to calculate the climate index. Evidently, we have to choose a reference site, for which we took Paris. We found then (see Van Praag 1988) Table 10.2.

Table 10.2 shows that the climate in Berlin is 11 percent more expensive than that of Paris. We have to take this interpretation with a pinch of salt. We saw that the price vector may depend on climate. Besides that, there may and will be other variables z that influence prices as well. For instance, prices will depend on the degree of urbanization, etc. In short, $p = p(C, z)$. Now it is obvious that the climate index covers only the climate effect in prices. It follows that this index has to be interpreted as that part of the household cost differences which may be attributed to climate differences.

Table 10.2. *Climate indices for some European cities*

Site	Climate
Paris	1.00
Berlin	1.11
London	1.08
Rome	0.95
Nice	0.91
Copenhagen	1.10
Sicily	0.94
Amsterdam	0.99
St. Hélier (Channel Islands)	0.87

Note: Paris is taken as the reference.

10.4. THE EFFECTS OF CLIMATE ON HOUSEHOLD COSTS AND WELL-BEING IN RUSSIA

The previous analysis has been repeated and extended by Frijters and Van Praag (1998) for a Russian data set[2] (CESSI, 1993–4). It will be understood that the quality of this data set is probably somewhat inferior to comparable western surveys at that time. Response behavior was less open than in the West. Given the consumption patterns, the fact that some major 'western' spending components were still heavily rationed in Russia in the survey period 1993–4 and/or supplied at unrealistic prices (e.g. housing costs), and the fact that part of the incomes were non-declared or in kind, we could not use all the observations. We used two waves of the Russian National Panel, for which we deleted the unreliable or too incomplete observations, and we ended up with an aggregate set of 2,508 households from the first wave and 1,904 observations from the second wave. We note that the observations were not wholly independent because of the panel character of the data set. However, Frijters and Van Praag found from unpublished analysis that the hypothesis of equal coefficients in both waves could not be rejected and that the correlation between error terms over both waves was negligible. Obviously, this was also caused by the chaotic circumstances in Russia, because usually we find in household samples a considerable household-specific random effect (see e.g. Chs. 3 and 4). The data set we use consists of 4,412 observations, in which the statistical significance of the estimated effects is slightly overestimated because of the neglect of the (slight) intertemporal correlation. We start by estimating the same μ-equation which we presented for western data in the previous section. For simplicity we repeat the figures for Europe from Table 10.1 in Table 10.3. For the European set we do not present the country-specific effects, and we drop the 1994 dummy for the Russian data set. As Russian temperatures are for some regions and periods below zero degrees Celsius, the logarithm is undefined for some observations. We repair this simply by adding 50 to the Russian numbers. This implies, however, that Russian figures and European figures cannot be directly compared.

From this table it is clear that the effects of non-climate variables do not differ dramatically from those found for Western Europe, although the family-size effect in Russia is much larger than in most of Western Europe. The climate effects, however, are very different and sometimes hard to interpret. Our conclusion is that we need a more refined climate description for Russia. It is of course very attractive to consider a Russian data set, because the climate

[2] The data set stems from a household panel survey held by the Institute for Comparative Social Research (CESSI) in Moscow under the guidance of Dr. Anna Andreenkova. It was designed and commissioned by Willem Saris of the University of Amsterdam with the financial support of the Dutch Foundation for Scientific Research (NWO).

Table 10.3. *Naive analysis of Russian data set*

Variable	Europe 1979	Absolute *t*-values	Russia 1993–4	*t*-values
Constant	6.94	20.6	2.17	2.1
Family size	0.11	10.8	0.22	12.5
Family income	0.57	57.0	0.65	60.2
Ln(temperature)	−0.15	5.0	−0.72	4.7
Ln(humidity)	−0.41	6.8	0.32	1.2
Ln(precipitation)	−0.10	10.0	0.16	4.7
N	—	13,428	—	4,412
R^2	0.6548	—	0.7254	

variation in Russia is much larger than in Western Europe. So a finer description of climate becomes possible.

Climate Variables
For the characterization of climate for such a climatically heterogeneous region as the Russian territory Frijters and Van Praag included more variables than for the previous analysis, which was restricted to Western Europe. The list of climate variables is shown in Table 10.4.

The tremendous differences between summer and winter temperatures in some regions make it necessary to introduce the winter and summer temperatures simultaneously. Given the chilly wind which frequently blows across the Russian steppe, we introduce the wind velocity as well. Given the availability of climate

Table 10.4. *Climate variables used for Russia*

Name	Description
JANTEMP	Average maximum daily temperature in January measured in C^0 plus 50
JULTEMP	Average maximum daily temperature in July measured in C^0 plus 50
TEMPAV	Average maximum daily temperature over a year measured in C^0 plus 50
TEMPDIF	JULTEMP–JANTEMP
RAINDAYS	Average number of days on which precipitation exceeded 0.1 mm
ALTITUDE	(Altitude in meters above sea level +50)/100
PREC	Average annual precipitation in mm
JANWIND	Average wind velocity in January in m/s
HUMIDITY	Relative humidity as a percentage
SUNHOURS	Average number of hours of sunshine per year
WINTERPREC	Average precipitation from October 1 to March 31
SUMMERPREC	Average precipitation from April 1 to September 30

data and the locations of our households it was possible to distinguish thirty-five different climate regions. The figures have been calculated as the averages from 104 weather stations in the USSR during the period 1931–60 (see Müller 1983).

A second point is that in Russia, as in America, the interstate mobility of labor is greater than in Western Europe. This is of course because it is one country, and international migration is culturally more difficult than that within a single country. However, migration comes at a price. If individuals have to be employed in Siberia (or Alaska) they have to be compensated in money, at least partially. It is obvious that a description of the Russian labor market is beyond our scope, but it is well known that the salary needed to seduce a worker to take on a job in Siberia or the Arctic region is frequently two or three times as high as the average over the country. This was also the case in Communist times, when the labor market was completely controlled from above. The same ratio is found for salaries in Alaska compared to US averages. It follows that we can expect that part of the climate effects will be compensated in the incomes. This, as we shall see in a moment, indeed happens to be the case. Let, for instance, $\ln(y) = \beta'x + \theta'C$, then the welfare index $\ln(y) - \mu$ gives an incorrect idea of the climate effect. For instance, if climate is 'exactly' compensated in income, we will not find any climate effect in $\ln(y) - \mu$. It follows that we will first see whether household incomes are partially determined by climate factors. We present the results in Table 10.5. It is obviously hard to interpret the non-climate effects, as the Russian labor market at that time was in a state of transition between a controlled economy and a more liberalized situation. The age profile is somewhat surprising, as the minimum household income is found at the age of 38, while most profiles in western economies are shaped with a maximum at about 50, not a minimum. We are interested in the climate effects. We see that climate plays a significant role. We have a combined effect

$$-1.53\ln(\text{JANTEMP}) + (\ln(\text{JANWIND})(5.35 - 1.54\ln(\text{JANTEMP})). \qquad (10.6)$$

We notice that on average $\ln(\text{JANTEMP})$ is about 4.7 and that $\ln(\text{JANWIND})$ is in the order of 1.8. It follows that both JANWIND and JANTEMP have a strong effect on wages. The harsher the weather is, the higher the household wages are. The same holds for extreme high temperatures as reflected in the JULTEMP effect. We note also the strong wave effect, which indicates that in one year nominal wages more than tripled. This reflects the rampant inflation in the period 1993–4.

In the Russian survey the income-evaluation question was also posed, this time with only five levels. The response was fairly good. We notice that, in spite of the hectic situation in Russia, the results of this equation do not look very different from western results. The family-size effect is more pronounced than in most western countries. The true effect equals about 0.45 (17/38), which is pretty high, reflecting the difficulties of families with children. This is also reflected by the very low Russian birth rate. We find significant climate effects, which look similar to the comparable effects on wages.

Table 10.5. *Household wages, μ, and general satisfaction for the Russian dataset*

Variable	Household wages	Absolute t-value	Financial satisfaction (μ)	Absolute t-value	General satisfaction	Absolute t-value
Intercept	13.2	4.3	−4.35	2.0	17.72	5.3
Ln(y$_c$)	—	—	0.62	56.6	0.25	16.9
Ln(adults)	0.68	28.9	—	—	—	—
Ln(family size)	—	—	0.17	8.7	—	—
Ln(age)	−3.41	5.4	2.14	5.1	−3.92	6.6
(Ln(age))^2	0.47	5.4	−0.30	5.4	0.53	6.6
Ln(education)	0.29	12.0	—	—	—	—
Dummies:						
Rural	−0.21	7.4	−0.08	4.3	2.17	4.7
Volga and South Russia	0.01	0.2	0.13	4.3	0.08	1.8
Wave 2	1.18	39.7	0.36	17.8	−0.22	7.9
Climate variables:						
Ln(JANTEMP)	−1.53	2.9	−1.30	3.3	—	—
Ln(JULTEMP)	4.09	4.2	3.84	5.4	—	—
Ln(TEMPDIF)	−2.62	5.7	−2.31	6.9	—	—
Ln(JANWIND)	5.35	4.7	4.07	4.9	−5.67	6.5
Ln(ALT)	0.04	1.3	0.11	5.5	−0.11	3.4
Ln(RAINDAYS)	—	—	—	—	0.86	6.1
Ln(SUNHOURS)	—	—	—	—	0.84	4.5
Ln(WINTERPREC)	—	—	—	—	−0.50	4.3
Ln(SUMMERPREC)	—	—	—	—	−0.35	4.6
Interaction effects:						
Ln(JANTEMP)*Ln(JANWIND)	−1.54	4.8	−1.12	4.8	1.59	6.7
Ln(PREC)*ln(TEMPAV)	0.002	0.2	0.06	5.5	0.21	4.3
Ln(HUMIDITY)*ln(TEMPAV)	—	—	—	—	−1.45	7.0
Rural*ln(PREC)	—	—	—	—	−0.34	4.6
N	—	4,127	—	4,112	—	4,112
R^2	0.577	—	0.731	—	0.094	—

Source: Frijters and Van Praag (1998). In the full specification we included twelve 'organization dummies' which described the type of employment, e.g. in a state organization, a private firm, a farm, etc.

Apart from the μ-equation we also estimated the equation for general satisfaction. In this Russian survey the responses were scaled on a discrete scale from 1 to 10. The transformation of responses was not done by using conditional expectations, but by taking conditional medians. We hinted at this alternative in Chapter 2. The relevant transform is given by $V_i^* = N^{-1}(\frac{-0.5+i}{10}; 0, 1)$, where $i = 1, \ldots, 10$.[3]

[3] It would have been more elegant if we had recomputed the results according to the COLS method. However, as it has been found that the trade-off ratios hardly change, we maintained the original computations in Frijters and Van Praag (1998). The estimated coefficients are comparable to those derived by the COLS method.

This equation is presented in the fifth column. We found that it partly depended on climate variables other than household income and μ. The number of rainy days has a positive effect, and the same holds for precipitation, if we take the interaction term into account.

10.5. CLIMATE EQUIVALENCE SCALES RECONSIDERED WITH INCOME CLIMATE-DEPENDENT

A climate-equivalence scale is the ratio by which household income has to be increased or reduced with respect to a reference level in order to maintain some welfare index at the same level. In section 10.3 we took financial satisfaction (as derived from the IEQ) as the welfare index. In this analysis we could also select the broader index, that is general satisfaction, as the index to be kept at the same level. It is clear that we then get two different climate-equivalence scales.

Let us consider first the index with respect to financial satisfaction. As before we write

$$\mu = \beta_1 \ln(y_c) + \beta'_2 x + \beta'_3 C, \tag{10.7}$$

where we distinguish between a 'preference-drift' effect depending on current income, an effect of 'other' variables x, and a climate effect of the climate vector C, measured in deviation from a reference climate C_0.

If our welfare index is $\ln(y_c) - \mu(y_c)$ we find that the compensating income behaves according to the equation

$$\ln(y_c) = \frac{1}{(1-\beta_1)} \{\beta'_2 x + \beta'_3 C\}, \tag{10.8}$$

in accordance with Van Praag (1988). The only point to note is that the Russian climate needs more descriptive dimensions than the Western European climate.

However, it was discovered that household income itself is partly determined by the climate. For instance, incomes increase if the wind velocity in January (JANWIND) increases. In Table 10.5 (first column) we presented the equation

$$\ln(y_c) = \theta_1 x + \theta'_2 C. \tag{10.9}$$

This relation may be caused by various factors. First, it may be that the labor productivity of individuals varies with the climate. For instance, in the building industry a harsh winter may interrupt the building process and cause idle days. The second reason may be that you have to pay individuals more to attract them to unpleasant climates. The first effect is the productivity effect and the second effect amounts to an internalization of the climate in the wage tariffs. It may also be that the quality of workers in harsh climates is worse than those living in moderate climates as a result of self-selection. The better workers move out to other regions of the country where they can live in a milder climate. We do not have means to distinguish between those effects, but our intuition says that it is plausible that the second effect prevails. When we follow that we see that climate works in two ways on financial satisfaction. First, it works through market income according to economic theory. But if the term $\theta_2'C$ deviates only slightly from zero, this indicates that the internalization through income is likely to be only partial if at all. The term $(\beta_3'C)$ in the μ-equation stands for the *residual* effect of climate, if climate-differentiated income does not give an adequate compensation for the climate. If it equals zero, it implies that compensation is total or that compensation is not needed. Let us assume a reference climate $C_0 = (0, \ldots,)$ after normalization. According to (10.9) an income at climate C will be corrected by the market by a factor $\exp(\theta_2'C)$. However, according to (10.8) that is insufficient to neutralize the climate difference. Therefore we need an additional correction by a factor $\exp(\beta_3'C/(1 - \beta_1))$. It follows that the total climate compensation is: $\exp(\theta_2'C).\exp(\beta_3'C/(1 - \beta_1)) = \exp(\tilde{\beta}_3 C))$ where $\tilde{\beta}_3 = \theta_2 + \frac{1}{(1-\beta_1)}.\beta_3$.

We may analyze in a similar way the climate effect on general satisfaction (GS) by looking at the fifth column of Table 10.5. We see that the climate effects on GS differ from the effects on financial satisfaction (FS). This may be expected, as the effects on various satisfaction domains are probably rather different. Also, the size of the market compensation may differ between domains. For instance, in some climatic situations you may get free housing or housing subsidies, in other cases there may be free health care.

For GS we see that part of the climate effects is compensated through market income. Using the same reasoning as above and assuming

$$GS = v_1 y + v_2'x + v_3'C$$
$$= v_1 \tilde{y} + v_2'x + (v_1\theta_2' + v_3')C$$

we see that the climate effect on GS may be broken down into a market-compensated and a residual-climate effect,[4] where $\tilde{y} = y - \theta_2'c$

Although this breakdown is interesting, it is irrelevant in practice. In practice, we are only interested in the residual effect, *after* the climate effect is partly internalized.

It is rather difficult to interpret the climate effects in Table 10.5, because of the interaction terms. Let us consider the expression (see (10.6))

$$-1.53\ln(\text{JANTEMP}) + 5.35\ln(\text{JANWIND})$$
$$-1.54\ln(\text{JANTEMP})^*\ln(\text{JANWIND})$$

in the income equation. We see that incomes increase if the January temperature falls and that this increase is more pronounced if the wind velocity increases. Alongside it there is an independent effect of JANWIND along the same lines.

---

[4] This does not exclude the possibility that climate may also affect other domains; we did not investigate this at the time.

As the effects are complex, we prefer to calculate the climate-index values at various specific sites in Russia, taking Moscow as the reference site. The chosen sites are Gurjew, at the northern tip of the Caspian Sea, St. Petersburg, near the Baltic Sea, Dudinka, on the Arctic Ocean, Novosibirsk, in the southern part of Siberia, and Cholmsk, in the extreme east of Russia near the Japanese border. We found the results listed in Table 10.6.

We see that incomes are highest in Dudinka, where they are on average more than four times as high as in Moscow. The lowest incomes are found in Gurjew, where incomes are on average 24 percent lower than in Moscow.

Consider now the μ-equivalence scale. We find that inhabitants of Gurjew are in income better off than the Moscovites, as they would require only 50.5 percent of the Moscow incomes to get equal financial satisfaction, but they get 76.3 percent of the Moscow incomes.

For general satisfaction we find the inverse result. The Gurjewians require 84.9 percent of Moscow income, but they only get 76.3 percent. Frijters and Van Praag (1998) tried to assess the effect of a global climate change for Russia. Although the result was that the Russian population would on average be better off by a global warming of a few degrees, this result must be taken with a pinch of salt, as the changes in production conditions caused by global warming were not taken into account. Global warming will change production conditions in, for example, agriculture, transport, and with respect to the availability of water. This will probably cause a change in factor prices, consumer prices, and labor incomes. Moreover, it may trigger regional migrations.

10.6. CONCLUSION

In this chapter we looked at the effect of climate on satisfaction. We found significant effects on μ and on GS. These effects are rather complex, as climate appears to be a multidimensional phenomenon. We can see this case as a particular instance of a more general problem: how to estimate the effect of an externality both in terms of satisfaction and in terms of a monetary compensation to neutralize externality differences.

Table 10.6. *Equivalence scales for several Russian sites*

Equivalence scales	Moscow	Gurjew	St. Petersburg	Dudimka	Novosibirsk	Cholmsk
Current incomes	1.0	0.763	1.133	4.157	1.353	0.995
Financial satisfaction	1.0	0.505	0.988	5.394	1.335	1.041
General satisfaction	1.0	0.849	1.085	2.463	1.069	0.743

Most external effects are neither completely internalized nor completely compensated through market incomes and prices. This method makes it possible to assess in how far the externality is compensated and what the size of the residual effect is.

In the next chapter we will apply the method to a totally different field; namely, the question of how far neighboring households are bothered by aircraft noise from Amsterdam Airport and what the monetary compensation for this would need to be.

11

How to Find Compensations For Aircraft Noise Nuisance

11.1. INTRODUCTION

In the previous chapter we considered climate effects. The approach developed there can also be used for the evaluation of other external effects. In this chapter we shall describe how to estimate the monetary compensation needed to neutralize aircraft noise for households living in the neighborhood of Amsterdam Airport (Schiphol). We start with a description of the setting. In Section 11.2 we consider the literature; in Section 11.3 we describe our 1999 data set; in Section 11.4 we describe the model and its estimates; in Section 11.5 we consider the resulting compensation schedule; and in Section 11.6 we conclude.

Many city dwellers are painfully aware of a nearby airport. They suffer from aircraft noise. Amsterdam Airport (Schiphol) is no exception. The air traffic has heavily expanded since the airport was opened in 1926. It is now one of the major hub airports in Europe and the only large-scale airport in the Netherlands. The aircraft noise around Schiphol is closely monitored by zip code. In 1999 noise was calculated in Kosten-units (Ku). This unit was called after the late Dutch professor Kosten, who chaired a government commission in the late sixties and early seventies. The task of the Kosten Commission (1967) was to derive an aircraft-noise measurement method. They developed an annual-noise-burden formula, where noise burden depends on the number of flights, differentiated according to the time of day or night and the number of decibels the flight produces. This formula of measurement has recently been replaced by the international L_{den}-measure. However, there is a strong empirical correlation between the results of both definitions of noise. That is, a zip-code, which scores high in Kosten-units, also scores high in terms of L_{den}. Maximum admissible noise

This paper is partly based on Baarsma (2000) and Van Praag and Baarsma (2001, published 2005). The work results from a study for the Dutch government. We are grateful to Prof. J. G. de Wit and the staff of the Directorate General of Civil Aviation of the Dutch Ministry of Transport (RLD for short) for giving us valuable comments. We thank Intomart, Hilversum (one of the leading polling agencies in the Netherlands) for their support in the data collection, Ingrid Overtoom, Marie-Louise Kok, and J. Peter Hop for their assiduous support in analyzing the data. Finally, this text also benefits from stimulating discussions with David De Meza.

norms are given for each zip-code area. In principle, noise should nowhere exceed the 35 *Ku* norm per year, although in practice in 2000 about 15,000 households endured a higher noise burden. As it is impossible to locate the airport elsewhere and it is equally impossible to relocate the inhabitants of the region involved, some parties defend the solution of monetary compensation for the inhabitants who are exposed to a noise overdose. Similar situations are found at many places in the world, e.g. Stockholm, Bangkok, Cologne, and several British cities.

The first question which comes to mind for economists is that of whether there is justification for such compensation. If we assume that the housing market is in equilibrium, individuals can choose where to live, and they will only choose a house near an airport if the lower rent/price of that house fully compensates the subjective noise damage. A house near an airport should be cheaper than a similar house with no noise. Let us denote noise by the variable K and the other housing characteristics by h, then we can assume that housing prices p are a function of the housing characteristics h and noise K. Let us assume, as in the previous chapter, that the individual evaluates his or her situation according to an (indirect) household-utility function $U(y; p(h, K), K)$ where K may influence utility directly and indirectly through prices. If individuals are free to move from one house to another, it is evident that all individuals with the same income will be at the same utility level. It may be that one house is subject to more noise than another, but this will then be reflected in the cheaper price or rent. For if they would enjoy different utility for the same income, they would move. It follows that in equilibrium there must hold

$$U(y; p(h, K), K) = \text{constant}.$$

Let us assume that we compare two locations, one of which has no noise at all; that is, $K = 0$. In the equilibrium case we have

$$U(y; p(h, K), K) = U(y; p(h, 0), 0)$$

and we can identify $p(h, K) - p(h, 0)$ as the noise compensation. We see that in this case the noise effect is completely internalized through prices. It is this assumption that there is an equilibrium in the housing market which is used by Blomquist, Berger, and Hoehn (1988) to price external effects. However, this method fails if there is no equilibrium. This is the case if $U(y)$ is observed to vary with the noise level K. In fact, this provides a test of whether there is an equilibrium or not. In the latter case the noise effect is not or not wholly internalized in prices; then the compensation for the external effect, as far as not accounted for by price differences, will have to be be partly through a direct income compensation Δy such that

$$U(y + \Delta y; p(h, K), K) = U(y; p(h, 0), 0).$$

It is well known that most mainstream economists are strongly attracted by the neoclassical paradigm, which almost always assumes equilibrium. We will not take this for granted. In fact, there was (1999) and is still much reason (in 2007) to assume that the housing market in the Amsterdam region is *not* in equilibrium, or at least to leave the possibility open. However, as this assumption is crucial for our analysis below, and the equilibrium assumption is mostly accepted as a matter of faith, we list some of our reasons for being doubtful about the realism of the equilibrium assumption in this instance.

Duration and Moving Costs

It seems reasonable to assume that individuals equalize utility contributions at the margin when they start living in their home. That means equalization, that is equilibrium, may be expected at the moment of opting for a specific dwelling. However, in our (representative) sample some of the respondents moved into their house thirty years ago. The average period since deciding to live there is 13.5 years. Given that incomes, preferences, the distribution pattern of flight paths, and noise level change over a lifetime, we cannot assume that under present conditions respondents would make the same choice as they made ten or twenty years before.

Also, relative housing costs have changed over the years. The reason that individuals stay where they are has much to do with the monetary and psychological costs of moving. For instance, when a house is sold the Dutch government levies a transfer tax of 6 percent on the transaction price. In fact, all these arguments make it doubtful that many markets for durables in general and for houses in particular are in equilibrium.

History and Legal Barriers

It is generally accepted in the Netherlands that the housing market in the wider Amsterdam area is not and has not been in equilibrium since World War II. There was and still is a terrible housing shortage. There are two sectors to the Dutch housing market. There is subsidized 'social housing', which includes about 75 per cent of the Amsterdam housing stock. One can rent a 'social house' (mostly an apartment) if the household income is below a specific income limit. In this sector you cannot be very choosy. A house is allotted to a family after a waiting time and if you refuse the offer you have to wait for another year or more. Moreover, for both the social and the private sector there is strict rent protection by law. The housing corporations or private owners are unable to terminate the lease or increase the rent if the tenant is not willing to leave. This leads to the odd result that many young people of modest means start by living in social housing, but stay on there when their income increases above the eligibility limit and continue to profit from the housing subsidies, although these are not intended for them. The rents increase by a percentage, fixed annually by parliament, mostly in line with general inflation. As housing prices soar year by year, it follows that the real housing costs of individuals fall when they stay in the same house. The waiting time to get a social house in the municipality of Amsterdam (i.e. the core of the region considered) has recently reached a record of eleven(!) years.

Absolute Scarcity, Political Influences, and Effects of Taxation
For the private sector there is also a rationing factor, as building plots are in scarce supply, mostly to be bought from the municipality, which puts a number of restrictions on building, the type of housing to be built, housing prices and rents, and sometimes imposes anti-speculation clauses. Frequently there are also waiting lists or even lotteries on the right to buy a new house. In Amsterdam nearly all building plots, even for private housing, are leased long-term (100 years) by the municipality and cannot be bought at all. In the private sector most houses are private property (excluding the plot in Amsterdam). Housing costs for owners are a strange mixture determined by, amongst others the historical buying price, the terms of the underlying mortgage, the repayment schedule, and the interest rate, which may be changed every five years.

The mortgage interest is wholly tax deductible, which implies that individuals with higher incomes can deduct a higher percentage of their interest payments as a result of the tax progression.[1] Hence, the net housing costs are partly income-dependent. Not surprisingly, housing prices in the private sector have increased each year by much more than the general price index. Housing costs 40 years ago were on average about 10 per cent of a one-earner household income for starters, while young couples starting out nowadays pay up to 35 percent of their joint two-earner household income for housing. That this causes major problems for young people is evident.

In fact, this is common knowledge for every Dutch person: buyer, seller, regulator, politician, or ordinary citizen. The permanent Dutch housing shortage since World War II, not only in Amsterdam but all over the country, is perceived as a big political problem. It is partly the result of political failures, partly of scarcity in the productive capacities of the building industry, and partly of the environmental conditions, whereby substantial parts of the region cannot be built on in the interests of conserving nature or historical city centers.

11.2. SHORT SURVEY OF THE LITERATURE

The valuation of external effects is a famous but difficult problem. Pigou (1920) and Coase (1960) are the pioneers on this subject. Early contributions on aircraft noise are by Plessas (1973) and Walters (1975). The problem is that an externality is not, or not adequately, priced in the market. According to our knowledge of the literature the problem has been approached along two roads. The first approach is that of hedonic price studies. The second road employs the contingent valuation method (CVM).

---

[1] There is an ever ongoing debate in Dutch politics on changing this tax schedule.

Hedonic Price Studies

Attempts to evaluate people's preferences for peace and quiet have centered on the use of the hedonic price method. The method assumes an underlying equilibrium. This method tries to impute a price for an environmental good by examining the effect that its presence has on a relevant market-priced good, like houses. In the case of aircraft-noise nuisance, the method attempts to identify how much of a difference in housing prices is the result of the level of noise nuisance.

Table 11.1 shows the results of various hedonic price surveys that have studied the effect of aircraft noise on residential property values. The price sensitivity with respect to aircraft noise is in most studies evaluated by the noise-depreciation index (NDI), which measures the change in property prices in terms of a percentage for each unit of change in the noise level. The NDI is derived on the basis of a survey of the changes in property values over particular periods or geographical areas (Nelson 1980: 40–2). A hedonic price equation is specified with the property value (V) on the one hand and a set of physical and locational housing characteristics (Z) and the level of noise nuisance (N) on the other: V = V(Z, N). The measures of noise-nuisance levels N differ between countries. For instance, the US noise descriptor is the noise-exposure forecast (NEF), the UK noise descriptor is the noise and number index (NNI), whereas the Dutch noise descriptor is the Kosten-unit (*Ku*) for the present study.[2] The NDI is derived from $\partial V / \partial N$.

Table 11.1. *A summary of hedonic price studies and aircraft-noise nuisance, measured in NDI (%)*

Study location	NDI estimate	Study location	NDI estimate
Australia:		*USA:*	
Sydney 1	0.40*	Atlanta	0.65*
Sydney 2	0.22*	Boston	0.83*
Canada:		Dallas 1	0.6*
Edmonton	0.51*	Dallas 2	2.3*
Toronto	0.52**	Los Angeles	0.8*
Vancouver 1	0.65*	Minneapolis	0.6*
Vancouver 2	0.90*	New Orleans	0.4*
UK:		New York	1.8*
Heathrow 1	0.25**	Rochester	0.55*
Heathrow 2	3.57**	San Francisco	0.5*
Manchester	0.15**	Washington DC	1.06*

*Noise nuisance is measured in NEF; **noise nuisance is measured in NNI.
Sources: Nelson (1980: 47–51); Pearce (1993: 72); Schipper (1997: 6).

[2] Recently, the US measure (NEF) has been replaced by the L_{den} measure, and the UK measure (NNI) has been replaced by the L_{eq}. The Dutch measure will be replaced by the L_{den} as well.

The consensus view that seems to have emerged from the hedonic price studies is that aircraft noise has a negative and statistically significant effect on housing prices; that is, NDI is around 0.6 percent on average (Collins and Evans 1994: 175; Nelson 1980: 46). This means that a house normally valued at, say, $200,000 would sell for 12 percent less, that is $176,000 if located in a noisier zone with 20 units more noise nuisance.

Looking at Table 11.1, which summarizes twenty studies, it is obvious that there is considerable variation, partly but not wholly caused by differences in the measurement method used and the choice of specific location. The use of the hedonic price method may have at least two drawbacks.

First, using property-price changes to elicit preferences for reducing noise nuisance does not encompass all the benefits of noise reductions. For instance, noise nuisance could entail health effects, and it is unlikely that individuals will be sufficiently aware of health risks to include those risks when choosing a house in a certain location. Secondly, hedonic pricing is dependent on some rather strict assumptions, which are in all probability not valid in the Schiphol region. The two most important assumptions are made explicit by Bateman (1993: 235):

1. The study area can be treated as a competitive market with freedom of access across the market and perfect information regarding housing prices and environmental characteristics.
2. The housing market in the study area is in equilibrium: individuals continually re-evaluate their location, and adjust their residential choice to changing circumstances.

These conditions do not apply to the Amsterdam area, as we argued above. This also holds for the non-applicability to the Amsterdam area of general equilibrium studies like that by Blomquist et al. (1988). A recent study by Morrell and Lu (2000) estimates the loss in housing value in the Schiphol area using an exogenously set NDI value of 0.40 percent.

Contingent Valuation Studies

The contingent valuation method (CVM) uses surveys to find the willingness to pay (WTP) or the willingness to accept (WTA) compensation for a change in the level of environmental service flows. There seem to be only a few studies with respect to airplane noise. We mention Feitelson et al. (1996) and more recently Carlsson et al. (2004).

There is a lively discussion of CVM in the literature (Pearce 1993; Hausman 1993). For a recent defense of CVM we refer to Carson, Flores, and Meade (2000). One of the problems of this approach is related to the direct method of questioning in CVM questionnaires, which may entail a strategic-response bias. For example, respondents are asked how much they are willing to pay for a reduction in noise nuisance during the night (WTP). This kind of questioning has two important drawbacks: strategic behavior and hypothetical bias. Although we do not deny that CVM analysis is informative, in the case of Schiphol considered in this study it would not have been very wise to use the

CVM-type method of questioning. Firstly, Schiphol Airport and noise nuisance are hot issues in the Netherlands. If it were known that a survey was being carried out with the aim of establishing monetary-compensation schemes for noise nuisance, this would definitely have led to organized strategic behavior (e.g. overestimation and/or a boycott of the survey). Secondly, respondents are not punished in any way if they do not express their true value but a value that is lower or higher than what they really feel (hypothetical bias), in an attempt to influence the provision or price of the environmental good under valuation. Hence, we cannot always take the CVM answer at face value.

The CVM has the advantage that it measures not just user values but the total economic value including non-user values. This is relevant because a non-user can assign a value to the conservation of the Brazilian jungle, the preservation of the polar bear or of wild birdlife in the Dutch 'polder'. Non-user values cannot be measured using the hedonic price method. For instance, noise nuisance has no effect in areas without houses, since in these 'empty' areas no housing prices exist that can reflect the impact of noise, whereas (non-)user values may be assigned to these non-housing areas as well.

A CVM study was conducted in Israel by Feitelson et al. (1996). It estimated the effect of changes in aircraft-noise exposure following an airport expansion on the willingness to pay (WTP) for residences. Home owners in three communities near a major airport where a significant expansion was planned were asked to state their WTP for a four-bedroom single-family residence located in an area with no aircraft noise at all. Next, they were asked to state their WTP for the same residence if it were located at sites subject to different levels of noise (expressed in L_{den}-units). A similar sequence of WTP questions was conducted for tenants in terms of monthly rent for a three-bedroom residence.

This Israeli study suggests that the difference in valuation for residences with no noise nuisance compared to residences with frequent and severe noise nuisance is 2.4–4.1 percent of the housing prices per L_{den} (for home owners) and 1.8–3.0 percent of the rents per L_{den} (for tenants). These noise-depreciation indices (NDI) are higher than the values obtained in most hedonic price studies (around 0.6 percent on average). This may be partly because CVM estimates include the loss of non-use values, whereas the hedonic price estimates only identify market premiums. However, given the nature of the question being asked in this CVM study, it is unlikely that non-user values are included.[3] Feitelson et al. also suggest another explanation; namely, the fact that the WTP structures are kinked. This implies that beyond a certain disturbance threshold households are unwilling to pay anything for the residences. Hence, their valuation of (the reduction of) noise nuisance is so high because they are not willing to pay anything for a residence at a noisy location.

---

[3] The manner of questioning in the Feitelson et al. study differs from the traditional CVM question in the sense that noise nuisance is not valued directly. Instead, it is valued indirectly, as the WTP is stated for a different good (namely, residences, a marketed good) of which noise nuisance is but one attribute.

In terms of utility CVM measures necessarily (*ex ante*) changes in decision utility, while acceptable public compensations should be based on (*ex post*) experienced utility. We saw in Chapter 2 that the decision utility is much steeper in the relevant region than the experienced utility function. It is this difference which may account for the marked difference between CVM and hedonic price studies.

11.3. THE DATA

In 1998 Van Praag and Baarsma participated in a postal survey[4] of the population living within a radius of 25 kilometers of Amsterdam Airport. Some of the respondents were subject to serious aircraft noise, while other respondents in the same overall area were not subject to such noise at all. This depends on the specific flight paths allocated to aircraft arriving at and leaving Schiphol.

The area consists of strongly urbanized parts like the city of Amsterdam, and of many villages and rural parts. The area is closely monitored for aircraft noise. The average noise burden for each zip code is known and monitored in terms of *Ku*. The measure, as we have already said, is a composite formula, built up from the maximum noise in decibels and the frequency of that noise level. A weighting system is applied, which differentiates between specific time periods during the day and night. Outside the monitored region the noise nuisance is negligible.

Asking people for their subjective opinion on noise nuisance in an area where there is a public outcry on this issue calls for specific precautions. Explicit questioning, as in a CVM study, is, as we stated earlier, out of the question, as it would lead to strategic-response behavior and probably a sample-selection bias with a heavy over-representation of partisans. In order to avoid such problems we embedded our relevant questions in a major postal questionnaire which did not focus on aircraft noise, but which dealt with the broad area of 'health, well-being, and living conditions in the Netherlands'. Of course the widening of the questionnaire to cover a broad variety of subjects was also done to enable use of the survey for other upcoming research questions as well.

The questionnaire,[5] which consists of fifty-one question modules, was mailed to a random sample of households in the area. When designing the data-collection method, we can choose various modes. At the one extreme we have the 'intensive' mode, with reminders in writing, phone calls and incentives in the form of gifts in money or in kind. If we send reminders and so forth it is obvious to the interviewee that there is no anonymity between him or her and the data-collection agency. This may be relevant if we send a sensitive questionnaire on

---

[4] The research was financed by the Dutch Ministry of Traffic and Transport. It was commissioned to the Foundation of Economic Research of the University of Amsterdam (SEO; since 2000 called Amsterdam Economics). The survey was designed by Van Praag, Baarsma, and the opinion agency GfK/Intomart, Hilversum.

[5] The complete text of the questionnaire can be found in Baarsma (2000).

individual well-being. The most 'extensive' method is to send off the questionnaire and simply wait for the anonymous response, without any monitoring of
who answers and who does not. Evidently, such monitoring is impossible if one
wants to preserve anonymity. Another point is that the more intensive the collection mode is, the more we run the risk of sample selectivity. We chose a compromise, in which we sent out only one 'anonymous' reminder to all adressees,
irrespective of whether they had already answered or not. The letter stated that in
the interests of anonymity we were contacting all the addresses. To somebody
who had already answered we offered our apologies for bothering them in ad-
vance. It is evident that the response rate depends on the collection method. Our
response was rather low, at 17 percent, but the sample appeared to be representative of the population. The sample, which is used for this study, consists of 1,400
respondents. Given the fact that this study is a pilot project, we decided that the
sample of 1,400 observations in the Schiphol area, that is in the monitored region,
was sufficiently large for a first analysis and an evaluation of the method.

One of our crucial tools of analysis was again the well-being question, originally devised by Cantril (1965). It asks for an evaluation of general well-
being or 'quality of life' (QOL). Except for differences in wording, it is identical
to the general-satisfaction question. The Cantril 'ladder-of-life' question runs as
follows:

*Here is a picture of a ladder, representing the ladder of life. Suppose we say that the top
of the ladder (step 10) represents the best possible life for you, and the bottom (step 1)
represents the worst possible life for you.*
Where on the ladder do you feel you personally stand at the present time?
(Please cross one box only.)

The marginal response distribution is given in brackets on the right-hand side
($N = 1,400$). We notice that only 3.9 percent are unable to answer the question.
Moreover, we see that all categories are filled in, with a majority at categories
7 and 8. Only about 10 percent rate life at 5 or lower.

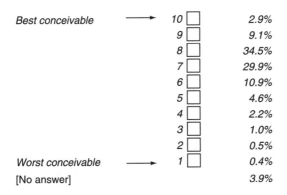

Figure 11.1. *The Cantril ladder-of-life question*

Table 11.2. *Noise-nuisance frequency (%)*

Sound sources	Never	Sometimes	Regularly	Often	Always	No answer
Cars, buses, mopeds, trucks	21.2	40.3	13.5	6.4	7.1	11.6
Electric trams/subway	69.4	6.1	1.9	1.0	2.1	19.5
Trains	65.9	9.1	2.1	1.5	1.8	19.6
Airplanes	11.4	32.9	18.6	18.8	13.2	5.1
Industry/business	67.1	9.0	2.0	1.2	0.4	20.4
Hotels, restaurants, pubs, and other places of entertainment	67.5	10.6	1.7	0.6	0.5	19.1
Noise nuisance from neighbors	38.9	32.1	7.1	3.8	1.8	16.4
Children/youngsters	43.1	29.8	5.3	2.6	0.9	18.4
Other sources	39.4	3.2	2.7	1.8	0.9	52.0

$N = 1400$ for respondents in the Schiphol area.

We shall explain the answer on the quality-of-life question by some other variables, including 'perceived aircraft-noise frequency'. Of the fifty-one question modules, question 25 is particularly relevant for our study. Question 25, which deals with a spectrum of noise sources, runs as follows:

Would you please indicate how many times the following sound sources are causing noise nuisance at your place of living?

By asking for nine possible sources of noise, aircraft noise is not singled out for special attention. The response rates for the questions are filled out in Table 11.2. We observe that the aircraft item gets a similar non-response rate as the other items (except 'other sources', for obvious reasons). This shows that the respondents are not strategically exaggerating the noise from aircrafts. The (verbal) frequency estimates reflect of course the subjective noise burdens. Apart from those 'subjective' questions there was asked for a host of other mostly factual variables like household income, age, family composition, education, and a typology of the dwelling including ownership. It was also asked whether the dwelling was insulated. More precisely, three types of insulation were distinguished: thermal insulation, noise insulation, and draught-proofing. Finally, the most detailed zip-code for each respondent was available. In the Netherlands there are on average twelve households with the same zip-code, although there is a considerable variation around that average. From that zip-code we could make a link with a list in which the aircraft-noise level in *Ku*, to be explained below, are described per zip-code. This list exists only for the Schiphol 50 km area. Summarizing, the special pieces of information used in what follows are: the question 25 on perceived noise nuisance; the question on general well-being; some demographic characteristics; and information on housing. The information is completed with the objective noise burden in *Ku* per zip-code.

11.4. THE MODEL ESTIMATED

The model is based on the Cantril question, which is a lookalike of the GS question used in earlier chapters. As a starter ordered probit was applied in order to estimate an equation $W = W(\ln(y), Ku, x)$, where $W(.)$ stands for the (latent) satisfaction variable, and x stands for a vector of 'intervening' variables.

We selected the following explanatory variables:

- net monthly household income $(\ln y)$[6]
- family size $\ln fs^2$ and $(\ln fs)^2$
- interaction term of income and family size $(\ln y^* \ln fs)$
- age of the respondent $(\ln age$ and $(\ln age)^2)$
- noise in terms of Kosten-units $(\ln Ku)$
- interaction term of a dummy for noise insulation (Ins) and noise in Ku $(Ins^*\ln Ku)$.

Using the variables listed above, the Cantril measure of well-being W is explained by the equation:

$$W = \beta_0 + \beta_1 \ln(y) + \beta_2 \ln(fs) + \beta_3 (\ln(fs))^2 + \beta_4 \ln(y).\ln(fs) +$$
$$+ \beta_5 \ln(age) + \beta_6 (\ln(age))^2 + \beta_7 \ln(Ku) + \beta_8 Ins.\ln(Ku). \tag{11.1}$$

The effect of income is of course expected to be positive. The family-size effect is ambiguous. For all parents there is a finite optimum, and if the number of children rises above that optimum children become more or less 'undesired'. From Equation 11.1, which specifies 'ln fs', it is obvious that the interaction term of 'ln$y$' with 'ln fs' is quite important. It presumes that the optimum number of children depends on the financial situation of the household. As earlier in this study, we added age as a variable.

Next, two variables in the respondents' living conditions are included in the model; namely the level of aircraft-noise nuisance, measured in Ku, and the presence of noise insulation. Obviously, the effect of aircraft-noise nuisance on well-being is expected to be negative. In the recent years, the literature has seen an increase on the number of studies that look at the relationship between individuals' well-being and the environment conditions where they live (e.g. Ferrer-i-Carbonell and Gowdy 2007; and Welsch 2006 and 2007). The interaction term $Ins^*\ln Ku$ is included in the model, since we assume that the size of the negative noise effect will do less harm if the house has noise insulation and, hence, that well-being is positively affected by the presence of noise insulation. The dummy variable Ins equals 1 when insulation is present and 0 otherwise. The resulting ordered-probit estimates for this equation (leaving out the nine threshold values) are presented in Table 11.3.

---

[6] In this chapter we sometimes write ln$y$ instead of, more formally, ln(y) and similarly ln$x$ instead of ln(x).

Table 11.3. *Estimation of the well-being equation with the variable Ku*

Variable	Parameter estimate	Standard error	Parameter estimate	Standard error
Lny	0.5093#	0.0849	0.5107#	0.0933
Ln fs	−2.3941#	0.8689	−1.8870#	0.9048
(Ln fs)^2	−0.1613	0.1297	−0.1787	0.1313
Lny*ln fs	0.3274#	0.1092	0.2582#	0.1154
Lnage	−4.2372#	1.1656	−3.7262#	1.2057
(Lnage)^2	0.5681#	0.1586	0.4896#	0.1656
LnKu	−0.0242	0.0252	−0.0213	0.0256
Ins*lnKu	0.0582#	0.0241	0.0546#	0.0244
Ln(He)	—	—	0.0443	0.0646
Home	—	—	0.0375	0.0980
Bal	—	—	−0.0633	0.0745
Gar	—	—	0.1650	0.0891
N	1,067	—	1,067	—
Pseudo-R^2	—	0.1614	—	0.1654

Note: Top of age at 42.

Significantly different from 0 at a 5% level.

Looking at the results in the second and third columns of Table 11.3, we see that the (external) effect of noise nuisance is not significant. It follows that our first attempt to identify the external effect has not been rewarded. We may think that additional variables might improve things. We added the following variables:

- monthly housing expenditures (ln*He*)
- dummy for presence at home during the day (*Home*)
- dummy for presence of balcony (*Bal*)
- dummy for presence of garden (*Gar*).

The first variable reflects the expectation that more expensive houses are of higher quality. The other three attempt to describe the noise exposure. If one is at home more, or if one has a balcony or a garden, one is more exposed to aircraft noise than when that is not the case. As we see from the last two columns in Table 11.3 the results do not improve at all.

The answer to this riddle is that the objective *Ku* measure does not describe *subjectively perceived* noise nuisance. After all, *Ku* is a calculated measure that does not include non-acoustic factors. In fact, it is possible that different individuals perceive noise differently. The objective measure *Ku* is certainly an explanatory variable, but not the only one. For instance, if an individual is at home during the day, it stands to reason that noise will have a larger impact than when he or she is working during the day. The same holds for family size. The larger the family, the higher is the family exposure to external factors. In short, the crucial variable is not the *objective* measurement of noise but the *subjective* perception of it. The concept that explains subjective well-being is the subjective variable *perceived noise*, which we shall call *noise* for short. Noise not only refers to noise nuisance *within* the house, but also to nuisance in the whole environment. Subjective perceptions were asked in the survey (see Table 11.2).

We notice that noise *hindrance* is subjectively evaluated on a discrete [1, 5] scale and we model it again by means of ordered-probit analysis. We assume that the latent variable noise can be explained by the equation

$$Noise = \alpha_1 \ln fs + \alpha_2 \ln He + \alpha_3 Home + \alpha_4 Bal + \qquad (11.2)$$
$$+ \alpha_5 Gar + \alpha_6 \ln Ku + \alpha_0 + \eta,$$

where η stands for the $N(0, 1)$-distributed error term. The resulting ordered-probit estimates for this equation are shown in Table 11.4.

Here nearly all the effects are significant and they have the expected sign. The influence of family size on *noise* is positive: the larger the household, the more annoyance perceived. There are more potential complainers in the household. If there is one complainer, this will be contagious among the other members of the household. Furthermore, the results indicate that the higher the housing expenses, the more aircraft-noise nuisance annoys someone. Obviously, if the house is more expensive one expects a higher housing quality, and absence of noise nuisance is one of the relevant quality dimensions. It may also be that richer people are more sensitive to negative factors influencing their life quality. In addition, individuals who are at home during the day on weekdays experience more aircraft-noise nuisance than people who leave the home during the day.

The next two variables describe the respondents' living conditions; namely, the presence of a balcony and the presence of a garden. The dummy variable *Bal* is 1 if a balcony is present and 0 otherwise. The same applies to the dummy variable *Gar* for garden. It appears that the presence of a garden significantly increases the extent to which individuals are annoyed by aircraft noise. The

Table 11.4. *Estimation of the intermediate variable 'noise'*

Variable	Parameter estimate	Standard error
Ln *fs*	0.1578#	0.0665
ln*He*	0.1457#	0.0543
Home	0.2120#	0.0805
Bal	0.0458	0.0685
Gar	0.2718#	0.0792
Ln*Ku*	0.3445#	0.0229
N	1,281	
Pseudo-R^2	0.2251	

Significantly different from 0 at a 5% level.

effect of the presence of a balcony is also positive but not significant at a 5 percent level. Our conclusion is that perceived noise does not only depend on the objective noise level, but the perception is 'colored' by intervening variables. Finally, we include the core variable: the level of aircraft-noise nuisance. Of course the effect of aircraft-noise nuisance on *noise* is strongly positive.

Respondents who are exposed to the same subjective *noise* level will be characterized by the same value of the latent variable *noise*. We may evaluate the expected noise level for each respondent by substituting his or her own values for the explanatory variables in Equation (11.2). We can reach an even finer approximation if we take account of the specific response category of question 25 which the respondent has chosen. Then, we may also assess the perceived *noise* by the conditional expectation of *noise*, given that the respondent has chosen a specific response category $I(I = 1, \ldots, 5)$ (see Maddala 1983; Terza 1987).

$$noise =$$
$$E(Noise \mid \mu_{i-1} < Noise \leq \mu_i) = \alpha_1 \ln fs + \alpha_2 \ln He + \alpha_3 Home + \alpha_4 Bal$$
$$+ \alpha_5 Gar + \ldots + \alpha_6 \ln Ku + \alpha_0 + E(\eta \mid \mu_{i-1} - E(Noise) < \eta \leq \mu_i - E(Noise)).$$
$$(11.3)$$

We notice that this variable *noise*,[7] which we operationalize by (11.3), is an ordinal index of subjective noise nuisance. If we include in Equation (11.1) the intermediate variable *noise* (specified in Equation (11.3)) instead of *Ku*, the specification of well-being reads as follows:

$$W = \beta_0 + \beta_1 \ln y + \beta_2 \ln fs + \beta_3 (\ln fs)^2 + \beta_4 \ln y^* \ln fs + \beta_5 \ln age+$$
$$+ \beta_6 (\ln age)^2 + \beta_7 noise + \beta_8 Ins^* noise. \qquad (11.4)$$

In this specification we suppose that well-being is indirectly, and not directly, influenced by changes in the level of *Ku*; that is, via the intermediate variable *noise*. We replace the objective variable *Ku* by a subjective translation of it. The *perceived* noise nuisance depends on objective noise *Ku and* on individual characteristics. The resulting estimates for this equation are presented in Table 11.5.

Let us start by noting that the coefficients in Tables 11.5 and 11.3 hardly differ, except for the noise coefficient. Net monthly income has a positive and significant impact on well-being. The family-size effects $\ln fs$ and $(\ln fs)^2$ are negative, but the latter is not significant. The coefficient of the interaction term with income $(\ln fs^* \ln y)$ is positive and significant. The age effect is quadratic with a minimum at 40 years.

The variable *noise* now has a significant and negative influence on well-being. The positive and significant interaction term of noise insulation with

---

[7] We note that this specification differs from the one used in Chapter 4, as we introduced *DS* variables on the right-hand side of the regression equation to explain *GS*. There we did not exploit the individual information in the conditional means. Also, we do not introduce a separate *z*-variable.

Table 11.5. *Estimation of the well-being equation with the intermediate variable 'noise'*

Variable	Parameter estimate	Standard error
Lny	0.5039#	0.0885
Ln fs	−2.1450#	0.8990
(Ln fs)^2	−0.1758	0.1326
lny*lnfs	0.3061#	0.1129
Lnage	−4.2718#	1.2025
(Lnage)^2	0.5788#	0.1636
Noise	−0.1126#	0.0331
Ins*noise	0.0736#	0.0270
N	1,031	
Pseudo-R^2	0.1662	

Significantly different from 0 at a 5% level.

noise nuisance (*Ins*noise*) indicates that if the house does *not* have noise insulation the effect of noise nuisance on well-being is −0.1126, whereas this effect reduces by more than half to −0.0390(− 0.1126 + 0.0736), if the house does have noise insulation. However, noise insulation does not fully mitigate the effects of aircraft noise on well-being.[8] It should be noted that insulation and *Ku* exposure are correlated. However, insulation is not purely exogenous, as Schiphol has the obligation to insulate all the houses in the most exposed residential quarters at no cost to the inhabitants. We see that replacing the objective measure *Ku* by an ordinal subjective analogue was worthwhile.

Since *noise* is positively related to the noise level in *Ku*, well-being is negatively related to the noise level in *Ku*. Using this specification of well-being, it is now possible to compute monetary compensations for changes in the noise level in *Ku*.

11.5. THE RESULTING COMPENSATION SCHEDULE

We are now able to derive shadow prices for changes in the noise level measured in *Ku* on the basis of Tables 11.4 and 11.5. Considering Tables 11.4 and 11.5 we may write schematically $W = W(y, noise (Ku, x), z)$, where *y* stands for income, *noise* is the perceived noise nuisance, being a function of the objective noise level in *Ku* and of other intervening variables *x*, and, finally, vector *z* includes family size (*fs*) and age. The shadow price Δy, needed to compensate for an increase of ΔKu, is now calculated from the equation

[8] This result, that insulation does not fully mitigate the effects of noise, was also found in the contingent valuation study conducted by Feitelson et al. (1996: 11) discussed in Section 11.2. In a study by the Dutch consultants Regioplan on the nature and the extent of the complaints about aircraft-noise nuisance in the Schiphol region a similar incomplete effect of noise insulation was found (Hulshof and Noyon 1997: 73).

$$W(y + \Delta y, noise\ (Ku + \Delta Ku,\ x),\ z) = W(y,\ noise\ (Ku,\ x),\ z). \tag{11.5}$$

Dropping all non-relevant terms, this boils down to the equation

$$(\beta_1 + \beta_4 \ln fs)^*(\ln y + \Delta \ln y) + (\beta_7 + \beta_8 Ins)^*(noise\ (Ku + \Delta Ku)) =$$
$$(\beta_1 + \beta_4 \ln fs)^* \ln y + (\beta_7 + \beta_8 Ins)^* noise\ (Ku)$$

or

$$(\beta_1 + \beta_4 \ln fs)^* \Delta \ln y = -(\beta_7 + \beta_8 Ins)^* 0.3445(\Delta \ln Ku)), \tag{11.6}$$

where β_1, β_4, β_7, β_8 are given in Table 11.5 and the coefficient 0.3445 is taken from Table 11.4. Equation (11.6) may be rewritten as

$$\frac{\delta \ln y}{\delta \ln Ku} = -\frac{(\beta_7 + \beta_8 Ins)}{(\beta_1 + \beta_4 \ln fs)} * 0.3445. \tag{11.7}$$

The first point, which follows from Equation (11.7), is that the shadow price is not constant; that is, the compensation is not linear in Ku, but it depends on the level of Ku. The change from $20Ku$ to $30Ku$ is equivalent to the change from $30Ku$ to $45Ku$. It is the relative change that counts. This is not surprising, as nearly every psychophysical stimulus is translated on a logarithmic scale.

Similarly, the compensation in money depends on the initial income level. Here also it is found that the relative changes count. The expression $\partial \ln y / \partial \ln Ku$ is an elasticity. Politically, this implies that the compensation for noise nuisance depends on income, where richer people are entitled to a higher compensation in absolute money terms. Politically, this is hard to defend, but not impossible. It is in fact the same mechanism that makes a progressive income tax acceptable. The pain of an income loss of €100 is smaller if one has an income of €2,000 than if one earns €1,000. Similarly, a compensation of €100 means less to somebody with €2,000 than to an individual earning €1,000. An alternative compensation scheme that may be acceptable to politicians is a scheme that differentiates for housing expenses. Although housing expenses may be more neutral in a political sense, the results will be similar, since housing expenses and income are strongly and positively correlated.

From Equation (11.7) it is obvious that the compensation (elasticity) depends on whether or not the house is insulated against noise. The compensation needed is much smaller when the house is insulated ($Ins = 1$).

Finally, the compensation depends on the family size. As this is not a politically relevant parameter, we fix the value of $\ln fs$ at the sample average, which equals 0.6743. There result two values for the elasticity ($\partial \ln y / \partial \ln Ku$); namely, a noise elasticity *without* noise insulation setting $Ins = 0$ in (11.7)

$$-\frac{(\beta_7)}{(\beta_1 + \beta_4 \ln fs)} * 0.3445 = -\frac{(-0.1126)}{(0.5039 + 0.3061*0.6743)} * 0.3445 = 0.0546$$

Table 11.6. *Monetary compensation as a percentage of net income for selected changes in noise level*

	20–30 *Ku*	30–40 *Ku*	40–50 *Ku*
Without insulation	2.24	1.58	1.23
With insulation	0.77	0.54	0.43
Value of noise insulation	1.47	1.04	0.80

and a noise elasticity *with* noise insulation of 0.0189.

The constant elasticities imply that there is a log-linear relationship between ΔKu and income Δy. That is, if *Ku* increases by *a* percent then the income *y* has to be increased by *b* percent to hold well-being constant. The percentages *b* are set out in Table 11.6 for the case both *without* and *with* noise insulation.

We see that in 1999 at a monthly net income of €1,500 a household would have to be compensated with 2.24 percent, that is €33.6 per month, for a noise increase from 20 to 30 *Ku*.[9] A change from 20 to 40 *Ku* would require approximately $33.6 + 23.7 = 57.3$ euros per month. The compensation amounts for houses *with* insulation are much smaller. For instance, at the same income level of €1,500 the compensation would be only 11.55 euros per month. This also implies that the value of insulation at that level would be $33.6 - 11.55 = 22.05$ euros. Under pressure of public opinion and of the government the Amsterdam Airport authorities have accepted the obligation to insulate dwellings which are in high *Ku* areas (> 45*Ku*). Now the question arises whether it would be cheaper to *pay* the compensation or to *insulate* the house. By subtracting the second row from the first row in Table 11.6 we find the value of the insulation. Clearly, noise insulation is a capital investment. Using an interest rate of 5 percent, a monthly amount of 22.05 euros is equivalent to a capital expenditure of $20 \times 12 \times 22.05 = 5,292$ euros. It follows that authorities should insulate the dwellings of households earning 1,500 per month experiencing a noise increase from 20 to 30*Ku*, if the once-only costs of insulation are below this amount of €5,292. It should be noted that the amounts are rather small. We remind the reader that these amounts refer to residual effects.

An important policy question is now what the total amount of compensation would be for compensating the population living around Schiphol for the noise nuisance they suffer from. This means that we have to compute the compensation per household in the area involved, taking into account that different households have different incomes and experience different *Ku* levels. Subsequently, the compensation amounts for all households concerned have to be added together.

[9] The exchange rate at the time of the survey was approximately $1 (US) = €1.

Suppose we set a critical *Ku* limit of X *Ku*, for example. What is the percentage of households having a noise-nuisance level higher than X *Ku*, and what would be the amount needed in order to compensate for the exceeding nuisance? In Table 11.7 this is calculated for some threshold levels.

To be precise, we have computed the total monthly compensation necessary to compensate the nuisance level for all people suffering from a damage level of over X *Ku*, to the chosen level of X *Ku*. Table 11.7 shows that the average monthly amount of compensation per household for a bottom level of 20*Ku* is higher than the average amounts for higher critical levels. That is logical, because the higher the critical level, the smaller the number of *Ku* that have to be compensated. This is shown even more clearly in column 3 of the table, where the total amount of annual compensation is given. This is because the number of households exposed to over 20*Ku* is much higher than the number of households exposed to higher critical levels.

To put the amounts in Table 11.7 into the right perspective we have to relate them to the number of commercial flights (which equalled about 397 thousand in 1999 at Schiphol) or to the number of passengers (which equalled about 36.8 million in 1999). Consequently, if we suppose that the government were to choose 20*Ku* as the critical level, the compensation per flight would amount to €253.45 and the compensation per passenger would be €2.73.

At the beginning of this chapter we observed that external effects can be partly internalized. In that case the relevant prices will depend on the external factor. In this context it would imply that housing costs would depend on the noise burden of the site. We did some additional regressions, in which we attempted to find a relationship between ln(housing costs) and noise, as measured by the Kosten-unit explained above. Housing costs are defined as the rent or the cost of the mortgage. The latter is somewhat difficult, as older loans may be amortized. We tried a number of equations, for tenants and for owners and for the two sub-samples taken together. We were not able to find a sensible (that is negative significant) noise effect. We present the simplest estimates in Table 11.8.

This table shows that the most important determinant of housing costs is the length of the period one has been living in the house, or in other words the date

Table 11.7 *Total yearly amount of compensation (euros)*

X *Ku*	Number of households[a] concerned (% in parentheses)	Average monthly compensation per household concerned	Total yearly amount of compensation (m.)
> 20*Ku*	148,063 (17.9)	56.63	100.62
> 25*Ku*	80,478 (9.7)	41.46	40.04
> 30*Ku*	26,734 (3.2)	29.90	9.59
> 35*Ku*	11,851 (1.4)	20.90	2.97
> 40*Ku*	6,030 (0.7)	17.13	1.24

[a] Out of the total population in the Schiphol region.

Table 11.8. *Ln(housing costs) explained*

Variable	Estimate	*t*-value
Constant	7.266	39.567
Dummies for housing type (ref. house in a row):		
Detached family house	0.12	1.60
Two under one roof	0.00	0.01
Corner family house	−0.05	−0.69
Flat	−0.28	−5.76
Other	−0.08	−0.67
Ln(age of the house)	−0.01	−0.17
Ln(years lived in the house)	−0.20	−10.98
Ln(K)	0.02	1.01
N	948	—
R^2	0.126	—

one started living there. The longer the person lives in the house, the lower the housing costs are. The reduction factor is 0.20. The noise effect is insignificant, which indicates that we are near the point of 'no internalization'. The dummy effects are reasonable, although most are non-significant.

We tried about twenty other specifications, including some with interactions between *Ku* and 'years lived in the house' and with the subjective variable 'noise'. We also tried those specifications on the two sub-samples of owners and tenants. All those specifications yielded similar results. Apart from the housing types, only 'years lived in the house' yielded a major effect, while the noise effect remained insignificant. We conclude that, referring to the reasons listed above, the noise burden is not internalized in the Schiphol area.

11.6. DISCUSSION AND CONCLUSION

In this chapter we estimated the money value of aircraft-noise nuisance. If we are able to observe an external effect, it is most likely a *residual* effect, as part of it will have been compensated for via the market price mechanism. In this case housing prices and rents already may partially reflect the impact of the external effect. We estimated the shadow price of this residual effect on the basis of two subjective questions about satisfaction with 'life as a whole' and about subjective noise hindrance. On the basis of our empirical estimates we conclude that the answers are interpersonally comparable for practical purposes. There is a residual effect. We estimated the monetary countervalue of that effect. Our second finding is that housing prices and rents in the Amsterdam region do not appear to internalize the external effect completely.

We used the Cantril ladder-of-life question as information on well-being, while recognizing the ordinal character of the Cantril index. Although there is an objective measure for noise nuisance available, we find that its explanatory value is not satisfactory, as it has to be corrected for individual circumstances like family size, age, and being at home during the day. Therefore, we replaced the objective measure by a subjectively corrected analogue. The monetary tariffs found, say shadow prices, are derived from that model and they differ according to whether or not the house is insulated against noise.

To our knowledge this is the first time that (residual) noise-nuisance effects have been monetarily measured by means of the well-being question. It is obvious that this external effect could only be measured because noise nuisance varies a lot over the Amsterdam area and the noise burden is pretty well registered according to zip codes, making it possible to link objective noise nuisance with the subjective feelings of the individuals living there.

The advantage of this approach compared to hedonic price analysis is that it does not assume equilibrium on the housing market and that it does not only include the external effect in so far as it concerns *housing* inconveniences, but that it includes *all* aspects, as we focus on satisfaction with 'life as a whole'. The advantage compared to the CVM approach is that the respondent is not aware that his or her responses may have any influence on decisions or compensations in which he or she has an interest. Hence, strategic-response behavior is highly unlikely in this survey design. As we need only a few questions, it will be easy to include them in routine surveys or opinion polls, which may imply a major cost reduction on data collection. It is evident that the method can be employed as well for the estimation of other external effects, where objective descriptions of the effect are at hand. The method also yields a test on market equilibrium. If noise does not influence general satisfaction, it implies that either noise has no influence on individual well-being or that individuals with same income but different noise burdens are wholly compensated via price differences.

One question which falls outside the scope of this study is the question whether a noise-compensation scheme is politically to be desired. On the one hand it is true to the idea that the polluter pays for the damage, and accordingly will reduce the pollution in line with a cost–benefit analysis. On the other hand it affects housing prices, since the compensated locations would be subsidized and hence would command a higher selling price than before. Given the fact that the Amsterdam housing market is characterized by soaring prices and a permanent housing shortage and that the size of the effects found is rather small, we do not believe that the compensation scheme derived from this study would affect or disturb the housing market to any significant extent. For reasons of justice there is much to say for the polluter-pays principle.

12

Taxation and Well-being

12.1. INTRODUCTION

There is no country without taxation. The *raison d'être* of the state as an organization is that there are a number of needs which citizens have in common and which can be met only at much higher cost or not at all if citizens do not associate into a state or a community. We mention the army, the police, justice, education, and the road system. We call the products *state services*. The production of those services requires human resources and capital, which cannot be used for the production of other commodities and services. The state has to buy these production factors or the finished products from the market at market prices. For instance, workers have the choice of working for a private firm, being self-employed, or becoming a civil servant. They only choose the civil service if the state is competitive with the private sector on the labor market. Similarly, the state has to pay the market rent if it wants to rent an office building.

Let us assume that via a parliamentary decision process the choice has been made that 30 percent of the national product must be spent by the state for the production of state services; then this implies that 30 percent of total national income has to be spent by the state and consequently that 30 percent of the factor earnings, that is salaries, profits, interest revenues, etc., has to be taxed away from the citizens. The ratio of 30 percent in this example we shall call the national tax ratio. Banknotes have to be seen as vouchers which stand for entitlements to a part of the productive efforts of the country. If we want those vouchers to be used for state production, it follows at the same time that the vouchers cannot be spent by citizens on food, housing, and other private purchases. In fact, the situation is very comparable to that of a football or golf club where the club provides fields, trainers, a club house, etc., which is paid for by contributions from the club members. The club members are the citizens and the contributions are the taxes the citizens are paying to the state.

We shall call the decision on the national tax ratio and on the distribution by the state of the tax revenue on various state services like army, police, and

This chapter is largely based on Plug, Van Praag, and Hartog (1999).

education *macro*-decisions. They are outcomes of the parliamentary process. Macro-decisions will not be the subject of this chapter.

Given the total tax revenue, our problem is how this tax revenue should be collected from the citizens. One may think of the poll tax, which amounts to an undifferentiated contribution rate per member, but this tax where every individual pays the same tax is problematic when some individuals are poor and others rich and the tax is substantial.

Another possibility is to differentiate the tax per individual according to the consumption of state services. However, this could imply that poor families with many children would have to pay a high education tax. As education has a strong beneficial effect on the production capacity of the country as a whole, it is by no means clear that the only positive effect of education accrues to the children who are educated. Moreover, in modern welfare states we see some state services as basic rights, which should be granted to every citizen. An education tax restricts the accessibility of the education system. Still more serious, it may stimulate children or their parents to 'buy' less education than would be optimal for them. Many other services provide a kind of insurance; for example, the fire brigade. It is very difficult to assess the consumption of the fire-brigade service for a specific individual. It follows that these earmarked levies are mostly felt to be undesirable for their income effects, the fact that specific consumption levels are difficult and costly to assess, and the fact that they may influence the use of those services in an unwanted manner.

It is mostly defended and accepted that citizens should be taxed according to their earning capacity. However, this is easier said than done, because we can measure income, but this is mostly a biased indicator for earning capacity.

There are indeed historic examples where earning capacity (or ability to pay) was proxied by other variables: occupation, social rank. In 1680 Holland moved from a tax on corn to a poll tax. The tax level was fixed for an individual, but differentiated by occupation. It was also differentiated by wealth though (see De Vries and Van der Woude 1995: 134). The Poll Tax Act of 1660 in England is an even better example. It was based on exogenously determined social rank: £100 for a duke, £60 for an earl, £30 for a baronet, £10 for a squire (Hahn 1973). In view of the high cost of income taxation, it is worthwhile to start thinking along those lines again, seeking better indicators of earnings capacity than simply realized earnings. The *ability tax* may then serve as a point of reference. In no way are we suggesting that the ability tax as we calculate it here is a scheme that should immediately be implemented.

In present-day reality the problem is solved by using a variety of taxes; for example, a tax on income, a tax on wealth, and taxes on consumption, which take the shape of excise taxes or value-added taxes. However, here we face similar problems. If individuals are taxed proportionally to earned income the incentive to work for money will be reduced. For instance, it may be that the tax causes the individual to reduce his work effort by 20 percent. Then, taxation influences behavior—that is that of labor supply—while the tax revenue for the state is reduced by 20 percent as well, if we assume a proportional income tax. This is called in economic literature the *dead-weight loss* effect. Similar effects are there if we apply a wealth tax or a consumption tax.

Nowadays, it is widely believed that income taxes in developed countries have large distortionary effects. About a decade ago several studies were published that found high excess burdens for the United States and other countries like Sweden and the Netherlands (Stuart 1981; Browning and Johnson 1984; Hausman and Ruud 1984; Stuart 1984; Browning 1987; Van Ravestijn and Vijlbrief 1988; Hartog 1989). Since that time many countries have implemented tax reforms and reduced marginal tax rates but, even so, in many countries dead-weight welfare losses must have remained at high levels.

The welfare loss is increased because of the large efforts that are made to avoid paying taxes, by adjusting behavior. Part of the adjustment is in the realm of perfectly legal behavior, another part is the shift of activities into the grey and black zones of semi-legal or outright illegal activities, like tax (and social-premium) fraud. The subterranean economy has absorbed a large share of the legal economy. For several countries estimates of up to 10 percent or even 20 percent of national income have been given (Gutmann 1977; Van Eck and Kazemier 1989; Schneider and Enste 2000). And on top of that there are substantial transaction costs: an army of tax inspectors, tax advisors, tax lawyers, all engaged in extensive debate on properly assessing the individual's income level.

Guidance on the structure and graduation of taxes has always been a prime topic of economics. Right from the start a fair distribution of the burden was a stated goal: 'the subjects of every state ought to contribute to the support of the government as nearly as possible in proportion to their respective abilities', according to Adam Smith. If we assume that income is proportional to earnings capacities and is not influenced by the income-tax schedule, it seems justified to take income as the tax base.

In the late nineteenth century the discussion opened on the proper graduation of the income tax. Should the tax be proportional, or should it increase for higher income levels? Taking individual income as given, tax rates were derived by applying John Stuart Mill's principle of equality of sacrifice to the welfare derived from the income (Mill 1965). The sacrifice was not yet defined. This is done in terms of a utility function of income $U(.)$. If we have a tax $T(y)$, then the *absolute* utility sacrifice is $[U(y) - U(y - T(y))]$. The tax amount is translated into a utility loss. Instead of the term utility we may also call it welfare or financial satisfaction. The *proportional* utility loss is $[\frac{U(y)-U(y-T(y))}{U(y)}]$. The norm for income taxation was differentiated into equal absolute or equal proportional utility losses. In the first case everybody is taxed in such a way that he or she incurs the same absolute utility loss, while in the second case the proportional losses are equalized over taxpayers. Of course each norm has a different implication for income-tax rates. However, apart from the question of the graduation of the tax tariff, there is the more primary question of what the tax base should be. Should it be income or should it be another personal index, which may proxy 'earnings potential' or, as we shall also call it, 'ability'.

The modern literature does not start out from given individual incomes. Taking into consideration the efforts needed to generate the income, neoclassical theory points out that efficiency losses can only be prevented by *lump-sum* taxation. Such a tax is not differentiated according to characteristics which can be changed by the individual him- or herself. For instance, the tax base could be gender and/or age. Only individually differentiated lump-sum taxation would allow costless attainment of desirable equity goals. It is felt that in an ideal (or just) system of taxation the lump-sum tax would have to be related to individual earning capacity. Tinbergen's calculation of an optimal income tax (Tinbergen 1975: ch. 7) and his proposal of a 'tax on talent' (Tinbergen 1970*a/b*) follow this argument. However, the first-best optimum can only be implemented if the government knows enough about individuals to determine their lump sums. The new literature on optimal taxation that has emerged in the wake of Mirrlees's seminal contribution (Mirrlees 1971) indeed starts out from the information problem.[1]

In this chapter an attempt is made to derive such lump-sum taxes, based on somewhat more specific information than is available in the traditional literature.

First, we employ our empirical results with respect to income utility, which we set equal in the context of this chapter to financial satisfaction. Taking individual incomes as given, we derive an income-tax schedule from a welfare function that has demonstrated its empirical strength in extensive research, the Leyden 'welfare function of income'. This welfare function is derived from the Income Evaluation Question (IEQ) presented in Chapter 2. The advantage over other approaches is the fact that individual welfare has been directly measured, rather than postulated or inferred from observed consumption/leisure choices. We apply four different 'sacrifice rules' and calculate the associated income taxes in Section 12.2. Then, we replace income as a tax base by 'ability', which is defined as a function of IQ and education. Then, we apply the same framework for the construction of an 'ability tax'. We know from the literature that equity could be served without dead-weight welfare loss if we were to set

---

[1] Mirrlees derives optimum conditions for a non-linear income-tax schedule in a model where individuals with different labor skills maximize a utility function in consumption and leisure, and where the government can observe earnings but not skills. So far, the practical implications for tax policy are quite limited. The key parameter of interest is the marginal income-tax rate, but the analyses generate no firm prescriptions on whether it should decrease, be constant, or increase. As Diamond has shown, acceptable cases can be constructed for each of these results (Diamond 1996). Neither has the literature determined a meaningful range over which it should vary, other than between 0 and 100 percent. Research along these lines is intellectually exciting but still seems far from settling the location of the compromise between equity and efficiency. For example, the rule proposed by Piketty (1993), of a tax schedule that not only depends on an individual's income but also on the distribution of income in society, is interesting but does not seem a ready candidate for implementation.

individuals' tax liability in relation to their ability or earning capacity. In Section 12.3 we consider the data set and we operationalize the empirical relationships; in Section 12.4 we consider the resulting ability tax tariffs; and in Section 12.5 we draw some conclusions.

12.2. INCOME TAXATION ON THE BASIS OF UTILITY SACRIFICES

In this section we consider the tax schedules, which result from the application of different taxation principles. We assume according to our findings in section 2.8 that incomes y are evaluated by a utility function

$$U(y; u(y_c, x), \sigma) = N\left(\frac{\ln(y) - \beta_1 \ln(y_c) - \gamma' x}{\sigma}; 0, 1\right),\qquad (12.1)$$

where y_c stands for current income, the vector x for a list of individual characteristics, and N for the standard normal distribution function. The subjective impact of a tax can then be assessed by using this instrument. The evaluation of current income y_c is

$$U(y_c; \mu(y_c, x), \sigma) = N\left(\frac{(1 - \beta_1)\ln(y_c) - \gamma' x}{\sigma}; 0, 1\right).\qquad (12.2)$$

We consider four taxation principles:

- absolute utility equality
- marginal utility equality
- imposition of equal proportional sacrifices
- imposition of equal absolute sacrifices.

The latter two rules are taken from the old, nineteenth-century literature. The first is a radical egalitarian norm, while the second follows from maximizing a Benthamite[2] social-welfare function (with pre-tax incomes fixed). We notice that all principles require a cardinal utility concept except for the first principle, where ordinal inter-individual comparability suffices. Let y_b and y_a stand for before- and after-tax income and let $(1 - t)y_b = y_a$ where t stands for the tax rate.

Absolute Utility Equality
Let us assume that we are strictly egalitarian and that we aim for the situation where after-tax income is evaluated equally by everybody. Say we require $U(y_a) = \alpha$. Let the utility function be

$$U(y_a; x) = N\left(\frac{\ln(y_a) - \beta_1 \ln(y_a) - \gamma' x}{\sigma}\right) = \alpha.\qquad (12.3)$$

---

[2] See Ch. 13 below for a definition.

This rule gives the same income to everybody except for individual character-istics x, (e.g. family size), for which a correction takes place. Hence, equal utility does not imply income equality. Notice that very poor people will get a higher income; that is, a negative tax. The resulting tax is $(y_b - y_a)$ where y_a is determined by (12.3).

Marginal Utility Equality

This principle is based on the idea that the marginal utility of income should be equal between individuals. We use the Leyden welfare function

$$\frac{d}{dy_a} U(y_a; x) = n\left(\frac{\ln(y_a) - \mu}{\sigma}\right) \cdot \frac{1}{y_a} = \alpha, \tag{12.4}$$

where $n(.)$ stands for the standard normal-density function. Taking logarithms at both sides and taking into account that we found that μ is a linear function in $\ln(y)$, we find a quadratic equation in $\ln(y_a)$. It has two roots of which we take the highest as after-tax income y_a. Notice that again very poor people will get a higher income; that is, a negative tax is possible.

Equal Proportional Sacrifices

In this case we have

$$(1 - \alpha) \cdot U(y_b) = U(y_a). \tag{12.5}$$

The relative utility loss is equal for every taxpayer, irrespective of his or her before-tax income y_a.

Equal Absolute Sacrifices

In this case we have

$$U(y_b) - U(y_a) = \alpha. \tag{12.6}$$

Obviously, this rule cannot be carried out if $U(y_b) \leq \alpha$, for in that case we would end up with negative utility, while we assumed utility to be between 0 and 1. Hence, at the lower end we have to make a requirement that after-tax income is still evaluated at a low positive value.

The schedules outlined above are all proposed in the taxation literature. However, the novelty here is that the utility functions involved, which of course determine the actual tax schedules, are approximately known from the estimation of the IEQ on real data, while in the traditional literature the utility functions are either not specified at all or just posited on the basis of intuition. Most frequently the function is specified as being logarithmic, following Bernoulli.

Although we have several tax rules which can be applied, we still face the problem that income is not an ideal tax base, given the fact that taxation affects actual income. We would like a variable like 'earning potential' or 'ability' which is not affected by taxation. But how to define and measure that concept? Griliches (1977) points to the restrictive nature of ability measures; according to him ability is something like a 'thing with feathers' (a Woody Allen quote). We assume that ability is multi-dimensional. The dimensions we would propose in the first place are the following candidates

- physical and mental health
- cognitive intelligence as measured by IQ
- social/emotional intelligence
- gender
- age
- education.

All these variables can be measured in a more or less satisfactory way. And, significantly, they are measured in practice in any western country for the great majority of children. There are two problems with those measures. First, they are subject to measurement error and vary during the development of the child. This can be repaired by repeated measurement over the childhood period, say from 6 to 14. A second objection that might be raised is that parents would strongly persuade their children to underperform on those dimensions to prevent high tax liabilities in the future. Here we refer to the famous quote: 'If we tax able men more than dunderheads, we open the door to all forms of falsification: we make stupidity seem profitable and any man can make himself seem stupid' (see De Villiers Graaf as quoted by Atkinson and Stiglitz 1980: 357). This objection is not devastating. As Mirrlees (1971) noted, the prestige effect may give a counter incentive. The same holds if desirable outcomes are linked to the test performance, such as school admission. In fact, as long as there will be systematic variation in the performance (that is, not every candidate will willingly score all zeros), we can model behavior and infer true ability from measured scores.[3] Also all (normal) parents will realize that 'making himself seem stupid' would be a damaging strategy for the children's career and the accumulation of their human capital.

There are two indices which need some further discussion. First, we include gender because the earning ability of females is reduced by the possibility of pregnancy and the obligations of motherhood. It is also reflected in the differences in lifetime income between males and females. In our application we will also use education as an indicator of ability. That is, we assume that education is not affected by the expectation that adults with much education will have to pay more taxes. We do not consider it realistic that parental and children's

---

[3] Psychologists acknowledge that people may show misleading behavior strategically. They have come up with tests accounting for these types of distortions. Unfortunately, there are no tests available yet detecting people who fake stupidity while taking IQ tests. However, in applications people who fake the ideal profile are detected by so-called social-desirability tests: see Crown and Marlowe (1964). A similar principle is easily transferred into an IQ setting. See also Jacob and Levitt (2003*a*, *b*) where tests are suggested to detect teachers who falsely improve the results of their pupils.

decisions on education are significantly affected by tax effects twenty years or more later, when the individual is grown up. Age is also a relevant differentiator, as almost all incomes are age-dependent. Finally, it might be argued that social parental background partially determines the earnings capacity of individuals. The same may hold for inherited wealth. We abstained from including those factors in order to avoid too many political and philosophical undertones in this first approach.

12.3. DATA AND OPERATIONALIZATION

As a matter of fact we do not have an ideal data set, in which all the variables listed above are known. However, we have at our disposal a unique data set in which both individual childhood IQ is measured and the IEQ is included. As an interesting starting point for the exercise to be developed in this chapter, we shall assume that ability is wholly determined by IQ, gender, and the number of years in education. At the end of the chapter we shall remind you of the fact that ability is only incompletely measured, but that it would be possible to repeat our exercise on a more satisfactorily defined ability measure. We notice that the concept 'ability' as it is introduced here is rather narrow. It refers only to ability in so far as human abilities determine earnings capacity.

In 1952 a quarter of the sixth-grade pupils (then about twelve years old) in Holland's southern province of Noord-Brabant were sampled.[4] At that time their scholastic achievement, intelligence, and family background were measured. Thirty years later the unique observations were still available. In 1983 the same individuals were contacted to collect data on education, labor-market status, earnings, and so on (some 4,700 out of 5,800 original observations). As the 1983 edition of the Brabant data turned out to be a very rich data set, the 1983 exercise was repeated in 1993 (see C. M. Van Praag 1992). In the latest version the questionnaire also included questions concerning subjective welfare measurement, one of these being the income-evaluation question (IEQ).

In this context we restrict ourselves essentially to this question for our analysis. The number of Brabant people who responded to the 1993 questionnaire is 2099. From these households a number of observations had to be removed from the analysis because of (partial) non-response. If we are aiming at taxing earnings capacity, we need variables to predict it. We only use observations on IQ for the individuals in the original 1952 survey, not for their spouses. In this chapter we do not want to get involved in the complications that arise if there is more than one income earner in the family. So we can only use the observations where the original respondent is now the single earner of the family. We will also restrict ourselves to individuals who work full-time. Of course the notion of taxing earning capacity rather than actual earnings is perfectly suited

---

[4] The description of the Brabant data set is partly taken from Hartog, Ridder, and Visser (1994).

to deal with the problem of variable hours, but that is not the purpose of the present investigation. Given all these restrictions and the loss of cases from missing observations on key variables, we end up with a sample of 525 observations. From the remaining IEQ answers we were able to identify 333 welfare functions.[5]

Finally, we corrected for extreme IEQ-response behavior by assuming that 'normal' response behavior has to satisfy

$$0.025 \leq N\left(\frac{\ln(y_c - \mu)}{\sigma}\right) \leq 0.975. \tag{12.7}$$

In other words, 'normal' respondents evaluate their own current net income between 0.025 and 0.975 on a [0, 1]-scale.[6] The final sample under analysis contains 301 observations. A short description of the other variables follows.

The IQ score was constructed from six sub-tests relating to numbers, words, analogies, and spatial orientation in one form or another. The educational variable represents the Dutch educational system. This system consists basically of two tracks, a vocational and a general or academic one. Although the different education types are difficult to compare, their respective names and durations give some indication of standing and difficulty. Beginning with the category 'elementary school', obligatory at six years of age, we distinguish seven levels with a corresponding total number of years:

- elementary school   6 years
- extended primary   8 years
- lower vocational   9 years
- intermediate vocational   10 years
- intermediate general   11 years
- higher vocational   15 years
- university   17 years.

This list describes the Dutch educational system as it was in the fifties and sixties. For all individuals education is set as equal to the normative length; that is, the additional minimally required schooling years beyond elementary school plus one year. In such a way the education variable can be defined as a natural logarithm of the number of years. All individuals are given the highest education level attended. The other variables used are family size fs and after- and before-tax household income y_a and y_b. Again, we notice that because of the genesis of the sample all respondents are roughly of the same age. So an age effect could not be distinguished. In the Dutch fifties participation in higher education was more restricted than in modern times. Education from

---

[5] The six IEQ answers are screened according to three criteria. The first requires that the answers increase, the second allows at most two answers to be missing, and the third criterion states that neither the first two nor the last two answers should be missing.

[6] Of course this is also a screening device pinpointing possible measurement errors in income or IEQ answers.

age 6–12 years was obligatory. The tuition fees were only a fraction of the real cost, with grants and loans available for poor families. Nevertheless, it has to be realized that poor families were confronted with a considerable opportunity cost, as the continuation of education after the obligatory age implied that the child could not contribute to the parental household income. In the context of trying to assess structural pre-career earning power this is not so much of a problem, as the decision on continued education in the Dutch 1952 situation was a parental decision, strongly guided by teachers' advice, on which the child itself had marginal influence only. The distribution of the sample according to IQ and education is presented in Table 12.1. In Table 12.1 IQ is subdivided. The 75-column represents those people with an IQ lower than 80. The 85 column scored between 81 and 90 on the IQ scale. All the columns are defined accordingly except for the 135 one. This column represents people with an IQ higher than 130. As expected, education increases with IQ score, but there is a large amount of dispersion in the relation.

Predicting Earnings Capacity
Because we aim at using 'earning capacity' as our tax base, we have to define and measure earning capacity. Before, we listed a set of basic individual-earnings determinants. Here, however, we are restricted by the data set and we have to do with the usual variables gender and education to which we can add IQ, measured at the age of 12. Unfortunately, as noted above, the age variable had to be dropped as an explanatory variable because all respondents in the sample are roughly the same age. They were about twelve years of age at the first sampling moment in 1952, and hence they are about fifty-three in 1993. In order to predict earnings capacity we assume

$$\ln(y_c) = \alpha_0 + \alpha_1 iq + \alpha_2 gender + \varepsilon, \tag{12.8}$$

where we take iq as the IQ test score divided by 100. To control for gender effects we add a gender dummy. The IQ measure and the gender dummy exclusively define earnings capacity as an exogenous variable. Unobserved ability determinants end up in the error. The earnings-capacity estimates may be inaccurate for

Table 12.1. *Distribution of the sample*

IQ	75	85	95	105	115	125	135	Subtotal
Elementary school	7	3	6	5	2	—	—	23
Extended primary	3	12	24	14	9	1	—	63
Lower vocational	—	5	9	22	8	4	1	49
Intermediate vocational	—	6	8	28	13	6	—	61
Higher vocational	—	7	7	28	19	12	2	75
University	—	—	—	5	4	7	4	20
SUBTOTAL	10	34	54	104	59	31	9	301

two reasons. First, the IQ measure is only an exogenous variable if people refrain from cheating in their IQ test. If not, we have to deal with the endogeneity of the IQ score. However, is it probable that twelve-year olds are able and willing to systematically cheat in an IQ test? Remember that cheating–if possible–can only be downwards. Secondly, we expect the impact of the measurement error on earnings capacity to be high; IQ is a rather narrow instrument to reflect a broad concept like earnings capacity. Alternatively, we add years of education to the list of variables and predict earnings capacity as follows:

$$\ln(y_c) = \alpha_0 + \alpha_1 iq + \alpha_2 \, gender + \alpha_3 \ln(e) + \varepsilon, \tag{12.9}$$

where we take e to be the total years of education. Thereby, we gain precision by reducing the measurement error, but we may lose with respect to the accuracy of OLS estimates. We realize that endogeneity of education may render our OLS estimate inadequate, as argued by Card (1994) and others. However, again we have to pose the question whether expected taxation over lifetime really is a strong determinant of educational choices when young. We do not believe that this was the case in the Netherlands in 1953.

We will continue to use both definitions as capacity predictors. In Table 12.2 we present the estimates of the net earnings function. The gender effect is quite strong; in this sample women's net earnings are about 60 percent of male earnings. The IQ parameter of net earnings is about 1 if we ignore education, and about a quarter if we add education. The education elasticity is about two-thirds. If we were to use the standard Mincer specification, the net return to education would be 6 percent–a conventional result for the Netherlands (cf. Hartog, Oosterbeek, and Teulings 1993).

It is now standard practice to use the Mincer specification, relating log earnings to years of education. In order to facilitate comparison of ours with other studies we also present the estimates for the traditional Mincer specification. In our model specification it is more convenient to use the (natural) logarithm of years educated. We feel justified in deviating from the Mincer specification for two reasons. First, the use of the (natural) logarithm of years

Table 12.2. *Net income functions*

	Estimate	Standard deviation	Estimate	Standard deviation	Estimate	Standard deviation
Intercept	7.232	0.152	6.426	0.146	7.307	0.127
Gender	−0.426	0.060	−0.415	0.050	−0.406	0.050
iq	0.953	0.144	0.246	0.135	0.259	0.134
Ln(years educated)	—	—	0.664	0.058	—	—
Years educated	—	—	—	—	0.060	0.005
R^2	0.205	—	0.444	—	0.449	—
N	301	—	301	—	301	—

educated is not rejected by the data. Whether we apply the Mincer specification or the specification in Equation (12.9) has no strong effect on the coefficients of the other variables, nor does it affect the correlation coefficient. Secondly, the Mincer specification implies a constant rate of return to education. In our specification there is a diminishing marginal return to years of schooling. We get

$$\frac{\partial \ln(y)}{\partial e} = \frac{\partial \ln(y)}{\partial \ln(e)} \frac{\partial \ln(e)}{\partial e} = \frac{\alpha_2}{e}. \tag{12.10}$$

A diminishing return for increasing education levels is one of the stylized features established in the international survey's by Psacharopoulos (1985) or Card (1994). The rate of return to education in our specification equals $0.664/e$ for net earnings. In Table 12.3 the corresponding gross-earnings estimates are presented. All coefficients are larger in absolute value than in the net specification. This may be interpreted as a reduction in ability-determined income inequality caused by the Dutch tax tariffs. We notice that this levelling attempt is not very impressive. The rate of return to education is $0.805/e$ for gross earnings.

It is also interesting to look at the substitution ratio between IQ and education. We find the constant yield curve

$$\alpha_1 iq + \alpha_2 \ln(e) = \ln(y_c) - \alpha_0. \tag{12.11}$$

The earnings function reveals the substitution ratios of IQ and years educated, keeping ability constant. We see that it becomes increasingly easy to replace a loss in education length by more IQ at higher levels of education. Or, to put it differently, an increase in IQ is harder to replace by more education at higher levels of education than at lower levels of education.

Extending the WFI
We found in Chapter 2 that the parameter μ depends on current net income y_c and family size *fs*. The Brabant data set allows us to extend this relation to other

Table 12.3. *Gross income functions*

	Estimate	Standard deviation	Estimate	Standard deviation	Estimate	Standard deviation
Intercept	7.395	0.182	6.417	0.173	7.485	0.151
Gender	−0.477	0.072	−0.464	0.060	−0.453	0.060
iq	1.224	0.172	0.366	0.161	0.386	0.160
Ln(years educated)	—	—	0.805	0.069	—	—
Years educated	—	—	—	—	0.073	0.006
R^2	0.206	—	0.451	—	0.454	—
N	301	—	301	—	301	—

variables. The variables of interest in the context of this paper are IQ and the education variable e. We suppose that the capacity to derive welfare (satisfaction) from income must be affected by one's education and by one's IQ. More precisely, we attempt to explain μ by the equation

$$\mu = \beta_0 + \beta_1 \ln(fs) + \beta_2 \ln(y_c) + \beta_3 iq + \beta_4 \ln(e). \tag{12.12}$$

Education deeply affects individuals, and one may expect strong influence on perceptions, tastes, and the art of spending income. IQ, standing for more or less innate properties, may operate as a taste shifter between individuals, although we are not sure a priori of the sign of the effect. People with a higher IQ may have more needs leading to an increase in μ, but on the other hand more intelligence may enhance the efficiency of the spending process as well.[7]

Estimation results are given in Table 12.4. We find first of all the usual income and family-size effects. The former is the well-established preference-drift effect. As stated earlier, there is a welfare leakage because part of additional income increases aspirations as well. A preference drift of 0.5–0.6 and a family-size elasticity of 0.11 are fully in line with the results commonly found for Dutch data (see Chapter 2). The interesting new variables in this context are IQ and years educated e. Increasing IQ by 10 points raises μ by 0.02 to 0.03, since iq $=$IQ/100. We have experimented with a quadratic function in IQ, but it turned out that a log-linear specification is sufficient. In the 'years-educated' specification we see that increasing education by 1 year raises μ by about 0.01. The effect of education is highly significant. In isolation IQ is also very significant, but with education added its effect is strongly diminished: with higher IQ

Table 12.4. *The relation between μ, IQ, and education*

	Estimate	Standard deviation	Estimate	Standard deviation	Estimate	Standard deviation
Intercept	2.638	0.266	2.882	0.276	3.052	0.306
Ln(household size)	0.116	0.028	0.116	0.028	0.116	0.028
Ln(household income)	0.596	0.034	0.539	0.039	0.542	0.040
iq	0.272	0.091	0.165	0.097	0.178	0.097
Ln(years educated)	—	—	0.143	0.049	—	—
Years educated	—	—	—	—	0.012	0.004
R^2	0.604	—	0.614	—	0.612	—
N	301	—	301	—	301	—

[7] We have not included gender in the welfare function. The motivation can be found in Plug and Van Praag (1998), where it was found that in one-earner families both spouses have a rather uniform opinion on their income. See also Chapter 6.

and more education, more income is needed to attain a given welfare level; intelligence and education raise 'needs'.

How do IQ and education affect the evaluation of income? In order to get an answer to this question we have to break down the effect of IQ and education into two separate effects. The first effect arises because the perception of welfare, as we just saw, is *directly* influenced by IQ and education. The second effect is that IQ and education affect welfare *indirectly via the market* through income. These welfare effects can be properly addressed by means of equivalence scales. Just as has been done for family-equivalence scales, it is possible to define IQ-equivalence scales or education-equivalence scales. If earnings capacity is defined by childhood IQ only, we can calculate how much money an individual with an IQ of iq_A must have in order to be as well off as an individual with an IQ of iq_B. If m is the equivalence scale, equality in utility reads as

$$U(m \cdot y(iq_A); iq_A) = U(y(iq_B); iq_B), \tag{12.13}$$

where we take into account that the income-evaluation function itself depends on iq as well (see Table 12.4 and Equation (12.13)). To present this within the Leyden framework, let us assume two individuals with IQ values iq_A and iq_B. Their incomes according to Equation (12.9) will be $y(iq_A)$ and $y(iq_B)$, other things being equal. Their welfare function will be described by μ_A and μ_B respectively, where according to (12.13)

$$\mu_A = \beta_0 + \beta_1 \ln(fs_A) + \beta_2 \ln(y_{c,A}) + \beta_3 iq_A. \tag{12.14}$$

The parameter μ_B is analogously defined. When σ is assumed constant over the sample, equivalence in welfare implies for the equivalence scale m

$$\ln(m \cdot y_A) - \mu(m \cdot y_A) = \ln(y_B) - \mu_B, \tag{12.15}$$

Assuming that $fs_A = fs_B$ we find:

$$(1 - \beta_2)\ln(y(iq_A)) - \beta_3 iq_A = (1 - \beta_2)\ln(m \cdot y(iq_B)) - \beta_3 iq_B. \tag{12.16}$$

Using the predicted earnings capacity in Equation (12.9), the Leyden IQ-equivalence scale m is defined as

$$\ln(m) = -\alpha_1 \Delta iq + \frac{\beta_3}{1 - \beta_2} \Delta iq, \tag{12.17}$$

where Δiq is the difference between the IQ levels iq_A and iq_B. We interpret the second term on the right-hand side as the pure-equivalence effect, while the first term reflects the market-correction effect. The pure-equivalence effect reflects the equivalence scale proper: additional income is needed for higher IQ levels in order to maintain welfare, acknowledging the welfare leakage caused by preference drift. The market-correction effect reflects the fact that an individual with a higher IQ earns on average $\alpha_1 \Delta iq$ more (see Equation (12.9)): it is the labour market's contribution to an individual's welfare, which can be deducted from the equivalence effect. In the case of a complete correction by the market we would end up with m = 0. Notice that we looked at ln (m), which can be broken down as the sum of two terms. If we look at the equivalence scale itself, it can be written as the product

$$m = e^{-\alpha_1 \Delta iq} \cdot e^{\frac{\beta_3}{1-\beta_2} \Delta iq}. \tag{12.18}$$

Table 12.5 presents both the pure and the market-correction effect associated respectively with the welfare function given in the first column of Table 12.4 and the net-earnings function given in the first column of Table 12.2. Our point of reference is set at an IQ equal to 105: the sample average. The first entry shows that individuals with IQ 75 reach the same utility level as individuals with average IQ (105) at 82 percent of the latter's income. They would be equally satisfied with their income as the reference person if they were to get 82 percent of the reference income. However, the market gives them 33 per cent less. If we combine both welfare effects, their present income should increase by 9 percent ($0.817 \times 1.331 = 1.088$). Hence, increasing IQ requires higher income to maintain welfare, but, as the market-compensation effect indicates, the labor market in 1993 generated overcompensation. Low-IQ people are worse off in terms of earnings capacity, earnings, and welfare compared to high-IQ people. In fact, what we observe here is the welfare effect of Mill's famous non-competing groups.

The exercise can be repeated after adding years educated as an explanatory variable. Now the point of reference is an intermediate general education and an IQ of 105 ($iq = 1.05$). The effects are now based on the third column in Tables 12.2 and 12.4. Results are given in Table 12.6. We note that, with IQ given, individuals need a higher income to maintain welfare if they have acquired more education, and that the pure difference between elementary education only and a university education is substantial. But we also note that the

Table 12.5. *Leyden equivalence scales—ability defined by IQ alone*

IQ	Pure	Market correction	Total
75	0.817	1.331	1.088
85	0.874	1.210	1.058
95	0.935	1.100	1.028
105	1.000	1.000	1.000
115	1.070	0.909	0.972
125	1.144	0.826	0.946
135	1.224	0.751	0.920

Note: Reference IQ = 105.

Table 12.6. *Leyden equivalence scales—ability defined by IQ and education*

IQ				Schooling			
IQ	Pure	Market correction	Total	Education	Pure	Market correction	Total
75	0.898	1.077	0.967	Elementary school	0.829	1.496	1.239
85	0.931	1.050	0.978	Extended primary	0.906	1.235	1.119
95	0.965	1.025	0.989	Lower vocational	0.940	1.143	1.074
105	1.000	1.000	1.000	Intermediate vocational	0.971	1.065	1.034
115	1.036	0.976	1.011	Intermediate general	1.000	1.000	1.000
125	1.074	0.952	1.023	Higher vocational	1.101	0.814	0.896
135	1.113	0.929	1.034	University	1.145	0.749	0.857

Note: Reference IQ = 105, education = intermediate general.

Dutch labor market undercompensates the lower educated and overcompensates the higher educated. The overcompensation of university educated relative to elementary schooling alone is quite substantial. More education pays off in terms of both earnings and welfare; the wage premium for schooling surpasses the compensating differential needed for constant utility. Table 12.6 also shows the effect of IQ when education is held constant. More able individuals still get a higher income, but now, conditional on given education, the labor market undercompensates. Note finally that the combined effects of IQ and years educated are the product of the two equivalence scales. For example, the joint welfare effect for an individual with university education and an IQ score of 135 adds up to an effect of -10 percent $(0.857 \times 1.034 = 0.905)$. If both years of schooling and childhood IQ define earnings capacity, we observe more or less similar findings to those described in Table 12.5. Highly educated people with high IQs are better off in terms of earnings capacity, earnings, and welfare.

12.4. THE RESULTS: TAX RATES

Now that we have all the ingredients, we operationalize our tax model as described in the opening paragraphs of Section 12.2. We will apply the tax norms listed above to earnings capacity. What would the ability tax be for the different ability classes, and how would the tax compare with the actual Dutch tax tariff? We assume that earnings capacity $y(a)$ is determined by ability a. We will perform our analyses using two ability measures, IQ alone and IQ with education. We assume that welfare $U(y; x)$ is derived from income y and that it also depends on intervening variables x other than income. The function $U(.)$ is the WFI. We assume that earnings y depend on ability and on other factors, which may be taken as random—at least, they are not correlated with ability. That is, we assume

$$\ln(y) = \ln(y(a)) + \varepsilon, \tag{12.19}$$

where $y(a)$ is the structural part representing earnings capacity. The error term ε reflects other variables and random factors. As we assume (and find) that ability and earnings capacity are monotonically related, it is not confusing to replace the latent variable 'ability' by $y(a)$.

As before, we apply four distinct optimality criteria for taxation: equal after tax utility, equal after tax marginal utility, equal proportional utility sacrifice, and equal absolute utility sacrifice. Let us now write the tax schedule as $t(a)$ where it is explicitly noted that $t(a)$ does not depend on actual income y but on earnings capacity $y(a)$. We then determine the tax function as in Section 12.3, with income replaced by earnings capacity $y(a)$, predicted either by IQ or by IQ and schooling combined. The total tax revenue is

$$R = \sum_{n=1}^{N} t(a_n)\, y\,(a_n). \tag{12.20}$$

The four tax schedules are calculated under the constraint that the total tax revenue will equal the current revenue in the 1993 data set.

Of course there is the possibility that a person does not earn enough to pay his ability tax. To prevent this, we allow for welfare payments.[8] Like the actual Dutch tax and welfare system, our model accounts for a minimum net income. This implies that whenever some tax payers get a net income below the threshold we activate a lower limit. In order to accommodate differences in household size, we also apply the Leyden household-equivalence scale. In Leyden-type poverty analysis (see e.g. Hagenaars 1986 and Ch. 15 below) the poverty threshold is set at a welfare value 0.4 (severe poverty) or 0.5 (poverty). These values correspond to verbal qualifications of 'insufficient' and 'nearly insufficient'. The value of 0.4 roughly coincides with the actual Dutch social minimum income. These levels are arbitrarily chosen, but are a standing convention. Of course, we might also have applied the actual social minimum as reflected in the Dutch minimum wage and minimum benefit levels, but applying the Leyden social minimum has all the charm of a coherent structure.

Results are presented in Tables 12.7 and 12.8. In Table 12.7 IQ serves as the single ability indicator. The column $y(a)$ presents actual net earnings capacity (income predicted from IQ) for the given IQ level. It is the average for men and women, weighted by the actual proportion of each at the given IQ level.

The next column gives the actual 'taxes' paid. We remind the reader of the fact that all the people in our data set are single earners in full-time work.

---

[8] If people are entitled to receive welfare payments, claims for enhancing efficiency gains are slightly damaged. However, given the exploratory nature of this chapter we will continue, and ignore these behavioral distortions. In our exercise only a few Brabant people were unable to pay their notional 'ability' tax. Therefore, we believe that in this situation these efficiency losses can be neglected.

Table 12.7. *Four different recipes for tax on ability as measured by IQ in % of gross income*

IQ	Actual net monthly earning capacity in Dfl (1993)	Actual taxes paid	Taxes under equal utility	Taxes under equal marginal utility	Taxes under equal proportional sacrifice	Taxes under equal absolute sacrifice
75	2,884	31	31	21	34	34
85	3,091	32	29	23	33	33
95	3,401	34	33	30	35	35
105	3,686	35	34	34	35	35
115	3,874	37	37	38	36	36
125	4,305	38	39	43	37	37
135	4,424	40	38	44	37	37

We have estimated gross and net earnings functions, and the gap between predicted gross and predicted net earnings equals predicted actual taxes. The tax is given as the amount paid and as a percentage of predicted gross income. Remember that the 'tax' is defined as the difference between gross and net earnings, so it includes both the Dutch income tax and the employee's social-security contributions.[9] In practice, it would be impossible to apply the official tax tariff in order to calculate the tax, because in reality there are a lot of exemptions, such that the official tax tariff does not give a proper reflection of the gap between gross and net earnings. The next four columns show the tax amounts under the four regimes: equal utility, equal marginal utility, equal proportional sacrifice, equal absolute sacrifice. A striking result is the remarkably small difference between actual taxes paid and 'optimal' taxes calculated under the four regimes. Imposing the rule of equal marginal utility would imply the largest change in the tax rates, with the range going from 31–40 percent to 21–44 percent.

In Table 12.8 we give the results for the case where earnings capacity is predicted from IQ and education together. The average tax rates are again quite close to the actual average rates for the two rules of equal sacrifice. Another striking result is the small difference emerging from the different optimum criteria. Taken together, these results suggest that applying any of these optimality rules leads to a tax structure with small effects on the tax rate for the average tax payer. The big change of course is in the elimination of tax dispersion within a group of (proclaimed) equal earnings capacity. But we now find large discrepancies if we impose equal utility or equal marginal utility. Indeed, in line with the earlier result, we find that the radical rule of equal post-tax utility implies a very progressive tax rate on earnings capacity. The results also fit in with those reported by Keller and Hartog (1977) explaining actual tax

---

[9] In the Netherlands social security is financed on a pay-as-you-go basis. The income tax and the social security contribution are formally distinct.

Table 12.8. *Four different recipes for tax on ability as measured by IQ and education in % of gross income*

	Actual net monthly earning capacity in Dfl (1993)	Actual taxes paid	Taxes under equal utility	Taxes under equal marginal utility	Taxes under equal proportional sacrifice	Taxes under equal absolute sacrifice
IQ = 75						
Elementary school	2,458	28	22	6	30	31
Extended primary	2,957	31	31	21	33	34
IQ = 85						
Elementary school	2,514	29	18	6	29	30
Extended primary	2,945	31	28	20	32	33
Lower vocational	3,066	32	25	22	31	32
Intermediate vocational	3,539	34	34	32	35	35
Intermediate general	3,760	35	26	31	31	32
Higher vocational	4,616	37	45	47	40	39
IQ = 95						
Elementary school	2,568	30	24	11	31	32
Extended primary	3,111	32	29	23	32	33
Lower vocational	3,243	33	28	25	32	33
Intermediate vocational	3,316	34	26	24	31	32
Higher vocational	4,733	38	47	49	42	41
IQ = 105						
Elementary school	2,463	30	18	9	27	30
Extended primary	3,179	33	26	23	31	32
Lower vocational	3,241	34	28	25	32	33
Intermediate vocational	3,605	35	32	32	34	34
Intermediate general	3,954	36	38	39	37	36
Higher vocational	4,725	39	44	48	40	40
University	5,273	40	46	53	41	40

Table 12.8. *(Contd.)*

	Actual net monthly earning capacity in Dfl (1993)	Actual taxes paid	Taxes under equal utility	Taxes under equal marginal utility	Taxes under equal proportional sacrifice	Taxes under equal absolute sacrifice
IQ = 115						
Elementary school	2,696	31	20	12	30	31
Extended primary	3,254	34	30	26	33	33
Lower vocational	3,066	34	25	20	31	32
Intermediate vocational	3,683	36	35	34	35	35
Intermediate general	3,697	36	34	33	34	35
Higher vocational	4,420	39	39	43	37	37
University	5,418	41	54	57	47	45
IQ = 125						
Extended primary	3,309	34	32	28	33	34
Lower vocational	3,297	35	27	25	32	33
Intermediate vocational	3,663	36	29	31	33	34
Intermediate general	4,108	37	42	42	38	38
Higher vocational	4,788	40	45	49	41	40
University	5,260	41	42	51	39	39
IQ = 135						
Lower vocational	2,439	33	14	5	27	29
Intermediate general	2,787	35	15	13	28	29
Higher vocational	5,173	41	42	51	39	38
University	5,667	42	48	56	42	41

rates from proportional sacrifice. In an earlier exercise we regressed individual actual after-tax income linearly on after-tax income derived from any of the four tax principles. Equal utility and equal marginal utility yielded correlation coefficients of 0.53, the sacrifice rules yielded 0.87 (all regressions had a significant negative intercept and a slope significantly above 1). Clearly, then, taxation according to the sacrifice rules implies taxation that on average would not deviate dramatically from actual taxation. But when we fix taxes as an individualized lump sum, the most interesting feature is the dispersion in the difference between actual and 'optimal' rates. We will investigate this only for the case of equal proportional sacrifice. We consider it an attractive principle of taxation as it imposes an equal relative burden on every taxpayer.

For each IQ-education combination we have taken the difference between reported gross and reported net income, and hence taxes paid, for all individuals observed in that group. Based on the individual's IQ and education, we have predicted the individual lump-sum tax, and we have calculated the difference between actual tax and lump-sum tax.

The main result is that those with low IQs have to pay extra taxes under the new system and that those with the highest IQs mostly gain. But there is no monotonic relation between tax changes and IQ or schooling: it is a rather mixed picture. In many cases the change is not really dramatic. For many entries the dispersion is not higher than Dfl150 per month. This means that for 95 percent of the individuals the effect is restricted to a gain or a loss of no more than Dfl300, roughly some 10 percent of net monthly income.[10] These small effects are caused by two factors. First, the actual tax rates in the Netherlands can quite well be interpreted from taxation by equal sacrifice. In that sense, there is no shift to a different principle. Second, we restrict our exercise to full-time employees, implying that the effect of a tax on leisure is not included. Hence, from this explorative analysis we can draw the conclusion that shifting to an ability-based earnings-capacity tax system does not have devastating effects on short-term net income positions.

12.5. CONCLUSION

In this chapter we investigated the question of whether the construction of a lump-sum tax built on 'ability' would be feasible. A tax on earnings capacity would bring great advantages in terms of economic efficiency, because taxing earning power does not affect the actual efforts. Taxing actual earnings does. In terms of fairness, it is felt by many that an income tax which levies the same amount on somebody who earns $30,000 by working 1 hour a day as on somebody who earns the same amount by working 8 hours a day is not acceptable. It is therefore worth searching for a viable measure of earnings capacity.

---

[10] For detailed results see table 10 in Plug, Van Praag, and Hartog (1999).

Such a measure should not only be based on IQ and years of education before starting work, but should also depend on other ability factors like physical state, gender, and social and emotional intelligence. Moreover, it should depend on age (which we had to exclude for our specific data set).

An obvious first step towards taxing earnings capacity is to eliminate the effect of hours worked. A tax on full-time earnings has been proposed before (see e.g. the well-known textbook by Musgrave 1959). We have experimented a little with variable labor supply, and for men we found only small consequences. Bigger consequences can be anticipated for women.

Our approach of aiming for a tax on ability, an answer to suggestions made by Tinbergen (1970*a/b*) and Mirrlees (1971, 1986), would need a much larger data set and more research before it could be operationalized or discussed as a political alternative to current tax practice. It could only be introduced gradually. However, our exercises show that an ability tax is not a *chimaera* but could be developed in earnest. Its advantage, from an ethical point of view embracing the notion of fairness, is obvious.

Tax perception costs would be greatly reduced, as the annual assessment of taxable income would be unnecessary. The same holds for the administration costs to the citizens to be taxed. If ability is measured early in life, the tax schedule would be known to any individual and uncertainty for individuals might be reduced as well.[11] As it were, individuals are classified early in life according to tax-ability. For practical reasons we have to aim at a discrete categorization. Such a tax schedule should be age-dependent as it is well-known that income and the evaluation of income varies with age. It might also depend on gender and, but this is a matter of debate, on one's family size. The reason for debate is clearly that family size is not a purely exogenous variable. For instance, if large families were to get a considerable tax deduction, it might cause taxpayers to have large families. We do not know for sure whether such a relationship is strong, and comparisons between different countries with different family-support systems do not suggest that the effect would be large, but here we have a strong political aspect. We may also think of the parental environment. It is obvious that, apart from inherited wealth, parental upbringing and the existence of a social network from being brought up in the right milieu facilitates a person's career considerably. A final aspect is that someone's income and earnings capacity is determined by his or her physical and mental health. Part of this is innate and more or less predictable and should be included in the tax base. Part of it is purely random. Individuals may become disabled for work. Obviously the tax should allow for hardship corrections. The individual him- or herself can influence another part of effective health. For instance, a heavy smoker may get lung cancer. We leave it for discussion

---

[11] Schooling levels should be reported to the tax authorities by the school administration, to prevent under-reporting by individuals. This is similar to banks reporting interest on savings, as required by Dutch tax law.

whether this kind of health deficit should be covered by the tax exemptions as well.

A tax pattern that is almost exactly known when starting one's career would facilitate career planning. Moreover, as taxes are independent of work effort, the incentive to work hard would be strengthened. Finally, the state tax revenue would be much less dependent on the business cycle.

Reservations about fixing lifetime tax liability from measured childhood ability can be based on a number of arguments. First, an individual's earnings are not only dependent on IQ, but on many other abilities: leadership, independence, creativity, ability to cooperate, commercial ability, and, last but not least, innate health. Tests for such abilities are available as well. A key issue is the problem of measurement error. Here, repeated measurement can help, and perhaps indicators other than test scores should be used, to allow for some system of error correction. Deliberate underachievement on the test–'playing the dunderhead'–is a problem that can be countered by linking positive incentives, such as linking IQ to admission to school (a common practice in many countries) and by estimating a test-behavior model. Mirrlees (1971) even suggests that the danger of evasion is not disturbing at all. If an individual capability like intelligence is valued highly in society, people will perform as best as they can, resulting in representative IQ scores.

Infringement of personal privacy is not an issue specific to ability testing. It also holds for modern income taxation, where income and reasons for exemption are annually assessed. Ability taxation may even be seen as an alleviation, as it does not require an annual impingement upon the individual's privacy. Moreover, nearly all individuals in western society have been tested repeatedly on their IQ and know the result of these tests. Obviously, the classification will reflect a social classification, but the present classification according to income is similar. Hence, we do not see why taxing ability would be socially and psychologically more damaging than the present income taxation is for many people.

A tax liability surpassing realized income is not a fundamental problem either. A social minimum can always be upheld, as we demonstrated in our exercises.

Perhaps the greatest reservation concerns the consequences of errors in measuring earnings capacity. Overestimation may set tax liabilities too high; underestimation would let millionaires get away with negligible taxes. First, such errors should be evaluated against the errors, injustices, and efficiency losses of the present system of taxing realized incomes. And, second, it may be worthwhile to investigate a mixture of systems, in which deviations between predicted earnings capacity and realized earnings could be taxed at a modest rate. This would provide an error-correction mechanism for fairness with a small efficiency cost.

We think there are good reasons to continue research along the line initiated here. Our first step would be to investigate the effect of eliminating the impact of working hours on tax liability. Secondly, we would bring in age as an indicator of earnings capacity, and a good one given its unquestionable exogeneity. In our exercise it is absent because age variation is absent from our data set. But we know that age is an important determinant of earnings capacity, and we know that it has a strong quadratic effect on the welfare parameter μ. And we should work at a structural model in which effort and innate ability are disentangled. Within such a model, the role of schooling will also be sharpened. Initial schooling is a constant over an individual's working life, and using it to set tax liability would surely bring efficiency gains. But of course individuals do have a choice, and this needs to be modelled more precisely. A final point which may pose a problem for future research is how schooling later in life, for example training on the job, should be accounted for in the tax system.

In laying out the problems of an ability tax, we should not forget that the present system of income taxation is a system with high costs. It is also a system with substantial errors, in the sense that taxable earnings is a far from perfect measure of earnings capacity, or ability to pay. Fairness is not upheld because high-income earners can spend more resources on setting up a negative bias in measured ability to pay. Given these drawbacks, we believe strongly that it is a sensible research effort to look into the consequences of shifting the tax base from realized earnings to predicted earnings capacity. This requires predictors that have sufficient reliability and are easy to measure. Using childhood IQ as a single indicator with a pervasive influence on lifetime tax liability would not receive great support in society, because of the vagaries of economic life in a market economy. Clearly, further work should address this and other issues. But we feel that it is a line of work that is a valuable extension to the theoretical work on optimal taxation in the footsteps of Mirrlees's ground-breaking contribution.

13

Subjective Income Inequalities

13.1. INTRODUCTION

Since Gini (1912) and Dalton (1920) the distribution and inequality of income has been an important subject of study for economic and social scientists. Recent surveys are offered in the handbooks edited by Atkinson and Bourguignon (1999), Silber (1999), and Salverda, Nolan, and Smeeding (2008). Let us assume a population with individuals $n = 1, 2, \ldots, N$ with incomes $y_1, \ldots, y_N$. Inequality may be defined in various ways. We may start with the well-known statistical spread formula, and we define the variance of the income distribution as

$$\sigma^2(y) = \frac{1}{N} \sum_{n=1}^{N} (y - \mu_y)^2, \tag{13.1}$$

where μ_y stands for *average* income. The problems with this measure are that it depends on the money unit chosen and that it depends on μ_y. If the money unit changes, for example because we take $100 as our new unit instead $1, all the amounts are divided by a hundred and consequently the variance is reduced by a factor $\frac{1}{10.000}$. It is obvious that this effect may be easily corrected in this setting, but there are situations where correction seems difficult; for instance, if we compare inequalities of two countries with different money systems or when we compare the development of income inequality over time in a country where there is price inflation. Another point which makes the definition rather problematic can be illustrated by the following example. Consider two populations, both consisting of three persons. The first three persons have incomes 9,000, 10,000, and 11,000, while in the second population the incomes are 99,000, 100,000, and 101,000. It is easily seen that the income variance will be the same for both populations. Nevertheless, we *feel* that the second distribution is much less unequal than the first one. The absolute differences are in both cases 1,000, but in the first case the rich person gets 10 percent more than the middle one and the middle one gets 10 percent more

This chapter is partly based on Ferrer-i-Carbonell and Van Praag (2003) and Van Praag (1978).

than the poor. In the second case those relative differences are a tiny 1 percent. Indeed, this demonstrates that inequality measurement is not only a matter of measurements but in the first place a matter of *feelings* towards inequality.

An inequality measure which does not suffer from these problems is the variance of log incomes

$$\sigma^2(\ln(y)) = \frac{1}{N} \sum_{n=1}^{N} (\ln(y) - \mu_{\ln(y)})^2. \tag{13.2}$$

As it is based on log differences, it reflects the relative income differences, which will appeal to most of us much more as reflecting inequality. From the wide literature on income inequality there is not one measure that emerges as theoretically or empirically superior to all other measures. One approach to selecting a plausible measure is to look for a set of criteria which the inequality measure should satisfy. Two criteria are rather self-evident. First, the measure should not depend on the money unit chosen. Second, the measure should not depend on the size N of the population. In particular, if we have two populations of size N with the same inequality in each, then the union of the two with size $2N$ will have the same inequality. It follows that the measure is a distribution parameter.

Beyond these two elementary criteria a number of other criteria have been suggested. A very popular one is the so-called Pigou-Dalton (P-D) condition, which requires that an income transfer from a richer person to a poorer person will reduce income inequality. Obviously, this criterion excludes a number of measures as inappropriate beforehand. At first sight the P-D condition looks very attractive. Who is not, in theory, for redistribution among the poor? However, it introduces a normative or even ethical element which is debatable. First, we are against adding ethical elements to our toolbox for empirical measurement. But even if you accept such an ethical coloring it is rather doubtful whether the P-D condition is so attractive.

Consider an income distribution where $y_1 = 10,000$, $y_2 = 11,000$, and $y_3 = 100,000$. Let us now redistribute such that the new distribution becomes $y_1 = 10,000$, $y_2 = 31,000$, and $y_3 = 80,000$. Although this redistribution should reduce the feeling of inequality, according to P-D, it is rather doubtful whether the first person will agree with that. The poverty status is always more tolerable together with others than when one is alone. This shows that even ethically the P-D condition is less than self-evident.

A second problem is that it is by no means clear whether an income y has the same significance for each household or individual. For instance, if two households have the same household income, but one household has five children to support and the second household consists of a single person, the household-income inequality may be formally zero but in reality will be considerable. This indicates that the way in which income is defined is crucial for the significance of the inequality concept. We have to replace nominal income by a concept of *equivalent* income. This means that incomes are made comparable between households, which are expected to derive different welfare or utility from the same nominal income as a result of objective differences in household characteristics.

The basic underlying question is why we are so interested in income inequality. It is not just an administrative statistic. The reason is that income or 'equivalent income' is taken as a proxy for welfare. It follows that income inequality is seen as synonymous with welfare inequality, a performance index of society.

Let us assume that we know how to measure *welfare* or *utility of income U*, then we have a welfare distribution $U_1, \ldots, U_N$ and we are looking for an inequality measure $I(U_1, \ldots, U_N)$. This, however, requires that welfare is a cardinal utility concept, for otherwise we cannot measure what an income increase does for a person in terms of an increase in welfare and consequently we cannot assess the effect of an income redistribution on inequality. In addition we have to accept the possibility of interpersonal comparison of welfare in order to assess the inequality between persons. If there is a one-to-one relation between (cardinal) welfare and income, say $U = U(y)$, then we may write $I(U_1, \ldots, U_N) = I(U(y_1), \ldots, U(y_n)) = \tilde{I}(y_1, \ldots, y_N)$. Hence, it looks as if we can define income inequality on the basis of the income distribution only, while interpreting it in terms of a welfare inequality *without* knowing the intermediate individual welfare function. Indeed, the difficulties with respect to the choice of the function $\tilde{I}(.)$ are partly caused by uncertainty about the function $I(.)$ and partly by ignorance about the function $U(.)$. These are two different ingredients with a totally different character. If we look at the measure $\tilde{I}(.)$ it is unclear how it is built up; we do not know on which utility function U and on which inequality concept I it is based.

The utility function $U(.)$ is something which, as we have seen earlier in this book, can be estimated with some degree of accuracy by satisfaction analysis. The inequality measure $I(.)$ is determined by statistical availability, tradition, ethics, and political decisions.

The literature bears witness that there is no generally accepted cardinal measure of welfare, because mainstream economics, at least until recently, did not accept the possibility of empirical utility measurement. Then, it is indeed difficult to operationalize the income-inequality concept, if it is intended to be more than just a statistical index like (13.2). As soon as we want to interpret it in the sense of welfare inequality, either implicitly or explicitly, we need to accept interpersonally comparable cardinal utility. Even if we accept that we know the utility function from empirical sources, this does not solve the problem of the choice of the welfare inequality definition of $I(.)$. This remains a political choice, as there is no 'natural' inequality measure. Kolm (1976) even suggests two measures: a 'rightist' and a 'leftist' definition of income inequality, which would reflect the views on inequality of the 'right' and the 'left'.

As another complication it is conceivable and even probable that individuals have different utility functions; for example, because they have different household sizes *fs*. In that case we have $U = U(y; fs)$ and the inequality will be $I(U(y_1; fs_1), \ldots, U(y_n; fs_N))$, or if there is a whole vector x of household-differentiating variables the relevant inequality measure would be

$$I = I(U(y_1; x_1), \ldots, U(y_n; x_N)). \tag{13.3}$$

In modern welfare states the vector x may include the regionally different availability of public services and collective goods like justice, roads, an education system, etc. We conclude that in order to compare incomes and to get some idea about income inequality it does not make much sense to define income inequality on nominal income only. Inequality should be measured with respect to *equivalent* incomes. It is evident that this will change income inequality. For instance, if we use the variance of log incomes as inequality measure and we assume that a nominal family income $y(2)$ for a two-person household is equivalent to an income $\tilde{y}(fs) = y(2).g(fs)$ for a household of size *fs* where $g(fs)$ stands for the equivalence scale, we have for the log variance of 'family-equivalence scale' corrected incomes

$$\text{var}(\ln(\tilde{y})) = \text{var}(\ln(y)) + \text{var}(\ln(g(fs)) + 2\text{cov}(\ln(\tilde{y}), \ln(g(fs))). \tag{13.4}$$

That is, the inequality of 'equivalized' incomes may be decomposed into inequality in nominal income, inequality in the correction factors, and a correction term reflecting the correlation between *fs* and equivalized incomes. A similar approach applies if we need to correct for a vector x. However, here again we touch on the problem of finding such equivalence scales, which is a hard job, if you ignore the validity of an approach which makes use of empirically measured welfare functions.

In this book we have already shown that we have confidence in empirical utility measurement, where we take 'satisfaction' as synonymous with 'utility' or 'welfare'. In the next section (13.2) we shall consider how we can construct a 'subjective' income-inequality measure, using two options: one where we assume a cardinal underlying utility function and one where we only make use of the trade-off coefficients derived from the ordinal information in satisfaction analysis. We start with the latter, less demanding, option, using the ordinal-probit model. Then we accept the additional assumption of cardinality as well.

In Section 13.3 we employ the information carried by the IEQ and the resulting individual welfare function to define a subjective income-inequality concept and especially to make a distinction between an experienced and a perceived income inequality. We will see that, depending on the position of the individual in the income distribution, he or she will *perceive* the income distribution as more or less unequal. In the sphere of perceptions it is impossible to find a unique measure, as perceptions differ between individuals across the board. We also consider how our concepts are related to the inequality concepts which have been introduced by Theil (1967) and Atkinson (1970). In Section 13.4 we draw some conclusions.

13.2. INCOME SATISFACTION INEQUALITY

In the usual approach to income inequality it is implicitly assumed that households[1] with the same income y derive the same financial satisfaction from that income. As we saw in Chapter 3 this assumption cannot be maintained when confronted with satisfaction data. We found in Chapter 3 that

$$Ln(FS^*_{nt}) = C_t + \alpha_y(y_{nt} - \bar{y}_n) + \alpha'_x(X_{nt} - \bar{X}_n) + (\alpha_y + \beta_y)\bar{y}_n$$
$$+ (\alpha_x + \beta_x)' \bar{X}_n + \varepsilon_{nt} + v_n, \tag{13.5}$$

where FS^*_{nt} stands for the latent financial satisfaction of household n at time t, y for log-income and X and Z for other variables. The variables $\bar{y}_n$ and $\bar{X}_n$ stand for long-term averages, which are termed the structural values of the variables. The difference terms are incidental shocks. The random variable v_n is individually fixed while C_t stands for time effects as inflation. As usual this equation is identified in the probit context if we add a normalizing condition. Traditionally we set the error variance equal to 1, or in this panel context $\sigma^2(\varepsilon_{n,t}) = 1$, but it is easily seen that we may set it at any value. For instance, if we were to postulate $\sigma^2(\varepsilon_{n,t}) = 4$, all estimated coefficients, their corresponding standard deviations, and the estimate of $\sigma(v_n)$ would have to be multiplied by $\sqrt{4} = 2$, while the corresponding t-values would not change. If we normalize by setting $\sigma^2(\varepsilon_{n,t}) = 1/(\alpha_y + \beta_y)^2$ and assume that there are no temporal fluctuations, or, which amounts to the same, we consider one-period inequality, then (13.5) becomes

$$Ln(FS_{nt}) = \bar{y}_n + \frac{(\alpha_x + \beta)'}{\alpha_y + \beta_y} \bar{X}_n + \tilde{\varepsilon}_{nt} + \tilde{v}_n \tag{13.6}$$
$$= \bar{y}_n + [\ln(g(\bar{X}_n))] + [\tilde{\varepsilon}_{nt} + \tilde{v}_n],$$

where we drop the asterisk for this restandardized variant. It may be read as log income *plus* a systematic log correction term *plus* a random error term $\tilde{\varepsilon}_{nt} + \tilde{v}_n$, where $\text{var}(\tilde{\varepsilon}_{nt} + \tilde{v}_n) = \dfrac{1}{(\alpha_y + \beta_y)^2}\text{var}(\varepsilon_{nt} + v_n)$. The correction term stands for the correction in order that the left-hand side for the household n is

---

[1] Our observation unit in this chapter will be the household, which is assumed to be adequately represented by the main breadwinner. Theoretically this is problematic, as it is not clear whether the household as such has a representative utility function. In Chapter 6 we saw that this hypothesis is empirically acceptable for German citizens, as husband and wife have broadly the same satisfaction levels and satisfaction functions.

equal to $\bar{y}_n$ for the reference household, for which by definition $\ln(g(\overline{X}_n) = 0$ and the random error equals 0 as well. The error term represents the omitted variables and the rounding-off error resulting from discrete observation of satisfaction in the satisfaction-question module. Notice that if there are only reference households for which the other structural and incidental variable X has no influence on financial satisfaction FS_n^*, then $\text{var}(Ln(FS_n^*)) = \text{var}(\bar{y}_n)$. We now propose to consider $\text{var}(Ln(FS_n^*))$ as the *subjective-income-inequality* concept. In fact, we are mostly interested in the structural part; that is, excluding the error term. We denote the structural part from now on by FS for short. The variance of objective log-income is embedded as a special case in the more general concept of the subjective income inequality. This clarifies precisely how we have to interpret our new inequality measure. It is the log variance of the corrected income distribution in which the corrections are empirically derived from satisfaction analysis instead of externally set according to some rule, as for instance the OECD family-equivalence scale.[2] Hence, the method is certainly an improvement on more traditional measures, but it does not incorporate cardinal elements; that is, the utility translation $U(.)$.

In fact, we may generalize any objective income-inequality index $I(y_1, \ldots, y_n)$, like Theil's entropy or Atkinson's index, in a similar way by defining the subjective analogue by $I(Fs_1, \ldots, Fs_n)$. The word 'subjective' implies that the incomes are replaced by 'corrected' incomes, where the correction is based on satisfaction analysis.

Let us now examine how this works out in practice by using the German GSOEP data set that we used in Chapters 3 and 4. We estimated in Chapter 3 the POLS regression equation (13.5); the results are found in Table 3.13. Essentially the same equation is used here, where we have renormalized in order that the two effects (shock and level) of income add up to 1. Table 13.1 presents estimates for the income-satisfaction inequalities in the four sub-samples, which we compare with the corresponding objective income inequalities. The number of observations refers to the observations per period. If the number of households is N and

Table 13.1. *Objective and subjective income-satisfaction inequalities, Germany*

	West workers	East workers	West non-workers	East non-workers
Variance of objective log incomes	0.218	0.173	0.284	0.218
Variance of log income satisfactions (structural part)	0.186	0.141	0.357	0.328
Structural part as percentage of total variance	6.03	8.94	12.41	12.70
N	30,356	11,256	20,510	8,501

[2] The Organization for Economic Cooperation and Development scale is an additive scale, where the first adult is set at 1.0, other adults at 0.7 and children at 0.5.

the number of periods is T, then we have here N^*T observations. We notice, however, that not every individual was observed for every period.

In the first line we present the objective income inequalities. In the second line we present the corresponding income-satisfaction inequalities, defined as the variances of the structural parts of the estimated income satisfactions. In the third line we present the structural variance as a percentage of the 'total' variance; that is, the structural variance *plus* the error variance $(\sigma^2(v) + \sigma^2(\varepsilon))$. For workers total variance is twenty times (!) the structural variance, while for non-workers the proportion is ten to one. This is of course because of the small explanatory power of these models in terms of R^2 or pseudo-R^2. This shows that by far the larger part of satisfaction inequality is caused by unobserved individual heterogeneity and/or random errors. We have to accept this as a fact of life. It does not imply that the structural inequalities have become devoid of interest.

Table 13.1 shows that the objective income inequality is larger in the West than in the East, and this holds both for workers and for non-workers. We also see that income inequality is larger within the group of non-workers than for workers. We note that for workers the satisfaction inequality is smaller than the inequality of objective incomes, while the opposite holds for non-workers. For instance, for western non-workers the objective inequality is 0.284 and the subjective analogue is 0.357.

Next, we present an income-inequality breakdown. In this way one can disentangle what is the contribution of each observable variable X and Z to income-satisfaction inequality. Since the income-satisfaction inequality is defined in terms of variance, studying the causes of this inequality is equivalent to breaking down the variance of the income satisfaction into contributing factors.

For those readers not well acquainted with this procedure, we give a short explanation. Let us consider a random variable Z, which is a sum

$$Z = \alpha X + \beta Y, \tag{13.7}$$

where X and Y are two other random variables. Then, the variance of Z, denoted by σ_Z^2 depends on the variances of X and Y, denoted by σ_X^2 and σ_Y^2 respectively. In the simplest case, where X and Y are stochastically independent, the relation is rather straightforward:

$$\alpha^2 \sigma_X^2 + \beta^2 \sigma_Y^2 = \sigma_Z^2. \tag{13.8}$$

It follows that the variance of Z is simply broken down into two variance contributions. Hence, if $\sigma_Z^2 = 10$ and the two terms at the left-hand side are 3 and 7 respectively, it follows that X determines 70 percent of the variance and Y 30 percent. Note that the term $\alpha^2 \sigma_X^2$ is a product of two factors. The variance σ_Z^2 depends partly on the variance of the variable X and partly on the magnitude of the effect α^2, which reflects the strength of the influence of X on Z. Now we will apply such an analysis to var(FS^*) as well.

If we consider Equation (13.6) we see that FS may be written as a sum of random terms, but things are not as easy as in the variance-breakdown example above, because the explanatory variables are as a rule correlated, except for the error term $(\tilde{\varepsilon}_{nt} + \tilde{v}_n)$, which is by assumption (and consequently by construction) not correlated with the explanatory variables. Let us now pursue our example and assume that X and Y are correlated and that their (non-zero) covariance is σ_{XY}. In that case we have

$$\sigma_Z^2 = \alpha^2 \sigma_X^2 + 2\alpha\beta\sigma_{XY} + \beta^2\sigma_Y^2 \tag{13.9}$$

and a straightforward breakdown is impossible. We cannot indicate the total effect of X, since Y is partly determined by X as well. However, we may break down Y by writing it as

$$Y = \beta_r X + \hat{Y}. \tag{13.10}$$

This equation is found by regressing Y on X. The coefficient β_X is simply the regression coefficient and $\hat{Y}$ is the residual, which is, as a result of the regression model, not correlated with X; that is, $\text{cov}(\beta_X X, \hat{Y}) = 0$. We may interpret the first term in Equation (13.10) as the part of Y which can be explained by X, and the second term as that part of Y which cannot be explained by X: the true own contribution of Y. Using Equations (13.7) and (13.10) we can then write

$$\begin{aligned} Z &= \alpha X + \beta(\beta_X X + \hat{Y}) \\ &= (\alpha + \beta\beta_X)X + \beta\hat{Y}. \end{aligned} \tag{13.11}$$

We can find the first effect by regressing Z on X and afterwards regressing the residual on Y. This method whereby a variable is broken down into non-correlated components is called in the literature 'stepwise regression'. Notice that the order in which the variables are introduced is not fixed. We can change the role of X and Y.

The previous procedure can be generalized to any number of explanatory variables. It follows that we can write

$$\sigma_Z^2 = (\alpha + \beta\beta_X)^2 \sigma_X^2 + \beta^2\sigma_{\hat{Y}}^2. \tag{13.12}$$

This is a straightforward and interpretable variance breakdown. The only problem is that the breakdown is not unique, as it depends on the order in which the explanatory variables are introduced. Two alternatives lie to hand. The first one is that in which the order is chosen in such a way that the first variable is that which yields the largest first term in Equation (13.12), the second variable to be introduced yields the second-largest variance contribution, and so on. We call it the 'peeling-off' or 'maximizing' method, which is a standard option in most multivariate software packages. The second option is the one in which we fix the order according to what variable we consider to be the most important one for explanation, on the basis of intuition, hypotheses, or even a theory.

In Table 13.2*a* we present for each of the four sub-samples the percentage-wise inequality breakdown according to the (sample-specific) maximizing order.

Table 13.2a. *Variance breakdown of income-satisfaction inequality (%)—stepwise regression, 'maximizing' approach**

Variable	West workers	East workers	West non-workers	East non-workers
$(Ln(age))^2$	2.59	1.30	2.62	1.62
Ln(age)	3.40	11.54	14.97	22.03
Ln(family income)	0.87	56.69	0.86	26.43
Gender (male)	0.17	1.05	3.48	1.14
Living together	2.07	1.75	3.06	2.42
Ln(years education)	1.17	0.01	0.76	8.68
Ln(family income)*ln(children +1)	0.15	0.00	0.56	0.00
Ln(adults)	1.26	11.44	0.12	22.17
Ln(children + 1)	0.17	8.16	0.08	13.95
Earner	0.05	0.59	—	—
Mean(ln(income))	65.63	6.06	35.13	0.62
Mean(ln(children + 1))	10.25	0.01	21.73	0.26
Mean(ln(adult))	12.21	1.41	16.62	0.69

*Procedure is stepwise regression, maximizing order.

Table 13.2b. *Variance breakdown of income-satisfaction inequality (%)—intuitive**

Variable	West workers	East workers	West non-workers	East non-workers
Ln(age)	0.12	5.68	9.18	2.72
$(Ln(age))^2$	1.34	1.77	23.41	50.06
Ln(family income)	56.60	61.55	42.99	29.68
Ln(years education)	6.48	1.32	1.43	0.68
Ln(adults)	10.32	14.20	5.75	11.98
Ln(children +1)	4.77	4.83	2.51	1.94
Ln(family income)*ln(children +1)	0.18	0.02	0.09	0.00
Gender (male)	0.28	1.12	3.88	1.00
Living together	3.41	2.06	3.63	0.38
Earner	0.21	0.94	—	0.00
Mean(ln(income))	13.12	5.14	5.05	0.62
Mean(ln(children + 1))	0.48	1.37	0.23	0.68
Mean(ln(adult))	2.68	0.01	1.85	0.25

*We chose the order for introducing variables on intuitive grounds.

In Table 13.2b we present the corresponding breakdowns in which we fix the order for each sample according to the order of variables in Table 3.13.

We find a number of interesting differences between the samples. For the western samples we find that the bulk of the inequality may be ascribed to permanent differences in income, and the number of children and adults to be supported. For the eastern samples we see the opposite pattern, as 'eastern' inequality is mostly caused by transitory fluctuations in income and the number of household members. For eastern and western non-workers we find a considerable age effect as well. For western workers we do not find this age effect, which may reflect the fact that western incomes are more inflexible and less age-dependent than in the East.

Finally, we can take a look at income-satisfaction inequality in the whole of Germany (G). This is more than the sum of the inequalities; say, I_W and I_E in both parts of the country. We have also to take into account that the two parts as such differ in average incomes. More precisely, let us assume for a moment that there are completely egalitarian distributions in both parts, but that the mean (equivalent) log incomes differ: say, they are $\tilde{y}_W$ and $\tilde{y}_E$ respectively. The mean log income for the whole country is $\tilde{y} = p_W \tilde{y}_W + p_E \tilde{y}_E$, where p_W, p_E stand for the population shares of the two German regions. Then, we would find for the income variance for the whole country $\sigma^2(\tilde{y}) = p_W(\tilde{y}_W - \tilde{y})^2 + p_E(\tilde{y}_E - \tilde{y})^2$. This variance component is called the 'between-group' variance or 'between-group' inequality, which we denote by $I_{between}$. Now we drop the assumption of the two egalitarian distributions. We have to add the two 'within'-inequality contributions, corresponding to the separate eastern and western distributions.

Then, we can break down the inequality of Germany as a whole according to the well-known variance decomposition

$$I(G) = p_W I_W + p_E I_E + I_{between}. \qquad (13.13)$$

The breakdown is tabulated in Table 13.3a. In fact, we perform the breakdown twice; that is, first for workers and non-workers in both parts of the country, and then when aggregating over the two parts.

Table 13.3a. *Inter-group breakdowns for income-satisfaction inequality*

Population shares	Group	Sub group	Variance of log income satisfaction	
$P_W = 0.803$	West			0.264
$P_{WW} = 0.549$		West workers (WW)	0.186	
$P_{WNW} = 0.451$		West non-workers (WNW)	0.357	
		Between WW and WNW	0.001	
$P_E = 0.197$	East			0.265
$P_{EW} = 0.528$		East workers (EW)	0.141	
$P_{ENW} = 0.472$		East non-workers (ENW)	0.326	
		Between EW and ENW	0.036	
	Between E and W		0.010	
	Germany			0.274

Table 13.3b. *Inter-group breakdowns for income inequality*

Population shares	Group	Sub group		Variance of objective log incomes
$P_W = 0.803$	West			0.261
$P_{WW} = 0.549$		West workers	0.218	
$P_{WNW} = 0.451$		West non-workers	0.284	
		Between WW and WNW	0.0132	
$P_E = 0.197$	East			0.219
$P_{EW} = 0.528$		East workers	0.173	
$P_{ENW} = 0.472$		East non-workers	0.218	
		Between EW and ENW	0.0248	
	Between E and W			0.0063
	Germany			0.259

Table 13.3*a* shows that the income-satisfaction inequality in Germany is 0.274, the inequality in the East being less than that in the West.

The same exercise is done for the objective income inequality. The results are presented in Table 13.3*b*. Again the reader can compare these results with the ones presented in Table 13.3*a*. The objective income inequality is 0.259, which is less than the income-satisfaction inequality. Now the westerners suffer from a larger inequality.

Cardinal approach

In Chapter 2.7 we also discussed the possibility of utilizing the cardinal information provided by a satisfaction question. If the response categories are 0, 1, 2, ..., 10, we argued that the fact that respondents are able to respond on such questions implies that they are evaluating their financial satisfaction on a cardinal finite-interval scale. Whether the categories are described by 1, ..., 5 or 1, ..., 7, or any other finite interval is obviously irrelevant. Let us assume that the individual evaluates his or her financial situation by a cardinal utility function $U = U(y; x)$, then the response $U = 7$ on a [0, 10] scale implies that the real U-value must be in the interval [6.5, 7.5] or, after rescaling to the unit interval, U must be in the interval [0.65, 0.75]. Then, we assumed that the utility function was specified as the normal distribution function

$$U(y; x, \varepsilon) = N(\alpha y + \beta' x + \beta_0 + \varepsilon; 0, 1). \tag{13.14}$$

In that case we found that

$$P[0.65 < U \le 0.75] = N(u_{0.75} - \alpha y + \beta' x + \beta_0) - N(u_{0.65} - \alpha y + \beta' x + \beta_0). \tag{13.15}$$

Equation (13.15) implies that the unknown parameters can be estimated by the so-called interval-(or censored) regression model. The nuisance parameters u do not have to be estimated but are exogenously fixed. We find an equation

$$ln(FS_{nt}^c) = C_t^c + \alpha_y^c(y_{nt} - \bar{y}_n) + \alpha_x^c(X_{nt} - \bar{X}_n) + (\alpha_y^c + \beta_y^c)\,\bar{y}_n$$
$$+ (\alpha_x^c + \beta_x^c)\,\bar{X}_n + \varepsilon_{nt}^c + v_n^c, \tag{13.16}$$

where the superscript c indicates the cardinal version. We found from Section 2.8 that there holds

$$ln(FS_{nt}^c) \equiv C\cdot ln(FS_{nt}) + D, \tag{13.17}$$

where C and D stand for parameters to be estimated from the sample as described in Chapter 2. We found for the specific German sample $C = 0.5359$. It follows that all coefficients of $Ln(FS_{nt}^c)$ in Equation (13.16) are equal to the corresponding coefficients of $Ln(FS_{nt}^*)$ in Equation (13.5) multiplied by the factor C. Hence $\alpha_y^c = C\alpha_y$ and $\beta_y^c = C\beta_y$. If we normalize $Ln(FS_{nt}^c)$ by dividing by $\alpha_y^c + \beta_y^c$ we find from Equation (13.17)

$$Ln(FS_{nt}^{c*}) \equiv \frac{CLn(FS_{nt})}{C(\alpha_y^c + \beta_y^c)} + \frac{D}{C(\alpha_y^c + \beta_y^c)}$$
$$= Ln(FS_{nt}^*) + \frac{D}{C(\alpha_y^c + \beta_y^c)}. \tag{13.18}$$

It follows that the satisfaction inequality derived from either the ordinal or cardinal version will be equal, as it should be; that is,

$$var(Ln(FS_{nt}^{c*})) = var(Ln(FS_{nt}^*)). \tag{13.19}$$

Consequently, the same holds for the breakdowns described above. However, we note that this holds only if we standardize with respect to $\ln(y)$. Now we shall consider whether we can probe deeper by means of the IEQ.

13.3. WELFARE INEQUALITY DERIVED FROM THE INCOME EVALUATION QUESTION AND THE INDIVIDUAL WELFARE FUNCTION

Up to this point in our analysis we have accepted the standard income-inequality definitions, which we refined by replacing nominal incomes y by 'corrected' incomes $\tilde{y}$, where the correction factor $g(x) = \tilde{y}/y$ is derived from the ordinal information in the financial-satisfaction question.[3] We can correct in a similar way all existing income-inequality measures, although here we only showed results for the log variance. If the population is homogeneous with respect to the variables x, and consequently no correction is needed, we get the old measures back.

In terms of the introduction to this chapter we have not looked at $I(U(y_1), \ldots, U(y_N))$ but only at $I(\tilde{y}_1, \ldots, \tilde{y}_N)$. The latter measure utilizes the

---

[3] The next sections are based on Van Praag (1977, 1978) and Van Batenburg and Van Praag (1980).

ordinal information but not the additional cardinal information. Now we shall try to exploit that information as well. However, before doing so we want to derive a basic principle according to which income or rather *welfare inequality* may be assessed. That is the *log-marginal welfare variance* principle.

If economists look at income inequality they practically never see it as a purely statistical measure. It has always an ethical flavor. Income inequality is essentially a measure to evaluate the equitability of the welfare distribution in society. We assume a social-welfare function of the Benthamite type (Bentham 1789); that is

$$SW(U_1, \ldots, U_N) = \frac{1}{N} \sum_1^N U_n(y_n).$$ (13.20)

This is average utility in the population, in which we assign equal weight to all households *n*. This equal weighting reflects, in our opinion, an ideal democracy. If we were to generalize this function to

$$SW(U_1, \ldots, U_N) = \sum_1^N w_n U_n(y_n),$$ (13.21)

where the unequal weights add up to 1, we could interpret the distribution $(w_1, \ldots, w_N)$ as the power distribution in society.

Let us assume that national income Y is fixed, then maximization of SW implies the solution of

$$\max_{y_1, \ldots, y_N} SW(U_1, \ldots, U_N)$$ (13.22)
$$sub \; y_1 + \ldots + y_N = Y.$$

The solution is derived from the Lagrange conditions

$$\frac{\partial SW_n}{\partial U_n} \cdot \frac{\partial U_n}{\partial y_n} = \lambda,$$ (13.23)

where λ is the Lagrange multiplier. If we have a democratic SW function, it follows that all households *n* should have the same marginal utility of income. We call this the *equitable* income distribution, as each household gets the same satisfaction of additional income. This does not necessarily imply equality of incomes, since we know that individuals may derive different degrees of satisfaction from the same amount of money. We denote the utility derivative by u_n, for short. Then, an equitable distribution implies $u_n = \bar{u}$, where $\bar{u}$ stands for average marginal utility. The same holds for log-marginal utility; that is, $\ln(u_n) = \overline{\ln(u)}$. Then, a measure of the non-equitability of the distribution is

$$s_u^2 = \sum (u_n - \bar{u})^2$$ (13.24)

or

$$\sigma_u^2 = \Sigma(\ln(u_n) - \overline{\ln(u)})^2. \tag{13.25}$$

As the first measure changes under a positive linear transform of U, we prefer the log variant. As soon as we substitute a utility function U, σ_u^2 can be evaluated.

We consider two examples. The constant-absolute-risk-aversion (CARA) function is $U(y) = 1 - e^{-\alpha y}(\alpha > 0)$. The resulting σ_u^2 can be calculated to be

$$\sigma_u^2 = \alpha^2 \frac{1}{N}\Sigma(y_n - \overline{y})^2 = \alpha^2 s_y^2. \tag{13.26}$$

It is simply the variance of incomes multiplied by the absolute risk aversion squared. In a similar way the constant-relative-risk-aversion (CRRA) function

$$U(y) = 1 + Cy^{-\alpha+1}/(1 - \alpha) \ (y \geq \delta > 0, \alpha > 1)$$

yields

$$\sigma_u^2 = \alpha^2 \Sigma(\ln(y_n) - \overline{\ln y})^2 = \alpha^2 \sigma_y^2 \tag{13.27}$$

or the log variance of incomes multiplied by the relative risk aversion α squared. Notice that for $\alpha = 1$ the utility function is a logarithmic function. It can be shown that Atkinson's and Theil's measures are approximately equal to $1 - e^{-\frac{1}{2}\alpha\sigma_y^2} \approx \frac{1}{2}\alpha\sigma_y^2$ and $\frac{1}{2}\sigma_y^2$ respectively. It would hold exactly if the income distribution were log-normal; in reality this is only approximately the case in most societies. We may see σ_u^2 in these cases as a subjectively colored version of σ_y^2, which is transformed by adding the influence of the personal utility parameter α.

There is a second *dual* way in which we can interpret σ_u^2. Let us assume that we had a non-democratic SW function with unequal weights w_n. In that case Equation (13.23) could be written as $w_n \cdot u_n = \lambda$. This implies that a non-equitable distribution, and hence unequal u's, is a sure sign that the social weights w_n differ between different households n. More precisely $w_n = (u_n^{-1}C)$, where C is chosen such that the weights add up to 1. There holds $\ln(w_n) = -\ln(u_n) + \ln(C)$. It follows that the power inequality equals the log-marginal welfare variance:

$$\text{var}(\ln(w_n)) = \text{var}(\ln(u_n)). \tag{13.28}$$

For instance, in the case of the CRRA utility function the weight function would be proportional to y_α. Power increases with income y. However, there may be a problem with this interpretation. If $n(y)$ stands for the density function of the income distribution, the sum of the weights or rather the integral of the weight function over the income distribution, that is $\int_0^\infty w(y)n(y)dy$, would have to be equal to 1, which implies that the integral converges. We will see later on that this is not always the case, although it holds for the two well-known CARA and CRRA utility functions.[4] This is the reason why we

---

[4] In practice, this is no problem because $n(y)$ has to be replaced by the true income density function, which has only finite support.

shall not pursue the idea that the true social-distribution process can be described as the result of a maximization of an SW function. The democratic SW function is useful as a benchmark to evaluate the deviation from the ideal.

The relevant point in this context is that we have available empirical estimates of the individual welfare function derived from the IEQ, as explained in Chapter 2. There we outlined how the utility function of income, when normalized to the [0, 1] interval, can be described by the log-normal distribution function $U(y) = N(\ln(y); \mu, \sigma)$, where μ and σ are personal parameters. We stress that this function is not a theoretical construct, but that it has been empirically estimated in a great number of large-scale surveys from a specific question module, the income-evaluation question (IEQ). Obviously, the description suffers from the inaccuracies common to all empirical-model studies; that is: a functional specification which is selected from a narrow set of flexible and tractable specifications; the possible exclusion of relevant variables; and the presence of random noise in the observations. Additional evidence is found in the COLS approach to financial satisfaction,[5] where we assumed that the latent evaluation of financial satisfaction was described by Equation (13.14). Now we have the opportunity to apply this utility function in the log-marginal welfare approach. This implies that we replace a theoretical, albeit attractive, function by an empirically estimated one.

When we use the log-normal distribution function there is one unusual difficulty. The function is not everywhere concave. That is, Gossen's First Law, stating that marginal utility falls throughout, does not apply everywhere for this function. The log-normal density function, which is identical to the marginal utility function, has its mode at $y_{mode} = e^{\mu - \sigma^2}$.

This implies that marginal utility would increase up to a threshold value, which for common values of σ is at a value of about $U \approx 0.3$; that is, a value which corresponds to 'very unhappy'. Some economists (see e.g. Seidl 1994) feel very uncomfortable about this non-concavity for very low incomes. In fact, they accept the overall concavity as a matter of faith. However, apart from some psychological intuitions, which are not well supported by psychological experiments, there is no factual evidence or proof that the utility function is everywhere concave. The assumption serves rather nicely in some fields of economic literature, because it can be shown that an everywhere-concave utility function has a unique maximum at an interior point of the choice set in the many optimization problems we economists are so fond of. In fact there is evidence to the contrary, that is non-convexities, from gambling experiments, investment analysis, and more broadly the work by psychologists and economists on decisions under uncertainty. There, an S-shaped cardinal utility function is fairly common (see e.g. Kahneman and Tversky 1979), because it is the only way to describe the reality of acceptance of lottery tickets at a higher

---

[5] See Sect. 13.2 and Ch. 2 above.

price than the mathematical expectation of the lottery concerned. We notice also that the lognormal may be seen as a generalization of the CRRA function, as the relative risk aversion for this function is linear in log-income (c.f. Van Praag 1971 and Hartog and Vijverberg 2003, who call it the translog-utility function).

However, the non-concavity at the lower end raises a problem for the maximization of the *SW* function, as some of the second-order derivatives may be non-negative. In those cases we get a corner solution, where the social-welfare function is increased by denying some people all of their small income and redistributing the incomes of the very poor to the better-off. Although this sounds crazy to the civilized reader it is a solution which has frequently been realistic in very poor economies. It explains also suicidal inclinations. Individuals below a certain threshold of material well-being may prefer death. However, for civilized and well-off western societies the national income Y is so high that nearly all or all individuals are above that threshold. Moreover, as we saw in Chapter 4, the individual is not driven by financial satisfaction only; financial satisfaction is only one domain of life among many others, and it is also only one component of general satisfaction. In the other domains income plays a role as well. By silently identifying financial satisfaction (welfare) with general satisfaction (general well-being) we commit an error.

So we assume that $U(y) = N(\ln(y); \mu, \sigma)$ and we notice that, as we saw, the parameters μ and σ vary with the individual characteristics y_n and x_n. If we neglect the (vector of) intervening variable(s) x, then a specific individual n evaluates income levels y by the function $U_n(y) = N(\ln(y); \mu(y_n), \sigma)$, where we assume that σ does not systematically depend on y_n and x_n but is constant over the population. This is a *virtual* welfare function. It describes how incomes are evaluated by n. It can be compared with the *decision*-utility-function concept introduced by Kahneman et al. (1997). The *true* welfare function is $U(y) = N(\ln(y); \mu(y), \sigma)$, which describes how individuals evaluate their own actual income y. It is comparable to Kahneman's *experienced* utility.

If each individual has his or her own utility function, it follows that individuals have their own inequality evaluation $\text{var}(\ln(u_n))$ as well, based on their own utility function. This finding is a very fascinating result. It shows that different individuals can have completely different evaluations of the same society, at least with respect to income distribution.

Let us now look at what the welfare inequality is if we assume a log-normal individual welfare function $U_n(y) = N(\ln(y); \mu(y_n), \sigma)$ and, moreover, assume that the income distribution itself is also log-normal with parameters μ_2 and σ_2 respectively. It is well known that the income distribution is only approximately log-normal. However, in order to get elegant results we assume that it holds exactly. It is of course possible to estimate the welfare variance numerically for any distribution from a sample, but in that case we do not get a neat formula. It is easily derived that

$$\ln(u) = -\ln(y) - \frac{1}{2\sigma^2}(\ln(y) - \mu(y_n))^2 - \ln\sigma - \frac{1}{2}\ln(2\pi). \tag{13.29}$$

We notice that this is a quadratic function in $\ln(y)$. Hence, its variance is a function in the first four moments of $\ln(y)$ (see Van Batenburg and Van Praag 1980). In the case of a log-normal income distribution we can restrict ourselves to the first- and second-order moments of the income distribution and we find after some calculations the formula

$$\sigma_u^2 = \text{var}(\ln u) = \frac{\sigma_2^2}{2\sigma^4}[\sigma_2^2 + 2(\sigma^2 + \mu_2 - \mu(y_n))^2]. \tag{13.30}$$

If we take account of the fact that we found that there is log-linear dependence on income, say $\mu(y_n) = \beta_0 + \beta_1 \ln(y_n)$, it follows that Equation (13.30) describes a parabola in $\ln(y_n)$. Its minimum value of $\frac{\sigma_2^4}{2\sigma^4}$ is reached at

$$\ln(y_a) = \frac{\sigma^2 + \mu_2 - \beta_0}{\beta_1}, \tag{13.31}$$

which corresponds to a position in the tenth quantile in the West German income distribution in 1997. We calculate σ_u^2 for the nine deciles in West Germany according to Equation (13.30). We see from Table 13.4 that the subjective perception of income inequality decreases with increasing income. The position where the feelings of inequality are minimal is fairly far to the right. This leads to a schizophrenia in society. The different income brackets have a different perception of inequality. A similar estimation and calculation has been performed by Van Batenburg and Van Praag (1980) on a data set referring to the Dutch income distribution 1971. These figures are listed in the third column of Table 13.4. It is remarkable how similar, but also how different, the two outcomes are. We see that Dutch inequality in 1971 was much larger than twenty-six years later in Germany. The individual coefficients are about the same. Differences in income-inequality perception between social classes in the Netherlands (1971) seem to be much more pronounced than in West Germany (1997).

13.4. CONCLUSION

In this chapter we extended the objective-income concept to define the subjective-income concept. We exploited the idea that the income utility that individuals experience depends on intervening variables like having children. It follows that any observations on income inequality have to be based on a corrected income concept, which satisfaction analysis provides for. Satisfaction questions give the key to how to compare incomes. The subjective measure I_{sub} includes objective income inequality as a special case; namely, when subjective-income satisfaction and income are identical. We elaborated this for the variance of log incomes, but the same refinement can be implemented for other measures of income inequality. We found that only a relatively small part of I_{sub} can be attributed to observed factors. This does not necessarily imply that there could be no other observable causes of inequality. It could be that the specification presented in Tables 13.2*a*/*b* omitted relevant observable variables. Nevertheless, this is hardly probable, given the large range of variables available in the GSOEP and the extensive research we undertook with different possible specifications. Even if the variance caused by observable factors is rather small, it is interesting to look at it, given that the objective variables are the only ones which policy makers can take into account. It appears that the role of income in explaining income-satisfaction inequality is not insignificant, but it is not the only factor. The number of people in the household and the age distribution are important as well. Thus, even if objective income inequality remains certainly an important statistic for monitoring the societal distribution process, this exercise shows that psychological feelings of inequality are relevant as well. Evidently, this research should be repeated for other populations before we can generalize our findings. We note that the ordinal and cardinal approaches which we outlined in Chapter 2 do not give different results.

A second step in this chapter was to use the individual-welfare-function approach. It is based on a decision utility function and, contrary to the experienced utility function, each individual has his or her own version of the utility function. Based on this concept, which coincides with the outlook of the individual, we found that individuals will also have a different evaluation of income inequality. We found the intuitively plausible result that individuals

Table 13.4. *Subjective inequalities for West Germany, 1997, and the Netherlands, 1971*

Income quantile	Monthly income	Subjective inequality for Germany 1997	Subjective inequality for the Netherlands 1971
1	1,797	2.336	8.423
2	2,261	1.842	6.013
3	2,668	1.535	4.633
4	3,074	1.308	3.613
5	3,508	1.123	2.883
6	4,004	0.965	2.325
7	4,613	0.826	1.902
8	5,444	0.703	1.684
9	6,849	0.602	1.826
Minimum	8,103		

Note: For Germany,
$\beta_0 = 3.20$; $\beta_2 = 0.59$; $\sigma_2 = 0.35$; $\mu_2 = 8.16$(monthly household income); $\sigma_2^2 = 0.27$.
For the Netherlands,
$\beta_0 = 3.16$; $\beta_2 = 0.64$; $\sigma^2 = 0.29$; $\mu_2 = 9.19$(annual household income); $\sigma_2^2 = 0.53$.

with a low income perceive a specific distribution as much more unequal than individuals in the well-off classes.

This chapter contributes to the literature of inequality by presenting an income-satisfaction concept which can be compared to objective measures of inequality. Income-satisfaction inequality differs from the established measures of inequality in using individual perceptions as a basis for making incomes comparable. The traditional measures of inequality introduce subjectivism via intuition by, for example, imposing family equivalence scales (such as the OECD scale) or by introspection in choosing a concrete welfare function specification (Atkinson 1970). The introduction of income satisfaction does not imply that objective measurement should be replaced by subjective concepts throughout, but only that each measure has a different role to play. The subjective concept is in our opinion a valuable addition to the family of inequality measures. In the next chapter we shall consider how far this approach can be generalized to other domains and to general satisfaction.

14

A Generalized Approach to Subjective Inequalities

14.1. INTRODUCTION

In the previous chapter we introduced the concept of a subjective income inequality. We replaced income in the usual inequality definition by its subjective counterpart *FS*, financial satisfaction. That gave us an income concept which is corrected for all intervening variables like age and family size, and we defined subjective income inequality in terms of inequality in *FS*. In Chapter 2 we saw that financial satisfaction may be quantified by taking conditional expectations $\overline{FS}_i$ of *FS*, given that it is found to be within the *i*th interval of the financial-satisfaction module. This expectation may be taken in the ordinal POLS variant or the cardinal COLS variant.

Now we can pose the question whether the subjective income inequality concept can be generalized to other domains such as, health and job satisfaction. It is obvious that there are large differences between individuals on these aspects as well. However, in the literature we do not find successful approaches. There are two problems which are, in our opinion, responsible for this lack of literature. First, how to measure health or job satisfaction in an objective way, as we use income to measure income inequality. It is obvious that such a basic variable is hard to find for those domains. Hence, it is impossible to measure objective health inequality in the same way as we can measure income inequality. In fact, we saw that income as such is also a rather meaningless variable, if we have in mind the mental state of satisfaction with income. This is because of the intervening variables for which nominal income has to be corrected. However, with respect to income we can assume a much closer link between nominal income and the ensuing satisfaction than between any objective health characteristic and health satisfaction. The second problem which makes health essentially different from income is that health is not transferable from one individual to another. We can think of a distribution of health, but it is impossible to realize a redistribution of health over the population as, at least theoretically, is conceivable for income redistribution. This makes ethical inequality measures like, for example, Atkinson's index unrealistic for the health domain. In Atkinson's index there is an optimum situation, which can be reached by redistribution. Inequality is defined by the deviation from the current to the optimal situation. It follows that such definitions are rather unrealistic if the satisfaction cannot be redistributed. We have to be content with the statistical interpretation of inequality.

That being said, there is no impediment to applying the methodology derived in Chapter 13 to operationalize subjective inequality with respect to domains of life other than finance.

14.2. SIMULTANEOUS INEQUALITIES

In the GSOEP and the BHPS we do not only find a question on financial satisfaction but also similar questions on health satisfaction, job satisfaction, etc. We can denote the answers of individual n by the satisfaction response vector $DS_n = (DS_n^{(1)}, \ldots, DS_n^{(k)})$. One of the components is financial satisfaction FS_n. Following Chapter 3, we estimate the k satisfaction equations separately. We get

$$DS_{i,n} = \alpha_i' x_{i,n} + \varepsilon_{i,n} \quad (i = 1, \ldots, k), \tag{14.1}$$

where we notice that each satisfaction equation has its own vector x_i of explanatory variables. We gain in notation if we assume an m-vector x of all explanatory variables, and a conform $(k \times m)$ matrix A where elements α are set at zero if the corresponding explanatory variables do not appear in the satisfaction equation.

Then, we can rewrite the system of domain-satisfaction equations (14.1) in matrix notation as

$$DS_n = Ax_n + \varepsilon_n \tag{14.2}$$

We notice that the error vector and the explanatory variables x are uncorrelated. However, the explanatory variables themselves can be correlated, and the same holds for the domain errors. Now we can calculate the sample covariance matrix of (14.2), which reads

$$\Sigma_{DS} = A\Sigma_x A' + \Sigma_\varepsilon. \tag{14.3}$$

We can see Σ_{DS} as the natural generalization of the one-dimensional financial-satisfaction inequality. It can be broken down into a *structural* part, which depends on the covariance matrix Σ_x of the explanatory variables and the estimated effect matrix A, and a *random* part, the covariance matrix of the disturbances. Notice that as a consequence of the discrete response formulation the latter matrix is the covariance matrix of the 'in-between' disturbances only. Hence, it is an underestimate of the total covariance matrix. In principle, it is possible to estimate the within-covariances from our knowledge of the 'in-between' covariance and the assumption of joint normality (see Maddala 1983:

368), but this is computationally very hard to perform on a large scale. Hence, we ignore in this multi-dimensional case the within-variances and -covariances from now on.

From Equation (14.3) two things are to be inferred. First, that satisfaction inequality depends partly on inequality with respect to the objective variables. For instance, let the first explanatory variable be log income y, then we see that each satisfaction inequality, that is the diagonal elements of Σ_{DS}, depends on the first diagonal element in Σ_r, as soon as the corresponding element of A is non-zero. Second, that inequalities are interdependent through two channels. The first channel exists because the domain satisfactions depend on the same x values. If, for instance, two domain satisfactions (e.g. finance and health) depend on the same variable y, it follows that if the variance in y increases then the variance in *both* satisfactions will increase. The second channel is there because the covariances between the random disturbances are non-zero. Those error covariances cannot be exactly estimated because of the discrete observation mode.

Let us now consider the additional question on satisfaction with life as a whole. We called it general satisfaction (GS). We denote the answers by GS_n.

We estimated[1] for the British data set the equation

$$GS_n = \alpha_{0,1}DS_{1,n} + \ldots + \alpha_{0,8}DS_{8,n} + \gamma Z_n + C + \varepsilon_{0,n}, \qquad (14.4)$$

where we defined the variable Z as the first principal component of the domain errors. It was included to correct for an imminent endogeneity bias (see Chapter 4).

Just as we can estimate domain-satisfaction inequalities, we can now assess the inequality in general satisfaction (overall inequality for short) by $\mathrm{var}(GS)$ and we have

$$\mathrm{var}(GS) = \alpha_0'\Sigma_{DS}\alpha_0 + \delta^2\mathrm{var}(Z) + \delta\alpha_0'\Sigma_{DS,Z} + \mathrm{var}(\varepsilon_0). \qquad (14.5)$$

It follows that overall inequality may be partly explained by domain inequalities. However, as Σ_{DS} is a non-diagonal matrix, we are unable to isolate the separate contributions of the $k(=8)$ domain inequalities and to write var (GS) as a sum of domain-satisfaction inequalities. We apply again (see section 13.2) a stepwise-regression procedure to get rid of 'double counting'. In this way we 'peel off' the overall inequality into independent contributions corresponding to the successive domains. This peeling off implies that the domain satisfactions are ordered and replaced by $\overline{DS}_1, \ldots, \overline{DS}_k$ where $\overline{DS}_1 = \alpha_{0,1}DS_1$, $\overline{DS}_2$ is the part of $\alpha_{0,2}DS_2$ which is not correlated with DS_1, and so on.

In terms of the new variables we may rewrite Equation (14.5) as

---

[1] We take here for $\bar{u}_{i,n}$ the conditional expectations without conditioning on x and taking $\sigma = 1$. In this way we approximate the rough observations as well as possible, instead of using 'calculated' observations.

$$\text{var}(GS) = \Sigma_{\overline{DS}} + \delta^2 \text{var}(Z) + \delta \Sigma_{\overline{DS}, Z} + \text{var}(\varepsilon_0), \tag{14.6}$$

where the first matrix is diagonal. We notice that var(GS) can be broken down further by substituting for the DS's the right-hand expressions in equations (14.2). Then, we can write the variance in terms of the variance matrix of the objectively measurable x-vector. Then, we see how the original inequalities affect the inequality of GS.

The inequalities for all the domains are presented in Table 14.1. Note that we use here the COLS specification. We do this because more than one domain is involved. We saw in Chapter 2 that in the ordinal specification (POLS) the unit of measurement is determined by the frequency distribution of the response frequencies. This also holds then for the domain variances. It follows that because of the ordinal specification it is hard to get a meaningful comparison between the inequalities of two domains. However, if we choose the unit of measurement on the basis of the cardinal evaluations, where we assume that an evaluation 5 on a [1, 7] scale corresponds with the same intensity of feeling, irrespective of the specific domain considered, the domain variances are comparable.

Table 14.1 shows that the inequalities with respect to health and the amount of leisure are the largest and that the inequality with respect to job satisfaction is the lowest. The inequalities can be explained, to a rather moderate extent. The major part has to be considered as random, at least with the choice of explanatory variables which we have used. When we compare the estimate[2] of the total (in-between *plus* within) error variance 0.6955 with the in-between variance for financial satisfaction, which equals 0.655, it follows that the within-error variance is about 0.040. Hence, the inaccuracy by group-wise observation seems almost negligible.

In Table 14.2 we present the *total* variance/correlation matrix between the domains for the subgroup of British married individuals with a paid job; that is, we present the total covariance matrix $\Sigma_{DS} = A\Sigma_r A' + \Sigma_{\tilde{\varepsilon}}$. The covariance

Table 14.1. *Inequalities per domain, individuals with job and married (BHPS)*

Domain	Structural inequality	In-between error variance	Total variance	Number of observations
Job satisfaction	0.023	0.625	0.648	6,408
Financial satisfaction	0.133	0.655	0.788	10,388
Housing satisfaction	0.094	0.667	0.761	10,361
Health satisfaction	0.047	0.858	0.905	10,371
Leisure-use satisfaction	0.083	0.719	0.802	10,347
Leisure-amount satisfaction	0.210	0.742	0.952	10,340
Marriage satisfaction	0.286	0.893	0.938	10,341
Social-life satisfaction	0.049	0.663	0.712	7,406

[2] This has been estimated based on the lognormality assumption.

Table 14.2. *Domain total variance/correlation matrix, individuals with job and married*

	Job satisfaction	Financial satisfaction	Housing satisfaction	Health satisfaction	Leisure-use satisfaction	Leisure-amount satisfaction	Social-life satisfaction	Marriage satisfaction
Job satisfaction	0.648							
Financial satisfaction	0.390	0.788						
Housing satisfaction	0.294	0.382	0.760					
Health satisfaction	0.292	0.338	0.238	0.905				
Leisure-use satisfaction	0.330	0.341	0.314	0.322	0.801			
Leisure-amount satisfaction	0.343	0.321	0.288	0.271	0.695	0.951		
Social-life satisfaction	0.407	0.385	0.343	0.332	0.694	0.629	0.712	
Marriage satisfaction	0.232	0.206	0.253	0.195	0.299	0.272	0.348	0.879

Table 14.3. *Domain structural-part variance/correlation matrix, individuals with job and married*

	Job satisfaction	Financial satisfaction	Housing satisfaction	Health satisfaction	Leisure-use satisfaction	Leisure-amount satisfaction	Social-life satisfaction	Marriage satisfaction
Job satisfaction	0.023							
Financial satisfaction	0.254	0.133						
Housing satisfaction	0.571	0.519	0.094					
Health satisfaction	0.050	0.423	-0.239	0.047				
Leisure-use satisfaction	0.391	0.399	0.810	-0.168	0.083			
Leisure-amount satisfaction	0.302	0.297	0.746	-0.317	0.935	0.210		
Social-life satisfaction	0.357	0.455	0.666	0.023	0.884	0.725	0.049	
Marriage satisfaction	0.511	0.200	0.654	-0.245	0.701	0.635	0.529	0.082

Table 14.4. *Domain error variance/correlation matrix, individuals with job and married*

	Job satisfaction	Housing satisfaction	Financial satisfaction	Health satisfaction	Leisure-use satisfaction	Leisure-amount satisfaction	Social-life satisfaction	Marriage satisfaction	
Job satisfaction	0.625	—	—	—	—	—	—	—	
Financial satisfaction	0.395	0.655	—	—	—	—	—	—	
Housing satisfaction	0.279	0.355	0.667	—	—	—	—	—	
Health satisfaction	0.292	0.357	0.251	0.858	—	—	—	—	
Leisure-use satisfaction	0.335	0.345	0.290	0.335	0.719	—	—	—	
Leisure-amount satisfaction	0.351	0.335	0.263	0.290	0.676	0.742	—	—	
Social-life satisfaction	0.411	0.370	0.313	0.341	0.681	0.609	0.663	—	
Marriage satisfaction	0.226	0.208	0.243	0.200	0.287	0.263	0.328	0.797	
Z	0.463	0.155	0.004	0.299	-0.043	0.187	-0.100	-0.393	0.267

matrix of the structural parts is presented in Table 14.3 and that of the random in-between errors $\Sigma_{\tilde{\varepsilon}}$ in Table 14.4. In the diagonal cells we present the inequalities themselves and in the lower-left cells we present the corresponding correlations. The upper half of the two symmetric matrices is left empty for convenience of presentation. In Table 14.4 we include in the last row the covariance with the Z-variable.

We see that there is a significant positive correlation between the domain satisfactions. However, there are some exceptions in Table 14.4. For instance, older people live in better houses or at least enjoy more housing satisfaction, while their health is worse than that of younger people. This may explain the negative correlation between health and housing. A similar explanation may hold for the negative correlation between health and marriage and for that between health and leisure satisfactions.

The sizeable correlation between domains implies that the domain inequalities cannot be seen as independent of each other. A high satisfaction in domain A predicts a high satisfaction in B, and consequently a strong inequality in domain A entails a strong inequality in domain B as well. This picture does not change very much when we take account of the fact that the structural variables X which play a role in one domain satisfaction also play a role in another domain. Therefore, we subtract the structural covariance matrix from the overall matrix. This leaves us with the matrix of the random errors $\Sigma_{\tilde{\varepsilon}}$ in Table 14.4. We see, perhaps not unexpectedly, that the major part of domain-satisfaction inequality cannot be explained by observed individual characteristics, and we also see that there is a significant correlation between the domain errors. This may be ascribed to latent psychological variables like optimism/pessimism, which affect the satisfaction of all domains of life in a similar way.

If we consider Equation (14.4), the estimates of which have already been presented in Chapter 4, we find that the general-satisfaction inequality can also be assessed and broken down into a structural and an error contribution. This is presented in Table 14.5 for the sub-sample of married individuals with a job. We use this sub-sample because only for this group do we have available the domains of job and marriage satisfaction.

From Table 14.5 two facts emerge. The first is that the variance explained is much higher than for the separate domains. In Table 14.1 we see that the percentage of variance explained is about 10%. For general satisfaction we find a percentage in the order of $(0.211/0.315)$ or roughly 65%. However, this percentage would be much lower if we were to replace domain satisfactions by

Table 14.5. *General-satisfaction inequalities, individuals with job and married*

	Structural inequality	In-between error variance	Sum of both	Number of observations
General satisfaction	0.211	0.104	0.315	5,041

their structural parts. The second thing is that the total inequality in *GS* is only about half or even less than the domain inequalities. This is because *GS* is a combination of domains and individuals may score badly on some domains, but mostly this underperformance on some domains will cancel out against the more-than-average performance on some other domains.

Given the considerable correlation of the terms in Equation (14.4) we get the risk of 'double counting'. We would like to know what the 'independent' contribution of finance is, after we have taken into account that a lower job satisfaction is correlated with lower financial satisfaction. Therefore, we apply the breakdown as outlined in Equation (14.5), where we have the domains ordered according to decreasing effects in Equation (14.4). We repeat that such an ordering entails an element of arbitrariness. We apply this breakdown to the structural covariance matrix. In this way we 'peel off' the inequality according to independent components, starting with the question of how much inequality in the second domain is *not* yet explained by the inequality in the first domain, and so on. The variances are given by the sequence in Table 14.6.

From Table 14.6 it is found that *job* satisfaction makes the largest contribution to general-satisfaction inequality, followed by *marriage* and *social life* roughly on a par. Next come finance and health, while the other domains make a negligible contribution. We note that the contribution of the auxiliary variable *Z* is less than 1 per cent. This breakdown is remarkable because it shows that general-satisfaction inequality cannot be identified with financial-satisfaction inequality. In reality, the financial aspect appears to be a rather modest component of general-satisfaction inequality. This is in contrast with conventional economic wisdom, which identifies well-being, welfare, etc. with the one-dimensional income concept.

14.3. DISCUSSION AND CONCLUSIONS

In line with the modern literature on satisfactions and happiness, we considered in this chapter whether we could define satisfaction inequalities.

Table 14.6. *Breakdown of general-satisfaction inequality, individuals with job and married*

	Variance	Contribution (%)
Job satisfaction	0.088	41.6
Marriage satisfaction	0.040	19.2
Social-life satisfaction	0.049	23.1
Financial satisfaction	0.012	5.6
Health satisfaction	0.012	5.6
Leisure-amount satisfaction	0.003	1.2
Housing satisfaction	0.002	1.0
Leisure-use satisfaction	0.005	2.6
Z	0.000	0.1
Total	0.211	—

It turned out that this is possible in a general way, not only for satisfaction with income, but with respect to satisfaction with every subject on which we can elicit evaluations on individual satisfaction. In this chapter we studied satisfactions with respect to eight life domains; such as financial situation, health, and social life. The information on these domain satisfactions is derived from questions which are now put as a matter of course in many socio-economic surveys, like the British Household Panel Survey and the German Socio-Economic Panel. When we try to explain those inequalities by objectively measurable variables, the explanation is meager in terms of variance explained. It follows that domain inequalities depend for a consider-able part on variables we are not yet able to measure. Unfortunately, they are covered under the heading of omitted variables and/or random errors.

Actually, we are considering for each individual a vector of domain satisfac-tions, the satisfaction vector for short. We showed that if we define satisfaction vector inequality as a variance-covariance matrix of a vector of individual satisfactions, those satisfaction dimensions are highly correlated, with correl-ation ratios in the order of 40 percent.

It also turns out that we can explain satisfaction with life as a whole as an aggregate of several domain satisfactions. Then, we may also define the in-equality of satisfaction with life as a whole, or *GS* for short, which is obviously a much more important index for evaluating the distribution of well-being in a population than inequality with respect to one domain. As the contributing components are highly correlated we employ a stepwise-regression procedure in order to avoid double counting. We find for the group of married people with a job that about two-thirds of satisfaction with life as a whole may be explained, and that within the explained part job satisfaction, satisfaction with marriage, and with social life count for about 80 percent.

It is obvious from this analysis that a number of choices had to be made which are open to debate. In the first place inequality can only be operational-ized if we assume the possibility of interpersonal comparability and a cardinal significance for the variables involved. Our choice is to assume that the numer-ical evaluations of satisfaction on a 1–7 scale (Likert 1932) are interpersonally comparable and have cardinal significance. The second point is that we have opted for the variance of the normally inverted answers. That we take the u's as our variable specification is not so strange as it appears, if we realize that probit analysis or interval-regression approach are also based on this specification. It is an empirical question whether another inversion trick and/or distributional specification for the error term might do better. If that were the case, the use of, for example, the logistic distribution would give no serious problems.

The choice of the variance as our inequality definition is clearly open for discussion. To begin with, we can consider generalized distance functions other than the Euclidean one, which would reflect different interpretations of inequality. It is obvious that the usual group breakdowns can be applied with respect to the variances or with respect to the covariance matrix of the satisfaction vector.

We did not require that the inequality concept satisfies a set of ethical normative restrictions like the Dalton transfer principle. This is for two reasons. First, we think that it does not apply in a positive-science approach. Second, we would not know how to do it. The inequality concept should be a neutral concept. In this chapter we leave it to the data and the estimated parameters to provide a description of how feelings of satisfactions and inequality are felt and how they depend on objective parameters. Moreover, in generalizing the inequality concept to a number of domains where transferability of satisfaction between individuals is inconceivable, and where a total store of satisfaction to be redistributed over individuals does not exist, we do not see how to define a benchmark of equality, except that all u's are equalized.

In our opinion the method and analysis here developed show beyond any doubt that satisfactions are data which can be handled by conventional econometric statistical methodology. Moreover, they can be used to define inequalities as well.

As this seems to be the first time that this approach has been used, we have not (yet) compared the empirical estimates with estimates from other countries or over time. It is obvious from the income-inequality literature that such comparisons are needed to interpret the figures and to get a feel for inequality differences. In this chapter we have made a first attempt to develop the basic methodology and instruments for the investigation of such satisfaction inequalities.

15

Poverty

15.1. INTRODUCTION

Since biblical times humanity has been preoccupied with the phenomenon of poverty. It is recognized that some individuals live more comfortably than others or, in harsher times or circumstances, that some of our neighbors are hungry and that others live in affluence. Although the phenomenon is widely recognized, it is difficult to agree on a definition of poverty. How can we recognize a poor household from a non-poor one? Usually, this is solved by specifying a net household income, which we denote by y_{min} and which we call the *poverty line*. If the household under consideration has an income smaller than y_{min}, then it is considered to be poor. It follows that it is rather crucial how we decide on where to place the poverty line. It is clearly a very relevant problem for modern societies, as one of the primary tasks of the modern welfare state is the creation and the running of a social-security system. That system boils down to a redistribution system where the non-poor pay a tax or contribute to a fund in order to alleviate the plight of the poor. It follows that the position of the poverty line is extremely important. If it is set at a high level such that, for example, 30 percent are poor, the volume of transfers will be high, while if the poverty line is set at a low level and, for example, 5 percent are poor, the transfer will be rather unsubstantial. It is evident that it will be much easier to get political support and acceptance for a relatively small redistribution than for a system which entails a rather large redistribution, unless in very inequitable societies, where a revolution is already simmering.

A number of poverty definitions have been suggested and put into practice; for example, in the USA and Europe. The difficulty with defining the concept of a poverty line is that poverty is a *feeling* and not an objective situation. Moreover, different individuals may have different feelings about the same objectively defined situation. Of course it has to do with 'command over commodities': we may describe a household consumption level either in terms of a commodity basket or more concisely by a net income level y. But how can we decide whether the level thus described causes a feeling of 'poverty'? Some households will feel 'poor' at a specific level whereas others do not. One way to overcome this problem is to appoint some experts to define the poverty line in terms of income, a commodity basket, or a specific food-share level, where we make use of Engel's Law (1895) that spending on food as a proportion of total expenditure falls with rising income. This approach is called the *objective approach*. It has paternalistic undertones. The other approach is to discover what income level individuals themselves associate with the poverty line. This is the so-called *subjective* approach, which is, as the reader will recognize, in the spirit of this book. Both approaches are based on the implicit assumptions that:

1. Similar individuals will use the same threshold income to define their situation as 'poor' or 'non-poor'.
2. The lack of well-being expressed by individual *A* when describing him- or herself as on the poverty line is comparable and equal to the lack of well-being expressed by individual *B* when saying that he or she is on the poverty line.

Both assumptions boil down to the idea that it is possible to make inter-individual welfare comparisons on the borderline of poverty/non-poverty. Frequently a distinction is made between various degrees of poverty, like 'poverty' and 'severe poverty'. In those cases we assume inter-individual welfare comparability throughout (see Sen 1976).

The discussion on poverty lines is frequently mixed up with the choice of a family-equivalence scale. Intuition dictates that a two-person-household poverty line, say $y_{min}(2)$, will be lower than the corresponding four-person line. However, what should be the ratio $e(4) = y_{min}(4)/y_{min}(2)$ in order that both household types suffer from the same degree of 'poverty'? It follows that the equivalence system used also has political implications. The definition of a poverty line involves in practice *two* problems. The first problem is how to define a poverty line for a reference household; say, the two-adults household. The second problem is how this poverty line should be 'equivalized' for various intervening variables, such that different household types perceive their poverty as equivalent. We notice that there may be more than one intervening variable, e.g., family size, age, region, urbanization, etc.

In the next section (15.2) we shall consider the concept of a poverty line. In Section 15.3 we shall consider some well-known-definitions. In Section 15.4 we shall consider the main equivalence systems in use. In Section 15.5 we look at the possibility of differentiating equivalence scales using variables other than merely household size. We do this on the basis of a household survey carried out in Belgium in the late eighties. In Section 15.6 we shall see how various poverty measures behave when combined with different equivalence systems. In 15.7 we also look at results from a Russian data set studied by Ferrer-i-Carbonell and Van Praag (2001). Section 15.8 concludes.

15.2. THE CONCEPT OF A POVERTY LINE

In applied poverty analysis, poverty is almost always described in terms of household income, that is, the total amount of income accruing to the household. This presupposes that the distribution within the household is such that all members enjoy roughly the same welfare level. Given a specific tax and social-security tariff it is usually possible to construct an approximate one-to-one relationship between net and gross income. As respondents frequently have a better knowledge of their net than of their gross income, we mostly prefer to use the *income net of taxes* concept.

Some objections may be raised:

1. Some of the household income may be *in kind* (e.g. gardening, baking, child-care, and exchanges in kind between the plumber and the dentist). If this type of income makes up a considerable part of household income, it does not make sense to take money income as a proxy for household welfare. This is particularly important in countries where some of the households depend on a single (mostly male) breadwinner and where other households are supported by two breadwinners. In that case the two-breadwinner households will have a larger money income than the one-breadwinner households, which are comparable to them in all other respects. The main difference between them is the amount of household production. Consider for instance the case where two women decide not to clean their own household any longer but to exchange roles, so that they act as paid cleaning women to each other. Household production has not changed at all, but the household incomes are much larger, suggesting greater welfare. Homans, Hagenaars, and Van Praag (1991) came to the conclusion that when we properly attribute a shadow price to household production the 'full' household income of the one-breadwinner family, including the value of household production, is about equal to the 'full' household income of the comparable two-breadwinner family. In fact, this is not so miraculous, as the decision on (female) labor participation is dictated by the comparison of 'full' household incomes. Hence, the female will not participate if the full household income is larger by adding 'home production' than if she were to participate in a paid job on the labor market and inversely she will participate if she can make more on the market than in her own house, taking account of the additional household amenities and help the household has to pay for. Similar problems are encountered when we compare one-parent families with two-parent families.

   When we compare urban families with rural families we face the same problem, as rural families have many more possibilities for the generation of income in kind. This is especially important if we compare developed and less-developed countries (see also Pradhan and Ravallion 2000).

2. The differentiation between gross and net income also raises problems. We may perceive our tax payments as paying our membership dues, for which

we get our share of the collective services like defense, security, education, national health, justice, etc. Still more complicating is the fact that income is frequently supplemented by income subsidies or price reductions on specific goods for low-income households; for example, in the form of food stamps, sickness insurance, social housing, reduced education costs, etc. This implies that the value of money may be different for low- and high-income households.

3. In many countries there is a considerable 'informal' or 'grey' economy. This is estimated for West-European economies to be between 16 and 30 percent of GNP. It is evident that official income becomes then an unreliable indicator of household welfare.

In most poverty literature these objections are ignored, and we will start by doing that as well. Taking the income concept y for granted, various types of poverty lines have been suggested. We want to consider several concepts which are in use, starting with the assumption that all households are equal with respect to size and other relevant variables, their only difference being their household income. By this assumption we have discarded the 'equivalence' problem for the moment.

A poverty line is frequently defined by determining the subsistence level in a society. However, there is a remarkable lack of discussion about which principle should form the basis for defining such a subsistence level.

15.3. POVERTY LINE DEFINITIONS

15.3.1. The Relative Approaches

The relative approach sees poverty as a relative concept. The poor are identified as belonging to the tail end of the income distribution, say the lowest 20 percent. If we denote the income-distribution function by $G(y)$, it follows that the poverty line y_{min} is at the lowest quintile of the distribution where $G(y_{min}) = 0.2$ holds.

The idea behind this definition is of socio-psychological origin. The poor are people who have the lowest income in society, *irrespective* of how rich this society is. It implies that any society, however rich in absolute terms, has 20 percent poor people in its midst. This concept can only be used to identify the poorest classes in a specific society. For international comparison it is rather useless, and the same holds for comparing developments over time. The number of poor is fixed at 20 percent.

This decile definition does not take into account the shape of the income distribution. For instance, consider a population of 100 families, where 81 families have $30,000 a year and 19 families have $29,999. The poverty line would be at $30,000. If the poor were to earn only $100 a year, the poverty line would still be at $30,000. In order to correct for this we can consider poverty line definitions that depend on average income and on skewness.

The half-median and half-mean lines

The median income $y_{0.5}$ is defined as that income such that 50 percent of the population has a lower income and 50 percent a higher income. In formula, $G(y_{0.5}) = 0.5$, where $G(y)$ stands for the income distribution function. The half-median line is defined at half the median income, that is $y_{min} = \frac{1}{2} y_{0.5}$.

A milder variant sets the poverty line at 60 percent of median income. This poverty concept is used for the European poverty statistics by EUROSTAT.

How this measure works is understood when we assume that the income distribution is log-normal. This approximation does not hold precisely, but it is frequently used as a roughly correct description. In that case the 60%-median line equals $0.6 e^\mu$ where μ stands for log-median income. The poverty rate according to this measure is then $N(\frac{\ln(0.6)}{\sigma}; 0, 1)$. It follows that the poverty rate would only depend on the standard deviation of log incomes σ. We saw in Chapter 13 that σ is a measure of income inequality. It follows that this measure does not change if the inequality remains constant. It follows that poverty will not decrease if all incomes increase but the inequality remains the same.

Another option is the half-mean line. Mean income under the lognormal distribution equals $\exp(\mu + 0.5\sigma^2)$. The half-mean equals $exp(\mu + 0.5\sigma^2 - \ln(2))$ with corresponding poverty ratio $N(\frac{0.5\sigma^2 - \ln(2)}{\sigma}; 0, 1)$. Also, for this measure we see that it is only determined by σ.

The value of these measures is doubtful. They are inequality measures in disguise.

15.3.2. The Absolute Approaches

The relative poverty line is useful to identify which families are poor according to the poverty definition used. The poverty definition itself does justice to the idea that individuals derive their idea of poverty (partly) from comparisons with fellow citizens. The relative concept is less acceptable, as it does not relate poverty to objective circumstances. For instance, the individual who feels hungry and is without a roof over his or her head in India may feel equally poor as the individual in the Netherlands who cannot pay for a bicycle. In material respects the conditions of poverty are completely different and the outsider would without hesitation stamp the Indian poor as much poorer than a member of the Dutch underclass.

The absolute approach takes account of this feeling. Forerunners were Rowntree (1901, 1941) and the monumental study by Peter Townsend (1979). The USA poverty-line definition, proposed by Milly Orshansky (1965), is in terms of a specific minimum food basket, which is priced by present-day prices. Orshansky defined such minimum baskets for various household types. Given that the food share, defined by this food basket, was about a third of total expenditure for households on the poverty line, the poverty line is set at three times the value of the minimum food basket. Since their original ·

introduction the poverty line has been annually adjusted for inflation. We notice that the definition of the food basket is rather arbitrary and subjective, being developed by a group involving nutritional experts. The *vox populi* is not heard in this definition. In fact, it is a rather paternalistic procedure to define a socially acceptable poverty line. Moreover, the commodity basket itself was left unchanged over the years. The multiplier procedure is also debatable. As previously noted, it is an experimental fact, known as Engel's Law, that the food share decreases with rising income. Hence, the choice of the value $\frac{1}{3}$ implies the definition of a poverty level. In fact, the food share itself may be seen as a welfare index. The lower the food share, the higher household welfare.

The Canadians Love and Oja (1977) proposed a refining of this measure by linking it explicitly to a budget share. Let E stand for the expenditures on clothing, food, and shelter, then their share E/y falls with income. The poverty line was then set by specifying the share E/y at a specific value. It is obvious that this definition entails arbitrary and subjective decisions as well.

15.3.3. Subjective Poverty Definitions

A third way to define poverty is called the 'subjective approach'. It is based on the idea that the population itself should define where the poverty line is situated. It makes use of the 'experienced-utility' or 'true-welfare' function $U(y)$ (see Ch. 2). It is estimated on the basis of a survey. We specify the poverty line y_{min} by the utility level 0.4 or 0.5 or, more generally, δ, and we solve the equation $U(y_{min}) = \delta$. Similarly, we may consider $U(.)$ to vary on a verbal range from 'worst' to 'best' and define the poverty line by an equation $U(y_{min}) =$ 'bad' or $U(y_{min}) =$ 'insufficient'. The last two (somewhat unusual) equations have to be read as: y_{min} is the income level which is evaluated by the verbal label 'bad' or 'insufficient'.

We saw before that there are (at least) two methods for estimating the experienced utility function. The first method uses the following satisfaction questions:

How satisfied are you today with the following areas of your life?
(Please answer by using the following scale, in which 0 means totally unhappy and 10 means totally happy.)
How satisfied are you with your household income...

Using the cardinal (CP) approach[1] and denoting log-income by y we estimate the welfare function

$$U = N(\alpha y - \gamma; 0, 1), \tag{15.1}$$

---

[1] Using the results in Ch. 2 it is obvious that we can work as well from the ordinal probit estimate.

which may be rewritten as

$$U = N(y; +\frac{\gamma}{\alpha}, \frac{1}{\alpha}). \tag{15.2}$$

The poverty line is then found by solving

$$N(y_{\min}; +\frac{\gamma}{\alpha}, \frac{1}{\alpha}) = \delta, \tag{15.3}$$

or, applying the inverse normal transformation,

$$y_{\min} = \gamma + \frac{u_\delta}{\alpha}. \tag{15.4}$$

The second method uses the income-evaluation question (IEQ):

Whether you feel an income is good or not so good depends on your personal circumstances and expectations.
In your case you would call your net household income:
a *very low* income if it equaled   DM _____
a *low* income if it equaled   DM _____
an *insufficient* income if it equaled   DM _____
a *sufficient* income if it equaled   DM _____
a *good* income if it equaled   DM _____
a *very good* income if it equaled   DM _____

This yields, as we saw in Chapter 2.8, the individual welfare function (decision utility)

$$U = N(y; \mu(y_c), \sigma), \tag{15.5}$$

where y_c stands for current income, and where we found the empirical relationship,[2] and

$$\mu(y_c) = \alpha y_c + \gamma. \tag{15.6}$$

We derive the true welfare function (experienced utility)

$$U(y_c) = N(y_c; \frac{\gamma}{1 - \alpha}, \frac{\sigma}{1 - \alpha}). \tag{15.7}$$

The poverty line is then found by setting

$$N(y_{\min}; \frac{\gamma}{1 - \alpha}, \frac{\sigma}{1 - \alpha}) = \delta, \tag{15.8}$$

or, applying the inverse normal transformation,

$$y_{\min} = \frac{\gamma}{1 - \alpha} + \frac{\sigma}{1 - \alpha} \cdot u_\delta. \tag{15.9}$$

This approach was introduced by Goedhart et al. (1977) and was called the 'Leiden poverty line' (LPL).

---

[2] The γ and α in (15.4) and (15.6) are not the same!

Goedhart et al., also gave a related alternative, which is termed the 'subjective poverty line' (SPL) in the literature. It is again based on a simple survey question, the so-called minimum income question (MIQ), which runs as follows:

What is in your opinion the minimum amount of income that your family in your circumstances would need to be able to make ends meet?
That would be DM...per month.

In this case we ask each respondent to solve the equation

$$N(y_{min}; \mu(y_c), \sigma) = make\ ends\ meet. \tag{15.10}$$

That is, we ask respondents to tell us what income level they identify with the situation of 'making ends meet', given their circumstances y_c. If we assume that the verbal label 'make ends meet' corresponds to a specific value $\delta \in [0, 1]$, in the welfare function context we solve the log-linear equation

$$\frac{y_{min} - \mu(y_c)}{\sigma} = u_\delta \tag{15.11}$$

or

$$y_{min} = \mu(y_c) + \sigma.u_\delta. \tag{15.12}$$

The interesting feature is that each respondent reveals his or her *own* poverty line, so to speak. This reflects the fact that individuals belonging to different social classes position the poverty line at different levels of income. How do we construct a socially acceptable poverty line from this set of widely differing opinions?

As we know $\mu(y_c)$ is a linear function in log-income y_c. Hence, we can regress the answers y_{min} directly on current individual income without any recourse to the welfare function context or the function $\mu(y_c)$ and we get the directly estimated equation

$$y_{min} = \alpha y_c + \gamma. \tag{15.13}$$

We observe that most respondents will situate the income level at which they would 'just make ends meet' at a level below their own income. For them,

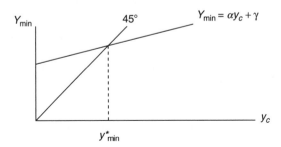

Figure 15.1. *The derivation of the poverty line*

$y_{min} < y_c$ holds. For the poor $y_{min} > y_c$ holds. It follows then quite naturally that the point of intersection at the value y^*_{min} of the two lines in Figure 15.1 is the socially accepted norm on the poverty line corresponding to the verbal label 'make ends meet'.

It is obvious that the same procedure can be repeated for any verbal label. The SPL version can be seen as specifying one point of the true welfare function, while the LPL version using the whole welfare function curve derives the whole true welfare function.

The advantage of the SPL-approach is that we can do the derivation and estimation without hypothesizing the existence of a lognormal individual welfare function and the estimation of its μ. The result, however, is theoretically and practically the same, apart from the level δ, generated by the Minimum Income Question, which in general will differ (mostly exceed) the exogenously fixed levels 0.4 or 0.5.

The poverty line resulting from the SPL approach is the familiar

$$y^*_{min} = \frac{\gamma}{1 - \alpha}. \tag{15.14}$$

There are two confusions in the practical literature, which should be mentioned.

The first one is that we should take the *average* of the responded log-income levels y_{min} instead of applying the somewhat indirect approach we just described. More precisely, we would have to look at

$$y^{**}_{min} = E(\gamma_{min}) = \alpha E(y_c) + \gamma = \alpha\mu_y + \gamma, \tag{15.15}$$

where μ_y is average log income in the sample. Comparing (15.14) and (15.15) it is obvious that in general both definitions will lead to different poverty lines. As we argued that (15.14) is the value such that households with more income than y^*_{min} qualify themselves as non-poor and households with less income than y^*_{min} qualify themselves as non-poor, and since in general $y^*_{min} \neq y^{**}_{min}$, the result is that adoption of y^{**}_{min} as the poverty line will create a class of 'poor' who are classified as 'non-poor' or a class of 'non-poor' which is stamped 'poor'. Another shortcoming of this approach is that the outcome depends on the income distribution in the sample. Frequently the average log income in the sample will not equal that of the population. This is especially so as so-called 'poor' are nearly always under-represented, resulting in a higher than actual poverty line.

A second confusing practice was followed, for instance, in Gallup polls between 1946 and 1989 (see e.g. Vaughan 1993). The relevant questions (see also Citro and Michael 1995 and Van den Bosch 2001) were:

1. *The 'get-along' question:* What is the smallest amount of money a family of four (husband, wife and two children) needs each week to get along in this community?

and

2. *The 'poverty-level' question*: People who have income below a certain level can be considered poor. That level is called the 'poverty line'. What amount of weekly income would you use as a poverty line for a family of four (husband, wife and two children) in this community?

Both questions suffer from the same weakness. Although the question tries to pin down a specific reference household, it is very dubious whether different respondents will consider the same household as their anchor type when answering the question. First, there is the fact that respondents who have a different household than the reference, say with more or fewer children, will have considerable difficulty in imagining themselves in the situation of the reference household. Second, there is the familiar problem that rich people do not have a realistic idea of what a poor situation is, and that 'get along' has a completely different meaning for households in different circumstances. In fact the reference household is undefined and, moreover, it is dependent on the respondent's own situation.

Questions have to refer to the respondent's *own* situation. Exploiting our knowledge about that 'own situation', we may then correct for the response bias towards the 'own situation' and find an answer which is representative for the population in the way we described above.

15.4. EQUIVALENCE SCALES

15.4.1. One-dimensional Equivalence Scales

Up to now we assumed that income is the only determinant of poverty. However, it makes a tremendous difference, for example, whether someone has to maintain only himself or a numerous family as well. Hence, nominal income has to be 'corrected' for family size and for other relevant factors to make the household welfare levels comparable. Only then can one decide in earnest which household is poor and which not. Traditionally it is assumed that a larger household needs more income than a small household to reach the same welfare level u.[3] In fact, household size is just one of the factors that influence financial satisfaction. We can think of age, of health status, education, urbanization, regional factors, climate, etc. as other factors as well. In short, we can conceive of a whole vector x. We start by looking at family size fs, because this is the traditional variable, mostly considered in this literature. A family-equivalence ratio is defined as

$$\frac{c(u; fs)}{c(u; fs_0)} = e(fs; u); \tag{15.16}$$

---

[3] The empirical figures in this section are borrowed from Van Praag and Flik (1992) and Van Praag, Flik, and Stam (1997).

that is, the ratio between the expenditures c(.) needed for maintaining a family of size *fs* at a utility level *u* and the expenditures needed for maintaining a reference family of size fs_0 at the same utility level *u*. Nearly always it is assumed that such a family scale does not depend on the specific utility level. That is, if a poor family of six persons needs twice as much as a family of two persons to reach the same poor level, the same ratio will hold for the rich family. In practice, this entails that we can write

$$c(u, fs) = e(fs).c(u, fs_0), \tag{15.17}$$

where we set $e(fs_0)$ at 1.

If we define a poverty line for the reference household either by identifying it with a minimum expenditure level c_{min} or by a minimum welfare level u_{min}, such that $c_{min} = c(u_{min})$, it is obvious that this translates into $c(u_{min}, fs) = e(fs).c(u_{min})$. Hence, for a good poverty line household-equivalence scaling is crucial. And, moreover, there is only one correct scale. Hence, if we apply a different one, the unavoidable consequence will be that poverty lines will refer to different utility levels, depending on family size. If the equivalence scale in use compensates less for having children than the true scale would prescribe, the number of large families that are poor will be underestimated. If the line is also used for deciding on whether specific households are eligible for social benefits, etc., those households may be very real victims of the wrong definition of the poverty line. On the one hand, it might be that this equivalence is intentionally chosen by the authorities to discourage households from becoming large. If that is true, we see that the poverty line is partly fixed on the basis of political predilections. On the other hand, if the equivalence scale is too 'steep', this may also be for the political reason of fighting underpopulation. In the case of a too steep scale many large families will be incorrectly identified as poor.

At the beginning of the twentieth century, or even earlier in some countries, schedules were already presented according to which households of different types were translated into 'consumer units'.

Within the scope of this chapter it cannot be the objective to give a comprehensive survey of this field. We refer, for example, to Van Praag and Warnaar (1997). Here we will give a brief sketch only. There are, roughly speaking, three approaches to the equivalence problem: the political, the objective, and the subjective ones.

The *political* approach is deceptive in its simplicity. It is not based on much research but on political decisions by parliament or civil servants. The predominant example is the so-called Oxford scale, which was later adopted by the OECD. It counts the first adult as one 'consumer unit', other adults as 0.7 'consumer unit' each, and children below 16 as 0.5 'consumer unit'. Obviously, this reflects certain economies of scale. However, the relative ratios are not based on scientific observations, except for some nutritional studies. The main attraction of the scale is its intuitive appeal and the fact that it is easy to work with it. It is widely used in OECD countries.

The second objective approach attempts to identify different utility levels by different spending patterns. It is obvious that various levels of well-being are linked to various spending patterns. For instance, as we have seen, Engel (1895) observed that the fraction of expenditures spent on food, the so-called food share, is high for poor people and low for rich people (Engels' Law). This led to the idea that the food share may be seen as a utility index U. We have then $U(y) = \dfrac{food\, \exp}{y}$. From there it is only one step to assuming that two households with fs_0 and fs_1 are at the same utility level if $U(y_0, fs_0) = U(y_1, fs_1)$. If this equality does not hold, the equation gives an easy method for finding which income y_1 is equivalent. In the US the food-share value at the minimum income level is put at one-third.

There are some questions with respect to this approach. First, it is not at all clear whether the food share can be interpreted as a welfare index. Second, what is the definition of food? Does it include wine, cigarettes, etc. It may be that 'food' stands for 'basic necessities', but there is ambiguity as to what is basic. Moreover, between poor individuals there are still differences in taste, such that one individual sees drinking milk as basic, while the other one sees beer drinking as indispensable. The problem becomes even more complex if we realize that the spending pattern of a family consisting of two adults will differ from that of a household with four young children.

In the same vein Rothbarth (1943) and later Deaton and Muellbauer (1986) identify household welfare by the consumption of the adults in the household. More specifically they define 'adult goods', for example a haircut, alcohol, tobacco, and they see the spending on these adult goods as a household welfare index. Two households of different composition enjoy an equal welfare level if the adults in the household consume an equal amount of adult goods. As spending on adult goods, say $A = A(y, fs)$, depends on income and family size, it is obvious that we may construct an equivalence scale on the basis of the relationship $A = A(y, fs)$. However, also, in this case it is very dubious whether two adults with the same consumption level of adult goods enjoy the same level of welfare and, moreover, it is very difficult to define what an 'adult good' is. The choice of those goods will affect how the relationship $A = A(y, fs)$ looks and hence what the equivalence scale will be.

A final more sophisticated example of the objective approach is the one using neoclassical demand analysis. The idea is that individuals spend their money y to buy quantities $q_1, \ldots, q_m$ of m commodities. Their aim is to maximize a utility function $U(q)$ where they are limited in their purchases by their budget constraint $p_1 q_1 + \ldots + p_m q_m = y$. It is possible to estimate the indifference curves from purchase behavior and to estimate from this information the indirect utility function $U(y; p)$. In its turn we can derive a price index, because a price change by Δp can be compensated for by an income change Δy such that $U(y; p) = U(y + \Delta y; p + \Delta p)$.

If households have different family sizes, we find purchase patterns which depend on prices *and* on family size. Then, it is also possible to estimate the utility function $U(q; fs)$. For a time it was thought that this approach yielded indifference curves between income and family size and hence family-equivalence scales. However, Pollak and Wales (1979) pointed out that these utility functions are conditional on family size. They say: 'The expenditure level required to make a three-child family as well off as it would be with two children and $12,000 depends on how the family feels about children. Observed differences in the consumption patterns of two- and three-child families cannot even tell us whether the third child is regarded as a blessing or a curse.' They argue that one should observe what they call unconditional preferences; that is, preferences on choices between consumer expenditures *and* changing family size. Children, so to speak, have to be seen as one of the commodities in the commodity bundle. They give as a possible way out: 'Unconditional preferences for demographic variables might also be obtained by analyzing responses to direct questions about preferences or hypothetical choices, although economists have traditionally been suspicious of this approach.' Then they refer to Kapteyn and Van Praag (1976) for an example of equivalence scales constructed on the basis of the IEQ. This is the subjective approach.

The *subjective* approach is the approach that we introduced informally in Section 2.4. We estimated the experienced utility function $U = U(y, fs)$. For any utility level U_0 and family size fs we can find the net household income $y_0(fs)$ needed to reach utility level U_0 by solving $U(y_0, fs) = U_0$. Notice that the resulting equivalence scale is

$$\frac{y_0^*(U_0; fs)}{y_0(U_0; fs_0)} = e(fs; U_0).$$

(15.18)

We note that in this general formulation the equivalence scale depends on the specific utility level U_0. In the specification $U(y, fs) = U(\alpha \ln(y) + \beta \ln(fs))$, which we use throughout this book, (15.18) simplifies to a non-utility-dependent equivalence scale.

As is obvious from Section 2.4, the equivalence scale defined on the basis of an estimated experienced-welfare function is the natural solution to the equivalence problem. The family-size-differentiated poverty line then follows in a very simple way. Let U_0 stand for the critical welfare level, say $U_0 = 0.4$. In that case the poverty line $y_{min}^*(fs)$ is found from the equation

$$U(y_{min}^*, fs) = U_0.$$

(15.19)

The resulting differentiated poverty line in money amounts is then

$$y_{min}^*(fs) = y_{min}^*(fs_0).fs^{-\frac{\beta}{\alpha}}.$$

(15.20)

We found in Chapter 2 that the power was about 0.3. We stress that the specific behavior of the scale, that is the value of $\frac{\beta}{\alpha}$, depends on the country for which this scale is estimated. In countries with a liberal family-allowance scale the power must be much lower than in countries with a rather meager allowance schedule.

If the state schedule yields an exact compensation we find $\beta = 0$. With overcompensation we would even find $\beta < 0$. The effect that we find is always a residual one. (Cf. the effect of noise in Ch. 11.)

15.5. MULTI-DIMENSIONAL EQUIVALENCE SCALES

It will be obvious to the reader that there may be more factors than family size alone which affect the feelings of financial poverty. Hence, it may be that poverty lines should be differentiated according to other variables as well. In Van Praag, Flik, and Stam (1997) a Belgian[4] data set was considered, in which the variable *age* of the head of the household was added. They included $\ln(age)$ and $(\ln(age))^2$. When people are young they collect and aspire towards a list of consumer durables; for example, a house and furniture. Later on in life one has the things one needs and consequently the need for new purchases falls. Similarly, in early life family size will rise with *age* but after a certain age family size will tend to fall with increasing age. In the same spirit two regional dummies were added to divide the country into three regions and finally working-situation dummies were included, where ONE indicates that either the head of the household or the spouse is working (part-time or full-time); ONETWO that both are working but at least one of them has a part-time job; and, finally, TWO that both are working in a full-time job. For an unemployed couple all dummies are zero. The resulting estimates for the μ-equation are given in Table 15.1.

We see that there is the familiar U-shape in age, with a maximum at 38. There is a marked difference between the three regions, where individuals in the reference region (Brussels) need 9.5 percent more than a person living in the second region and 17 percent more than those living in the third region. This is partly because of the differences in the regional price levels, for example in housing, and partly perhaps because of differences in preferences, as there are cultural differences between the Flemish and the Walloon regions. Two-full-time-breadwinner families need 14 percent more than families without workers to reach the same welfare level. Comparing the three specifications we see how remarkably constant the effects stay from one specification to the other.

From this μ-equation we can easily derive a multi-dimensional equivalence scale. Let

$$\ln(y) - \mu = \ln(y) - \alpha \ln(y) - \beta_1 \ln(fs) - \gamma_1 x_1 - \ldots - \gamma_k x_k - \gamma_0, \quad (15.21)$$

---

[4] The sample used is not completely representative. It did not include the self-employed and farmers. For our methodological investigations this makes no difference.

Table 15.1. *Different specifications for* μ

Variables	Equation 1		Equation 2		Equation 3	
	Effect	*t*-value	Effect	*t*-value	Effect	*t*-value
Constant	5.768	38.3	3.029	3.5	3.258	3.5
y_c	0.424	29.0	0.412	28.8	0.372	24.3
Fs	0.177	13.8	0.149	11.0	0.166	12.4
Ln(age)	—	—	1.615	3.5	1.704	3.7
$(Ln(age))^2$	—	—	−0.223	−3.6	−0.227	−3.7
REG1	—	—	—	—	−0.157	−8.8
REG2	—	—	—	—	−0.091	−4.8
ONE	—	—	—	—	0.033	1.8
ONETWO	—	—	—	—	0.090	3.4
TWO	—	—	—	—	0.130	5.2
N	1,917					
R^2	0.56		0.57		0.59	

where $x_1, \ldots, x_k$ stand for factors other than *fs* which affect the evaluation of income. If we now solve the equation

$$\ln(y) - \alpha \ln(y) - \beta_1 \ln(fs) - \gamma_1 x_1 - \ldots - \gamma_k x_k - \gamma_0 = u_{0.4}, \qquad (15.22)$$

we get the poverty line

$$\ln(y^*_{min}) = \frac{\beta_1 \ln(fs) + \gamma_1 x_1 + \ldots + \gamma_k x_k + \gamma_0 + u_{0.4}}{1 - \alpha}. \qquad (15.23)$$

Let us assume a reference household with characteristics $fs^{(0)}, x_1^{(0)}, \ldots, x_k^{(0)}$. Then, we find for the ratio of the poverty lines for an arbitrary household and the reference household

$$y^*_{min}/y^{*(0)}_{min} = \left(\frac{fs}{fs^{(0)}}\right)^{\left(\frac{\beta_1}{1-\alpha}\right)} * \left(\frac{x_1}{x_1^{(0)}}\right)^{\left(\frac{\gamma_1}{1-\alpha}\right)} * \ldots * \left(\frac{x_k}{x_k^{(0)}}\right)^{\left(\frac{\gamma_k}{1-\alpha}\right)} \qquad (15.24)$$

$$= e(fs)^* e_1(x_1)^* \ldots^* e_k(x_k).$$

We notice that the multi-dimensional equivalence scale has an extremely simple structure. It is the product of one-dimensional indices (.). It is evident that this simple structure is caused by the log-linear specification of the μ-equation. However, that specification has been chosen on the basis of empirical fit. Hence, there is an empirical basis for this multiplicative index. Given this structure the index may be computed, if we know the separate one-dimensional indices. We give them in Table 15.2.

By means of these findings it is possible to assess poverty lines for various subgroups in the population. The methodology may also be used to discover whether a specific characteristic has a measurable effect on feelings of poverty.

If the effect is estimated to be zero or non-significantly different from zero, there is no argument to include it in the equivalence scale and to differentiate the poverty line for that factor. However, if a factor has a significant effect, this is not enough reason to differentiate the poverty line for that factor. The choice to 'equivalize' for a specific factor is a *political* choice in the last instance. For instance, we can differentiate with respect to the number of breadwinners, but there is also an argument not to do so. We can argue that it is the free decision of the household which and how many members are employed outside. Hence, is it reasonable that the state assumes a responsibility for alleviating financial poverty if the poverty is caused by the choice of the household? In practice, the differentiation is restricted to family size. Outside academic poverty analysis and international comparative statistics many nations use their own family-equivalence scales, which are mostly but not always based on political intuition and nutritional studies. We refer to Van Praag and Warnaar (1997) for a comprehensive overview of about a hundred different scaling systems.

It is obvious that the same equivalence scales may be estimated on the basis of the *minimum-income*-question (MIQ), where we replace μ by y_{min}. It will be no surprise that the scales derived are in both cases almost the same. This is witness to the fact that such scales are extremely robust estimates. The drawback of the MIQ and the resulting *subjective poverty line* (SPL) compared to the LPL, derived from the IEQ, is that the MIQ is a one-level question while the IEQ mostly includes six levels. Hence, the answers to the IEQ are better calibrated than the response to the one-shot minimum-income question. Therefore, the LPL estimate is somewhat more reliable than the SPL one. A second and more important point is that the LPL method may yield poverty lines for 'severe' poverty, 'moderate' poverty, 'near' poverty, etc., by varying the threshold value 0.4 to 0.5 or, for example, 0.6. It is obvious that the SPL does not offer this possibility. Moreover, it is unclear which utility value corresponds to 'making ends meet'. Similar considerations and results hold for the financial-satisfaction question. The equivalence scales derived from that question are practically identical with those derived from the IEQ and the MIQ (see also Sect. 2.4).

Table 15.2. *Equivalence scales for family size, age, region, and breadwinners*

Family size	1	2	3	4	5	6
Equivalence scale	1.00	1.20	1.34	1.44	1.53	1.60
Age	25	35	45	55	65	75
Equivalence scale	1.00	1.10	1.11	1.09	1.05	1.00
Region	1	2	3	—	—	—
Equivalence scale	1.00	1.11	1.28	—	—	—
Number of breadwinners	0	1	1.5	2.0	—	—
Equivalence scale	1.00	1.05	1.16	1.23	—	—

15.6. POVERTY LINES AND EQUIVALENCE SCALES COMPARED

It is interesting to compare the frequently used OECD scale with the subjective LPL scale. This gives Table 15.3.

From Table 15.3 it is clear that the OECD scale exaggerates the scale effects enormously. That this has its consequences for the resulting poverty ratios we will now see. We compare various poverty lines for the same Belgian sample in which we apply side-by-side the OECD and the subjective family-equivalence scales. The difference is that the household incomes are standardized according to two different scales: the subjective scale, which we dare to call the *true* scale, and the OECD scale. After standardization it is obvious that the ranking order of households in the income distribution will have changed. Large households become much poorer under the OECD scaling compared to the one-person household than under subjective scaling. For instance, a two-adult-two-children household with $1,000 will get an OECD-standardized one person household income of 1000/2.7 = $370 and a subjectively standardized income of 1000/1.53 = $654.

In Table 15.4 we consider the first decile instead of the two-decile measure. Moreover, we introduce alongside the SPL two LPL levels; namely $U = 0.4$ and $U = 0.5$. In addition, we consider three units of observation. The first is the sample of *households*. Second, we consider the number of poor *individuals*. Third, we consider the population of children alone and we count how many are situated in poor households. As the OECD scaling exaggerates the poverty in large families (with many children) compared to the 'subjective' outcomes it is not surprising that the OECD scale exaggerates child poverty considerably. Table 15.4 illustrates that the choice of the equivalence scale is critical in the determination of the poverty ratio.

Similarly, it is not guaranteed that the poverty line corresponds with the same welfare level for every household type. We compared the outcomes of the first decile, the half median, the LPL 0.4 and the SPL more precisely for various family sizes in Table 15.5.

Two things may be inferred from Table 15.5. The first thing is that OECD scaling is very much to the advantage of large families. We may even say that

Table 15.3. *OECD and LPL scales compared*

Household type	Scale	
	OECD	Subjective LPL
Single	1.00	1.00
Couple	1.70	1.23
Couple with 1 child	2.20	1.40
Couple with 2 children	2.70	1.53
Couple with 3 children	3.20	1.63

Table 15.4. *Poverty ratios based on different*
principles and two different scales

	Scale	
	OECD	Subjective
Households		
First decile	10.00	10.00
Half median	4.05	6.44
SPL	5.26	6.67
LPL 0.4	2.02	3.37
LPL 0.5	4.32	5.81
Individuals		
First decile	11.71	6.54
Half median	5.55	3.96
SPL	6.73	4.16
LPL 0.4	3.08	1.92
LPL 0.5	5.81	3.51
Children		
First decile	16.09	3.42
Half median	8.03	1.83
SPL	9.33	2.00
LPL 0.4	4.55	0.40
LPL 0.5	8.19	1.53

the result, which is found in many countries, that poverty is largely concentrated in large families, may be seen as an artefact, caused by the use of the OECD scale. Obviously, this statement is based on the assumption that the subjective scale is the 'true' scale. If we accept that the individuals give a true assessment of their feelings of satisfaction, this is a rather acceptable assumption. It is seen that the choice of the equivalence index, given its impact on taxes, social security benefits, and subsidies to families in money and in kind, is not a minor choice. It is extremely relevant for the evaluation of social welfare policy.

The second point of interest is that the SPL scale ('making ends meet') seems to correspond in Belgium with a welfare level of 0.53; that is, higher than the usual 0.4.

There are numerous poverty indices. We considered just the most simple one, the poverty ratio. That is the percentage of households in the population below the poverty line. This index does not take into account that there is a difference between those who are situated just below the poverty line and those who are far below the poverty line. There is a whole literature (see e.g. Hagenaars 1986: ch. 6) which tries to establish poverty indices by requiring them to satisfy certain theoretical requirements. This literature resembles the literature on income inequality, as those axioms mostly have an ethical content. The most striking example is the 'transfer axiom', according

Table 15.5. *Welfare evaluations of family-size-dependent poverty lines*

Family size	First decile		Half median		LPL 0.4		SPL	
	OECD	Subjective	OECD	Subjective	OECD	Subjective	OECD	Subjective
1	0.41	0.60	0.29	0.52	0.22	0.40	0.33	0.53
2	0.61	0.60	0.49	0.52	0.40	0.40	0.53	0.53
3	0.72	0.60	0.61	0.52	0.52	0.40	0.64	0.53
4	0.79	0.60	0.68	0.52	0.60	0.40	0.72	0.53
5	0.84	0.60	0.75	0.52	0.67	0.40	0.78	0.53
6	0.90	0.60	0.83	0.52	0.76	0.40	0.85	0.53

Note: The two-adult family is the reference household type.

to which a transfer from a richer person to a poorer person should reduce the poverty index. In fact, the whole problem can be seen as a specific illustration of the income-inequality literature. We try to evaluate a specific income distribution with distribution function $F(y)$, where we assume that households differ only with respect to income y. The population is split up into two subgroups A_p and A_{np}: the poor and the non-poor. For the poor it holds that $y \leq y^*_{\min}$ and for the non-poor $y > y^*_{\min}$; the fraction of poor (the poverty ratio) is $p = F(y^*_{\min})$ and the fraction of non-poor is $(1 - p)$. Now three points are of interest.

First, how is satisfaction or utility measured? We can think of absolute income y, log income $\ln(y)$, or any utility function $U(y)$. In the last case we can think of the *ex ante* decision-utility function or the *ex post* experienced-utility function, denoted by $U(y; y_c)$ and $U(y; y) = \tilde{U}(y)$ respectively. Second, we are interested in the relative fraction p. Finally, we are interested in the utility gap between the poor and the rich.

An attractive measure for that gap would be the in-between variance; that is,

$$\sigma^2_{between} = p(\overline{U}_p - \overline{U})^2 + (1 - p)(\overline{U}_{np} - \overline{U})^2, \tag{15.25}$$

where $\overline{U}_p$ stands for the average utility among the poor and $\overline{U}_{np}$ for the average utility among the non-poor. It is obvious that we can conceive of an infinite variety of specifications, depending on the definition of the utility function. It stands to reason that we should depart from our empirical estimates, which indicate that a log-normal distribution function, both for the decision and the experienced utility function, seems appropriate. We notice that here again we can distinguish between poverty as perceived by individuals, say *virtual* poverty based on the virtual welfare function, and *true* poverty, based on the *true* or *experienced* welfare function.

We will not get into this normative problem of defining a poverty index. It is a branch of the normative income-inequality literature.

15.7. OTHER POVERTY DEFINITIONS, WITH AN EXCURSION TO RUSSIA

When we talk about subjective poverty, literature and practice refer to the SPL or, to a lesser extent, the poverty definition which is based on the IEQ. When we look at the Internet we see that there are tens of countries in the world where studies with respect to subjective poverty have been carried out like in Latin America and China (see, for example, Rojas 2006*b*; and Gustafsson, Shi, and Sato 2004). However, we do not know of countries where the methodology has been accepted as *the* official instrument to define and measure poverty. Apart from its relative novelty, the main reason is presumably that the outcomes of such studies are beyond the control of the political authorities. Poverty is a politically sensitive issue, as one of the established indicators of how well the society functions and, moreover, poverty is linked with social assistance and security and hence with public finance. No wonder that politicians want to have the measurement instrument firmly under their control.

One of the countries in which the authors carried out a poverty study is Russia (see Ferrer-i-Carbonell and Van Praag 2001). We refer also to Ravallion and Lokshin (2002), who performed a study on another Russian data set. Ravallion and Lokshin do not define a poverty line but study 'self-rated economic welfare' based on an economic-ladder question that is roughly comparable to the Cantril question, where the categories range from 'poorest' to 'richest'. Our main conclusions are also found in Ferrer-i-Carbonell and Van Praag (2001). We used the IEQ and alongside it we tried two other approaches to establish a poverty line. (See also the earlier study by Frijters and Van Praag 1997.)

It is evident that the study, which was based on two waves of a household panel, collected in 1997 and 1998, suffers from peculiar difficulties related to the then prevailing Russian situation. First, Russian society was (and is) rather chaotic. Hence, even if individual respondents were as willing as western respondents to give careful and true answers to the questions posed, which may be doubted in view of the recent history and social culture of mutual spying, respondents are very frequently in a situation which is much more difficult to describe and much more complex than that of citizens in a western welfare state. People frequently do not know their own situation very well, when there are several adults living in a house and each adult has two or more jobs. There may be considerable uncertainty about earnings because one does not know whether one will be employed next month; it may also be that one is employed but that the payment of wages is indefinitely postponed. There are all kinds of informal income components. Moreover, there was rampant inflation in those years. These facts suggest that the data will be much less accurate than those of comparable contemporary surveys in the West. A third point is that the economy was much less monetarized than in the West. The income in kind, for example vegetables from a garden, may be considerable. This type of income is difficult to observe accurately. All in all, household income was much less reliably observed than in comparable western data sets. This does not imply that the fieldworkers did a worse job than their western colleagues. Quite the contrary; the survey was carried out with as much care and reliability.

Our data set is the RUSSET panel data set, organized by the University of Amsterdam. The initiator and leader of the project was William Saris, while the fieldwork was carried out by CESSI (Institute for Comparative Social Research, Moscow) and coordinated by Dr. Anna Andreenkova. The survey was financed by the Dutch National Science Foundation.

Among others, the questionnaire contained the following three questions (Fig. 15.2). In the first and the third one every respondent has to locate his/her own position on an interval scale. In the second question, which is the IEQ with five levels, the respondent has to specify five income levels.

The first and the third question were analyzed by means of ordered probit, while the IEQ was analyzed in the traditional way described above. We found Table 15.6.

When comparing the financial-satisfaction question and the results of the IEQ we find again, as in Chapter 2, that the family effects derived from both questions are very similar. For instance, in wave 5 the family-size elasticity is found

A. How satisfied are you with the financial situation of your family?

0	1	2	3	4	5	6	7	8	9	10

$\mu_0=-\infty$ μ_1 μ_2 μ_3 μ_4 μ_5 μ_6 μ_7 μ_8 μ_9 $\mu_{10}=+\infty$

Not at all satisfied — Very satisfied

B. Assuming prices to be constant, what monthly income (net of taxes) would you consider for your household as:

Thousands of rubles per month

Very bad ....
Bad ....
Not bad/not good ....
Good ....
Very good ....

C. How satisfied are you with your life as a whole?

0	1	2	3	4	5	6	7	8	9	10

$\mu_0=-\infty$ μ_1 μ_2 μ_3 μ_4 μ_5 μ_6 μ_7 μ_8 μ_9 $\mu_{10}=+\infty$

Not at all satisfied — Very satisfied

Figure 15.2. *Income-satisfaction questions in the RUSSET panel*

Table 15.6. *Estimation results for waves 5 (1997) and 6 (1998)*

Variable	Wave 5 (1997)			Wave 6 (1998)		
	FSQ	IEQ(μ)	SWB	FSQ	IEQ(μ)	SWB
$\ln y_c$	0.722	0.370	0.503	0.570	0.365	0.352
	(0.039)	(0.018)	(0.080)	(0.044)	(0.020)	(0.091)
$\ln fs$	−0.522	0.422	1.164	−0.328	0.392	0.579
	(0.061)	(0.032)	(0.427)	(0.066)	(0.033)	(0.470)
$(\ln fs)^2$	—	—	0.021	—	—	−0.085
			(0.120)			(0.114)
$\ln y_c \ln fs$	—	—	−0.167	—	—	−0.050
			(0.074)			(0.078)
Adjusted R^2 (IEQ), (pseudo)-R^2 (FSQ, SWB)	0.210	0.400	0.185	0.205	0.403	0.186
		SFS $-\gamma_2/\gamma_1$			IEQ $\beta_2/(1-\beta_1)$	
Wave 5	—	0.724	—	—	0.670	—
Wave 6	—	0.575	—	—	0.618	—
Delta method used to calculate the standardized difference between the two ratios[5]	—	0.574	—	—	−0.251	—

to be 0.724 when using the FSQ, while the elasticity is estimated at 0.670 when derived from the IEQ. There is no statistically significant difference between the two estimates. It is, however, remarkable that the size of these elasticities is much higher than the values of about 0.3 we found for western-European countries. This indicates that children and other family members are felt as much more of a financial burden in Russia than, for example, in Germany. It follows that the OECD scale, which we found too steep for most countries on the Western European continent, may be a more suitable candidate for Russia. The reasons for this relatively high elasticity can only be conjectured. The main reasons may be that the state is less liberal in family allowances and especially that most of the urban population lives in a rather small space, sometimes with two families or one extended family in one house or apartment. We should also realize that the Soviet social-assistance network has been replaced to a considerable extent by a capitalist market-distribution system. The less socialist a social structure is, the less we may expect that families are compensated by the state to alleviate welfare differences caused by differences in family size, health, or education. Van Praag, Hagenaars, and Van Weeren (1982) found similar results in the eighties when comparing a range of European countries, where England, Greece, and Portugal showed markedly higher elasticities than the richer countries in the (at that time) core of the European Union.

[5] The standard error is $\left(\dfrac{(-\gamma_2/\gamma_1)-(\beta_2/1-\beta_1)}{\sqrt{\sigma^2_{-\gamma_2/\gamma_1+\sigma\beta_2/1-\beta_1}}} \right)$

In contrast, the income effect (preference drift) 0.37 is much lower than is mostly found in Western Europe. This is probably caused by several factors. First, Russian incomes vary greatly over time, both in real and in nominal terms. Moreover, there is more income in kind or of an 'informal' nature than in the West. Frequently, the standard of living is less related to income available than to having the right kind of relations. Both factors point to the fact that own current income is less stable as an anchor-point than in the West. The Subjective Well-Being question (SWB) results are somewhat different from the western-type results as well. The income coefficient is much higher than is usual, which suggests that for most people primary needs, which have to be satisfied by spending money, are still very important, while for western people income is not such a pressing factor for well-being, to be clearly distinguished from economic welfare.

It is not evident what number on the various scales should be identified with poverty. When we consider the bounds 3, 4, and 5 respectively we get Table 15.7a/b, by counting how many respondents consider their household level as being below level 3, 4, or 5.

From Table 15.7a/b it is evident that poverty in Russia at those times was shockingly high. The contrast becomes clear by comparing it with the corresponding responses by German respondents on the same questions. Indeed, more than 50 percent of the population appears to live in poverty, with an increasing tendency from 1997 to 1998. For 'life as a whole' we find smaller figures, but they are also very high.

Now we try to define the poverty lines. For LPL this is simple, as explained above. For the financial-satisfaction question we can follow a similar philosophy. The latent variable Z explaining the response follows an equation

$$Z = \alpha \ln(y) + \beta_1 X_1 + \ldots + \beta_k X_k, \tag{15.26}$$

and a response i implies that $\mu_{i-1} < Z \leq \mu_i$. Those nuisance parameters μ_i are estimated by the probit approach. Notice that if a person evaluates his or her financial satisfaction at exactly 4, then it implies that his or her $Z = \mu_4$. This is tantamount to a recardinalization. Hence, the poverty line for this person is situated at

$$\ln(y^*_{min}) = \alpha^{-1}[\mu_4 - (\beta_1 X_1 + \ldots + \beta_k X_k)]. \tag{15.27}$$

Similarly, we can construct a poverty line for the subjective well-being question. In Table 15.8 we reproduce the corresponding poverty ratios, where we took for the financial-satisfaction question 'level 3' as the poverty boundary to bring the FS and LPL estimates in line. The poverty ratios refer to individuals, counted irrespective of their age, such that the contribution of large households is proportional.

For comparison, we give the so-called objective poverty lines based on the half-mean[6] and half-median criteria. From these figures it is again evident that

---

[6] For an elaboration of this theme we refer to Van Praag and Ferrer-i-Carbonell (2007b).

Table 15.7*a*/*b*. Primary results on poverty in Russia (1997/1998), compared with Germany (%) measured by subjective financial satisfaction and subjective well-being

	FSQ		SWB	
(a) RUSSET	Wave 5 (1997)	Wave 6 (1998)	Wave 5 (1997)	Wave 6 (1998)
Below 3	57.8	67.8	23.0	40.7
Below 4	67.6	77.6	32.5	51.2
Below 5	82.9	89.3	57.6	72.5
(b) GSOEP	West Germany* (1997)		East Germany* (1997)	
	FSQ	SWB	FSQ	SWB
Below 3	5.8	4.4	6.4	5.6
Below 4	11.2	8.5	12.6	10.5
Below 5	24.2	20.4	32	29.9

*Number of individuals who live in a poor household.

Table 15.8. *Poverty ratios for Russia 1997/1998 according to various criteria (%)**

Family size	Half mean		Half median		FSQ(3)		LPL(4)		SWB(4)	
	1997	1998	1997	1998	1997	1998	1997	1998	1997	1998
1	33	18	17	14	84	93	84	86	57	91
2	23	20	19	14	73	86	73	77	16	51
3	27	31	22	25	63	90	61	74	17	36
4	34	35	27	25	64	91	63	79	20	31
5	17	56	9	45	87	92	57	90	4	40
6	67	48	50	43	100	86	83	86	50	43
7	33	80	33	60	100	100	100	100	33	60
TOTAL	29.5	34.2	22.9	26.3	67.8	90.3	65.9	79.9	20.5	41.2

*Number of individuals who live in a poor household.

subjective poverty is at levels completely unknown in the West. The objective figures are also comparatively high, but much less so. This shows, in our view, again that the rather arbitrary definitions 'half mean' or 'half median' do not relate very well to actual feelings of poverty. It is remarkable that the SWB figures are much lower than the corresponding LPL and FS figures. The reason is clearly that the quality of life as a whole is not identical with *financial* satisfaction. The difference between the two figures indicates that the situation with respect to general well-being in Russia is less dire than that with respect to financial satisfaction.

15.8. CONCLUSION

In this chapter we have tried to define poverty. Discussion of the definition is a first and necessary step in the struggle against poverty. We need an agreed-upon measurement procedure by which we can estimate the size of the problem and identify poor individuals or households. We recognized that all 'objective' definitions lack credibility, because poverty is a *feeling*. If we do not base our poverty definition on the subjective feelings of individuals, we run the risk that our poverty definition will lead to results that do not reflect reality. Households which are defined as poor may feel 'non-poor' and vice versa. This holds especially for the 'equivalizing' operation. If household situations are characterized by their net household income, it is obvious that households that differ in composition and probably other (politically accepted) characteristics will not be equally satisfied with the same income. This calls for a 'correction procedure'. We saw that it is very important that this procedure reflects the individual's feelings. The only way to estimate the correction factor needed is to base our work on observations about the feelings of the persons involved. The 'persons involved' are not only those people who are expected to be poor. This would cause a circularity, as we would need for that an a priori definition, and that is just what we are looking for. We need the opinion of the whole population on poverty.

As we showed in Chapter 2 and in this chapter, the derivation of the equivalence scales does not require a specific cardinal-utility-function concept (see also Van Praag and Van der Sar 1988). However, we need a cardinal utility function if we want to define poverty. For instance, if we choose the value 0.4 as our poverty boundary this only makes sense if we adopt a specific utility function $S_j(x_j)$ which is the same for all individuals that are compared. As seen above, it is possible to choose another cardinalization, but then the value 0.4 has to be replaced by μ_4. The choice of the poverty boundary is of course a political choice. The choice of 0.4 on a unit-interval scale or the fourth rung of an economic-ladder scale with ten rungs is acceptable to most people, although the values 0.3, 0.5, or even 0.6 in liberal welfare states can be defended as well. Needless to say, this leads to varying populations of poor.

We have ended this chapter in a somewhat less optimistic tone. We realized that when we talk about poverty this is almost invariably cast in terms of lacking income. However, there are a number of domains which are not or are only slightly determined by household income. Hence, when talking about poverty in the traditional sense, this implies a narrow restriction to the (private) financial domain. For instance, it may be that public expenditures on collective services like public health and education can do much more for the household's well-being than increasing private income. Second, in less-developed countries money income as such may be only a secondary determinant of household welfare, as many households depend very much on income in kind. Another problem is how to define the extended family. In our surveys we may stick to the assumption that the respondent represents the opinion of the household (see also Ch. 6), but this becomes increasingly difficult when the household widens to a kind of mini-community.

In our opinion the definition and measurement of poverty is of primary importance. However, notwithstanding the progress made by others and ourselves in coping with this scientific problem, work in this area remains at an early stage.

16

Multi-dimensional Poverty

16.1 INTRODUCTION

Let us now reconsider and generalize the poverty concept. Up to now we have, more or less automatically and in line with the bulk of the literature, assumed that poverty refers to a lack of financial satisfaction and that someone's situation can always be described by his or her income level, corrected if necessary for some individual characteristics like family size. In fact, this is a rather one-dimensional approach, irrespective of whether we choose for an objective or a subjective approach. We saw in this book that the financial domain is just one aspect of subjective well-being. So it lies at hand to generalize the concept of financial poverty to *domain* poverty.

We can conceive of more than one poverty concept. Alongside financial poverty we can think of health poverty, job poverty, leisure poverty, and so on. Finally, we may define a poverty concept in terms of General Satisfaction with life. These generalizations will be the subject of this chapter. This implies a generalized poverty concept, which is not necessarily cast in monetary terms of a poverty line.

The examples above are already illustrative for the practical relevance of such a generalization. However, if we leave the framework of our Western societies, based on money as the medium of exchange, and think of the situation in the rest of the world, the relevance of this conceptual generalization becomes even greater. The income poverty concept that most of us have in mind is too restrictive. In many developing countries, where the poverty problem is most acute, the concept cannot be satisfactorily operationalized. Not only for the reason that income and consumption statistics may be unreliable or non-existent in such countries, but more basically, because such economies are only partly monetarized. The citizens' well-being does not depend so much on their income, but on their production in kind, their skills and those of their family, their health, how many children there are and in what measure they support the common household, their possibilities for exchange and the available social network for mutual assistance.

This chapter is partly based on Van Praag and Ferrer-i-Casbonell (2007).

In the literature the multi-dimensionality of the poverty concept has been acknowledged by several authors. We mention Maassoumi (1986), Slottje (1991), Pradhan and Ravallion (2000), Case and Deaton (2002), Bourguignon and Chakravarty (2003), Deutsch and Silber (2005), and more recently Duclos, Sahn, and Younger (2006), as authors who stress that poverty is a multi-dimensional phenomenon. Pradhan and Ravallion, among others, take an intermediate position, as they assume that in the end the poverty gaps in the various dimensions can be reduced to money gaps. However, a good part of the recent literature deals with the axiomatic side and will be difficult to operationalize.

The domain satisfaction approach as developed in Chapters 3 and 4 of this book offers a good starting point for an empirically viable and intuitively plausible approach to multi-dimensional poverty. Perhaps needless to say, we start from the fact that poverty is a feeling and not an objective condition of living. What is felt to be poverty depends on the individual.

As we saw that individuals can numerically evaluate their domain satisfaction on an interval scale, say, from 0 to 10, or, after rescaling, on [0, 1], we can define an individual as being subjectively poor with respect to a specific domain j, if his or her satisfaction with respect to that domain is smaller than 0.4; that is, satisfaction $S_j \leq 0.4$. Obviously, the number 0.4 may be replaced by 0.5 or, more generally, by any number $\delta \in [0, 1]$. Accordingly, we will distinguish between (0.4) or (0.5)-poverty or, more generally, δ-poverty. If δ is increased, the severity of the poverty measure becomes less and the corresponding poverty ratio increases.

Now we recall that there are several alternative models and estimation methods, used in this book, by means of which domain satisfactions may be described. We consider here: Ordered Probit, POLS, and COLS.

In all three models we assume that the individual's domain satisfaction is described by

$$DS_j = \beta'_j x_j + \beta_{0j} + \varepsilon_j \quad (j = 1, \ldots, k) \tag{16.1}$$

where the domain j is described by a vector of characteristics x_j and a random disturbance term ε_j, standing for unobserved heterogeneity, individual random effects, and observation errors. The cardinal satisfaction (using COLS) with respect to the domain j is

$$S_j(Z_j) = N(\beta'_j x_j + \beta_{0j} + \varepsilon_j; 0, 1). \tag{16.2}$$

The β's and the variance of ε are estimated.

The estimated trade-offs may, as we saw before, be estimated by the various methods with similar outcomes. The only difference is in scaling and the location of the intercept.

The poverty regions are differently defined in the alternative models. In OP the response Categories correspond to a partition of the real line by the cutoff parameters μ_i. If $(-\infty, \mu_5)$ corresponds to the union of the response categories 0, 1, ..., 4, somebody is poor if $DS_j \leq \mu_5$. In the POLS-model this equation corresponds to $DS_j \leq u_5$, where u_5 is the normal sample quantile, such that $N(u_5) = p_0 + \ldots p_4$. In the COLS-setting the equivalent is $DS_j \leq v_{0.4}$, where $v_{0.4}$ is defined by (2.38). We will use the COLS- setting as our frame of reference here.

The poorness of the individual is now described by k poverty indicators $(P_1, \ldots, P_k)$, corresponding to the k domains, where

$$P_j = 0 \quad \text{if } DS_j \leq v_{0.4} \quad (j = 1, \ldots, k)$$

and $P_j = 1$ otherwise.

Obviously the number 0.4 may be replaced by δ. If δ increases, the poverty concept becomes less and less severe and the number of poor people will consequently increase.

The vector P is just a simple transformation of the vector S of domain satisfactions. Similarly, we may derive from General Satisfaction GS an index of overall or general poverty, say, GP. Actually, if we take the satisfaction levels 0, $\ldots$, 4 together as one response class, say A, and we call the set of the other response classes B, we may apply a Bi- Probit to explain poverty.

Counts

A simple count for the GSOEP 1996 wave yields the following results (see Table 16.1) for domain poverties, that is, the individuals in the level groups 0, 1, $\ldots$, 4 taken together. We see that financial poverty is 6.76 percent but that with respect to health the poverty is 11.34 percent while job scores 10.44 percent.

Table 16.1 *A simple count of domain poverties, SOEP, 1996 West Germany workers (in %)*

Level of satisfaction	Life as a whole	Financial situation	Health	Work	Leisure	Environment	Housing
0	0.23	0.31	0.68	0.80	1.02	0.81	0.93
1	0.25	0.33	0.54	0.55	1.33	0.71	0.50
2	0.71	0.77	2.03	1.73	3.57	1.78	1.51
3	1.35	1.89	3.59	3.04	5.49	4.73	2.49
4	2.76	3.46	4.51	4.32	6.32	6.64	3.50
5	9.72	9.35	12.13	10.93	13.68	16.95	7.89
6	11.07	10.62	10.11	9.96	11.51	14.56	7.68
7	23.98	22.19	17.49	17.97	16.86	22.15	14.85
8	33.51	30.10	26.06	27.89	21.40	20.29	25.72
9	11.63	13.46	13.25	13.73	10.01	7.68	17.87
10	4.77	7.53	9.62	9.08	8.81	3.69	17.06
Are poor							
<=4	5.31	6.76	11.34	10.44	17.73	14.67	8.93

Table 16.1 shows that 'non-financial' poverty is a very realistic phenomenon, especially because it is frequently hard or even impossible to compensate for the lack of satisfaction by giving more money to the individual.
Apart from the fact that enormous money amounts may be needed for such
compensations, money is hardly a determinant of some domain satisfactions.
In fact, as we observed before, financial poverty is a coarsened version of
income inequality. In the same way this multidimensional poverty concept
can be seen as a coarsened version of the multidimensional inequality concept considered in Chapter 14. We saw there that domain satisfactions are
strongly correlated. It follows that individuals, who are poor with respect to
one domain, run a good risk of being poor in other domains as well. The
analysis using the model developed in Chapters 3 and 4 can be applied to
poverty as well.

The poverty region with respect to domain j is a collection of domain char-
acterizations (x_j, ε_j) defined by the inequality

$$DS_j = \beta'_j x_j + \beta_{0j} + \varepsilon_j \leq v_{0.4} \quad (j = 1, \ldots, k) \tag{16.3}$$

16.2. PREDICTION OF POVERTY

The first question is now how well these models predict poverty. The naïve
setup in the COLS-framework is to test for each individual whether the inequal-
ity $DS_{nj} = \beta'_j x_{nj} + \beta_{0j} \leq v_{0.4}$ holds. That is we set the error term at zero. As
$(\beta'_j x_{nj} + \beta_{0j})$ is the expectation of DS, the inequality $\beta'_j x_{nj} + \beta_{0j} \leq v_{0.4}$ would
imply inequality (16.3); it follows that poverty would be considerably overesti-
mated. Predicting on the basis of $DS_{nj} = \beta'_j x_{nj} + \beta_{0j} \leq v_{0.4}$ is what we call the
prediction at an *individual* level. Now we saw in Chapters 3 and 4 that the
explanatory value of the models in terms of correlation coefficients or pseudo-
correlation coefficients in the case of OP was very small. This finding may be
interpreted as that our variables x have a significant effect on satisfaction, but
that this effect is rather tiny, compared to a number of factors we do not or
cannot observe, and which are included in the error term. As a result the
predictions at an individual level are very bad, irrespective of whether we
choose OP, POLS, or COLS. Some figures are presented in Table 16.2.

Another approach is what we call the *macro*-approach. Here we calculate for
each individual n what would be his or her *chance* of being poor, given his or
her X-variables. Then those individual chances on poverty are averaged over
the sample, yielding the overall poverty ratio in the sample or the population
for which the sample is representative.

In the COLS-setting this means that we look for the chance on the event that
$DS_{nj} = \beta'_j x_{nj} + \beta_{0j} + \varepsilon \leq v_{0.4}$. That is, if we assume that ε is normally distributed, the chance on poverty for individual n is $N(v_{0.4} - (\beta'_j x_{nj} + \beta_{0j}); 0, \sigma(\varepsilon_j))$,
where $\sigma(\varepsilon_j)$ is estimated in the COLS-estimation. The chance may be interpreted

Table 16.2. *Job and financial poverty ratios as observed and predicted, according to three models (1996 GSOEP)*

	Job satisfaction			Financial satisfaction		
	OP	POLS	COLS	OP	POLS	COLS
Poverty ratio observed	10.44%	10.44%	10.44%	6.76%	6.76%	6.76%
Individual poverty ratio predicted	0%	0%	0%	0%	0%	0%
Macro- poverty ratio predicted	10.41%	7.54%	10.14%	6.64%	4.28%	6.31%

	House satisfaction			Health satisfaction		
	OP	POLS	COLS	OP	POLS	COLS
Poverty ratio observed	8.93%	8.93%	8.93%	11.34%	11.34%	11.34%
Individual poverty ratio predicted	0%	0%	0%	0%	0%	0%
Macro- poverty ratio predicted	8.92%	6.15%	8.28%	11.31%	8.05%	10.95%

	Leisure satisfaction			Environment satisfaction		
	OP	POLS	COLS	OP	POLS	COLS
Poverty ratio observed	17.73%	17.73%	17.73%	14.67%	14.67%	14.67%
Individual poverty ratio predicted	0.002%	0%	0.001%	0%	0%	0%
Macro- poverty ratio predicted	17.75%	13.76%	16.89%	14.64%	10.79%	14.52%

	General satisfaction		
	OP	POLS	COLS
Poverty ratio observed	5.31%	5.31%	5.31%
Individual poverty ratio predicted	1.14%	0.49%	0.81%
Macro-poverty ratio predicted	5.22%	4.93%	4.69%

as how poverty-prone an individual is. If we take the average chance over the population, this equals the *expectation* of the poverty ratio in the sample. We see that this estimate is rather close to reality for all domains and that this holds for all three methods OP, POLS, or COLS, although POLS performs definitely worse than the two other methods.

Using our findings in Chapters 4 and 14 we see that it is possible for someone to be 'poor' with respect to some domains and not with respect to others. We also see that one can be poor with respect to life as a whole although one is financially rich. The same analysis as for specific domains is performed for general satisfaction on the basis of the two-layer model.

16.3. PERSISTENT AND TRANSITORY POVERTY

Poverty analysts sometimes differentiate between *persistent* and *transitory* poverty. The basic idea is that some individuals are temporarily poor while others are constantly poor. The first situation is unpleasant, but much less dramatic than when the situation is permanent. This differentiation may be studied when we have a panel data set like the GSOEP. If we define the poverty profile for individual n at time t as $P_{n,t} = (P_{n,t,1}, \ldots, P_{n,t,k})$, the maximum number of switches between poverty and non-poverty per domain j is (T-1) and the volatility for a specific domain for individual n may be characterized by $V_{n,j} = \frac{1}{T-1} \sum_{t=1}^{T-1} (P_{n,j,t} - P_{n,j,t-1})^2$. The volatility is thus a percentage that can vary from 0 to 1.

In Table 16.3 we present the average volatilities for the various domain satisfactions over the GSOEP-data set during the period 1992–6. For example, the volatility for financial satisfaction is 12.42 percent. The volatility is calculated by using the total number of individuals in the panel (as opposed to the total number of observations). After deleting individuals who are only one year in the panel and those who are in multiple but not subsequent years, we are left (for financial satisfaction) with 5,536 individuals. From all these individuals, the vast majority (4,221) do not experience any change in their rich or poverty status in any of the years. Only 1.18 percent of these individuals (50) are poor in all the years. The rest (4,171) are always reporting a financial satisfaction of 5 or more. From the total of 5,536 individuals, there are 202 (3.65 percent) that change from poor to rich or from rich to poor every single year they are in the panel. Nevertheless, 130 out of the 202 (64 percent) are only 2 years in the panel, which means that they only switch once. Actually, there are only four individuals who are six years in the panel and who switch every single year. The volatility index if we only take the individuals who are present in the panel in all the 6 years (2,333) equals 11.76 percent, which is fairly similar to the volatility index when we take all the observations (12.42 percent).

Table 16.3. $P_{poor,\ rich},\ P_{rich,\ poor},$ *and the corresponding*
$V_{n,\ j}$ *for all domains and GS*

	P→R	R→P	Volat.
	%	%	%
Job satisfaction	60.32	6.92	12.06
Number observations	18,453		5,434
Financial satisfaction	68.99	6.92	12.42
Number observations	18,811		5,536
Health satisfaction	56.31	8.27	13.4
Number observations	18,904		5,553
House satisfaction	59.91	5.56	11.29
Number observations	18,747		5,508
Leisure satisfaction	48.61	12.21	20.05
Number observations	18,785		5,533
Environment satisfaction	56.25	11.68	19.78
Number observations	18,812		5,538
General satisfaction	61.87	3.92	7.02
Number observations	18,879		5,526

In Table 16.3 we present the volatilities. Next, we differentiate between the (conditional) chance on an upwards shift from 'poor' to 'non-poor,' say $p_{p\rightarrow r}$ and the (conditional) chance on a downwards shift, say $p_{r\rightarrow p}$. These chances are also tabulated based on simple counting. The main difference between the volatility index and these conditional chances is that while the first measure was calculated at the individual level, these conditional chances are calculated as averages over annual observations at the sample level. Therefore, we use all the observations available. Of course, the last year that an individual is in the panel cannot be used, as we do not know how satisfied the individual will be next year. Similarly, the first year can also not be used, as we do not know how satisfied the individual was the year before. In addition, we cannot use individuals who are only one year in the sample and those who are present in non-sequential years. Let us take financial satisfaction as an example. The total number of yearly observations available to calculate the conditional chance is 18,811. In 1993, there were 83 individuals who were poor in 1992 and stayed poor, 162 who were poor in 1992 and became rich, 174 who were rich in 1992 and became poor, and 3,277 who were rich in both years. Therefore, the conditional chance of an upward shift (coming out of poverty) in 1993 is $162/(162 + 83) = 66.12\%$. Similarly, the chance on a downward shift is $5.04\% = 174/(174 + 3277)$. The mean across years is 68.99 percent and 6.92 percent, respectively. These are the numbers presented in Table 16.3.

Our conclusion is that, fortunately, most cases of subjective poverty may be stamped as transitory poverty.

16.4. APPLICATION TO POVERTY ALLEVIATION

Finally, we look how we may influence poverty and well-being by specific policy measures. For, if we change the *x-variables* we may in fact change the satisfaction distributions. For instance, if we change the income distribution of the population we may change the financial poverty ratio. The same holds for other variables such as working hours, education, and health. We perform now a few of those exercises, where we stress to begin with that the political value of these exercises should not be exaggerated yet. This is a *caveat*. They are just academic exercises at this moment, but they may hold promises for policy making in the future. What we will look after are just the direct effects. For instance, if we change the net income distribution by changing taxes and/or social security this may affect the supply and demand for labour and a whole sequence of secondary effects may be triggered off. Hence, a realistic assessment would require a comprehensive model of all indirect effects. However, this does not change the point that an ultimate evaluation of the social effect of such measures would have to be done in terms of domain satisfactions and/or general satisfaction.

Reducing the Chance of Poverty

Let's look at the chance that an individual is poor by using the COLS estimation method. The point of departure is the difference $(v_{0.4} - \beta' x_n - \beta_0 - \varepsilon)$. As soon as this expression is positive for a specific domain or for 'life as a whole' we call the person poor with respect to that domain or for 'life as a whole'. We

Table 16.4   *Chance of being poor, West Germany, 1996*

	Job satisf.	Finan. satisf.	Health satisf.	House satisf.	Leisure satisf.	Environ. satisf.	General satisf.
With current situation	10.14%	6.31%	8.28%	10.95%	16.89%	14.52%	4.69%
Education							
People with years education <=10		7.61%	13.71%				
People with 11 years of education		6.87%	12.76%				
Work							
People work 20% less hours	4.69%						
Health							
People with Health sat.<= 5							12.41%
People with Health sat. = 6							3.79%

might call this difference the *poverty gap* for the specific domain. For individual n holds that the chance on the event $\{\varepsilon < (v_{0.4} - \beta' x_n - \beta_0)\}$ is $N\left(\frac{(v_{0.4} - \beta' x_n - \beta_0)}{\sigma(\varepsilon)}\right) = p_n$. Table 16.4 shows these chances, averaged over the population, for each domain in 1996 for West Germany (notice that these results are identical to the ones presented in Table 16.2).

The question we are interested in is whether we can reduce the chance to be poor by modifying the situation of the individual. Therefore, we first have to know which x-variables can be influenced or determined by the authorities.

Hours of work, health, and education are possible candidates. This is clearly an institutional and political problem, and the answer will vary from society to society. Table 16.4 shows the results for some variables.

If all West German workers would work 20 percent fewer hours than they do now, the chance of being poor in job satisfaction would reduce from 10.14 percent to 4.69 percent. This result takes only into account the direct effect and we thus ignore all the indirect effects that reducing working hours would have. For example, the fact that a working week reduction or the dropping of night work may have effects on general satisfaction. A nasty question is caused by the fact that a reduction of the working week may have a fall in income as effect. Hence, we have to model precisely the link between hours of work and income. If the working week is reduced in the framework of government policy, like in France where the working week is maximized by law at 35 hours for most jobs, then it is not necessarily the case that labor income is reduced proportionally or at all.

Similarly, labor laws may affect job security in the sense that individuals are more or less easily fired. This may affect the supply and the demand for jobs and hence influence unemployment. The effect on individual satisfaction is only one aspect of such policy measures, but the overall effect depends as well on the labor market effects.

Two other measures are in the dimensions of health and education. We saw that both factors have sizeable effects on satisfaction and productivity. Both may be influenced in most countries by government policy. Compulsory health insurance and health subsidies are very important for well-being. The costs of such policies are also considerable. The same holds for education. It is then a matter of cost–benefit analysis to decide which measures or mix of measures would be most productive in poverty reduction. The ultimate criterion would be a social welfare function, which is a weighed sum of the individual satisfactions. The weighting of individuals is a purely political choice, where a leftist regime may overweight the feelings of the poor and where a more rightist regime would incline towards weighing citizens equally or even overweighing the 'haves', compared to the 'have-nots'.

Table 16.4 shows that for individuals with low education (i.e. 907 individuals who have ten or fewer years of education), the average financial satisfaction poverty chance is 7.61 percent and for health satisfaction poverty is 13.71 percent. These are the only two domain satisfactions for which we found a statistically significant effect of education (see Chapter 3). If we would now give 11 years of education to all these individuals, the chance for financial poverty for those sub-groups of low education would be reduced to 6.87 percent and for health to 12.76 percent. Relatively speaking this implies a reduction of about 9 percent for financial poverty and for health of about 7 percent.

We next look at the effect that improving health satisfaction would have on poverty with respect to general satisfaction. Taking only individuals with a health satisfaction of a 5 or lower, the chance of general satisfaction poverty is 12.41 percent (see Table 16.4). This chance of GS-poverty would be reduced to 3.79 percent if all these individuals would be lifted to a health satisfaction level of 6. This would be a reduction of GS-poverty by about 70 percent.

As already said, at this stage in our argument it would be presumptuous to draw hard conclusions for practical policy. Therefore we need a detailed empirical model of how various measures affect the different sub-groups of citizens. However, if we have reliable knowledge in this area, we may link it with our knowledge on well-being, collected in this book and elsewhere, to assess political measures in terms of individual satisfactions.

Income transfers: How much it will cost?

Let's now do another exercise, in which we focus on financial satisfaction and look at how much income is necessary to reduce poverty. If an individual is poor, how much money do I need to give him or her to lift him or her out of poverty? Let us assume for the purpose of exposition that the only relevant variable is net log-income y. An individual is then 'financially poor' if $(\beta_1.y + \beta'x + \beta_0) + \varepsilon < v_{0.4}$ or $\varepsilon < v_{0.4} - (\beta_1.y + \beta'x + \beta_0)$.

It follows that, if we would increase log-income by $\Delta y = \frac{1}{\beta_1}(v_{0.4} - (\beta_1.y + \beta'x + \beta_0) - \varepsilon)$, we would have lifted the individual considered out of poverty. Hence, we may interpret Δy as the *relative poverty gap* for $\Delta y > 0$.

As $\varepsilon \sim N(0, \sigma(\varepsilon))$, where $\sigma(\varepsilon)$ has been estimated, we may assess the *expected* poverty gap $\overline{\Delta y}$ for individual n under the condition that $\Delta y < 0$.

Using the now well-known formula for the conditional expectation, given in Chapter 2 we find

$$E(\varepsilon|\varepsilon < v_{0.4} - (\beta_1.y_n + \beta'x + \beta_0)) = \sigma(\varepsilon).E\left(\left(\frac{\varepsilon}{\sigma(\varepsilon)}\Big|\frac{\varepsilon}{\sigma(\varepsilon)} < \frac{v_{0.4} - (\beta_1.y_n + \beta'x + \beta_0)}{\sigma(\varepsilon)}\right)\right)$$

$$= -\sigma(\varepsilon).n\left(\frac{v_{0.4} - (\beta_1.y_n + \beta'x + \beta_0)}{\sigma(\varepsilon)}\right) \Big/$$

$$N\left(\frac{v_{0.4} - (\beta_1.y_n + \beta'x + \beta_0)}{\sigma(\varepsilon)}\right)$$

The expected relative poverty gap for individual n is then

Table 16.5. *Average transfers needed to remove financial poverty, West Germany, 1996*

		Mean	Minimum in the sample	Maximum in the sample
Average transfer amount (D-marks/month)	$\sum_n p_n . \Delta y_n . y_n$	390	64.45	1505.66

$$\overline{\Delta y_n} = \frac{1}{\beta_1}(v_{0.4} - \beta_1 . y - \beta_0 - E(\varepsilon | \varepsilon < v_{0.4} - (\beta_1 . y_n + \beta_0)))$$

The *absolute* poverty gap for individual n is $\overline{\Delta y_n} . y_n$. Now the chance that for individual n holds $\varepsilon < v_{0.4} - (\beta_1 . y + \beta_0)$ is, as before,

$$N\left(\varepsilon < \frac{v_{0.4} - (\beta_1 . y_n + \beta_0)}{\sigma(\varepsilon)}\right) = p_n.$$

The *social absolute* poverty gap is found by weighting the individual gaps by the chances p_n that there is a gap. We get the amount $\sum_n p_n . \Delta y_n . y_n$, this is the *social absolute* poverty gap. We give for West Germany in the year 1996 the figures in Table 16.5.

What is the meaning of this exercise? As a statistical index of poverty and the severity of poverty it is an interesting index. Apart from that, would a transfer as described above really eliminate the financial poverty problem? We are doubtful about it, as we ignored the reference effect. We saw in Chapter 8 that the income distribution of the social environment plays a powerful role in determining one's individual satisfaction.

Hence, if every poor family gets the transfer, the individual impact will be much less than when only one individual will get it. In order to cover this reference effect we should redefine the poverty gap as $\Delta y = \frac{1}{\beta_1}(v_{0.4} - \beta' x - \beta_{ref}\Delta y_{n,ref} - \beta_0 - E(\varepsilon | \ldots))$, where $\Delta y_{n,ref}$ is the relative distance of n's income to the reference income. At this stage we will abstain from extensive modeling, as it is still empirically unclear what is the exact size of the reference effect.

16.5. CONCLUSIONS

In this chapter we extended the subjective poverty definition to a multi-dimensional concept. We see that the analytical model, developed in Chapters 3 and 4 provides an intuitively plausible basis for defining the poverty concept. Actually, poverty may be considered as a dichotomized version of the original satisfaction concept, where a continuous satisfaction scale is mapped on two points, viz. poverty or non-poverty. The threshold version is set in this chapter at 0.4, but this threshold is purely arbitrary. We may defend 0.5 or 0.6 just as well. Hence, analytically the poverty concept, developed here, does not add new insights to the models developed in this book. However, it demonstrates the political relevance of the happiness concept. Politically, the poverty concept is very relevant.

The charm of this concept is that it is intuitively plausible, that it does not require tedious and costly observations of material household welfare, like having a fridge, etc., that it does not require rather arbitrary definitions of poverty, and, last but not least, that it is straightforwardly applicable to non-monetary aspects and consequently it is relevant for economies in development. It is obvious that this subjective concept differs from all other measures and concepts of poverty in the literature.

17

Epilogue

No book is complete without an epilogue. Let us now look back to see how far we have come in this book, and let us also look ahead.

17.1. WHAT DID WE FIND?

In this book we embarked on a systematic exploration of so-called satisfaction questions. Satisfaction questions probe feelings of satisfaction with various domains of life. They refer to our health, our job, our financial situation, etc. Similar questions can be posed referring to matters which are not so directly related to our own situation. For instance, we can ask for an evaluation of government policy. There, we can distinguish between how government policy affects our own situation and how the policy affects the situation of the country. It could also be that we ask people for an evaluation of a fictitious situation, such as how they would evaluate an income 20 percent below their actual income. In the latter case, when we ask for an evaluation of the prevailing and/or fictitious situations, etc., we try to get insight into the individual *norms* of individuals. We can also ask for evaluations of events like a concert, a football match, etc. Such questions provide information on personal feelings, the character of the respondent, and, last but not least, about the appreciation by the respondent of the item which has to be evaluated, say the *evaluandum*.

There already exists a long tradition in psychology and sociology with respect to this type of questions. Apart from primary analysis, the answers have also been analyzed by means of multivariate models like factor analysis and principal components, but economists have always distrusted the validity and the information value of such questions. As a consequence, the typical tools of econometrics, namely the regression-type models in which dependent variables are singled out and 'explained' by a set of explanatory variables, are just beginning to be systematically applied for the analysis of satisfaction questions, in the last decade. These questions have just started to be systematically analyzed by means of models in the sense that economists give to this word. In the years since the first edition of this monograph in 2004 hundreds of papers have been written where 'happiness equations' are estimated. However, the 'two-layer model', as introduced in Chapter 4, is still a novel approach. In this book we tried to develop and to apply a methodology by which we can analyze satisfaction along lines similar to those whereby econometricians now analyze all kinds of 'objective' variables as a matter of routine. We think that this book provides evidence that this attempt has succeeded. Indeed, it proved possible to deal with satisfaction variables in a way which did not differ very much from ordinary econometric practice.

It appeared that there are two additional difficulties. The first is that the responses to such questions are mainly in terms of ordered numerical or verbal categories. Traditionally, economists tackle this by using the ordered-probit (or logit) model. However useful this model may be for single-equation models, it is not very tractable for more complex multi-equation models. In Chapter 2 we developed the POLS and COLS methodology to free ourselves from the traditional methodological bodice. It turns out that these methods, although not as general as ordered-probit, in practice yield almost always very similar results in our context. This is certainly also helped by the relatively large number of categories used, mostly seven or eleven. The second more difficult nut to crack is the ordinality/cardinality issue. We do not wish to repeat the whole discussion anew. Let it suffice to say that we followed the way of physics, where many concepts only became measurable after researchers had defined the unit and the measurement procedure in a somewhat arbitrary way. The only requirements were that the outcomes of the measurement procedure are not influenced by the observer, that the procedure may be repeated with, in general, a similar outcome except for measurement errors, and, finally, that the measurement results could be fitted into empirical relationships with other variables, sometimes called empirical 'laws'. Famous examples in physics are the laws of Ohm or of Boyle-Gay Lussac. In our field of sciences such laws are evidently much less exact and much more ridden with intervening variables than in physics. Nevertheless, we see that this physical approach to the cardinality issue works miracles. We find that the measurement can be realized without observer effects, that it can be repeated, and, finally, that empirical laws like the preference drift (and hedonic treadmill) can be derived. It follows that there is no cardinality issue left. It is only an apparent but not a real obstacle.

And, indeed, we found empirical laws and were able to define new concepts based on our empirical measurements, such as, the inequality measures we defined in Chapters 13, 14, 15, and 16.

From 1968/1971 onwards, Van Praag worked with the income-evaluation question and the resulting income-evaluation function, also called the 'Welfare Function of Income'. This line of research is known as the Leyden School. Up to now the difference and the similarity between this earlier Leyden approach and the satisfaction-question approach, initiated in economics by Oswald and Clark, have remained unclear. In this book we have closed the gap, and we find that there is a link and a complementarity between both approaches (see also Van Praag 2007).

The complementarity may be sketched as follows. The Leyden School estimates both the decision and experienced-utility function in the sense of Kahneman et al. (1997) with respect to income or the financial situation, but the
Leyden approach, which is based on individual income *norms*, has thus far not
been applied to other domains of life. The satisfaction approach estimates only
the experienced utility but is applicable to all kinds of domains.

17.2. WHAT LIES AHEAD?

The first point which we have to look for is for methods whereby we can
estimate decision-utility functions for other domains as well. For, we saw that
decision- and experienced-utility functions are different concepts. Since the
publication of the first edition, we have progressed in this line by designing
a measure of ex-ante (or decision) subjective job utility (Ferrer-i-Carbonell,
Thedossiou, and Van Praag 2007). Satisfaction questions do not yield decision-
utility functions, although we expect that the observed domain satisfaction functions can be derived from the underlying decision function coupled with an
adaptation process, characterized by a domain-specific preference drift. However,
at the moment this is still to be discovered. We have to design new measurement
procedures; in particular, we have to devise question modules by means of
which we can measure individual norms. Such question modules may be generalizations of the income-evaluation question.

More precisely, let a domain, other than the financial, be described by a
vector x and the individual's current situation by x_c, then the individual's
(virtual) domain-satisfaction function is $U(x; x_c)$ and the (true) satisfaction
function is $\tilde{U}(x_c) = U(x_c; x_c)$. At this stage we are able to observe $\tilde{U}(x_c)$ but
not[1] the individual's $U(x; x_c)$. We shall have to find methods to estimate
$U(x; x_c)$ per person (see Ferrer-i-Carbonell, Thedossiou, and Van Praag 2007).
Moreover, we shall have to investigate the nature of the adaptation process to
changing circumstances. What is its velocity? Is it similar to the process
sketched in Chapter 7, or is it different? It may well be that our relatively
simple longitudinal model, following Mundlak, as elaborated in Chapters 3–6,
would have to be made more complex, to include lags and leads.

The second major issue on which we need to focus research is the question
of optimality. We are curious as to whether decision processes follow the path
predicted by the decision-utility structure. If that were true, individuals would
be in equilibrium when marginal satisfactions with respect to their $U(x; x_c)$ in
all directions were equalized. In practice, this neoclassical situation is a benchmark but frequently not a reality. For instance, on the labor market many
workers would like to work more or less or in a different job than in their
actual situation. It may be that they are rationed. It may also be that their
preferences have changed since they made their job decision, but that they are
unable—or only at high material and/or non-material transaction costs—to

[1] Except for income.

change their present situation into a better or optimal alternative. An example was found in Chapter 11, where we considered a non-optimal housing situation around Amsterdam Airport. If the relationship presumed above between $U(x; x_c)$ and $\bar{U}(x)$ is true, the study of true satisfaction functions can inform us about whether the individual is in equilibrium or not.

17.3. THE RELEVANCE OF THE NEOCLASSICAL EQUILIBRIUM ASSUMPTION

In fact, the direct observation of utility functions opens a whole new area of research. In neoclassical theory the basic assumption is that individuals are in equilibrium. That is, they are in the situation that is optimal for them. However, if one is able to observe utility functions directly, then we can check whether the neoclassical marginalist assumption holds. If not, we can evaluate how far away the individual is from the situation of equilibrium, what is the utility loss associated with the disequilibrium, and what is the most efficient way to reduce the gap. In fact, we can consider the set of neoclassical equilibria as a subset of our observation space, containing equilibria *and* disequilibria. We refer to our analysis of airport noise and the housing market in Chapter 11 as an example. It implies that we do not always have to take the neo-classical equilibrium assumptions for granted to make identifiable statements.

As we explained, there is a difference between the approach of mainstream economics and other social scientists within and outside economics with respect to the kind of data that are acceptable as sources of information for research. Up to now there is a kind of schism between both approaches. Mainstream economics is only interested in *revealed preferences*; that is, what people *do*. Others are also interested in what people say they would do or prefer to do if they were in specific circumstances. This type of information is mainly called *stated preferences*. This book is mainly based on the latter type of information. At the moment it seems appropriate to merge both sources of information—both toolboxes—and to look at how far both approaches may be combined. For consumer behavior, for instance, this implies a combined study of purchasing behavior and of purchasing intentions. There can be no doubt that a merger will lead to novel results which the two approaches cannot deliver on their own.

17.4. THE NEED TO JOIN WITH SISTER DISCIPLINES

In Chapters 7, 8, and 10 we were out of the traditional area of economic science. In Chapter 7 we considered the processes of memory and anticipation, which are usually considered to be in the heartland of psychology, and we investigated in Chapter 8 the basic problem of the definition and observation of social reference groups, mainly thought to be one of the core problems of sociology. We do not claim that we have made major contributions, but we claim that we have demonstrated one thing; that is, that the observation of satisfactions and norms is a relevant source of information for economic science, sociology, and psychology. The social sciences share the information sources and in fact, to a large part, consider the same questions. Hence, it should be very desirable to join forces between psychologists, sociologists, and economic and political scientists. It is not clear why these sciences should march apart.

17.5. CONCLUSION

We have to wait and see whether our enthusiasm for our findings and even more for our methodologies will be shared by other researchers. We believe, however, that this book might be a significant step in a new scientific adventure in social research, which is now, witness the prolific recent literature, coming into full swing. Before the findings of happiness economics in general, and our own findings in particular, are sufficiently refined and proven stable so that they can be applied for practical purposes, still more thought and time will be required. Many steps will come after us, and perhaps we may contribute some ourselves. The path that lies ahead is long and thorny, but also extremely rewarding.

References

Aitchison, J., and Brown, J. A. C. (1960), *The Lognormal Distribution*, Cambridge: Cambridge University Press.

Alesina, A., Di Tella, R, and MacCulloch, R. (2004). 'Inequality and Happiness: Are Europeans and Americans Different?', *Journal of Public Economics*, 88: 2009–42.

Alessie, R., Crossley T., and Hildebrand, V. (2006), 'Estimating a Collective Household Model with Survey Data on Financial Satisfaction', Institute for Fiscal Studies, IFS Working Papers: W06/19.

Atkinson, A. B., (1970), 'On the Measurement of Inequality', *Journal of Economic Theory*, 2: 244–63.

—— and Bourguignon, F. (1999) (eds.), *Handbook of Income Distribution*, Amsterdam: North Holland.

—— and Stiglitz, J. E. (1980), *Lectures on Public Economics*, Maidenhead: McGraw-Hill.

Baarsma, B. E. (2000), 'Monetary Valuation of Environmental Goods: Alternatives to Contingent Valuation', Amsterdam: Thela Thesis Publisher.

Bateman, I. J. (1993), 'Valuation of the Environment, Methods and Techniques: Revealed Preference Methods', in R. K. Turner (ed.), *Sustainable Environmental Economics and Management*, London: Belhaven Press, 192–265.

Bender, K. A, Donohue, S. M., and Heywood, J. S. (2005), 'Job Satisfaction and Gender Segregation', *Oxford Economic Papers*, 57: 479–96.

Bentham, J. (1789), *An Introduction to the Principles of Morals and Legislation*, (London), repr. Oxford: Blackwell (1948).

Benz, M. (2005), 'Not for the Profit, but for the Satisfaction?—Evidence on Worker Well-Being in Non-profit Firms', *Kyklos*, 58: 155–76.

Bertrand, M., and Mullainathan, S. (2001), 'Do People Mean What They Say? Implications for Subjective Survey Data', *American Economic Review*, 91: 67–72.

Björn G., Shi, L., and Sato, H. (2004), 'Can Subjective Poverty Line be Applied to China? Assessing Poverty Among Urban Residents in 1999', *Journal of International Development*, 16: 1089–107.

Blanchflower, D. G., and Oswald, A. J. (2004), 'Well-being Over Time in Britain and the USA', *Journal of Public Economics*, 88: 1359–86.

—— and —— (2007), 'Hypertension and Happiness across Nations', forthcoming in *Journal of Health Economics*.

Blomquist, G. C., Berger, M. C., and Hoehn, J. P. (1988), 'New Estimates of Quality of Life in Urban Areas', *American Economic Review*, 78/1: 89–107.

Bonke, J, Deding, M., and Lausten, M. (2006), 'Time and Money: Substitutes in Real Terms and Complements in Satisfactions', The Levy Economics Institute Working Paper No. 451.

Borooah, V. K. (2006), 'What Makes People Happy? Some Evidence from Northern Ireland', *Journal of Happiness Studies*, 427–65.

Bourguignon, F., and Chakravarty, S. (2003), 'The Measurement of Multidimensional Poverty', *Journal of Economic Inequality*, 1: 51–65.

Bradburn, N. M. (1969), *The Structure of Psychological Well-being*, Chicago: Aldine.

Brickman, P., and Campbell, D. T. (1971), 'Hedonic Relativism and Planning the Good Society', in M. H. Apley (ed.), *Adaptation-level Theory: A Symposium*, New York: Academic Press, 287–302.

Browning, E. K. (1987), 'On the Marginal Welfare Cost of Taxation', *American Economic Review*, 77/1: 11–23.

Browning, E. K., and Johnson, W. R. (1984), 'The Trade-off between Equality and Efficiency', *Journal of Political Economy*, 92/2: 175–203.

Browning, M. (1992), 'Children and Household Behaviour', *Journal of Economic Literature*, 30: 1434–75.

Bruni, L., and Porta, P. L. (2005) (eds.), *Economics and Happiness: Framing the Analysis*, Oxford: Oxford University Press.

— and Sugden, R. (2007), 'The Road Not Taken: How Psychology Was Removed from Economics, and How It Might be Brought Back', *Economic Journal*, 117: 146–73.

Buhmann et al. (1988), 'Equivalence Scales, Well-Being, Inequality, and Poverty: Sensitivity Estimates across Ten Countries Using the Luxembourg Income Study (LIS) Database', *Review of Income and Wealth*, 34: 115–42.

Burchardt, T. (2005). 'Are One Man's Rags Another Man's Riches? Identifying Adaptive Preferences Using Panel Data', *Social Indicators Research*, 74: 57–102.

Camerer C., and Loewenstein G. (2004), 'Behavioural Economics: Past, Present, Future', in: Camerer C., Loewenstein G., and Rabin M. (eds), *Advances in Behavioral Economics*, Princeton University Press and Russell Sage Foundation, 3–52.

Cantril, H. (1965), *The Pattern of Human Concern*, New Jersey: Rutgers University Press.

Card, D. (1994), 'Earnings, Schooling and Ability Revisited', NBER Working Paper 4832, Cambridge, Mass.

Carlsson, F., Lampi, E., and Martinsson, P. (2004), 'The Marginal Values of Noise Disturbance from Air Traffic: Does the Time of the Day Matter?', *Transportation Research Part D*, 9: 373–85.

Carson, R. T., Flores, N. E., and Meade, N. F. (2001), 'Contingent Valuation: Controversies and Evidence', *Environmental and Resource Economics*, 19: 173–210.

Case, A., and Deaton, A. (2002), 'Consumption, Health, Gender and Poverty', World Bank Policy Research Working Paper No. 3153.

Chamberlain, G. (1980), 'Analysis of Covariance with Qualitative Data', *Review of Economic Studies*, 47: 225–38.

Citro, C. F., and Michael, R. T. (1995) (eds.), *Measuring Poverty: A New Approach*, Washington DC: National Academy Press.

Clark, A. E. (1997), 'Job Satisfaction and Gender: Why are Women so Happy at Work?', *Labour Economics*, 44: 341–72.

— (1999), 'Are Wages Habit-forming? Evidence from Micro Data', *Journal of Economic Behavior and Organization*, 392: 179–200.

— (2001), 'What Really Matters in a Job? Hedonic Measurement Using Quit Data', *Labour Economics*, 8: 223–42.

— (2003), 'Unemployment and Social Norms: Psychological Evidence from Panel Data', *Journal of Labor Economics*, 21: 323–51.

— and Oswald, A. J. (1994), 'Unhappiness and Unemployment', *Economic Journal*, 104: 648–59.

— and — (1996), 'Satisfaction and Comparison Income', *Journal of Public Economics*, 61: 359–81.

——, Etilé, F., Postel-Vinay, F., Senik, C., and Van der Straeten, K. (2005). 'Heterogeneity in Reported Well-being: Evidence from Twelve European Countries', *Economic Journal*, 115: C118–32.

——, Frijters, P., and Shields, M. A. (2006), 'A Survey of the Income Happiness Gradient', forthcoming in *Journal of Economic Literature*.

Coase, R. (1960), 'The Problem of Social Cost', *Journal of Law and Economics*, 3: 1–44.

Collins, A., and Evans, A. (1994), 'Aircraft Noise and Residential Property Values: An Artificial Neural Network Approach', *Journal of Transportation Economics and Policy*, 28: 175–97.

Crown, D. P., and Marlowe, D. (1964), *The Appraisal Motive: Studies in Evaluative Dependence*, New York: Wiley.

Cuellar, I., Bastida, E., and Braccio, S. M. (2004), 'Residency in the United States, Subjective Well-being, and Depression in an Older Mexican-Origin sample', *Journal of Aging and Health*, 16: 447–66.

Culyer, T., and Newhouse, J. P. (2000) (eds.), *Handbook of Health Economics*, i (a) and i (b), Amsterdam: Elsevier.

Cutler, D., and Richardson, E. (1997), 'Measuring the Health of the US Population', *Brooking Papers: Microeconomics*, 217–71.

—— and —— (1998), 'The Value of Health: 1970–1990', *American Economic Review*, 88: 97–100.

Dalton, H. (1920), 'The Measurement of the Inequality of Incomes', *Economic Journal*, 30: 348–61.

Das, M., and Van Soest, A. (1999). 'A Panel Data Model for Subjective Information on Household Income Growth', *Journal of Economic Behavior and Organization*, 40: 409–26.

Deaton, A., and Muellbauer, J. (1986), 'On Measuring Child Costs: With Application to Poor Countries', *Journal of Political Economy*, 94: 720–44.

—— and Paxson, C. H. (1998), 'Aging and Inequality in Income and Health', *American Economic Review*, 88: 248–53.

Deutsch, J., and Silver, J. G. (2005), 'Measuring Multidimensional Poverty: An Empirical Comparison of Various Approaches', *Review of Income and Wealth*, 51: 145–74.

De Vries, J., and Van der Woude, A. (1995), *Nederland 1500–1815: De eerste Ronde van moderne economische Groei*, Amsterdam: Balans.

Dhrymes, P. J. (1970), *Econometrics: Statistical Foundations and Applications*, New York: Harper & Row.

Diamond, P. (1996), 'Optimal Income Taxation: An Example with a U-shaped Pattern of Optimal Marginal Tax Rates', *American Economic Review*, 88: 83–95.

Diaz-Serrano, L. (2006), 'Housing Satisfaction, Homeownership and Housing Mobility: A Panel Data Analysis for Twelve EU Countries', IZA discussion paper 2318.

Diener, A., O'Brien, B., and Gafni, A. (1998), 'Health Care Contingent Evaluation Studies: A Review and Classification of the Literature', *Health Economics*, 7: 313–26.

Diener, E. (2006), 'Guidelines for National Indicators of Subjective Well-being and Ill-being', *Journal of Happiness Studies*, 7: 397–404.

—— and Lucas, R. E. (1999), 'Personality and Subjective Well-being', in D. Kahneman, E. Diener, and N. Schwarz (eds.), *Well-Being: The Foundations of Hedonic Psychology*:

Scientific Perspectives on Enjoyment and Suffering, New York: Russell Sage Foundation, Ch. 11.

— and Seligman, M. E. P. (2002), 'Very Happy People', *Psychological Science*, 13: 80–3.

Di Tella, R., and MacCulloch, R. J. (2006), 'Some Uses of Happiness Data in Economics', *Journal of Economic Perpectives*, 20: 25–46.

— and — (2005), 'Partisan Social Happiness', *Review of Economic Studies*, 72: 367–93.

—, —, and Oswald, A. J. (2001), 'Preferences over Inflation and Unemployment: Evidence from Surveys of Happiness', *American Economic Review*, 91: 335–41.

—, —, and — (2003), 'The Macroeconomics of Happiness', *The Review of Economics and Statistics*, 85: 809–27.

Dolan, P., Peasgood, T., and White, M. P. (2006), *Review of research on the influences on personal well-being and application to policy making*. Project Report for Department of Environment Food and Rural Affairs (DEFRA) & to Government's Sustainable Development Unit, UK.

Dolan, P., Peasgood, T., and Tsuchiya, A. (2005), 'Health Priorities and Public Preferences: The Relative Importance of Past Health Experience and Future Health Prospects', *Journal of Health Economics*, 24: 703–14.

Donohue, K. C., and Ryder, R. G. (1982), 'A Methodological Note on Marital Satisfaction and Social Variables', *Journal of Marriage and the Family*, 44: 743–7.

Drakopoulos, S. A., and Theodossiou, I. (1997), 'Job Satisfaction and Target Earnings', *Journal of Economic Psychology*, 186: 693–704.

Drummond, M. F., O'Brien, B., Stoddart, G. L., and Torrance, G. W. (1997), *Methods for the Economic Evaluation of Health Care Programs*, 2nd edn, Oxford: Oxford University Press.

Duclos, J.-Y., Sahn, D., and Younger, S. D. (2006), 'Robust Multidimensional Poverty Comparisons with Discrete Indicators of Well-being', in: S. P. Jenkins and J. Micklewright (eds.), *Poverty and Inequality Re-examined*, Oxford: Oxford University Press.

Duesenberry, J. S. (1949), *Income, Saving and the Theory of Consumer Behavior*, Cambridge, Mass.: Harvard University Press.

Easterlin, R. A. (1974), 'Does Economic Growth Improve the Human Lot? Some Empirical Evidence', in P. A. David and M. W. Reder (eds.), *Nations and Households in Economic Growth: Essays in Honor of Moses Abramowitz*, New York: Academic Press, 89–125.

— (1995), 'Will Raising the Incomes of All Increase the Happiness of All?', *Journal of Economic Behavior and Organization*, 27/1: 35–47.

— (2001), 'Income and Happiness: Towards a Unified Theory', *Economic Journal*, 111: 465–84.

— (2002) (ed.), *Happiness in Economics*, Cheltenham, UK: Edward Elgar Publ. Ltd.

— (2005). 'A Puzzle for Adaptive Theory', *Journal of Economic Behavior and Organization* 56: 513–21.

Eggink, E., Hop, J. P., and Van Praag, B. M. S. (1994), 'A Symmetric Approach to the Labor Market with the Household as Unit of Observation', *Journal of Applied Econometrics*, 9: 133–61.

Elster J., and Loewenstein G. (1992), 'Utility from Memory and Anticipation', in: J. Elster and G. Loewenstein (eds.), *Choice over Time*, New York: Russell Sage Foundation, 213–34.

Engel, E. (1895), 'Die Lebenskosten belgischer Arbeiterfamilien frueher und jetzt. Ermittelt aus Familienhaushaltsrechnungen und vergleichend zusammengestellt', *Bulletin of the International Institute of Statistics*, 9: 1–124.

Falk, A., and Knell, M. (2004), 'Choosing the Joneses: On the Endogeneity of Reference Groups', *Scandinavian Journal of Economics*, 106: 417–35.

Feitelson, E. I., Hurd, R. E., and Mudge, R. R. (1996), 'The Impact of Airport Noise on Willingness To Pay for Residences', *Transportation Research, D*, 1: 1–14.

Ferrer-i-Carbonell, A. (2005), 'Income and Well-being: An Empirical Analysis of the Comparison Income Effect', *Journal of Public Economics*, 89: 997–1019.

— (2003), 'Quantitative Analysis of Well-being with Economic Applications', Amsterdam; Thela Thesis Publisher.

— and Gowdy, J., (2007), 'Environmental Degradation and Happiness', *Ecological Economics*, 60: 509–16

— and Van Praag, B. M. S. (2001), 'Poverty in Russia', *Journal of Happiness Studies*, 2: 147–72.

— and — (2002), 'The Subjective Costs of Health Losses due to Chronic Diseases: An Alternative Model for Monetary Appraisal', *Health Economics*, 11: 709–22.

— and — (2003), 'Income Satisfaction Inequality and its Causes', *Journal of Economic Inequality*, 1: 107–27.

Ferrer-i-Carbonell, A., and Frijters, P. (2004), 'How Important is Methodology for the Estimates of the Determinants of Happiness?', *The Economic Journal*, 114 (497), 641–59.

—, Theodossiou, I., and Van Praag, B. M. S. (2007), 'Image and Reality: The Case of Job Satisfaction', Working paper, University of Amsterdam.

Frank, R. G. (1985), *Choosing the Right Pond*, Oxford: Oxford University Press.

Frederick, S., Lowenstein, G., and O'Donoghue, T. (2002), 'Time Discounting and Time Preference: A Critical Review', *Journal of Economic Literature*, 40: 351–401.

Frey, S. and Stutzer, A. (2000), 'Happiness, Economy and Institutions', *Economic Journal*, 110: 918–38.

— and — (2002*a*), *Happiness and Economics*, Princeton, NJ: Princeton University Press.

— and — (2002*b*), 'What Can Economists Learn from Happiness Research?', *Journal of Economic Literature*, 40: 402–35.

Friedman, M. (1957), *A Theory of the Consumption Function*, Princeton, NJ: Princeton University Press.

Frijters, P. (2000), 'Do Individuals Try to Maximize General Satisfaction?', *Journal of Economic Psychology*, 21: 281–304.

— and Van Praag, B. M. S. (1997), 'Estimates of Poverty Ratios and Equivalence Scales for Russia and Parts of the Former USSR', Tinbergen Institute Discussion Paper N. 95/149, the Netherlands.

— and — (1998), 'The Effects of Climate on Welfare and Well-being in Russia', *Climatic Change*, 39: 61–81.

—, Geishecker, I., Shields, M. A., and Haisken-DeNew, J. P. (2006), 'Can the Large Swings in Russian Life Satisfaction be Explained by Ups and Downs in Real Incomes?', *Scandinavian Journal of Economics*, 108: 433–58.

—, Shields, M. A., and Haisken-DeNew, J. P. (2004), 'Money Does Matter! Evidence from Increasing Real Incomes in East Germany Following Reunification', *American Economic Review*, 94: 730–41.

—, —, and — (2005), 'The Effect of Income on Health: Evidence from a Large Scale Natural Experiment', *Journal of Health Economics*, 24: 997–1017.

Frisch, R. (1932), *New Methods of Measuring Marginal Utility*, Tübingen: Mohr.

Frisch, R. (1964), 'Dynamic Utility', *Econometrica*, 32: 418–29.

Gardner, J., and Oswald, A. J. (2006), 'Do Divorcing Couples Become Happier By Breaking Up?', *Journal of the Royal Statistical Society Series A*, 169: 319–36.

Gerdtham, U.-G., and Johannesson, M. (2001), 'The Relationship between Happiness, Health, and Socio-economic Factors: Results Based on Swedish Microdata', *Journal of Socio-Economics*, 30: 553–7.

Gini, C. (1912), *Variabilita e Mutabilita*, Bologna: Tipografia di Paolo Cuppins.

Goedhart, T., Halberstadt, V., Kapteyn, A., and Van Praag, B. M. S. (1977), 'The Poverty Line: Concept and Measurement', *Journal of Human Resources*, 12: 503–20.

Gourieroux, C., and Montfort, A. (1995), *Statistics and Econometric Models*, Cambridge: Cambridge University Press.

Graham, C. (2006), 'The Economics of Happiness', in: S. Durlauf and L. Blume (eds.), *The New Palgrave Dictionary of economics*, Forthcoming.

Greene, W. H. (1991), *Econometric Analysis*, New York: MacMillan.

—— (2000), *Econometric Analysis*, 4th edn., New Jersey: Prentice-Hall.

Griliches, Z. (1977), 'Estimating the Returns to Schooling: Some Econometric Problems', *Econometrica*, 45: 1–22.

Groot, W. (2000), 'Adaptation and Scale of Reference Bias in Self-assessments of Quality of Life', *Journal of Health Economics*, 19: 403–20.

—— and Maassen Van den Brink, H. (1999), 'Job Satisfaction and Preference Drift', *Economics Letters*, 63 3: 363–7.

——, ——, and Plug, E. (2004), 'Money for Health: The equivalent Variation of Cardiovascular Diseases, *Health Economics*, 13: 859–72.

Grzeskowiak, S., Sirgy, J. M., and Widgery, R. (2003), 'Residents' Satisfaction with Community Services: Predictors and Outcomes', *Journal of Regional Analysis and Policy*, 33: 1–36.

Gustaffson, B., Shi, L., and Sato, H. (2004), 'Can a Subjective Poverty Line be Applied to China? Assessing Poverty Among Urban Residents in 1999', *Journal of International Development*, 16: 1089–107.

Gutmann, P. M. (1977), 'The Subterranean Economy', *Financial Analysts Journal*, Nov.–Dec.: 26–7.

Hagenaars, A. J. M. (1985), *The Perception of Poverty*, Ph.D. thesis (University of Leyden).

—— (1986), *The Perception of Poverty*, (revision of the above thesis) Amsterdam: North-Holland.

—— and Van Praag, B. M. S. (1985), 'A Synthesis of Poverty Line Definitions', *Review of Income and Wealth*, 31: 139–53.

—— and de Vos, K. (1988), 'The Definition and Measurement of Poverty', *Journal of Human Resources*, 23: 243–66.

Hahn, F. H. (1973), 'On Optimum Taxation', *Journal of Economic Theory*, 6: 96–106.

Hajivassiliou, V. A., and Ruud, P. A. (1994), 'Classical Estimation Methods for LDV Models Using Simulation', in: R. F. Engle and D. L. McFadden (eds.), *Handbook of Econometrics*, iv; *Handbooks in Economics*, ii, Amsterdam/London/New York: Elsevier/North-Holland, 2383–441.

Hartog, J. (1989), 'Distribution Policies in the Netherlands', in F. Muller and W. J. Zwezerijnen (eds.), *The Role of Economic Policy in Society*, The Hague: UPR, 17–46.

— Oosterbeek, H., and Teulings, C. (1993), 'Age, Wages and Education in the Netherlands', in P. Johnson and K. Zimmermann (eds.), *Labour Markets in an Aging Europe*, Cambridge: Cambridge University Press.

— Ridder, G., and Visser, M. (1994), 'Allocation of Individuals to Job Level under Rationing', *Journal of Applied Econometrics*, 9: 437-52.

— and Vijverberg, W. P. M., (2003), 'Do Wages Really Compensate for Risk Aversion and Skewness Affection?', Manuscript, University of Dallas.

Hausman, J. A. (1993) (ed.), *Contingent Valuation—A Critical Assessment*, Amsterdam: Elsevier.

— and Ruud, P. (1984), 'Family Labor Supply with Taxes', *American Economic Review*, 74: 242-8.

Healy, J. D. (2003), 'Housing Conditions, Energy Efficiency, Affordability and Satisfaction with Housing: A Pan-European Analysis', *Housing Studies*, 18: 409-24.

Helson, H. (1947). 'Adaptation-Level as a Frame of Reference for Prediction of Psychophysical Data', *American Journal of Psychology*, 60, 1-29.

Hicks, J. R., and Allen, R. G. D. (1934), 'A Reconsideration of the Theory of Value, i, ii', *Economica*, 1: 52-75, 196-219.

Homans, E., Hagenaars, A., and Van Praag, B. M. S. (1991), 'Income Inequality Between One-earner and Two-earner Households: Is it Real or Artificial?', *De Economist*, 139: 530-49.

Houthakker, H. S. (1961), 'The Present State of Consumption Theory', *Econometrica*, 29: 704-40.

Hulshof, M., and Noyon, R. (1997), *Klagen over Schiphol: Oorzaken en Gevolgen Van Geluidhinder (Complaining about Schiphol: Causes and Consequences of Noise Nuisance)*, Amsterdam: Regioplan Stad en Land.

Jacob, B., and Levitt, S. (2003*a*), 'Rotten Apples: An Investigation of the Prevalence and Predictors of Teacher Cheating', *Quarterly Journal of Economics*, 118: 843-77.

— and — (2003*b*), 'Catching Cheating Teachers: The Results of an Unusual Experiment in Implementing Theory', NBER Working Paper No. 9414

Joo, S., and Grable, J. E. (2004), 'An Exploratory Framework of the Determinants of Financial Satisfaction', *Journal of Family and Economic Issues*, 25: 25-50.

Kahneman, D. (1999), 'Objective Happiness', in D. Kahneman, E. Diener, and N. Schwarz (eds.), *Well-Being: The Foundations of Hedonic Psychology: Scientific Perspectives on Enjoyment and Suffering*, New York: Russell Sage Foundation, Ch. 1.

— and Tversky, A. (1979), 'Prospect Theory: An Analysis of Decisions under risk', *Econometrica*, 47: 313-27.

— Wakker, P., and Sarin, R. (1997), 'Back to Bentham? Explorations of Experienced Utility', *Quarterly Journal of Economics*, 2: 375-405.

— Diener, E., and Schwarz, N. (1999), (eds.), *Well-Being: The Foundations of Hedonic Psychology: Scientific Perspectives on Enjoyment and Suffering*, New York: Russell Sage Foundation.

Kahneman, D., and Krueger A. B. (2006), 'Developments in the Measurement of Subjective Well-being', *Journal of Economic Perspectives*, 20: 3-24.

—, —, Schkade, D., Schwarz, N., and Stone, A. (2006), 'Would You be Happier if You Were Richer? A Focusing Illusion', *Science*, 312: 1908-10.

Kapteyn, A. (1977), A Theory of Preference Formation, Ph.D. thesis (University of Leyden).

Kapteyn, A. and Van Herwaarden, F. G. (1980), 'Interdependent Welfare Functions and Optimal Income Distribution', *Journal of Public Economics*, 14: 375–97.

— and Van Praag, B. M. S. (1976), 'A New Approach to the Construction of Equivalence Scales', *European Economic Review*, 7: 313–35.

—, —, and Van Herwaarden, F. G. (1978), 'Individual Welfare Functions and Social Reference Spaces', *Economics Letter*, 1: 173–8.

Katona, G. (1951), *Psychological Analysis of Economic Behavior*, Amsterdam: Elsevier.

— (1975), *Psychological Economics*, New York: McGraw-Hill.

Keller, W. J., and. Hartog, J. (1977), 'Income Tax Rates and Proportional Sacrifice', *Public Finance*, 3: 321–32.

Kerkhofs, M., and Lindeboom, M. (1995), 'Subjective Health Measures and State Dependent Reporting Errors', *Health Economics*, 4: 221–35.

Kolm, S. C. (1976), 'Unequal Inequalities', *Journal of Economic Theory*, 41: 416–42.

Layard, R. (2005). *Happiness. Lessons from a New Science*, London: Allen Lane.

Leu, Robert G., Burri, St., and Priester, T. (1997), *Lebensqualität und Armut in der Schweiz*, Bern: Haupt.

Likert, R. (1932), 'A Technique for the Measurement of Attitudes', *Archives of Psychology*, 140/5.

Loewenstein, G., and Prelec, D. (1991), 'Negative Time Preference', *The American Economic Review*, 81/2: 347–52.

Love, R., and Oja, G. (1977), 'Low Income in Canada', *Review of Income and Wealth*, 23: 39–61.

Luchini, S., Protière, C., and Moatti, J.-P. (2003), 'Eliciting Several Willingness to Pay in a Single Contingent Valuation Survey: Application to Health Care', *Health Economics*, 12: 51–64.

Luttmer, E. F. P (2005), 'Neighbors as Negatives: Relative Earnings and Well-Being', *Quarterly Journal of Economics*, 120: 963–1002.

Maddala, G. S. (1983), *Limited Dependent and Qualitative Variables in Econometrics*, Cambridge: Cambridge University Press.

Maassoumi, E. (1986), 'The Measurement and Decomposition of Multidimensional Inequality', *Econometrica*, 54: 991–7.

McBride, M. (2001), 'Relative-income Effects on Subjective Well-being in the Cross-section', *Journal of Economic Behavior and Organization*, 45: 251–78.

McFadden, D. (1974), 'The Measurement of Urban Travel Demand', *Journal of Public Economics*, 3: 303–28.

Mill, J. S. (1965), *Principles of Political Economy, Collected Works, iii*. Toronto: University of Toronto.

Mirrlees, J. A. (1971), 'An Exploration in the Theory of Optimal Taxation', *Review of Economic Studies*, 38: 175–208.

— (1986), 'The Theory of Optimal Taxation', in: K. J. Arrow and M. D. Intriligator (eds.), *Handbook of Mathematical Economics, iii*, Amsterdam: North-Holland, 1198–249.

Morrell, P., and Lu, C.-H. Y. (2000), 'Aircraft Noise Social Cost and Charge Mechanisms: A Case Study of Amsterdam Airport Schiphol', *Transportation Research*, 5 (pt. D): 305–20.

Müller, M. J., and Baltes, K. (1979), *Handbuch ausgewählter Klimatstationen der Erde*, Trier: Gerold Richter.

Mundlak, Y. (1978), 'On the Pooling of Time Series and Cross Section Data', *Econometrica*, 46: 69–85.

Musgrave, R. A. (1959), *The Theory of Public Finance*, New York: McGraw-Hill.

Nelson, J. P. (1980), 'Airports and Property Values: A Survey of Recent Evidence', *Journal of Transport Economics and Policy*, 14/1: 37–52.

Orshansky, M. (1965), 'Counting the Poor: Another Look at the Poverty Profile', *Social Security Bulletin*, 28: 3–29.

Oswald, A. J. (1997), 'Happiness and Economic Performance', *Economic Journal*, 107/445: 1815–31.

—— and Gardner, J. (2007), 'Money and Mental Wellbeing: A Longitudinal Study of Medium-Sized Lottery Wins', *Journal of Health Economics*, 26: 49–60.

Parducci, A. (1995), *Happiness, Pleasure and Judgment*, New Jersey: Lawrence Erlbaum.

Pareto, V. (1909), *Manuel d'économie politique*, Paris: Giard & Brière.

Parkes, A., Kearns, A., and Atkinson, R. (2002), 'What Makes People Dissatisfied with Their Neighbourhoods?', *Urban Studies*, 39: 2413–38.

Pearce, D. W. (1993), *Economic Values and the Natural World*, Cambridge, Mass.: MIT Press.

Persky, J., and Tam, M-Y. (1990), 'Local Status and National Social Welfare', *Journal of Regional Science*, 302: 229–38.

Pigou, A. (1920), *The Economics of Welfare*, London: Macmillan.

Piketty, T. (1993), 'Implementation of First-best Allocation Via Generalized Tax Schedules', *Journal of Economic Theory*, 61: 23–41.

Plug, E. J. S. and Van Praag, B. M. S. (1995), 'Family Equivalence Scales within a Narrow and Broad Welfare Context', *Journal of Income Distribution*, 4: 171–86.

Plug, E. J. S. and Van Praag, B. M. S. (1995), 'Welfare and Intelligence', Tinbergen Discussion Paper TI 1-95-196, University of Amsterdam.

—— and —— (1998), 'Similarity in Response Behavior between Household Members: An Application to Income Evaluation', *Journal of Economic Psychology*, 19: 497–513.

——, ——, and Hartog, J. (1999), 'If We Knew Ability, How Would We Tax Individuals?', *Journal of Public Economics*, 72/2, 183–211.

Pollak, R. A., and Wales, T. J. (1979), 'Equity; the Individual Versus the Family: Welfare Comparisons and Equivalence Scales', *American Economic Review*, 69: 216–21.

Pradhan, M., and Ravallion, M. (2000), 'Measuring Poverty using Qualitative Perceptions of Consumption Adequacy', *Review of Economics and Statistics*, 82: 462–71.

Psacharopoulos, G. (1985), 'Returns on Education: A Further International Update and Implications', *Journal of Human Resources*, 20: 583–97.

Ravallion, M., and Lokshin, M. (2002), 'Self-rated Economic Welfare in Russia', *European Economic Review*, 46: 1453–73.

Robbins, L. (1932), *An Essay on the Nature and Significance of Economic Science*, London: Macmillan.

Rojas, M. (2006a), 'Life Satisfaction and Satisfaction in Domains of Life: Is it a Simple Relationship?', *Journal of Happiness Studies*, 7(4): 467–97.

Rojas, M. (2006b), 'Well-being and the Complexity of Poverty: A Subjective Well-being Approach', in: M. McGillivray and M. Clarke (eds.), *Understanding Human Well-Being*, Chapter 9, United Nations University Press.

Rojas, M. (2007a), 'A Subjective Well-Being Equivalence Scale for Mexico: Estimation and Poverty and Income-distribution Implications', *Oxford Development Studies*, forthcoming.

Rojas, M. (2007*b*), 'Heterogeneity in the Relationship between Income and Happiness: A Conceptual Referent Theory Explanation', *Journal of Economic Psychology*, 28(1): 1–14.

Rothbarth, E. (1943), 'Notes on a Method of Determining Equivalent Incomes for Families of Different Composition', app. 4 in C. Madge (ed.), *War-time Patterns of Saving and Spending*, Cambridge: Cambridge University Press.

Rowntree, B. S. (1901) *Poverty: A Study of Town Life*, Policy Pr; 2nd edition (December 2000).

Rowntree, B. S. (1941), *Poverty and Progress*, London: Longmans, Green.

Salverda, W., Nolan, B., and Smeeding, T. (2008) (eds.), *Oxford Handbook on Economic Inequality*. Oxford: Oxford University Press, forthcoming.

Samuelson, P. A. (1947), *Foundations of Economic Analysis*, Cambridge, Mass.: Harvard University Press.

— (1979), *Foundations of Economic Analysis* (1st pub. 1954). New York: Atheneum.

Sandvik, E., Diener, E., and Seidlitz L. (1993), 'Subjective Well-being: The Convergence and Stability of Self-report and Non-self-report Measures', *Journal of Personality*, 61: 317–42.

Schipper, Y. (1997), 'On the Valuation of Aircraft Noise—A Meta-analysis', *Journal of Air Transport Management*, 4: 117–24.

Schneider, F., and Enste, D. (2000), 'Shadow Economies Around the World—Size, Causes, and Consequences', IMF Working Papers 00/26, Washington DC: IMF.

Seidl, C. (1994), 'How Sensible is the Leyden Individual Welfare Function of Income?', *European Economic Review*, 38/8: 1633–59.

Sen, A. K. (1976), 'Poverty and Ordinal Approach to Measurement', *Econometrica*, 44: 219–31.

— (1995). 'Rationality and Social Choice', *American Economic Review*, 85: 1–24.

— (1999), 'The Possibility of Social Choice', *American Economic Review*, 89: 349–78.

Senik C. (2005), 'What Can We Learn from Subjective Data? The Case of Income and Well-Being', *Journal of Economic Surveys*, 19: 43–63.

— (2006). Is Man Doomed to Progress?. IZA working Paper, 2237.

Shields, M. A., and Price, W. S. (2005), 'Exploring the Economic and Social Determinants of Psychological Well-being and Perceived Social Support in England', *Journal of the Royal Statistical Society, Series A*, 168: 513–38.

Shizgal, P. (1999), 'On the Neutral Computation of Utility: Implications from Studies of Brain Simulation Reward', in: D. Kahneman, E. Diener, and N. Schwarz (eds.), *Well-Being: The Foundations of Hedonic Psychology, Scientific Perspectives on Enjoyment and Suffering*, New York: Russell Sage, ch. 26.

Silber, J. (1999) (ed.), *Handbook of Income Inequality Measurement*, Dordrecht: Kluwer Academic.

Slottje, D. (1991), 'Measuring the Quality of Life Across Countries', *The Review of Economics and Statistics*, 73: 684–93.

Smith, J. P. (1999), 'Healthy Bodies and Thick Wallets: The Dual Relation between Health and Economic Status', *Journal of Economic Perspectives*, 13/2: 145–66.

Sobal, J., Rauschenbach, B. S., and Frongillo, E. A. (1995). 'Obesity and Marital Quality—Analysis of Weight, Marital Unhappiness, and Marital Problems in a US National Sample', *Journal of Family Issues*, 16: 746–64.

Stewart, M. (1983), 'On Least Squares Estimation when the Dependent Variable is Grouped', *Review of Economic Studies*, 50: 141–9.

Stone, A., Shiffman, A. S., and De Vries, M. W. (1999), 'Ecological Monetary Assessment', in D. Kahneman, E. Diener, and N. Schwarz (eds.), *Well-Being: The Foundations of Hedonic Psychology, Scientific Perspectives on Enjoyment and Suffering*, New York, Russell Sage, ch. 2.

Stuart, C. E. (1981), 'Swedish Tax Rates, Labor Supply and Tax Revenues', *Journal of Political Economy*, 89/5: 1020–38.

—— (1984), 'Welfare Costs per Dollar of Additional Tax Revenue in the United States', *American Economic Review*, 74/3: 352–62.

Stutzer, A. (2004), 'The Role of Income Aspirations in Individual Happiness', Forthcoming in *Journal of Economic Behavior and Organization*, 54: 89–109.

Stutzer, A., and Frey, B. S. (2006), 'Does Marriage Make People Happy, or Do Happy People Get Married?', *Journal of Socio-Economics*, 35: 326–47.

Suppes, P., and Winet, M. (1954), 'An Axiomatization of Utility Based on the Notion of Utility Differences', *Management Science*, 1: 259–70.

Taylor, M. P. (2006), 'Tell Me Why I Don't Like Mondays: Investigating Day of the Week Effects on Job Satisfaction and Psychological Well-Being', *Journal of the Royal Statistical Society: Series A (Statistics in Society)*, 169: 127–42.

Terza, J. V. (1987), 'Estimating Linear Models with Ordinal Qualitative Regressors', *Journal of Econometrics*, 34/3: 275–91.

Thaler, R. H. (1981). 'Some Empirical Evidence on Dynamic Inconsistency', *Economic Letters*, 8: 201–7.

Theil, H. (1967), *Economics and Information Theory*, Amsterdam: North-Holland.

—— 'The Measurement of Inequality by Components of Income', *Economics Letters*, 2: 197–9.

Theodossiou, I. (1998), 'The Effects of Low-Pay and Unemployment on Psychological Well-Being: A Logistic Regression Approach', *Journal of Health Economics*, 17: 85–104.

Tinbergen, J. (1956), 'On the Theory of Income Distribution', *Weltwirtschaftliches Archiv*, 77: 155–75.

—— (1970a). 'A Positive and Normative Theory on Income Distribution', *Review of Income and Wealth*, 16: 155–75.

—— (1970b), 'Belasting op bekwaamheid', (*Tax on Ability*), *Intermediair*, 30/6: 1–3.

—— (1972), 'Some Features of the Optimum Regime', in *Optimum Social Welfare and Productivity*, the Charles C. Moskowitz lectures, New York: New York University Press.

—— (1975), *Income Distribution, Analysis and Policies*, Amsterdam: North-Holland.

Townsend, P. B. (1979), *Poverty in the UK*, Allen Lane and Penguin Books, London.

Tsou, Meng-Wen, and Liu, Jin-Tan (2001), 'Happiness and Domain Satisfaction in Taiwan', *Journal of Happiness Studies*, 2: 269–88.

Tsuchiya, A., and Dolan, P., (2005), 'The QALY Model and Individual Preferences for Health States and Health Profiles Over Time: A Systematic Review of the Literature', *Medical Decision Making*, 2005, 25: 460–7.

Van Batenburg, P. C., and Van Praag, B. M. S. (1980), 'The Perception of Welfare Inequality, a Correcting Note', *European Economic Review*, 13: 259–63.

Van den Berg, B., and Ferrer-i-Carbonell, A. (2007). 'Monetary Valuation of Informal Care: The Well-being Valuation Method'. Forthcoming in *Health Economics*.

Van den Bosch, K. (2001), *Identifying the Poor, Using Subjective and Consensual Measures*, Aldershot: Ashgate.

Van Eck, R., and Kazemier, B. (1989), Zwarte arbeid, een empirische en methodologische studie (*Hidden Labour: An Empirical and Methodological Study*), Ph.D. thesis (University of Amsterdam).

Van Herwaarden, F. G., and Kapteyn, A. (1981), 'Empirical Comparison of the Shape of Welfare Functions', *European Economic Review*, 15: 261–86.

Van Klaveren, C. (2002), Political Satisfaction and Economic Policy, MA thesis, (University of Amsterdam).

— Maassen Van der Brink, H, and Van Praag, B. M. S. (2002), 'Political Satisfaction and Economic Policy', Working Paper, University of Amsterdam.

Van Praag, C. M. (1992), 'Zomaar een dataset; een beschrijving Van 15 jaar onderzoek met het Brabant-cohort', University of Amsterdam.

Van Praag, B. M. S. (1968), *Individual Welfare Functions and Consumer Behavior*, Amsterdam, North-Holland.

— (1971), 'The Welfare Function of Income in Belgium: An Empirical Investigation', *European Economic Review*, 2: 337–69

— (1976), 'The Individual Welfare Function of Income and its Offspring', in J. S. Cramer, A. Heertje, and P. Venekamp (eds.), *Relevance and Precision: Essays in Honour of Pieter de Wolff*, Amsterdam, North-Holland.

— (1977), 'The Perception of Welfare Inequality', *European Economic Review*, 10: 189–207.

— (1978), 'The Perception of Income Inequality', in: W. Krelle and A. F. Shorrocks (eds.), *Personal Income Distribution*, Amsterdam: North-Holland, 113–36.

— (1981), 'Reflections on the Theory of Individual Welfare Functions', report 81.14, Centre for Research in Public Economics, Leyden University, Proceedings of the American Statistical Association.

— (1988), 'Climate Equivalence Scales; An Application of a General Method', *European Economics Review*, 32: 1019–24.

— (1991), 'Ordinal and Cardinal Utility: An Integration of the Two Dimensions of the Welfare Concept', *Journal of Econometrics*, 50: 69–89.

— (1994), 'Ordinal and Cardinal Utility', in R. Blundell, I. Preston, and I. Walker (eds.), *The Measurement of Household Welfare*, Cambridge: Cambridge University Press.

— (2007), 'Perspectives from the Happiness Literature and the Role of New Instruments for Policy Analysis' *CESifo Economic Studies*, 53: 42–68.

— and Baarsma, B. E. (2005), 'Using Happiness Surveys to Value Intangibles: The Case of Airport Noise', *The Economic Journal*, 115: 224–46.

— and Ferrer-i-Carbonell, A. (2002), 'Age-differentiated Health Losses Caused by Illnesses', Discussion Paper 02–01513, Tinbergen Institute, Amsterdam.

— and — (2007), 'A Multi-dimensional Approach to Subjective Poverty', in J. Silber and N. Kakwani (eds.), *Quantititative Approaches to Multidimensional Poverty Measurement*, Palgrave-MacMillan, forthcoming.

— and Flik, R. J. (1992), 'Poverty Line and Equivalence Scales: A Theoretical and Empirical Investigation', in *Poverty Measurement for Economies in Transition in Eastern Europe*, International Scientific Conference, Warsaw, 7–9 October, Polish Statistical Association, Central Statistical Office.

— and Frijters, P. (1999), 'The Measurement of Welfare and Well-being: The Leyden Approach', in D. Kahneman, E. Diener, and N. Schwarz (eds.), *Well-Being:*

The Foundations of Hedonic Psychology, Scientific Perspectives on Enjoyment and Suffering, New York: Russell Sage.

— and Kapteyn, A. (1973), 'Further Evidence on the Individual Welfare Function of Income: An Empirical Study in the Netherlands', *European Economic Review*, 4: 33–62.

— and Plug, E. J. S. (1995), 'New Developments in the Measurement of Welfare and Well-being', Discussion Paper TI 95-60, Tinbergen Institute, University of Amsterdam.

— and — (1998), 'The Costs and Benefits of Children', in S. Ringen and P. R. de Jong (eds.), *Fighting Poverty: Caring for Children, Parents, the Elderly and Health*, Aldershot: Ashgate, 53–70.

— and Spit, J. S. (1982), 'The Social Filter Process and Income Evaluation–An Empirical Study of the Social Reference Mechanism', Report 82.08, Center for Research in Public Economics, Leyden University.

— and Van der Sar, N. L. (1988), 'Household Cost Functions and Equivalence Scales', *Journal of Human Resources*, 23: 193–210.

— and — (1991), 'Social Distance on the Income Dimension', in: R. Vermunt and H. Steensma (eds.), *Social Justice in Human Relations*, ii. *Societal and Psychological Consequences of Justice and Injustice*, New York, Plenum, 209-28.

— and Van Weeren, J. (1988), 'Memory and Anticipation Processes and their Significance for Social Security and Income Inequality', in S. Maital (ed.), *Applied Behavioral Economics*, ii: 731–51, Brighton: Wheatsheaf.

— and Warnaar, M. F. (1997), 'The Cost of Children and the Use of Demographic Variables in Consumer Demand', in: M. R. Rosenzweig and O. Stark (eds.), *Handbook of Population and Family Economics*, Amsterdam: Elsevier North-Holland, i (a): 241–74.

— Dubnoff, S., and Van der Sar, N. L. (1988), 'On the Measurement and Explanation of Standards with Respect to Income, Age and Education', *Journal of Economic Psychology*, 9: 481–98.

Van Praag, B. M. S., Flik, R. J., and Stam, P. A. J. (1997), 'Poverty Lines and Equivalence Scales: A Theoretical and Empirical Evaluation', in N. Keilman, J. Lyngstad, H. Bojer, and I. Thomsen (eds.), *Poverty and Economic Inequality in Industrialized Western Societies*, Oslo: Scandinavian University Press.

— Frijters, P., and Ferrer-i-Carbonell, A. (2003), 'The Anatomy of Subjective Well-being', *Journal of Economic Behavior and Organization*, 51: 29–49.

— Hagenaars, A., and Van Weeren, J. (1982), 'Poverty in Europe', *Review of Income and Wealth*, 28: 345–59.

— Kapteyn, A., and Van Herwaarden, F. G. (1979), 'The Definition and Measurement of Social Reference Spaces', *The Netherlands' Journal of Sociology*, 15: 13–25.

Van Ravestijn, A., and Vijlbrief, H. (1988), 'Welfare Cost of Higher Tax Rates', *De Economist*, 136/2: 205–19.

Van der Sar, N. L. (1991), 'Applied Utility Analysis', Ph.D. thesis (Erasmus University, Rotterdam).

Van de Stadt, H., Kapteyn, A., and Van de Geer, S. (1985), 'The Relativity of Utility: Evidence from Panel Data', *The Review of Economics and Statistics*, 67: 179–87.

Varady, D. P., and Carozza, M. A. (2000), 'Towards a Better Way to Measure Customer Satisfaction Levels in Public Housing', Cincinnati, *Housing Studies*, 15: 797–825.

Vaughan, D. R. (1993), 'Exploring the Use of the Public's View to Set Income Poverty Thresholds and Adjust Them Over Time', *Social Security Bulletin*, 56/2: 22–46.

Veblen, T. (1909), 'The Limitations of Marginal Utility', *Journal of Political Economy*, 17: 620–36.

Veenhoven, R. (1989), *Conditions of Happiness*, Dordrecht/Boston: Kluwer Academic.

—— (1996), 'Happy Life-expectancy: A Comprehensive Measure of Quality-of-Life in Nations', *Social Indicators Research*, 39: 1–58.

Veenhoven, R. (1999), 'Quality-of-Life in Individualistic Society: A Comparison of Forty-three Nations in the Early 1990 s', *Social Indicators Research*, 48: 157–86.

Vieira, J., and Cabral, A. (2005), 'Skill Mismatches and Job Satisfaction', *Economics Letters*, 89: 39–47.

Walters, A. A. (1975), *Noise and Prices*, Oxford: Clarendon Press.

Welsch, H. (2006), 'Environment and Happiness: Valuation of Air Pollution Using Life Satisfaction Data', *Ecological Economics*, 58: 801–13.

—— (2007), 'Environmental Welfare Analysis: A Life Satisfaction Approach, *Ecological Economics*, forthcoming.

Whiteford, P. (1985), 'A Family's Needs: Equivalence Scales, Poverty and Social Security', Research Paper 27, Department of Social Security, Australia.

Wottiez, I., and Theeuwes, J. (1998), 'Well-being and Labor Market Status', in: S. P. Jenkins, A. Kapteyn, and B. M. S. Van Praag (eds.), *The Distribution of Welfare and Household Production: International Perspectives. New York and Melbourne*, Cambridge: Cambridge University Press, 211–30.

Index

Figures and tables are denoted by the letters 'f' and 't' in bold print.

Index